In Search of Liberty

Race in the Atlantic World, 1700–1900

SERIES EDITORS

Richard S. Newman, *Rochester Institute of Technology*
Patrick Rael, *Bowdoin College*
Manisha Sinha, *University of Connecticut*

ADVISORY BOARD

Edward Baptist, *Cornell University*
Christopher Brown, *Columbia University*
Vincent Carretta, *University of Maryland*
Laurent Dubois, *Duke University*
Erica Armstrong Dunbar, *Rutgers University*
Douglas Egerton, *LeMoyne College*
Leslie Harris, *Northwestern University*
Joanne Pope Melish, *University of Kentucky*
Sue Peabody, *Washington State University, Vancouver*
Erik Seeman, *State University of New York, Buffalo*
John Stauffer, *Harvard University*

In Search of Liberty

AFRICAN AMERICAN
INTERNATIONALISM IN THE
NINETEENTH-CENTURY
ATLANTIC WORLD

EDITED BY
Ronald Angelo Johnson and
Ousmane K. Power-Greene

The University of Georgia Press
ATHENS

© 2021 by the University of Georgia Press
Athens, Georgia 30602
www.ugapress.org
All rights reserved

Set in 10.5/13.5 Adobe Caslon Pro Regular
by Kaelin Chappell Broaddus

Most University of Georgia Press titles are
available from popular e-book vendors.

Printed digitally

Library of Congress Cataloging-in-Publication Data

Names: Johnson, Ronald Angelo, 1970– editor. |
   Power-Greene, Ousmane K., editor.
Title: In search of liberty : African American internationalism in the
   nineteenth-century Atlantic world / edited by Ronald Angelo Johnson
   and Ousmane K. Power-Greene.
Other titles: African American internationalism in the nineteenth-century
   Atlantic world
Description: Athens : The University of Georgia Press, [2021] |
   Series: Race in the Atlantic world, 1700–1900 | Includes bibliographical
   references.
Identifiers: LCCN 2020055867 | ISBN 9780820360089 (hardback) |
   ISBN 9780820360102 (paperback) | ISBN 9780820360096 (ebook)
Subjects: LCSH: African Americans—History—19th century. | African
   Americans—Foreign countries—History. | Free blacks—America—
   History—19th century. | Antislavery movements—History—19th
   century. | United States—Race relations—Political aspects—History—
   19th century. | Internationalism—History—19th century. | African
   diaspora.
Classification: LCC E185.18 .I525 2021 | DDC 304.8096—dc23
LC record available at https://lccn.loc.gov/2020055867

CONTENTS

Prologue
JAMES SIDBURY *vii*

Introduction
RONALD ANGELO JOHNSON AND
OUSMANE K. POWER-GREENE *1*

PART 1. *North America*

ONE   On the Edge of Freedom: The Reenslavement of Elizabeth Watson in Nova Scotia
FRANCO PAZ AND HARVEY AMANI WHITFIELD *17*

TWO   A Scheme to Desert: The Louisiana Purchase and Freedom Seekers in the Louisiana-Texas Borderlands, 1804–1806
MEKALA AUDAIN *40*

THREE   Looking for Freedom in the Borderlands: U.S. Black Refugees from Slavery in Early Independent Mexico, 1821–1836
THOMAS MAREITE *57*

PART 2. *Africa*

FOUR   The International Migration of South Carolinian Free People of Color, 1780–1865
LAWRENCE AJE *89*

FIVE   Liberia as a Theater: Performance, Race-Making, and the Liberian Nationality
CAREE A. BANTON *112*

SIX The Making of a Pan-Africanist: George Henry Jackson and the Lukunga Mission in the Congo Free State
MARCUS BRUCE *142*

PART 3. *Caribbean*

SEVEN The British Emigration Scheme and the African American Emigration Movement to the Caribbean
DEXTER J. GABRIEL *165*

EIGHT A Reinterpretation of African Americans and Haitian Emigration
BRANDON R. BYRD *197*

NINE Frederick Douglass and Debates over the Annexation of the Dominican Republic
CLAIRE BOURHIS-MARIOTTI *224*

PART 4. *Europe*

TEN African American Women in Europe
PIA WIEGMINK *253*

ELEVEN Black Abolitionists in Ireland and the Challenge of Universal Reform
ANGELA F. MURPHY *279*

Epilogue
GERALD HORNE *297*

Contributors *303*

PROLOGUE

JAMES SIDBURY

Questions centering on separation and integration structure many of the ways we understand the histories of African-descended people in colonial British America and the United States. That is perhaps most obviously true of our attempts to make sense of the long struggle for civil rights, first for Black people's right to recognized civic personalities and then, once that was achieved, the ongoing battle for civic equality. But if the focus on questions of separation and integration emerged out of the brute presence of legal segregation in American history—of Jim Crow—one need not look long to find the themes of separation and integration arising elsewhere in interesting variations. They are integral to W. E. B. Du Bois's meditation on the "two-ness" of "the Negro People" embodied in "an American, a Negro; two souls, two thoughts, two unreconciled strivings." Du Bois's impassioned plea for a society that would allow "a man to be both a Negro and an American without being cursed and spit upon by his fellows, without having the doors of opportunity closed roughly in his face" arose out of a rapidly segregating America and has remained central to our understanding of African American history because it speaks in an idiom rooted in the turn of the twentieth century to issues that reach back into the seventeenth century and push forward to the twenty-first. Those issues are unavoidably both national and international, as Du Bois emphasized by beginning *The Souls of Black Folk* with the prescient observation, made at the dawn of the new century, that "the problem of the Twentieth Century is the problem of the color line."[1]

Du Bois's insight has offered generations of scholars a powerful lens through which to read the rich literature on the cultures forged by enslaved and free Black people during the eighteenth and nineteenth centuries. That may be most obvious and controversial in the opening sentence of the first chapter of Eugene D. Genovese's *Roll, Jordan, Roll*—"Cruel, unjust, exploitative, oppressive, slavery bound two peoples together in bitter antagonism while creating an organic relationship so complex and ambivalent that neither could express the simplest human feelings without reference to the other"—but scholars who reject both *Roll, Jordan, Roll*'s insistence on paternalism and its Black nationalist interpretation of slave culture nonetheless engage a similar dialectic of separation and integration.[2] The struggle to make sense of that tension lies at the heart of the creolization scholarship that has been produced by followers of the theoretical model developed by Sidney Mintz and Richard Price, and it is equally at play in interpretations that foreground cultural separation, including interpretations offered by those who reject creolization and insist on ways of understanding enslaved people's lives and communities that foreground West and West Central African cultures. For scholars working in both traditions—for scholars working in any tradition, even that associated with mid-twentieth-century Howard University sociologist E. Franklin Frazier—one of the central challenges of African American history involves interpreting the contradictory impulses toward separation and integration.[3]

Analogous themes run through the histories of periods preceding and following Du Bois's formulation of the trope of double consciousness. Almost anywhere we turn—to the study of urban residential patterns, of occupational segmentation, of popular culture, of organized labor, or of political behavior in the twentieth century—issues of racial separation and integration, of inclusion and exclusion, weave through accounts of African American history in ways that profoundly shape understandings of American society, economy, and culture.[4] The complex interplay of patterns of inclusion and exclusion is particularly heightened at this moment as we look back on eight years during which the son of a black Kenyan and a white American served as president of the United States. That obviously represents evidence of inclusion—evidence of inclusion that stunned many who believed they would die without witnessing it—but the story is anything but straightforward. Despite being the first presidential candidate in two decades to win two popular majorities and only the third to do so since 1952, Barack Obama suffered unprecedented attacks on his legitimacy, attacks that helped fuel the rise of a successor who campaigned on barely disguised promises of racial exclusion, promises he has kept since assuming office. Inclusion and exclusion, separation and integration have moved in complicated and contradictory directions throughout American history.

The important essays in this book contribute to a new departure in African American history, but one with roots in perennial questions about American history. The move to internationalize African American history confronts what is, on the one hand, a long-standing tendency within much American historiography to separate "general" American history—the histories of high politics, of foreign relations, of ideas—from the history of "minorities." ("Special interest" history is a term sometimes used by those hostile to such work.) In doing so, these essays connect to the deeply transnational way that historians of race and of slavery and of African Americans have almost necessarily approached the Black experience.[5] This "transnational tendency" begins with the coerced migration from African societies to the Americas of Black victims of the Atlantic slave trade, which serves as the empirical starting point for a wide range of interpretations of the relationships among the cultures of West and West Central African societies, on the one hand, and the cultures of the enslaved in colonial British America, on the other. It continues with the links among North American slave societies and slave societies elsewhere—especially those in the Caribbean— and with the transnational engagement of Black American activists in the abolition movement. It encompasses the related but distinct emigration and colonization movements and the ways in which Black writers looked beyond the American nation-state when envisioning possibilities for collective progress. None of these is a new topic. None has been ignored by previous scholars.

Nonetheless, as the essays in this volume illustrate, many of these questions take on a different hue when their transnational qualities are seen as fundamental rather than incidental to the story. A quick and necessarily superficial survey of the relationship between these essays and the existing literature suggests how.

Black history has played a crucial but bounded role in the historiography of North America. Histories of slavery, of the enslaved, and of various forms of postbellum (white) repression and (Black) resistance to oppression are staples of American historical writing. Their very prominence in the literature has, however, had an ironically segregating effect. Many historians are attracted by and write to and within the well-established subfields that comprise African American history. This can effectively distance the study of state politics, of geographical expansion through the dispossession of Native peoples, of economic development, of ideas, and of foreign relations from the study of Black people. This tendency should not be overstated. One cannot study antebellum politics and continental expansion without close attention to problems tied to the existence of slavery in the South, nor do people study postbellum politics without attending to the rise of Jim Crow, the disenfranchisement of the freed people, or the rise of racially repressive regimes throughout and beyond the South. The study of scientific racism is central to much of intellectual history, and the American version of the "white man's burden" is an unavoidable aspect of any history of American foreign relations during the rise of the American Empire. In short, the problems created by slavery and race and the issues growing out of racial diversity in America have long attracted the attention of American historians.[6] However, it remains too often true that sophisticated and insightful efforts to explore those problems focus appropriately critical attention on white racist actions, a focus that can have the unintended effect of turning Black Americans into passive victims. They can too easily become objects in stories about white oppression, or, more commonly, resistance to Jim Crow and racism can come to look like the single defining feature of Black life in the United States.

How do the essays in this volume point in a promising new direction? Several do so by bringing the approaches that have long informed scholars of African American history to the study of topics that have more often fallen under the province of historians working on politics or foreign relations. These essays do not study the problems that slavery created for politicians or those that the presence of Black people created for other state actors, or, at any rate, they do not cordon off those questions. Instead, they look at the ways that Black people sought to negotiate the possibilities and dangers created by the changing and sometimes fluid national boundaries drawn by different imperial powers in North America. They embrace the focus that has long been central to African American history—a focus on the lived experiences of Black people—to shed new light on questions that historians of politics and foreign relations have often approached with a sharp but narrow focus on the perspectives of state actors. Most of those state actors, it could probably go without saying, have been white men. By bringing the perceptions and choices of new actors—Black actors—to the fore, these essays do more than broaden the cast of characters, though the way that they do that is much needed. They also show that the choices made by different (white) state actors—whether Nova Scotian court officials or various Mexican and Louisianan politicians—can only be fully understood when the choices made by Blacks who have too often been cast as passive victims are included in the story.

The case studies that focus on Africa do similar work. Africa is, of course, the continent that has most consistently brought Black people into a transnational narrative of American history. Questions about the nature and extent of cultural continuity between the cultures of enslaved Americans and the cultures of West and West Central Africa have a genealogy that reaches back to openly racist accounts of the American past. U. B. Philips famously conceived of the plantation as analogous to a benevolent school that civilized the supposedly savage Africans brought to the Americas.[7] Historians have long since jettisoned Philips's explicitly racist assumptions when tracing the Old World origins of African American cultures, but the dominant treatments of American connections to Africa have told a story of the transmission and transformation of African cultures in the Americas. That is an inherently transnational story. A different strand of scholarship has focused primarily on elite white efforts to create colonization movements designed to resettle free Black people in settler societies founded on the west coast of Africa. Historians of colonization generally note the resistance of African Americans to these movements, but their focus tends to be on the political maneuvering of white leaders of the movement.[8] The essays in this volume link to a different and shorter strand of historiography, one that focuses on the experiences of Black people who visited or moved from the United States to an African society. African American historiography has delved into such stories, but the temporal focus of much of that work has been the twentieth century.[9] The essays in this volume, with their focus on nineteenth-century Black actors and agency, highlight an emerging focus on earlier Black engagement with Africa, engagement that sits beside the more conventional story of African cultural influences on the nineteenth-century United States. Such work is stimulating scholars to conceive of the relationships among African and African American societies in more holistic and reciprocal terms; these essays contribute a much-needed push in that direction.

The essays that comprise part III of this volume deal with a set of relationships that has been more neglected in the existing literature. While there are canonical studies exploring the ties linking U.S. Black people to African-descended people and cultures in the Caribbean—work by Julius S. Scott, Rebecca Scott and Jean Hébrard, and Joseph Roach come immediately to mind—there are more invocations of a "Greater Caribbean" or of a "Greater Gulf" region than there are empirical studies of the links between African-descended peoples living on the islands and those on the mainland.[10] The essays in this volume contribute to a small but vibrant body of work that has insisted on the complicated role that Caribbean societies played in nineteenth-century free Black communities and culture as people who escaped the scourge of slavery in the United States searched for ways to reckon with the realization that freedom from slavery did not offer an escape from U.S. racism. Much of that work has explored the symbolic importance of Haiti as the first free Black American nation-state. Its practical importance as a potential site for free Black emigration may be familiar, but Brandon Byrd in his chapter shows that there is much still to learn about it.[11] The other essays in this section of the book complement Byrd's argument by showing the degree to which prominent nineteenth-century African Americans—the internationally famous, as well as those who enjoyed more limited local renown—looked to create ongoing links to other Caribbean places, whether through formal political affiliation or through voluntary migration that would help mitigate the injustices visited upon nineteenth-century people of African descent in and beyond the United States. This work underscores the importance for the history of Black people in the United States of the serial acts of emancipation in the Caribbean (1794, 1833, 1848, etc.), as well as the aftermaths of those acts.[12]

The essays in part IV of the volume turn to Europe, and in doing so they broaden the preexisting picture of American Black people in Europe. Much of the existing literature focuses on the twentieth century and the ways that many African Americans (especially African American artists) left U.S. racism behind to find greater acceptance—and often great celebrity—in European capitals (especially in Paris).[13] There is interesting work on the earlier era, including, for example, attention to the Black Shakespearian actor Ira Aldridge, who left New York City to tour Europe for much of the first half of the nineteenth century, and a more extensive body of scholarship looking at Black abolitionists in Europe.[14] The essays in this volume push beyond these relatively familiar stories to examine Black people in Europe—some activists, some simply travelers—and the ways they responded to different European people and settings as thinking and acting individuals rather than as self-styled "representatives" of their race. The travelers engaged with people ranging from Irish politicians to members of the tsar's court in Russia, and while the essays always acknowledge the roles that their subjects' racial identities played in those interactions, they never treat these Black travelers as people whose humanity was defined by their race.

It is, in fact, the way that all of the essays in this volume foreground Black people as the subjects (rather than the objects) of these historical narratives that offers their clearest collective contribution to the internationalization of African American history and, through that, to American history. In this regard, the essays follow in the well-respected but too rarely followed path of scholars like James Campbell, Wilson Jeremiah Moses, Manisha Sinha, Sterling Stuckey, and others, all of whom have produced penetrating studies of different Black Americans' engagement with the world beyond the United States.[15] All of this work, like so much of the study of African-descended people in the United States, stretches back to Du Bois.

On the one hand, the efforts to internationalize Black history that are represented in this volume add important new elements to this existing historiography. They push the main lines of inquiry into African American history—especially of nineteenth-century African American history—beyond their concentration on domestic events and on the struggle against slavery and its legacies in the United States. They simultaneously push the main lines of inquiry into the history of American foreign relations away from traditional issues involving state-to-state interactions, and they broaden more recent scholarly concerns with often elite patterns of cultural interaction. By foregrounding the way largely forgotten people of African descent—people existing scholarship often passively assumes must have lived lives defined by local issues and concerns—engaged with the peoples and cultures found in distant parts of the globe, these essays contribute to the efforts of scholars studying America and the world to widen the lens through which we perceive the influence of the United States on the rest of the globe and, of course, of different parts of the globe on the United States. In both of these senses, this work helps build on and expand earlier scholarship.

Compensating for things missing in previous scholarship—making new bricks to fill empty spaces in an already defined wall—is a time-honored and important goal. These essays do that, but they also point toward something more. Integrating people of African descent into the history of the way the United States has related to the rest of the world does more than add black bricks to a previously all-white wall. On the one hand, the essays in this book deliver on the implied promise of the volume's title: they internationalize the history of nineteenth-century African Americans. In the process, they do less obvious but even more important work integrating American history by uncovering the ways that African Americans, from the famous to the obscure, helped to shape the place of America in the world, even in a period when most Black Americans remained enslaved.

NOTES

1. W. E. B. Du Bois, *The Souls of Black Folk*, https://www.gutenberg.org/files/408/408-h/408-h.htm#chap01.

2. Eugene David Genovese, *Roll, Jordan, Roll: The World the Slaves Made* (New York: Random House, 1972), 3.

3. The literature is enormous. See Sidney W. Mintz and Richard Price, *The Birth*

of African-American Culture: An Anthropological Perspective (1976; repr., Boston: Beacon Press, 1992), for a founding case for creolization; Michael A. Gomez, *Exchanging Our Country Marks: The Transformation of African Identities in the Colonial and Antebellum South* (Chapel Hill: University of North Carolina Press, 1998), for the best broad synthetic case for the longer-term persistence of ethnic cultures and identities among African-descended people in the United States. E. Franklin Frazier, *The Negro Family in the United States* (Chicago: University of Chicago Press, 1939) posited that the Middle Passage stripped enslaved people sold into the United States of their ancestral cultures.

4. Works that illustrate these themes include Thomas J. Sugrue, *The Origins of the Urban Crisis: Race and Inequality in Postwar Detroit* (Princeton, N.J.: Princeton University Press, 1996); Thomas J. Sugrue, *Sweet Land of Liberty: The Forgotten Struggle for Civil Rights in the North* (New York: Random House, 2008); Joe William Trotter Jr., *Black Milwaukee: The Making of an Industrial Proletariat, 1915–1945* (Urbana: University of Illinois Press, 1985); N. D. B. Connolly, *A World More Concrete: Real Estate and the Remaking of Jim Crow South Florida* (Chicago: University of Chicago Press, 2014); and Karl Hagstrom Miller, *Segregating Sound: Inventing Folk and Pop Music in an Age of Jim Crow* (Durham, N.C.: Duke University Press, 2010). For contrasting syntheses of labor history's engagement with race that underscore the centrality of issues of separation and integration, see Herbert Hill, "The Problem of Race in American Labor History," *Reviews in American History* 24, no. 2 (1996): 189–208; and Eric Arnesen, "Black and White Workers, Race, and the State of Labor History," *Reviews in American History* 26, no. 1 (1998): 146–74.

5. Much of the recent work internationalizing our understanding of Black culture and politics has focused on the twentieth century. See, for example, David Levering Lewis, *W. E. B. Du Bois: Biography of a Race, 1868–1819* (New York: Henry Holt and Company, 1993); David Levering Lewis, *W. E. B. Du Bois: The Fight for Equality and the American Century, 1919–1969* (New York: Henry Holt and Company, 2000); Robin D. G. Kelley, *Africa Speaks, America Answers: Modern Jazz in Revolutionary Times* (Cambridge, Mass.: Harvard University Press, 2012), and Kelley, *Freedom Dreams: The Black Radical Imagination* (Boston: Beacon Press, 2002); Carol Anderson, *Eyes Off the Prize: The United Nations and the African American Struggle for Human Rights, 1944–1955* (New York: Cambridge University Press, 2003); Paul Gilroy, *The Black Atlantic: Modernity and Double Consciousness* (Cambridge, Mass.: Harvard University Press, 1993); Kevin K. Gaines, *American Africans in Ghana: Black Expatriates and the Civil Rights Era* (Chapel Hill: University of North Carolina Press, 2006); and Frank Andre Guridy, *Forging Diaspora: Afro-Cubans and African Americans in a World of Empire and Jim Crow* (Chapel Hill: University of North Carolina Press, 2010). For work looking at earlier transnational political thought among African Americans, see Julius S. Scott, *The Common Wind: Afro-American Currents in the Age of the Haitian Revolution* (Brooklyn: Verso Books, 2018); Wilson Jeremiah Moses, *Afrotopia: The Roots of African American Popular History* (New York: Cambridge University Press, 1998); Floyd J. Miller,

The Search for a Black Nationality: Black Emigration and Colonization, 1787–1863 (Urbana: University of Illinois Press, 1975); and James Sidbury, *Becoming African in America: Race and Nation in the Early Black Atlantic* (New York: Oxford University Press, 2007). Sterling Stuckey's pioneering *Slave Culture: Nationalist Theory and the Foundations of Black America* (New York: Oxford University Press, 1987) sought to bridge the eighteenth, nineteenth, and twentieth centuries, as does James T. Campbell, *Songs of Zion: The African Methodist Episcopal Church in the United States and South Africa* (New York: Oxford University Press, 1995), and Campbell, *Middle Passages: African American Journeys to Africa, 1787–2005* (New York: Penguin Press, 2006), which pushes into the twenty-first.

6. Again, the literature that I am superficially summarizing here is far too extensive to be cited, so I will list a few important works. It bears noting that I am citing excellent work, most of which does not suffer from the exclusion of Black actors found in the literature as a whole. See David W. Blight, *Race and Reunion: The Civil War in American Memory* (Cambridge, Mass.: Harvard University Press, 2001); Matthew Karp, *This Vast Southern Empire: Slaveholders at the Helm of American Foreign Policy* (Cambridge, Mass.: Harvard University Press, 2016); and Edward J. Larson, *Sex, Race, and Science: Eugenics in the Deep South* (Baltimore, Md.: Johns Hopkins University Press, 1996). Manisha Sinha, *The Slave's Cause: A History of Abolition* (New Haven, Conn.: Yale University Press, 2016), integrates Black and white actors of widely varying interests in a unified analysis.

7. U. B. Phillips, "The Plantation as a Civilizing Factor," *Sewanee Review* 12, no. 3 (1904): 257–67.

8. Among books focused specifically on colonization, this is most true of older books like P. J. Staudenraus, *The African Colonization Movement, 1816–1865* (New York: Columbia University Press, 1961); and Early Lee Fox, *The American Colonization Society, 1817–1840* (Baltimore, Md.: Johns Hopkins University Press, 1971). More recent books pay equal or greater attention to Black engagement, but they are often written as African American history; for example, see Ousmane K. Power-Greene, *Against Wind and Tide: The African American Struggle against the Colonization Movement* (New York: New York University Press, 2014). The colonization movement is most often discussed as part of a study of antebellum thought or politics, and it is there that the focus often falls almost exclusively on white actors. Sinha, *The Slave's Cause,* is an important recent exception.

9. For work on the twentieth century, see works cited in note 5 above. For exceptions to the focus on the twentieth century, see Miller, *The Search for a Black Nationality*; and Sidbury, *Becoming African in America.* For a study that crosses centuries and ties together themes too often left unconnected, see Campbell, *Middle Passages.*

10. Scott, *The Common Wind*; Rebecca Scott and Jean Hébrard, *Freedom Papers: An Atlantic Odyssey in the Age of Emancipation* (Cambridge, Mass.: Harvard University Press, 2012); Joseph Roach, *Cities of the Dead: Circum-Atlantic Performance* (New York: Columbia University Press, 1996).

11. For example, see Ronald Angelo Johnson, *Diplomacy in Black and White: John Adams, Toussaint Louverture, and Their Atlantic World Alliance* (Athens: University of Georgia Press, 2014); Sara Fanning, *Caribbean Crossing: African Americans and the Haitian Emigration Movement* (New York: New York University Press, 2015); and Ashli White, *Encountering Revolution: Haiti and the Making of the Early Republic* (Baltimore, Md.: Johns Hopkins University Press, 2010).

12. For important work in this vein, see Edward Bartlett Rugemer, *The Problem of Emancipation: The Caribbean Roots of the American Civil War* (Baton Rouge: Louisiana State University Press, 2008); Christa Dierksheide, *Amelioration and Empire: Progress and Slavery in the Plantation Americas* (Charlottesville: University of Virginia Press, 2014); and Edward Bartlett Rugemer, *Slave Law and the Politics of Resistance in the Early Atlantic World* (Cambridge, Mass.: Harvard University Press, 2018). The first two books focus on white actors, while the third pays equal or greater attention to Black actors.

13. Much of this work is found in biographies of Black artists. See, for example, Sherry Jones, *Josephine Baker's Last Dance* (New York: Gallery Books, 2018).

14. Bernth Lindfors, ed., *Ira Aldridge: The African Roscius* (Rochester, N.Y.: University of Rochester Press, 2011). For an example of the literature on Black abolitionists in Europe, see Sirpa Salenius, *An Abolitionist Abroad: Sarah Parker Remond in Continental Europe* (Amherst: University of Massachusetts Press, 2016).

15. See the works cited in notes 5 and 6 above.

In Search of Liberty

INTRODUCTION

RONALD ANGELO JOHNSON AND
OUSMANE K. POWER-GREENE

"SOMEWHERE."

Is there a place that hides from sight
Where daytime never turns to night?
Somewhere, somewhere?
There must be, else we could not bear
The pain, the anguish we have here.
Tell me! Tell me! Is it not true?
A place exists where we're made anew,
Somewhere, somewhere?

—WILLIAM FRANK FONVIELLE

Three months after the Continental Congress approved the Declaration of Independence, Lemuel Haynes, a former indentured servant and soldier of color in the Massachusetts militia, cited it when he drafted a scathing critique against slavery. In "Liberty Further Extended," Haynes invoked Thomas Jefferson's proposition that "all men are created equal" to conclude that "an African, or, in other terms, that a Negro may Justly Chalenge, and has an undeniable right to his Liberty: Consequently, the practise of Slave-keeping, which so much abounds in this Land is illicit."[1] According to his biographer, "the eradication of slavery and the extension to blacks of the liberty and security of an antislavery republican state were, in Haynes's mind, essential to republican governance."[2] Haynes pushed the founding generation beyond its limited vision of freedom and challenged white American audacity to clamor for liberty while holding humans of color in chains.[3]

Yet, white slaveholders' resistance to liberating millions of Black people left Haynes to preach of freedoms on "judgment day" in "a future state" beyond U.S. borders that would present "a striking contrast between this and the coming world."[4]

Inspired by the Age of Revolutions, African-descended people scattered throughout the European colonies interpreted the central concepts in the U.S. Declaration of Independence and France's Declaration of the Rights of Man as foundational to the establishment of the social, political, and economic relations of the modern world.[5] For this reason, the independence movements that spawned revolutions, most importantly the Haitian Revolution, encouraged African Americans to consider "Liberty or Death" an axiom when rising up against slaveholders, escaping enslavement, and organizing in opposition to discriminatory policies, such as segregation on public conveyances in the North.[6]

In the early republic, discussions raged within communities of color about whether to fight for freedom in the United States or to seek freedom beyond American shores.[7] Abolitionists, as Manisha Sinha shows in *The Slave's Cause*, demonstrated the crucial role transnational networks of British philanthropists and reformers played in antislavery and emigration movements, such as providing them with eager audiences for Black lecturers who challenged proslavery philosophical arguments, as well as procolonization perspectives.[8] For the enslaved, the questions involved seeking freedom through violent rebellion, through fugitive flight, or by passing from this life to the next. Acts of resistance and self-emancipation proved brick and mortar in what historians such as Ira Berlin call "the Long Emancipation," culminating in the Civil War or, as Frederick Douglass framed it, "an Abolition war."[9]

It is within this context that African Americans, enslaved and free, looked beyond U.S. borders for political rights, social equality, and economic prosperity.[10] Black internationalism, in this context, is understood as both linking up with a global struggle against racial oppression in the United States and leaving the "empire of liberty" to settle abroad. African Americans' willingness to fight, flee, forge, and foil illustrated a quest that, as Stephen Kantrowitz points out, "infused the word citizen with meaning beyond a common set of rights and obligations—with a vision of solidarity, regard, and even love that continued to reverberate for generations to come."[11]

Black abolitionists with an Atlantic worldview shared a sense of cosmopolitanism with white reformers. Yet, as scholar Ifeoma Kiddoe Nwankwo has shown, they understood their mobility as centered on resistance rather than as an expression of class privilege. Frederick Douglass and others used their cosmopolitan ties and international networks to protest systematic racial oppression in the United States while holding fast to their citizenship and belief in American ideals.[12] Though Douglass's shadow looms large over nineteenth-century Black activism, African American women traveled to enlist European allies in their fight for liberty and equality. However, antislavery lecturer Sarah Parker Remond remarked in 1858 that, whether she sailed to Europe on an American or a British steamer, "I know the spirit of prejudice will meet me."[13] Female travelers of color faced obstacles based on gender and race, as Elizabeth Stordeur Pryor has described, yet deftly negotiated these restrictions through white alliances and class pretensions.

With the demise of Reconstruction, once again, African Americans, now free citizens of former slave states, participated in a series of emigration initiatives in search of freedom from a level of racial violence that led scholar Rayford Logan to identify this period as the nadir of Black life in the United States.[14] African Americans found themselves in pitched battles outside polling stations with the Ku Klux Klan or the Red Shirts, who sought to deny Black citizens the liberty they had fought for from the Revolutionary War through the Civil War. As lawmakers of the U.S. South passed successive legislation to further restrict paths for African Americans to pursue equality and citizenship after the Civil War, Black people questioned how free they could ever truly be in the United States. The conversations among Black activists and community leaders did not take place within a societal vacuum. White Americans simultaneously argued among themselves over the extent to which they were willing to live with Black people in the United States and permit them to exercise their "unalienable rights." Despite persistent agitation, African Americans continued to search for equality through the end of Reconstruction and into the age of European colonialism in Africa.[15]

As the dawn of the twentieth century approached, African American writer William Frank Fonvielle endured a patronizing address by former white American congressman Stephen White, encouraging Fonvielle and other Black undergraduates at Livingstone College in Salisbury, North Carolina, to "be just to slaveholders and white men" as the latter cohort enacted post-Reconstruction laws that placed the lives of recently acknowledged U.S. citizens of color in "a condition little preferable to that of slavery."[16] This ominous forecast prompted Fonvielle to travel through the Deep South to observe white Americans' efforts to curb Black freedoms. His education in these Jim Crowisms came soon after he arrived in Spartanburg, South Carolina, one hundred miles south of Livingstone. Fonvielle saw "two sign boards at the train station, which told me that 'This room is for colored people. This room is for white people.'" The signs' meaning was evident: "The Negroes must stay in here... and the superior civilization goes where it pleases."[17] Later, as the train lumbered "through a beautiful stretch of mountainous country" and Fonvielle was not confined to a "Jim Crow car," he sat back and, with a sense of despair, penned the poem "Somewhere." In verse he looked away, as had Lemuel Haynes, to a place beyond U.S. shores "where we're made anew," where for Black people "daytime never turns to night," where they could live in dignity and peace.[18]

※※※

The writings of Lemuel Haynes and William Fonvielle reveal what African Americans within the United States understood: their freedoms would not be secured without an arduous, persistent fight. This volume explores their transnational struggle for freedom and citizenship by exploring the ways in which African Americans since the founding of the United States have viewed their struggle for freedom and liberty as a feature of changes within the Atlantic world.[19]

Building upon the rich scholarship in a transnational approach to African American history that decenters the United States within narratives of Black life, *In Search of Liberty* is the first volume to bring together international and interdisciplinary approaches to examine U.S.-based activists' fight against race and class exploitation through the establishment of an international network of allies.[20] This volume extends the long and important tradition of internationalism among historians of the Black American experience represented in Robin D. G. Kelley's pivotal essay "'But a Local Phase of a World Problem': Black History's Global Vision, 1883–1950."[21] Not only did African Americans locate their freedom dreams within a global context, but they also exhibited interest in the impact of international actions and events on U.S. life and movements.[22]

In order to explore the broad ways in which African Americans searched for liberty across the Atlantic world, this book charts African Americans' internationalism both spatially and topically in original ways. From emigration abroad, to lecture tours in Europe denouncing slavery, to missionary activity in King Leopold's Congo, the collection explores the complicated encounters in which notions of "Blackness" and "Africanness" manifested themselves. Indeed, as scholar James Sidbury shows in his work on the early nineteenth century, while Black Americans used racialist concepts of "Africanness" to inspire, unify, and resist racist oppression in the United States and the diaspora, these alliances remained fragile, causing some Black leaders to mix biblical notions of "oneness" with more recent histories of enslavement to justify nation-building projects in North America, Latin America, and Africa.[23] Activists and intellectuals like Mary Ann Shadd Cary shifted their ideas about emigration, colonization, and the international dimensions of Black freedom struggles based on changing national circumstances. However, what becomes clear through these chapters is that the local became a part of the transnational, and the transnational became a feature of how African Americans understood themselves and their notions of progress, equality, and democracy in their quest toward liberty and away from race-based oppression in the United States.[24]

In Search of Liberty is divided into four geographic sections to analyze Black internationalism through the diverse motives and methods free and enslaved Black people employed to realize and to expand freedom for themselves and their posterity across the Atlantic world. Part I focuses on the disparate experiences of Black people pursuing freedom across North America. The chapter by Franco Paz and Harvey Amani Whitfield is situated within the historical literature on the Black Loyalist diaspora to direct our attention toward the gripping and complex struggles for liberty of Black individuals in Canada.[25] It paints a jarring portrait of the reenslavement of Elizabeth Watson, a Black woman from the United States, and the arduous legal battles to restore her freedom. The analysis of Paz and Whitfield adds texture to the historical literature addressing the memory of Black flight to the "promised land" by underscoring the "fragile freedom" of Black life in Canada due to a common practice of seizing a Black person and enslaving them.[26] Leading off the collection, the essay serves as a reminder that the path toward freedom for Black people across the Atlantic world, rather than a straight line, was at times fraught with uncertainty and obstruction from relentless proslavery forces.

Mekala Audain's chapter describes the experiences of Black people who fled enslavement in Natchitoches, Louisiana, to illuminate the contours of a southern Underground Railroad that developed after the Louisiana Purchase. Building on the evolving scholarship of freedom seeking to the south, it treats Black internationalism southward into Spanish America colonial territory in ways comparable to the extensive literature on Black Americans' northern escape routes toward Canada.[27] Audain presents a path to liberty in Spanish Texas populated by sympathetic Spaniards to the plight of Black freedom seekers who traveled the Camino Real (Royal Road) connecting Natchitoches to Nacogdoches to conclude that the Spanish-speaking world was an important destination for Black liberty in the nineteenth century.

Similarly, Thomas Mareite's exploration of Black fugitives from slavery in Mexican Texas places the southern Underground Railroad within postindependence Mexico, where general emancipation appeared on the horizon. The chapter features Black people who fled to northern Mexico between 1821, the year of Mexican independence, and 1836, when Texas seceded from Mexico, and encountered a society on the brink of eradicating slavery. However, because Mexican authorities failed to enforce abolition laws among Anglo migrant slaveholders, Black refugees in Mexico faced threats to their freedom when Texas seceded. Placing runaways from slavery within the context of the early Mexican republic, Mareite demonstrates the diplomatic challenges that gradual abolition posed for Mexican authorities who protected refugees and free Black people from U.S. kidnappers.

The essays in part II bring Africa into sharp relief as a complicated refuge of Black freedom and governance. Lawrence Aje's chapter explores the push-and-pull factors that encouraged free people of color to emigrate from South Carolina within the context of competing emigration movements between 1780 and 1865. It suggests that certain members of the state's free Black population shared a vision of contributing to the establishment of a Black nation-state without slavery and racial caste.[28] Aje follows emigrants in a long view of colonization in West Africa that considers various factors, such as gender balance and the mean age of free Black South Carolinians, in determining which inhabitants departed the state and which returned from these emigration initiatives.

Caree A. Banton examines Liberia as a theater using an interdisciplinary approach to the study of race and race-making. Her method provides a nuanced exploration into ways abolitionists, colonizationists, Black nationalists, diplomats, and migrants in Liberia performed notions of freedom in the way they carried themselves and how they spoke. Situated within a historical literature that acknowledges how Harriet Beecher Stowe's story of American slavery serves as a paradigm for understanding oppression, this chapter studies how debates about race and emigrants provided physical and imaginative venues for combatting popular ideas of Black racial inferiority.[29] Banton's analysis outlines how, by embodying liberty literally, Black

Americans used performance and theatrics to assert their humanity and to demand respect from European powers en route to Liberian independence and statehood.

Marcus Bruce's chapter considers the religious motivations of African Americans for venturing to Africa at the end of the nineteenth century. It critically examines the journals and correspondence of Yale University student George Henry Jackson, who believed, like other postemancipation African American students, that he had a responsibility for the redemption of Africa through Christianity.[30] Bruce employs Jackson's recorded memories of his tenure in Congo Free State during the 1890s to reveal a rare glimpse into the conscience of an African American emigrant in Africa who, in working to spiritually "save" Africa, experienced what Michel Foucault describes as the "cultivation of the self."[31]

In part III of the collection, the Caribbean serves as the setting for historical analysis of the ways in which emancipation, Black governance, and the lure of citizenship inspired Black American emigration efforts to the region. Dexter J. Gabriel's chapter focuses on Black Americans who emigrated to Trinidad in the wake of Britain's Slavery Abolition Act. It tells the story of free Black people looking to the British West Indies to escape Baltimore's racialized caste system. Gabriel charts the trek of Nathaniel Peck and Thomas Price across British Guiana and Trinidad to demonstrate how abolition and emigration intersected. His analysis augments the burgeoning scholarship on the modified white power structures Black emigrants confronted in the postemancipation Caribbean.[32]

Brandon R. Byrd's chapter on Haiti reappraises the historiography of this well-known destination for Black emigrants. It calls for greater use of Haiti-based sources by scholars to evaluate the Black American emigration movements of the latter nineteenth century. Byrd proposes interdisciplinary approaches, with an emphasis on anthropological methods and oral histories from within Haiti, to provide more accurate assessments of emigration, life, and contributions of Black Americans in Haiti.

Claire Bourhis-Mariotti's chapter moves east across the Haitian border to examine critically the diplomatic role of Frederick Douglass in U.S. debates surrounding the annexation of the Dominican Republic.[33] Through interrogating Douglass's reasons for accepting his position on the exploratory mission, Bourhis-Mariotti answers the enduring question: Why would a man who devoted his life to the liberty of Black people and their right to self-determination be complicit in U.S. imperialism in the Caribbean? The essay contextualizes Douglass's role by analyzing his rise within the Republican Party and a desire to leverage his participation in the mission to build legitimacy and power within a shaky U.S. political landscape. Alongside recent scholarship on Douglass, Bourhis-Mariotti's analysis offers a fresh interpretation of the conflicting efforts of an international abolitionist who condemned the federal government for insufficient protections of freed Black people who resettled in Kansas before accepting a controversial presidential appointment as minister to Haiti.[34]

The essays in part IV, set in Europe, explore Black female activism and travel writing and the trail Frederick Douglass blazed through reform circles for Black Americans up to the twentieth century. Pia Wiegmink's chapter on African American women in Europe analyzes the way in which African American women's travels to England, France, and Russia shaped their racial consciousness and ideas about progress. These female activists traversed the Atlantic world as thinkers and actors, building transnational coalitions within the European communities to fight slavery and to secure liberty for Black Americans. Through these experiences, Wiegmink identifies how each writer developed key elements of her ideas on Black womanhood, identity, and the freedom struggle.

Angela F. Murphy's chapter on Frederick Douglass's activism in Europe, specifically Ireland, places Douglass's trip within the context of earlier Black abolitionists who built a foundation of antislavery sentiment among the "liberty-loving" Irish people.[35] This chapter departs from the treatment of Douglass as a "representative man" and focuses on how he confronted detractors who failed to grasp the difference between race-based suffering and oppression rooted in class and religion. Murphy details the setbacks Douglass faced in Ireland, illustrating the limitation of transnational connections and the difficulty of linking Irish activism for home rule with the struggle of Black people against U.S. slavery and racial injustice.[36]

※

From those who fled slavery for liberty beyond U.S. borders to those who left of their own accord to agitate for human rights, African Americans remained wedded to networks within the Atlantic world. For this reason, they searched for places and spaces where they could realize their freedom dreams. "Many black Americans subscribed," Sylvia Jacobs explains, "to the concept of a common brotherhood among blacks the world over and saw the need to maintain the African nexus."[37] *In Search of Liberty* is a collection of historical analyses of the ideals, efforts, and sacrifices of African Americans toward their freedom and equality within an international context.

NOTES

Fonvielle's poem, which serves as the epigraph for this introduction, was reprinted in the official newspaper of the African Methodist Episcopal Zion Church, the *Star of Zion* (Charlotte, N.C.), November 12, 1964, 5.

1. Spelling as in the original. Lemuel Haynes, quoted in Ruth Bogin, "'Liberty Further Extended': A 1776 Antislavery Manuscript by Lemuel Haynes," *William and Mary Quarterly* 40, no. 1 (1983): 95.

2. John Saillant, *Black Puritan, Black Republican: The Life and Thought of Lemuel Haynes 17533–1833* (New York: Oxford University Press, 2003), 49.

3. See Manisha Sinha, *The Slave's Cause: A History of Abolition* (New Haven, Conn.: Yale University Press, 2016); Richard Newman, *Freedom's Prophet: Bishop Richard Allen, the A.M.E. Church, and the Black Founding Fathers* (New York: New York University Press, 2009); Annette Gordon-Reed, *Thomas Jefferson and Sally Hemmings: An American Controversy* (Charlottesville: University of Virginia Press, 1997).

4. Lemuel Haynes, *The Important Concerns of Ministers, and the People of Their Charge, at the Day of Judgment* (Rutland, Vt., 1798), 3–5, 9–10, 12–13.

5. See Gerald Horne, *The Counter-revolution of 1776: Slave Resistance and the Origins of the United States of America* (New York: New York University Press, 2014), 20; David Brion Davis, *Slavery in the Age of Emancipation* (New York: Vintage, 2014).

6. Christopher Leslie Brown, *Moral Capital: Foundations of British Abolitionism* (Chapel Hill: University of North Carolina Press, 2006); Patrick Rael, *Eighty-Eight Years: The Long Death of Slavery in the United States, 1777–1865* (Athens: University of Georgia Press, 2015). For studies of African Americans' challenge to the formation of the United States, see Horne, *The Counter-revolution*; and Douglass Egerton, *Death or Liberty: African Americans and Revolutionary America* (New York: Oxford University Press, 2011).

7. For a history of Black Americans' struggle for citizenship, see Stephen Kantrowitz, *More Than Freedom: Fighting for Black Citizenship in a White Republic, 1829–1899* (New York: Penguin Books, 2012); Erica Armstrong Dunbar, *A Fragile Freedom: African American Women and Emancipation in the Antebellum City* (New Haven, Conn.: Yale University Press, 2008); and Leslie M. Harris, *In the Shadow of Slavery: African Americans in New York City, 1626–1863*.

8. Sinha, *The Slave's Cause*, 339.

9. See Ira Berlin, *The Long Emancipation: The Demise of Slavery in the United States* (Cambridge, Mass.: Harvard University Press, 2015); Rael, *Eighty-Eight Years*; W. Caleb McDaniel, *The Problem of Democracy in the Age of Slavery: Garrisonian Abolitionists and Transatlantic Reform* (Baton Rouge: Louisiana State University Press, 2013).

10. See Betty Fladeland, *Men and Brothers: Anglo-American Antislavery Cooperation* (Urbana: University of Illinois Press, 1972); J. R. Oldfield, *Transatlantic Abolitionism in the Age of Revolution: An International History of Antislavery, c. 1787–1820* (New York: Cambridge University Press, 2013).

11. See Eric Williams, *Capitalism and Slavery* (1944; repr., Chapel Hill: University of North Carolina Press, 1994); Betty Fladeland, *Men and Brothers: Anglo-American Antislavery Cooperation* (Urbana: University of Illinois Press, 1972); Kantrowitz, *More Than Freedom*, 9. For a thorough exploration of this struggle for citizenship, see Martha Jones, *Birthright Citizens: A History of Race and Rights in Antebellum America* (New York: Cambridge University Press, 2018). For how the quest for citizenship intersects with Black mobility in the Atlantic world, see Elizabeth Stordeur Pryor, *Colored Travelers: The Fight for Citizenship before the Civil War* (Chapel Hill: University of North Carolina Press, 2016).

12. Ifeoma Kiddoe Nwankwo, *Black Cosmopolitanism: Racial Consciousness and Transnational Identity in the Nineteenth-Century Americas* (Philadelphia: University of Pennsylvania Press, 2005).

13. Sarah Parker Remond quoted in Pryor, *Colored Travelers*, 141. For the important role of nineteenth-century Black women internationalists in the transatlantic struggle against slavery, see Kathryn Kish Sklar and James Brewer Stewart, eds., *Women's Rights and Transatlantic Antislavery in the Era of Emancipation* (New Haven, Conn.: Yale University Press, 2007).

14. Rayford W. Logan, *The Negro in American Life and Thought: The Nadir, 1877–1901* (New York: Dial Press, 1954).

15. James T. Campbell, *Middle Passages: African Americans' Journeys to Africa, 1787–2005* (New York: Penguin Random House, 2007); Robin Winks, *The Blacks in Canada: A History*, 2nd ed. (Montreal: McGill-Queen's University Press, 2000); Richard West, *Back to Africa: A History of Sierra Leone* (New York: Holt, Reinhart, Winston, 1970); Harvey Amani Whitfield, *Blacks on the Borders: The Black Refugees in British North America, 1815–1860* (Burlington: University of Vermont Press, 2006); Bronwen Everill, *Abolition and Empire in Sierra Leone and Liberia* (New York: Palgrave Macmillan, 2013); Kenneth C. Barnes, *Journey of Hope: The Back-to-Africa Movement in Arkansas in the Late 1800s* (Chapel Hill: University of North Carolina Press, 2004); Kendra T. Fields, "'No Such Thing as Stand Still': Migration and Geopolitics in African American History," *Journal of American History* 102, no. 3 (2015): 693–718.

16. Stephen V. White, *Address of Hon. S. V. White upon the Race Question in the South Delivered at Salisbury, N.C., before the Literary Societies of Livingstone College* (Salisbury, N.C., 1890), 8, 10–11.

17. Fonvielle, "The South as I Saw It," *A.M.E. Zion Church Quarterly* 4 (1894): 151, 157.

18. Ibid., 156.

19. Joanne Pope Melish, *Disowning Slavery: Gradual Emancipation and "Race" in New England 1780–1860* (Ithaca, N.Y.: Cornell University Press, 1998); Mia Bay,

White Image in the Black Mind: African-American Ideas about White People, 1830–1925 (New York: Oxford University Press, 2000); Ibram X. Kendi, *Stamped from the Beginning: The Definitive History of Racist Ideas in America* (New York: Nation Books, 2016).

20. Michelle M. Rief's scholarship continues to inspire research on Black women's internationalism. See Michelle M. Rief, "Thinking Locally, Acting Globally: The International Agenda of African American Clubwomen, 1880–1940," *Journal of African American History* 89, no. 3 (2004): 203–22; Sarah L. Silkey, *Black Woman Reformer: Ida B. Wells, Lynching and Transatlantic Activism* (Athens: University of Georgia Press, 2015); Laura Renee Chandler, "Black Women and the World: African American Women's Transnational Activism, 1890–1930" (PhD diss., Rice University, 2015).

21. See Robin D. G. Kelley, "'But a Local Phase of a World Problem': Black History's Global Vision, 1883–1950," *Journal of American History* 86, no. 3 (1999): 1045–77; Thomas Bender, "The 'La Pietra Report': Project on Internationalizing the Study of American History," *Amerikastudien / American Studies* 48, no. 1 (2003): 33–40; Nemeta Blyden, "Relationships among Blacks in the Diaspora: African and Caribbean Immigrants and American-Born Blacks," in *Africans in Global Migration: Searching for Promised Lands*, ed. John A. Arthur, Joseph Takougang, and Thomas Owusu (Lanham, Md.: Lexington Books, 2012), 161–74.

22. Sylvia M. Jacobs's pioneering study of Black American internationalism is the cornerstone of scholarship on late nineteenth- and early twentieth-century Black internationalism. See Sylvia M. Jacobs, *The African Nexus: Black American Perspectives on the European Partitioning of Africa, 1880–1920* (Westport, Conn.: Greenwood Press, 1981).

23. James Sidbury, *Becoming African in America: Race and Nation in the Early Black Atlantic* (New York: Oxford University Press, 2007), 6, 38, 119.

24. Scholars Keisha Blain and Tiffany Gill have traced the vital role of Black women internationalists across the late nineteenth and twentieth centuries. See Keisha Blain and Tiffany Gill, eds., *To Turn the Whole World Over: Black Women and Internationalism* (Urbana: University of Illinois Press, 2019).

25. Maya Jasanoff, *Liberty's Exiles: American Loyalists in the Revolutionary World* (New York: Vintage Books, 2011), 12–13. For an excellent transnational examination of Black emigration to Canada within an Atlantic world context, see Ikuko Asaka, *Tropical Freedom: Climate, Settler Colonialism, and Black Exclusion in the Age of Emancipation* (Durham, N.C.: Duke University Press, 2017).

26. Dunbar, *A Fragile Freedom*.

27. See Sean Kelley, "'Mexico in His Head': Slavery and the Texas-Mexico Border, 1810–1860," *Journal of Social History* 37, no. 3 (2004): 709–23; Damian Alan Pargas, ed., *Fugitive Slaves and Spaces of Freedom in North America* (Gainesville: University Press of Florida, 2018).

28. See Eric Burin, *Slavery and the Peculiar Solution: A History of the American Colonization Society* (Gainesville: University Press of Florida, 2005); Penelope

Campbell, *Maryland in Africa: The Maryland State Colonization Society, 1831–1857* (Chicago: University of Chicago Press, 1971); Claude Clegg, *The Price of Liberty: African Americans and the Making of Liberia* (Chapel Hill: University of North Carolina Press, 2004); Alan Huffman, *Mississippi in Africa: The Saga of the Slaves of Prospect Hill Plantation and Their Legacy in Liberia* (New York: Gotham Books, 2004); Marie Tyler-McGraw, *An African Republic: Black & White Virginians in the Making of Liberia* (Chapel Hill: University of North Carolina Press, 2007); Beverly C. Tomek, *Colonization and Its Discontents: Emancipation, Emigration, and Antislavery in Antebellum Pennsylvania* (New York: New York University Press, 2010); Susan E. Lindsey, *Liberty Brought Us Here: The True Story of American Slaves Who Migrated to Liberia* (Lexington: University Press of Kentucky, 2020); Bronwen Everill, "Experiments in Colonial Citizenship in Sierra Leone and Liberia," in *New Directions in the Study of African American Recolonization*, ed. Beverly C. Tomek and Matthew J. Hetrick (Gainesville: University Press of Florida, 2017), 184–205.

29. See Marcy J. Dinius, "'I Go to Liberia': Following *Uncle Tom's Cabin* to Africa," in *Uncle Tom's Cabins: The Transnational History of America's Most Mutable Book*, ed. Tracy C. Davis and Steak Mihaylova (Ann Arbor: University of Michigan Press, 2018); Randall Miller, "Mrs. Stowe's Negro: George Harris' Negritude in *Uncle Tom's Cabin*," *Colby Quarterly* 10, no. 8 (1974): 521–26; David Reynolds, *Mightier Than the Sword: "Uncle Tom's Cabin" and the Battle for America* (New York: W. W. Norton and Company, 2011).

30. See Nemata Amelia Ibitayo Blyden, *African Americans and Africa: A New History* (New Haven, Conn.: Yale University Press, 2019); Elliot P. Skinner, *African Americans and U.S. Policy toward Africa 1850–1924: In Defence of Black Nationality* (Washington, D.C.: Howard University Press, 1993); Jacobs, *The African Nexus*; James T. Campbell, *Songs of Zion: The African Methodist Episcopal Church in the United States and South Africa* (New York: Oxford University Press, 1995); David Killingray, "The Black Atlantic Missionary Movement and Africa, 1780s–1920s," *Journal of Religion in Africa* 33, no. 1 (2003): 3–31.

31. Michel Foucault, *Technologies of the Self: A Seminar with Michel Foucault* (Amherst: University of Massachusetts Press, 1988), 5.

32. See Claudius K. Fergus, *Revolutionary Emancipation: Slavery and Abolitionism in the British West Indies* (Baton Rouge: Louisiana State University Press, 2013); Gale Kenny, *Contentious Liberties: American Abolitionists in Post-emancipation Jamaica, 1834–1866* (Athens: University of Georgia Press, 2011).

33. For a useful exploration of Frederick Douglass in the Caribbean, see Millery Polyné, "Expansion Now! Haiti, 'Santo Domingo,' and Frederick Douglass at the Intersection of U.S. and Caribbean Pan-Americanism," *Caribbean Studies* 34, no. 2 (2006).

34. See David Blight, *Frederick Douglass: Prophet of Freedom* (New York: Simon and Schuster, 2018), 544.

35. Fionnghuala Sweeney, *Frederick Douglass and the Atlantic World* (Liverpool:

Liverpool University Press, 2007); Tom Chaffin, *Giant's Causeway: Frederick Douglass's Irish Odyssey and the Making of an American Visionary* (Charlottesville: University of Virginia Press, 2014); Laurence Fenton, *Frederick Douglass in Ireland: The "Black O'Connell"* (Cork: Collins Press, 2014).

36. W. Caleb McDaniel, "Repealing Unions: American Abolitionists, Irish Repeal, and the Origins of Garrisonian Disunionism," *Journal of the Early Republic* 28, no. 2 (2008): 243–69.

37. Sylvia M. Jacobs, "Three African American Women Missionaries in the Congo, 1887–1899: The Confluence of Race, Culture, Identity, and Nationality," in *Competing Kingdoms: Women, Mission, Nation, and the American Protestant Empire, 1812–1960*, ed. Barbara Reeves-Ellington, Kathryn Kish Sklar, and Connie A. Shemo (Durham, N.C.: Duke University Press), 321.

PART I

North America

CHAPTER 1

On the Edge of Freedom
*The Reenslavement of
Elizabeth Watson in Nova Scotia*

FRANCO PAZ AND
HARVEY AMANI WHITFIELD

It was early March 1778, seven o'clock in the morning. Elizabeth Watson lay shackled to the floor of a dark cellar.[1] She had been enslaved in Halifax, Nova Scotia, by Elias Marshall, master shipwright of the Royal Naval Dockyard.[2] Marshall had beaten her for six hours. Elizabeth Watson was pregnant. He had known for eight days.

Watson went into labor likely as a result of Marshall's assault. When she asked him for "help to have her delivered," Marshall beat her once again. Hours later, Watson crawled out of the house toward a latrine inside the stable. In that outhouse, surrounded only by Marshall's cattle, she delivered her own child "without assistance from any earthly being."

Marshall found her there the following morning. He wanted Watson to work, ordered her to wash herself, but Watson told Marshall she was cold. "I will soon cure you," Marshall said. He sent Durdsly, another servant, to fill two buckets with snow and ice water, which Marshall emptied over her body. He left Watson there.[3]

The next day, Marshall took Watson back into the house, where his wife waited with a fire iron. Upon entering, Marshall's wife seized Watson and split open her skull. Afterward, Marshall dragged her down the stairs and into the cellar once more, tied her hands and feet to a beam, and beat her for one hour. Then he walked upstairs to eat dinner.

Marshall went back to the cellar once he had finished eating. This time he beat Watson well into the night, until her body was no longer bound by skin. She could not even lie down. Her exposed flesh forced Watson to remain on her hands and knees. Realizing her life was in peril, Marshall was at last forced to call a doctor. When Halifax surgeon Phillips saw Watson, he fainted.[4]

The doctor pronounced Elizabeth Watson dead.

Elias Marshall did not accept this. He called a second, unnamed doctor, who was ultimately able to stabilize her, though this entailed severing large patches of skin and flesh from her body. Once Watson's life was no longer in immediate danger, Marshall refused to feed her anything but "peas or what [she] could get out of the Hog's Trough."[5]

Soon after, Marshall sold Elizabeth Watson to John Woodin.[6] Recognizing this opportunity to escape enslavement, Watson petitioned the Halifax Inferior Court of Common Pleas. She claimed she had been born a free woman in Boston and had been abducted there "under false pretense." As her witness she brought Elizabeth Reed, another Boston-born Halifax slave. Reed attested to the veracity of Watson's testimony, testifying that she "well knew ... Elizabeth Watson to be a Free Woman." She added that Watson lived with a Mrs. Lobdell prior to her abduction. Following Reed's deposition, the court declared Watson a free woman.[7]

Watson's liberty only lasted thirty-one days. On April 23, 1779, Halifax butcher William Proud seized Elizabeth Watson and claimed she was his "Right and Property."[8]

The explicit portrayal of the violence Elizabeth Watson suffered at the hands of Elias Marshall might strike some readers as over the top, an altogether too graphic depiction of an event that constituted, at the end of the day, a shocking aberration in the generally "benign" form of slavery that existed in the Canadian Maritimes. This is simply not true.[9] But it is also beside the point. Whether or not this base brutality is indicative of the experience of the majority of Maritime bondspeople is incidental. This assault—this particular assault—happened. The account of it comes from Elizabeth Watson's deposition. These are her words. To omit or otherwise sanitize her story would have done her and others like her a disservice.[10]

Although the individual lives of enslaved people may have been erased by the archive's quiet tyranny, their presence in pre-Loyalist Nova Scotia remains evident. Beyond attesting to the brutal world in which she and others like her lived, Watson's story, particularly her petitioning of the lower court, reveals her keen understanding of the legal world she inhabited and of her rights as a British subject. But her actions alone do not account for the trial's occurrence. Watson's ability to stand in a court of law against white men suggests a legal apparatus that to some extent enabled Black people to assert themselves. A full ensemble of institutions, regulations, and customs must come together for such a trial to take place: lawyers willing to take a slave's case, judges inclined to hear it, juries amenable enough to not make the act futile. This apparatus is worth exploring, as is its role in regulating the conditions of possibility for both Black and white Maritime populations.

Watson's story is an early example of reenslavement in the region.[11] Her story departs from well-known narratives of African American freedom in Canada. Likewise, it complicates and nuances historical analyses of the Black Atlantic world and reveals the porous, fragile nature of the boundary between slavery and freedom. Watson's protean story, time and again oscillating between freedom and slavery, is emblematic of this history. Elizabeth Watson was likely the first enslaved woman to seek her freedom in a Maritime court of law, but she was not the last. Watson's legal fight was followed by those of two other enslaved Black women: Mary Postell in 1791 and Nancy, with no surname, in New Brunswick nine years later.[12] Elizabeth Watson oscillated from slavery to freedom and back to slavery in the space of thirty-one days. Tracing the genealogy of her search for liberty and exploring her path to enslavement in Nova Scotia broaden our perception of the Maritime world's unique syntax. Elizabeth Watson brings this world of unfreedom into a fuller, more vivid light. Her life complicates our understanding of the threads that bound freedom and slavery in the Atlantic world.

Slavery in the Maritimes

Even as early as the seventeenth century, Africans had a presence in the Maritimes. Mathieu da Costa, an early free Black man in colonial Canada, was a member of Pierre Dugua's 1605 exploratory party.[13] He likely worked as a translator between the French and Mi'kmaq, but it is unclear how Costa "might have travelled to North America, how long he stayed, for whom he worked, and with whom he interpreted."[14] His last name reveals some connection to Portugal. His story links him to the Atlantic Creoles, who were well versed in "the commerce of the Atlantic, fluent in its new languages, and intimate with its trade and cultures."[15] It is likely that Costa spoke multiple languages, including French and Mi'kmaq, and that he was familiar with the culture of the latter. Though his life remains obscured by a lack of extant sources, the known fragments of his life connote links between distant regions of the Atlantic world. Other Africans arrived in Nova Scotia during the seventeenth century. Little is known about their lives or whether they were enslaved. The archives hold a few scattered stories, most notably that of La Liberté, who lived in Cape Sable (an island off the southern coast of Nova Scotia) around 1686 and was likely "a slave who had escaped from one of the colonies to the south."[16]

Most enslaved Black Canadians during the first half of the eighteenth century lived in Île Royale, known eventually as Cape Breton.[17] At least 266 enslaved people populated Île Royale between 1713 and 1758, with the majority of them living in Louisbourg.[18] They came from a variety of backgrounds, including Africa, the West Indies, and the American colonies. In contrast to other areas of New France, where the enslaved were largely Indigenous, over 90 percent of Île Royale's enslaved population was Black.[19] They worked predominantly as domestic servants. They cleaned, cooked, nursed, gardened, and more.[20] Only nineteen of Île Royale's bondspeople worked outside the household: one fisherman, two cabin boys, fifteen sailors, and one executioner.[21] There were only a few enslaved people per household. The small-scale nature of Île Royale slavery, where close contact between slaveholders and the enslaved was the norm, led to a deep-rooted culture of sexual violence.[22]

In 1749 Edward Cornwallis and twenty-five hundred settlers sailed into the waters of Chebucto on a sloop of war and thirteen transport ships. They disembarked along the harbor's spruce-lined shore and founded Halifax.[23] Enslaved Black people became a habitual sight soon thereafter, having made their way to Nova Scotia with Cornwallis's first settlers, as well as through the business dealings of early Halifax merchants. In 1750 Captain Bloss, a Royal Navy officer, brought sixteen bondspeople to Nova Scotia possibly from Antigua. They built him "a very good house."[24] It is likely that the people Bloss enslaved worked as agricultural laborers and domestic servants.[25]

In September 1751, the *Boston Post-Boy* advertised the sale of "ten strong hearty Negro men mostly tradesmen, such as caulkers, carpenters, sailmakers, and ropemakers."[26] This advertisement reveals the type of skilled labor that characterized Maritime slavery, as well as the existence of established trade routes between newly founded Halifax and Massachusetts. The following year, Thomas Thomas, "late of New York, but now of Halifax," wrote a will in which he bequeathed "all my plate and my negro servant Orange that now lives with me at Halifax . . . to my son."[27]

The diversity of skills Maritime bondspeople possessed was once again displayed in merchant Joshua Mauger's 1752 sale notice in the *Halifax Gazette*. Mauger's advertisement was published shortly after his return from the West Indies and describes "several Negro slaves . . . a likely Negro Wench, of about thirty-five years of Age ... capable of doing Needle-Work of all sorts ... Washing, Ironing, Cookery and every other Thing that can be expected of such a Slave ... Likewise two healthy Negro Slaves about 18 years of Age, of agreable [sic] Tempers, and fit for any kind of Business."[28] This advertisement indicates both the existence of a viable slave-trading market in Halifax—Mauger would likely have sold them during the return voyage otherwise—and the city's growth as an urban center, by then part of a larger Atlantic trading network between North America and the West Indies.[29] Coupled with the 1751 *Boston Post-Boy* sale notice, the advertisements display the versatile, multioccupational nature of Maritime slavery and reveal labor patterns that would echo in the lives of the enslaved brought to the province by the New England Planters in 1760 and the Loyalists in 1783.[30]

Following the brutal expulsion of the Acadians from the Maritimes between 1755 and 1764, Governor Charles Lawrence offered land expropriated from the Acadians to English-speaking settlers from New England. The government granted an additional fifty acres of land to these settlers for each Black person they brought into the colony, encouraging slavery in the region. Between 1759 and 1774, approximately eight thousand Planters settled in Nova Scotia. Historians do not know the exact number of enslaved people who arrived in the Maritimes during this time, but it is clear that a number of prominent planters were slaveholders.[31]

The New England Planters' use of enslaved labor and their efforts to strengthen slavery in the Maritime colonies underlined their similarity to other slaveholding areas throughout New England and New York. Like the enslaved in Île Royale, close contact between slaveholders and the enslaved was the norm. Most enslaved people worked in a range of tasks, such as planting crops, repairing fences, cooking, cleaning, and caring for children. Nova Scotia's Black population increased as a result of the New England Planters' arrival, but it remained small. For example, a colonial census taken in 1767 shows that Nova Scotia's Black population hardly exceeded one hundred, though this census almost certainly excluded the enslaved population.[32] The exact number of the enslaved population in Nova Scotia prior to the arrival of the Loyalists is impossible to calculate and will more than likely remain unknown.[33]

However, the experiences of the enslaved remain buried in the letters and diaries of white slaveholders and newspaper advertisements submitted by those who sought to buy or sell a person. In 1759, for example, a Halifax merchant named Malachy Salter wrote to his wife, Susanna Mulberry, and asked her to buy a slave while she was traveling in Boston. As Salter explained, a young enslaved boy had proven troublesome. "Jack is Jack still," he wrote, "but rather worse. I am obliged [to beat him] almost every day."[34]

One year later, the *Halifax Gazette* advertised for the sale "at public auction on Monday the 3rd of November, at the house of Mr. John Rider, of two slaves, viz. a boy and a girl, about eleven years old."[35] Rider was a surveyor of highways who later managed—perhaps owned—the Wolfe Tavern, deemed in its day a "very elegant resort ... [whose] wines were noted for excellence."[36] It is not known, however, whether Rider owned the two children sold at his home in the spring of 1760.

A Halifax assemblyman named Charles Proctor sold a "Mulatto girl" to Mary Wood of Annapolis, wife of missionary Reverend Thomas Wood, in the summer of 1767.[37] The girl's name was Louisa. She cost fifteen pounds. Mary Wood transferred ownership of Louisa to her daughter Mary Day, and Louisa then disappeared from history.[38] According to the January 1771 census, there were seven other bondspeople in Annapolis. Ebenezer Messenger owned one of them. Nothing is known about the man Ebenezer Messenger owned. Elsewhere in Annapolis, Magdalen Winniett owned a man, a woman, and a girl. Joseph Winniett owned a woman and a boy. Ann Williams owned one man. One is struck by how often all that remains of a Black life is the name of the white life that professed to own it.

Like those of Jack, Louisa, and other enslaved Black Canadians, the details surrounding Elizabeth Watson's arrival remain uncertain. Most likely, Watson arrived in Halifax sometime in the 1770s. Although the nature of slave labor in the region remained relatively unchanged following the arrival of the New England Planters, there is one contemporary local slave advertisement that denotes the particular skills she may have been expected to possess. In May 1776, a man published a notice in the *Nova Scotia Gazette and Weekly Chronicle*. He hoped to acquire "a Negro Woman, about 25 or 30 years of age, that understands country work ... the management of a dairy ... and domestic labor."[39] The breadth of skills that the enslaved—particularly women—were expected to have would likely have included "farming, cooking, cleaning, washing clothes, and looking after children."[40] Physical tasks might have been as diverse as "cutting, carting, threshing ... milling wheat ... husking corn ... cutting cornstalks; mowing, raking, and carting hay; digging ... sledding stones and building stone walls; building fences; cutting and scowing wood; hoeing and picking peas, beans, and turnips."[41] Watson and others enslaved in Nova Scotia prior to the American Revolution would have experienced a form of slavery with many of the characteristics found in the province's New England counterpart.

Both New England and the Maritime region maintained slaveholding connections and trading relationships with the West Indies. Yet, the small number of bondspeople per household implies an inherent level of proximity between the enslaved and slaveholders that contrasts with the Caribbean and southern United States; low population density in turn indicates a greater difficulty in forming Black communities and producing distinct Black cultures compared to the large-scale plantations of the southern colonies and the Caribbean.[42] But this is not to say that the enslaved women and men of Nova Scotia were unable to develop communities or distinct cultures. Certain aspects of low-density, small-scale slavery with multioccupational, semiskilled, and skilled labor patterns might even have lent themselves to cultural diffusion in a way that large plantations did not. "Abroad" marriages and romantic relationships, for example, were likely far more common in Nova Scotia than South Carolina. In addition, skilled workers were often able to travel unsupervised. All of these represented valuable opportunities to network and build communities across large distances.[43]

Though the number of bondspeople brought to Nova Scotia by the New England Planters will almost certainly remain elusive, there are enough extant sources to suppose it modest.[44] The New England Planters came largely from overcrowded areas of southern New England. They were above all else attracted to Nova Scotia by the promise of free developed land. They did not have much money; they were likely to have bought land in New England if they had the financial resources to do so.[45] Governor Lawrence's offer included subsidies to cover the cost of resettlement, further enticing New Englanders of lower socioeconomic status.[46] All of this amounts to the unlikelihood that slaveholding was widespread among Planters. But slavery had an influence far more pervasive than bare numbers might suggest. Planters who had the greatest financial resources were likely to take on positions of leadership within the province. These same men were the most likely to enslave Black people. Slaveholders may have been a minority, but—as evidenced by Malachy Salter and others—they tended to have outsized influence over public and legislative policy. In outright political terms, it did not matter whether the New England Planters brought twenty or two thousand bondspeople so long as the right people enslaved them.

Nova Scotia never had a statute law that recognized or regulated slavery.[47] Indeed, Prince Edward Island was the only Maritime province ever to enact slavery into law.[48] In 1762, Nova Scotia came as close as it ever would to acknowledging the existence of slavery within its territory. The second session of the Third General Assembly convened that year and passed the

Innholders Act, which banned the sale of alcohol on credit for "any sum exceeding five shillings . . . to any soldier, sailor, servant, apprentice, bound servant, or negro slave."[49] It is not beyond reason to speculate that the language of the bill might have been engineered in such a way as to give slavery a legal footing in the province. After all, the Third General Assembly counted slaveholders among their rank. Slaveholders were present in the Nova Scotia Assembly as late as 1808.[50]

Lacking statute law, the legitimacy of slavery in Nova Scotia was predicated on the notion that custom attains the force of law and as such remained "implicitly lawful . . . until adjudged or legislated to be explicitly illegal."[51] This rationale began to be challenged in the 1780s following the arrival of the Loyalists. But even then, these challenges were rare and often unsuccessful. Fruitful legal challenges on the basis of title defect did not become the norm until the 1792 exodus to Sierra Leone. Elizabeth Watson's court cases should not be confused with these actions, which were explicitly designed to test the legality of slavery within the province.

From Slavery to Freedom

When Elizabeth Watson petitioned the Halifax Inferior Court of Common Pleas in March 1778, she claimed she had been "brought from Boston [to Halifax]" and there, unknown to herself, had been sold to Elias Marshall as a slave. By petitioning the court, she became the first Black woman to seek possession of her freedom in a Nova Scotia court of law.[52] Elizabeth Watson's keen understanding of the legal world she inhabited and of her rights as a British subject may well point to her New England origins. Indeed, freedom suits were a well-established legal recourse for the enslaved population of New England around the time Elizabeth Watson likely arrived in Nova Scotia.[53]

In New England, Joan Jackson was the first Black woman to win her freedom through judicial proceedings. She was declared free in 1716 in Cambridge, Massachusetts, and spent the remainder of her life seeking freedom for her children.[54] By 1750, three other enslaved women had obtained their legal freedom—one in South Kingstown, Rhode Island, and two in Portsmouth, New Hampshire.[55] These women seized their liberty through "freedom suits," civil actions brought by bondspeople, which often culminated in a lower court trial.[56] In other words, New England's freedom suits were traditionally brought in the exact fashion that Elizabeth Watson sought her freedom in March 1778. Though freedom suits originated in colonial Virginia, where six such actions had been brought by 1670, the loopholes that allowed enslaved women and men to sue for freedom in the South did not remain open for long.[57]

By the eighteenth century, New England's legal system was unique in granting judicial access for such actions to enslaved and free Black people. Even in the northern colonies there were few freedom suits outside of New England. None occurred in Pennsylvania or New Jersey prior to the end of the American Revolution. Likewise, there is no record of a freedom suit brought by an enslaved woman or man in New York.[58] By contrast, fourteen Massachusetts women filed civil lawsuits to secure their freedom between 1716 and 1783.[59] All of this points to Elizabeth Watson's New England origins and establishes her case as a transnational example of New England's freedom suits.

Elizabeth Watson's petition and subsequent freedom, however brief, can be interpreted as the ultimate assertion of her rights as a British subject, as well as a powerful statement to her self-perception and identity.[60] It can also be interpreted as a violent reminder of the aporia that permeated Blackness and slavery in New England, which Elizabeth Watson embodied as she stood astride her status of legal personhood and chattel. On the other hand, her reenslavement at the hands of Halifax butcher William Proud and the jury's decision to reaffirm her slave status can be interpreted as symbolic of the ideological battle over the meaning of freedom—and therefore the meaning of slavery—that seized British North America around the time of the Revolutionary War.[61] Indeed, the 1765 Stamp Act coincided with a sharp rise in the incidence of freedom suits. This has twofold importance: while Elizabeth Watson clearly knew about and was influenced by these suits, so were the Loyalist judges and lawyers who later proved instrumental to ending slavery in Nova Scotia during the 1790s.

The Reenslavement of Elizabeth Watson

Proceedings at the Supreme Court began on July 13, 1778.[62] George Thomson, in front of Chief Justice Bryan Finucane and his assistant justices, declared in a writ of replevin that "William Proud ... alias Butcher" had unlawfully seized Elizabeth Watson on April 24, 1778, and held her captive still at that very moment. Thomson declared that Watson was suing Proud for damages of £100—almost £20,000 today. Richard Gibbons's avowry on behalf of William Proud admitted to "the force and Injury" Proud had used when he abducted Elizabeth Watson but nonetheless affirmed that he had been justified in his actions, as Watson was "a Negro Slave and Servant [who] ... without the consent and against the Will of the Said William Proud did desert and abscond from his service." Gibbons went on to say that "the Said female Negro Slave and Servant [was] truly called and known by the name of Phillis but [is] falsely and pretendedly calling herself Elizabeth Watson." He finished his avowry by asserting that Elizabeth Watson was William Proud's "absolute Slave and Servant, Right and Property and part of the proper Goods Chattels and Estate of the said William Proud and not a good Lawful and Free Woman." Thomson's replication maintained that Proud could not have abducted Watson lawfully because "she was and Yet is a Good Lawful and Free Woman justly and truly named Elizabeth Watson." "Without this," Thomson finished, "She is a Slave and Servant." Once Gibbons and Thomson had finished laying out their respective cases, the court commanded that a jury of "twelve free and lawful Men" convene at a later date to decide Elizabeth Watson's fate.

On August 1, 1778, a Court of Special Sessions of the Peace sat for the trial.[63] The judges were John George Pyke, Thomas Bridge, George Smith, and John Newton, the first three of whom had heard Watson's original suit against Elias Marshall. Elizabeth Watson secured the services of George Thomson, the most junior attorney in the province.[64] William Proud, by contrast, was represented by Solicitor-General Richard Gibbons Jr., the senior member of the bar and its most prominent attorney—which points, perhaps, to the potentially high-profile nature of the trial. Elizabeth Watson's sworn deposition, signed with an X, is quoted here:

> Justices. —
> Elizabeth Watson, being duly Sworn Deposeth and Saith that on, or about the 16th Day of July last, about three of the Clock in the Morning being Warm, and much fatigued by Cooking &ca. in the House of Mr. William Proud, she went out to the necessary, when said Mr. Proud came out thither with a Candle, and this Deponent being in the necessary ask'd who came there. And immediately [Proud] asked who this Deponent had with her, and Demanded her to open the Door, and come out Directly, and this Deponent came into the House accordingly, and one Mr. Barn being in the House much in Liquor with this Deponent taking Notice of by Expressing the same. Mrs. Proud the wife of the said William Proud immediately Struck this Deponent in the face with her Hand after which this Deponent went up the Stairs and said Mr. Proud and his Wife both follow'd this Deponent. And the said Mr. Proud flogged, or Beat, this De-

ponent Violently with a Horse Whipp he had brought with him until he broke it & after got another and continued to repeat the same for a long time, and then kicked her this Deponent with his feet down the Stairs, or some part thereof.[65]

The Supreme Court of Nova Scotia took over the case through a writ of certiorari filed by Richard Gibbons after Watson's assertion that she had suffered "damage to the value of One Hundred Pounds."[66]

George Thomson applied for and obtained a writ de homine replegiando. This writ is crucial to understanding the significance of Elizabeth Watson's trial. De homine replegiando is an old medieval writ—perhaps one of the oldest, first appearing in the pipe rolls of 1165–66.[67] The writ de homine replegiando "lies to replevy a man out of prison, or out of custody of any private person—in the same manner that chattels in distress may be replevied—upon giving security to the sheriff that the man shall be forthcoming to answer any charge against him."[68] The writ was "a popular remedy to obtain release from simple custodies" and evolved through medieval times into the customary common law method to replevy villeins seized by a lord by writ de nativo habendo.[69] By the eighteenth century, the writ de homine replegiando had long been rendered obsolete by habeas corpus.[70] The two writs worked in much the same fashion, and both could be brought on behalf of the detainee by a third party. But habeas corpus and de homine replegiando differed in one crucial point. Where the former called for a bench trial, the latter called for a jury trial.[71] That Watson sought to take an obsolete action that guaranteed her a trial by jury may well speak to Nova Scotia's ideological state at the time of the Revolutionary War. Clearly, she thought a jury would be more likely to grant her freedom than the Supreme Court justices, pointing, perhaps, to schisms between the political elite and people likely to serve in a jury. Of course, the jury would still comprise landowning white men, but it has already been established that this segment of Nova Scotia's population prior to the arrival of the Loyalists had, at least to some extent, been drawn from New England's lower socioeconomic strata.[72]

The case's pivotal moment, however, came two months later. William Proud's key witness, Samuel Laka, was deposed by the court at the home of Chief Justice Finucane on September 14, 1778. Richard Gibbons questioned him.[73]

"Did you at any time... purchase a Negro woman by the name of Phillis in Boston and from whom and for what sum?" Gibbons asked.

"I did purchase such a woman from Nicholas Lobdell in Boston, but when I paid the money and received her Nicholas was not present. Do not recollect the time. Believe the sum to be twenty-seven pounds," Laka replied.

"When and to whom and where did you dispose of this Woman?"

"I disposed of her in Halifax to Mr. Elias Marshall."

"In the Bill of Sale now shown to you with a receipt signed with your name—a Bill of Sale transferring this woman from you to Elias Marshall—is the name Samuel Laka, here signed, your handwriting?"

"It is," Laka answered.

"Is the Bill of Sale now shown to you under seal, signed 'Agnes Lobdell on behalf of my husband Nicholas Lobdell,' the original Bill of Sale of this Negro woman to you?" Gibbons continued.

"It is."

"Did this Negro woman at or before the time of her sale to you or at any time afterward while she was with you declare herself to be a free woman and not a slave, or claim to be set free as such, or object to being sold by you to Mr. Marshall as a slave?"

"She expressed uneasiness at coming to Halifax, but neither she nor anybody else ever said that she pretended to be Free or that I had no right to dispose of her as my property until my arrival at this time in Halifax," Laka answered.

"How long have you known this Negro woman, and what reasons have you to believe her a slave and not a free woman?"

"I knew her as a servant in Mr. Lobdell's family for about six months before I purchased her. I was told by Mr. and Mrs. Lobdell that they had bought her from one Ebenezer Gorham, from whom I have a Bill of Sale to Lobdell."

"Other than Phillis, did you ever hear or know of any other name by which this Negro woman was at any time called or known—if yes, what was the name and where, and when, and by whom was she so called?" Gibbons asked.

"Never heard of any other than Phillis," Laka replied.

"Did this Negro Woman at the time of being sold to you and at the time of your selling her to Mr. Marshall know she was being sold as a slave?"

"Yes."

"Did you ever hear or know that either of this Negro woman's parents were Free persons? What were their names and, if slaves, to whom were they or either of them slaves?"

"I do not know."

"Are you eventually interested in Phillis's freedom or slavery?"

"I am not interested," Laka said.

George Thomson declined to question Laka on Elizabeth Watson's behalf. Samuel Laka was in the end the only witness at the trial. Elizabeth Reed, on the strength of whose testimony Watson had secured her freedom one year earlier, was not summoned to appear before the court.[74]

The trial concluded on October 20, 1779. George Thomson's failure to act on Watson's behalf—in terms of questioning Samuel Laka, objecting to any part of his testimony, or bringing a witness of his own—meant that William Proud's attorney presented all the evidence that the jury was to consider. Having heard no evidence to the contrary, the Supreme Court of Nova Scotia ruled that "said *Elizabeth Watson* is [William Proud's] property and slave." At least she won her name.[75]

From Freedom to Slavery

Elizabeth Watson's story is not the only story of reenslavement in Nova Scotia.[76] The incidence of such kidnappings in Nova Scotia is well documented, particularly in the wake of the Loyalist diaspora.[77]

There was Mertilla Dixon, who fled her enslaver's Virginia home during the Revolutionary War and found her way to Nova Scotia, where again she was impelled to flee from an employer who "threatened to ship her to the West Indies, and ... dispose of her as a Slave." Dixon took refuge with her father and invited her old employer to "prove his claim."[78]

There was Lydia Jackson, whose poverty forced her to indenture herself to a Loyalist. He took advantage of her illiteracy and signed her to a thirty-nine-year term instead of the one year she had agreed to. He later sold Jackson to Dr. William Bulman, who beat her "with tongs, sticks, pieces of rope about the head and face ... [and] in the most inhuman manner stamped upon her whilst she lay upon the ground ... though she was in the last month of pregnancy."[79] The courts did not help her, silenced as they were by Dr. Bulman's overbearing influence. For three more years Jackson lived with him, until at last she "made her escape in a wonderful way through the woods."[80]

And there was Mary Postell. Likely born enslaved in South Carolina, she fled to British lines during the American Revolution with her daughters Flora and Nell.[81] They were reenslaved in 1785, when Jesse Gray destroyed Postell's certificate of freedom. He took her and her two daughters to Nova Scotia, where he forced them to "Work and Labour ... as the Slave and Slaves of him."[82] Postell grew fearful that Gray intended to sell her away from Flora and Nell. They fled his home, and Postell went to court. Though he submitted paltry evidence—a bill of sale from his own brother Samuel— the court ordered that Postell and her daughters return to Gray's home "on condition that he give Security for not Selling her ... in Twelve Months from this Day."[83] One year later, Gray sold Mary Postell for a hundred bushels of potatoes. Three years later, he sold Flora south to North Carolina for five pounds.[84] Afraid that Nell would suffer the same fate, Postell returned to court and "complained against Jesse Gray ... for taking away her children."[85]

Mary Postell had a much stronger case than Elizabeth Watson. Two separate witnesses testified to her freedom and her work for the Loyalist cause. But the court still decided that Postell had not proven her freedom, and it returned her to slavery.[86] Her bitter end should not cast a shadow over the fact that Postell fought tooth and nail for five years.

Mertilla Dixon, Lydia Jackson, Mary Postell, and Elizabeth Watson. These four admirable women stand for countless others of all ages and genders whose names are lost to history. Neither their names nor their number will ever be known with any degree of certainty. Nova Scotia may not have been a place of widespread slavery, but it was a place of rampant unfreedom.

Conclusion

Ultimately, it would be easy to blame Elizabeth Watson's wretched fate on George Thomson's inability or unwillingness to represent his client with any semblance of integrity. But there is another possibility, one to which much of the evidence points: Elizabeth Watson lied.

Say she did not. Say Samuel Laka conspired with William Proud to deliver false testimony. Say that together they falsified three bills of sale, the genealogy of her unfreedom: from Ebenezer Gorham to Nicholas Lobdell, to Samuel Laka, to Elias Marshall. Say Elizabeth Reed did in fact know her as Elizabeth Watson, a free woman born of a free mother.
Here is another version. A young enslaved woman named Phillis landed on the shores of a foreign land and sensed an opportunity to fashion herself anew. She had heard stories of women in Boston who had sued for their freedom and won. She used this knowledge and her natural intelligence to navigate Nova Scotia's fledgling legal system. She gave herself a new name.

Whether or not she lied in the end does not matter. These are questions without answers. And answers, of course, would not change a thing. This is what history is. Nothing could change what happened to Elizabeth Watson.

Here is all that we know with certainty. Elizabeth Watson arrived in Halifax from Boston sometime in the mid-1770s. In March 1778 she suffered an atrocious beating at the hands of Elias Marshall. The Halifax Court of Quarter Sessions granted her freedom on March 23, 1778. She was seized by the butcher William Proud thirty-one days later. The Supreme Court of Nova Scotia returned her to slavery on October 20, 1779.

Nothing else is certain. The archive silenced her, as it has done to so many others. Elizabeth Watson's story comes to us like a frantic, solitary shout amid a sea of silence, a light that flashed once and was never seen again. The child she carried almost certainly died.[87] Its body was likely buried somewhere in Elias Marshall's land—four hundred acres bounded by Washmill Lake to the east and Fox Lake to the west.[88] There are no plaques here, no memorials or remembrances, no markers or headstones.[89] Only the soil remains; still bucolic, by now idyllic, long reclaimed by balsam firs and red spruce. Past the western shore of Fox Lake there is primeval forest, taller and heavier—the sole reminder that people lived in this place.

NOTES

1. The following account comes from Elizabeth Watson's sworn testimony in *Woodin v. Watson*, 22/45, Record Group (RG) 37, Nova Scotia Archives (hereafter NSA).

2. For details on Elias Marshall's employment, see W. A. B. Douglas, "COFFIN, Sir ISAAC," in *Dictionary of Canadian Biography*, ed. Frances G. Halpenny (Toronto: University of Toronto Press, 1988), 7:196–97; Julian Gwyn, *Ashore and Afloat: The British Navy and the Halifax Naval Yard before 1820* (Ottawa: University of Ottawa Press, 2004), 107.

3. Whether Dursdly was enslaved is unknown.

4. There were three surgeons in Halifax by the name of Phillips—George, John, and William. Which of the three men this incident involved is unknown. A. E. Marble, *Surgeons, Smallpox, and the Poor: A History of Medicine and Social Conditions in Nova Scotia, 1749–1799* (Montreal: McGill-Queen's University Press, 1993), 86, 107.

5. *Woodin v. Watson*, 22/45, RG 37, NSA.

6. Woodin was then keeper of the Halifax Poor House, which was essentially an early version of a Victorian workhouse. Thomas B. Akins, *History of Halifax City* (Halifax: Nova Scotia Historical Society, 1895), 78.

7. *Woodin v. Watson*, 22/45, RG 37, NSA.

8. *Watson v. Proud*, C/21, RG 37, NSA.

9. Thomas Peters, for example, related the story of a man who, once reduced to slavery, "did actually lose his Life by the Beating and Ill Treatment of his Master and another who fled the like cruelty was inhumanly shot and maimed." Thomas

Peters to Lord Grenville, "The Humble Petition of Thomas Peters, a Negro," 1790, FO 4/1, C 308757, National Archives, London (hereafter NA).

10. For several examples of cruelty toward the Maritimes' enslaved population, see Harvey Amani Whitfield, *North to Bondage: Loyalist Slavery in the Maritimes* (Vancouver: University of British Columbia Press, 2016), 78–80; Whitfield, ed., *Black Slavery in the Maritimes: A History in Documents* (Peterborough: Broadview Press, 2018), 106, 116.

11. For more on the fluidity of the unfree condition, see Hardesty, *Unfreedom*. For a discussion of the onerous methodological difficulties a high rate of reenslavement presents, see Whitfield, *North to Bondage*, 13–16.

12. On the Mary Postell and Nancy cases, see Whitfield, *Black Slavery in the Maritimes*, 107, 114.

13. Pierre Dugua, along with Samuel de Champlain, founded Acadia's first capital at Port-Royal. It was France's first North American colony. Aside from a few trading outposts, Port-Royal was then the only European settlement in Nova Scotia. See John G. Reid, ed., *The "Conquest" of Acadia, 1710: Imperial, Colonial, and Aboriginal Constructions* (Toronto: University of Toronto Press, 2004); Phillip Buckner, ed., *Canada and the British Empire* (Oxford: Oxford University Press, 2008); Elizabeth Mancke, "Early Modern Imperial Governance and the Origins of Canadian Political Culture," *Canadian Journal of Political Science* 32, no. 1 (1999): 3–20.

14. A. B. J. Johnston, "Research Note: Mathieu Da Costa along the Coasts of Nova Scotia: Some Possibilities," *Journal of the Royal Nova Scotia Historic Society* 4 (2001): 152–64.

15. Ira Berlin, *Many Thousands Gone: The First Two Centuries of Slavery in North America* (Cambridge, Mass.: Harvard University Press, 1998), 17. For more on Atlantic Creoles, see Linda Heywood and John Thornton, *Central Africans, Atlantic Creoles and the Foundation of the Americas, 1585–1660* (New York: Cambridge University Press, 2007); Jane G. Landers, *Atlantic Creoles in the Age of Revolutions* (Cambridge, Mass.: Harvard University Press, 2010); James H. Sweet, *Domingos Alvares, African Healing, and the Intellectual History of the Atlantic World* (Chapel Hill: University of North Carolina Press, 2011); Ira Berlin, "From Creole to African: Atlantic Creoles and the Origins of African American Society in Mainland North America," *William and Mary Quarterly* 53, no. 2 (1996): 251–88.

16. See doc. 28, vol. II, NSA, in C. B. Fergusson, *A Documentary Study of the Negroes in Nova Scotia between the War of 1812 and the Winning of Responsible Government* (Halifax: Public Archives of Nova Scotia, 1948), 1.

17. Donovan, "Slaves in Île Royale."

18. Louisbourg was a cod fishing port and later a fortress of formidable reputation. It was founded after the Treaty of Utrecht forced the French out of Nova Scotia. See A. J. B. Johnston, "From Port de Peche to Ville Fortifiee: The Evolution of Urban Louisbourg, 1713–1758," *Proceedings of the Meeting of the French Colonial Historical Society* 17 (1993): 24–43; Robert Emmet Wall Jr., "Louisbourg, 1745," *New England Quarterly* 37, no. 1 (1964): 64–83; A. J. B. Johnston, "To Mark and to Celebrate: Commemoration Efforts at Eighteenth-Century Louisbourg," *French Colo-

nial History 1 (2002): 161–75. For more on the Treaty of Utrecht, see Renger E. de Bruin, Cornelis van der Haven, Lotte Jensen, and David Onnekink, eds., *Performances of Peace: Utrecht 1713* (Leiden, the Netherlands: Brill, 2015).

19. Donovan, "Slaves in Île Royale."

20. Donovan, "A Nominal List"; Kenneth Donovan, "Slaves in Cape Breton, 1713–1815," *Directions: Canadian Race Relations Foundation* 4, no. 1 (Summer 2007): 44–45.

21. Donovan, "Slaves in Île Royale," 26.

22. Donovan, "Female Slaves."

23. George T. Bates, "The Great Exodus of 1749: or, The Cornwallis Settlers Who Didn't," *Collections of the Nova Scotia Historical Society* 38 (1973): 227–62; see also John Grenier, *The Far Reaches of Empire: War in Nova Scotia, 1710–1760* (Norman: University of Oklahoma Press, 2008).

24. Letter from Governor Cornwallis about Captain Bloss and his slaves, September 22, 1750, doc. 25, vol. 35, RG 1, NSA; Douglas Brymner, *Report on Canadian Archives* (Ottawa: S. E. Dawson, 1895), 280; Harvey Amani Whitfield, *Blacks on the Border: The Black Refugees in British North America, 1815–1860* (Burlington: University of Vermont Press, 2006), 15.

25. Letter from Governor Cornwallis about Captain Bloss, doc. 25, vol. 35, RG 1, NSA. Ken Donovan notes that a schooner brought nine slave men, the property of Captain Bloss, to Nova Scotia from Antigua; see Donovan, "Slaves in Île Royale," 32.

26. *Boston Post-Boy*, August 8, 1750, September 23, 1751. It is clear that Captain Bloss and Benjamin Hallowell knew each other.

27. Smith, "The Slave in Canada," 9.

28. *Halifax Gazette*, May 30, 1752.

29. See Gregory E. O'Malley, *Final Passages: The Intercolonial Slave Trade of British America, 1619–1807* (Chapel Hill: University of North Carolina Press, 2014).

30. Jerry Bannister, "Atlantic Canada in an Atlantic World? Northeastern North America in the Long 18th Century," *Acadiensis* 43, no. 2 (2014): 28. For a general overview of the major demographic shifts, see Margaret Conrad and James Hiller, *Atlantic Canada: A History* (Toronto: Oxford University Press, 2010), chaps. 6–8.

31. T. Stephen Henderson and Wendy G. Robicheau, eds., *Nova Scotia Planters in the Atlantic World, 1759–1830* (Fredericton, N.B.: Acadiensis Press, 2012); Lucille H. Campey, *Planters, Paupers, and Pioneers: English Settlers in Atlantic Canada* (Toronto: Dundurn Press, 2010); George Rawlyk and Gordon T. Stewart, *A People Highly Favoured of God: The Nova Scotia Yankees and the American Revolution* (Toronto: Macmillan, 1972); Margaret Conrad, ed., *Making Adjustments: Change and Continuity in Planter Nova Scotia, 1759–1800* (Fredericton, N.B.: Acadiensis Press, 1991); Conrad and Barry Moody, eds., *Planter Links: Community and Culture in Colonial Nova Scotia* (Fredericton: Acadiensis Press, 2001); Conrad, ed., *They Planted Well: New England Planters in Maritime Canada* (Fredericton, N.B.: Acadiensis Press, 1988); Conrad, ed., *Intimate Relations: Family and Community in Planter Nova Scotia, 1759–1800* (Fredericton, N.B.: Acadiensis Press, 1995).

32. 1767 Nova Scotia Census, RG 12, NSA.

33. As Barry Cahill writes, "Collection of quantifiable data is complicated by Black people not being enumerated in extant early census records. Blacks as a rule were slaves, slaves were chattels (movable property), and personality was not censual" ("Colchester Men: The Pro-slavery Presbyterian Witness of the Reverends Daniel Cock of Truro and David Smith of Londonderry," in Conrad and Moody, *Planter Links*, 134).

34. Malachy Salter to Susanna Mulberry, September 2, 1759, doc. 27, vol. 217, MG 100, NSA. Malachy Salter was one of Halifax's most prominent early entrepreneurs. A ruthless businessman, he was described by contemporaries as "a Litigious troublesome Man . . . who has treated us in a Barbarous cruel manner." He was the most litigious man of his time, having been "plaintiff in 110 actions and a defendant in 30" (James Muir, *Law, Debt, and Merchant Power: The Civil Courts of Eighteenth-Century Halifax* [Toronto: Osgoode Society for Canadian Legal History, 2016], 38).

35. *Halifax Gazette*, November 1, 1760. The advertisement continues: "Likewise [for sale] a puncheon of choice cherry brandy with sundry other articles." For more on the commodification of Black people, see Walter Johnson, *Soul by Soul: Life inside the Antebellum Slave Market* (Cambridge, Mass.: Harvard University Press, 1999). For a controversial look at the economics of slavery, see William Robert Fogel and Stanley L. Engerman, *Time on the Cross: The Economics of American Negro Slavery* (Toronto: Little, Brown and Company, 1974). For a lengthy rebuttal of Fogel and Engerman's methods and conclusions, see Herbert G. Gutman, *Slavery and the Numbers Game: A Critique of "Time on the Cross"* (Urbana: University of Illinois Press, 1975). For more recent studies, see Sven Beckert and Seth Rockman, eds., *Slavery's Capitalism: A New History of American Economic Development* (Philadelphia: University of Pennsylvania Press, 2016); Christy Clark-Pujara, *Dark Work: The Business of Slavery in Rhode Island* (New York: New York University Press, 2016); Edward Baptist, *The Half Has Never Been Told: Slavery and the Making of American Capitalism* (New York: Basic Books, 2014).

36. Akins, *History of Halifax City*, 63; James S. MacDonald, *Annals of the North British Society in Halifax, Nova Scotia with Portraits and Biographical Notes 1768–1903* (Halifax, N.S.: McAlpine Publishing Company Ltd., 1905), 17.

37. For background on Charles Proctor, see Ronald Rompkey, ed., *Expeditions of Honour: The Journal of John Salusbury in Halifax, Nova Scotia, 1749–53* (Montreal: McGill-Queen's University Press), 173. For Thomas Wood, see C. E. Thomas, "WOOD, THOMAS (1711–78)," in Halpenny, *Dictionary of Canadian Biography*, vol. 4.

38. See Smith, "The Slave in Canada," 15n2.

39. *Royal Gazette*, May 28, 1776.

40. Whitfield, *North to Bondage*, 41.

41. Joanne Pope Melish, *Disowning Slavery: Gradual Emancipation and "Race" in New England, 1780–1860* (Ithaca, N.Y.: Cornell University Press, 1998), 14.

42. For slave culture in the North, see William D. Piersen, *Black Yankees: The Development of an Afro-American Subculture in Eighteenth-Century New England* (Amherst: University of Massachusetts Press, 1988); Gary B. Nash, *Forging Freedom: The Formation of Philadelphia's Black Community, 1720–1840* (Cambridge, Mass.: Harvard University Press, 1988); Shane White, "'It Was a Proud Day': African Americans, Festivals, and Parades in the North, 1741–1834," *Journal of American History* 81 (1994): 13–50; for slave life and culture more broadly, see Sterling Stuckey, *Slave Culture: Nationalist Theory and the Foundations of Black America* (New York: Oxford University Press, 1987); John W. Blassingame, *The Slave Community: Plantation Life in the Antebellum South* (New York: Oxford University Press, 1972); George P. Rawick, *From Sundown to Sunup: The Making of the Black Community* (Westport, Conn.: Greenwood Press, 1972). On slavery in New England, see Jared Ross Hardesty, *Unfreedom: Slavery and Dependence in Eighteenth-Century Boston* (New York: New York University Press, 2016); Hardesty, *Black Lives, Native Lands, White Worlds: A History of Slavery in New England* (Amherst: University of Massachusetts Press, 2019); Harvey Amani Whitfield, *The Problem of Slavery in Early Vermont, 1777–1810* (Barre: Vermont Historical Society, 2014); Allegra di Bonaventura, *For Adam's Sake: A Family Saga in Colonial New England* (New York: W. W. Norton, 2013); Clark-Pujara, *Dark Work*; Lorenzo J. Greene, *The Negro in Colonial New England* (1942; repr., New York: Atheneum, 1968); Berlin, *Many Thousands Gone*, 177–94; Robert K. Fitts, *Inventing New England's Slave Paradise: Master/Slave Relations in Eighteenth-Century Narragansett, Rhode Island* (New York: Garland, 1998); Melish, *Disowning Slavery*, 1–49; Peter Benes, ed., *Slavery/Antislavery in New England: The Dublin Seminar for New England Folklife Annual Proceedings, 2003* (Boston: Boston University, 2005).

43. One may look at the American South itself for examples of these processes at work; indeed, the history of slavery in the mountains of southern Appalachia may well hold some promise for future comparative studies of Maritime slavery. See Wilma A. Dunaway, *Slavery in the American Mountain South* (Cambridge: Cambridge University Press, 2003); John C. Inscoe, ed., *Appalachians and Race: The Mountain South from Slavery to Segregation* (Lexington: University Press of Kentucky, 2001).

44. Historian Karolyn Smardz Frost argues that there may have been as many as two hundred Black people brought enslaved into the region by the New England Planters, though she notes that the enslaved continued to be brought in after the initial migration. Cited in Harvey Amani Whitfield, "The African Diaspora in Atlantic Canada: History, Historians, and Historiography," *Acadiensis* 46, no. 1 (Winter/Spring 2017): 213n1.

45. Graeme Wynn, "A Province Too Much Dependent on New England," *Canadian Geographer* 31, no. 2 (1987): 98–113.

46. Robert McLaughlin, "New England Planters prior to Migration: The Case of Chatham, Massachusetts," in Conrad and Moody, *Planter Links*, 17.

47. See Bell, "Slavery and the Judges"; Jack, "The Loyalists and Slavery"; Winks,

The Blacks in Canada, 24–60; Cahill, "Slavery and the Judges"; Cahill, "Habeas Corpus."

48. "An Act, declaring that Baptism of Slaves shall not exempt them from Bondage," 1781, CO 228, Colonial Office Acts No. 1, Prince Edward Island, 1770–81, MS 1–66, Public Archives and Records Office of Prince Edward Island. See also Whitfield and Cahill, "Slave Life."

49. "1762 Innholders Act," in *Statutes at Large, Nova Scotia* (Halifax, 1805), 77.

50. Whitfield, *North to Bondage*, 68–109.

51. Cahill, "Slavery and the Judges," 79.

52. *Woodin v. Watson*, 22/45, RG 37, NSA.

53. The date of her arrival is unknown, though it was likely sometime in the mid-1770s.

54. See Bonaventura, *For Adam's Sake*; Allegra di Bonaventura, "It's Complicated," *Historically Speaking* 14, no. 3 (2013): 7–8.

55. Catherine Adams and Elizabeth H. Pleck, *Love of Freedom: Black Women in Colonial and Revolutionary New England* (New York: Oxford University Press, 2010), 127.

56. Graham Russell Hodges, *Root and Branch: African Americans in New York and East Jersey, 1613–1863* (Chapel Hill: University of North Carolina Press, 1999), 129–30.

57. For more on the history of freedom suits, see Paul Finkelman, *Slavery in the Courtroom: An Annotated Bibliography of American Cases* (Washington, D.C.: Library of Congress, 1985); Finkelman, *Imperfect Union: Slavery, Federalism, and Comity* (Chapel Hill: University of North Carolina Press, 1981); Ariela Gross, *Double Character: Slavery and Mastery in the Antebellum Southern Courtroom* (Princeton, N.J.: Princeton University Press, 2000); Edlie L. Wong, *Neither Fugitive nor Free: Atlantic Slavery, Freedom Suits, and the Legal Culture of Travel* (New York: New York University Press, 2009); William E. Foley, "Slave Freedom Suits before Dred Scott: The Case of Marie Jean Scypion's Descendants," *Missouri Historical Review* 79 (1984): 1–23; Loren Schweninger, "Freedom Suits, African American Women, and the Genealogy of Slavery," *William and Mary Quarterly* 71, no. 1 (2014): 35–62; Jason A. Gillmer, "Suing for Freedom: Interracial Sex, Slave Law, and Racial Identity in the Post-revolutionary and Antebellum South," *North Carolina Law Review* 82, no. 2 (2004): 535–619. For a first-person account of a freedom suit, see Lucy Delaney, *From the Darkness Cometh the Light, or Struggles for Freedom* (St. Louis, Mo.: J. T. Smith, 1891).

58. Hodges, *Root and Branch*, 129–30.

59. Adams and Pleck, *Love of Freedom*, 127.

60. See Van Gosse, "As a Nation, the English Are Our Friends: The Emergence of African American Politics in the British Atlantic World, 1772–1861," *American Historical Review* 113, no. 4 (2008): 1003–28.

61. See Edmund Morgan, *American Slavery, American Freedom: The Ordeal of Colonial Virginia* (New York: W. W. Norton, 1975); David Brion Davis, *The Problem of*

Slavery in the Age of Revolution, 1770–1823 (Ithaca, N.Y.: Cornell University Press, 1975); Winthrop D. Jordan, *White over Black: American Attitudes toward the Negro, 1550–1812* (Chapel Hill: University of North Carolina Press, 1968); Jack P. Greene, *All Men Are Created Equal: Some Reflections on the Character of the American Revolution, an Inaugural Lecture* (New York: Oxford University Press, 1976); Greene, "Slavery or Independence: Some Reflections on the Relationship among Liberty, Black Bondage, and Equality in Revolutionary South Carolina," *South Carolina Historical Magazine* 80 (1979): 193–214; Holly Brewer, "Slavery, Sovereignty, and 'Inheritable Blood': Reconsidering John Locke and the Origins of American Slavery," *American Historical Review* 122, no. 4 (2017): 1038–78.

62. The following account comes from *Watson v. Proud*, C/21, RG 37, NSA.

63. Justices typically held "special" sessions between regularly scheduled Courts of Quarter or General Sessions of the Peace; they were intended to prevent delays in the administration of justice. See J. H. Baker, "Criminal Courts and Procedure at Common Law 1550–1800," in *Crime in England 1550–1800*, ed. J. S. Cockburn (Princeton, N.J.: Princeton University Press, 1977), 30.

64. For mentions of *Watson v. Proud*, see Cahill, "Slavery and the Judges," 80; and Julian Gwyn, "Female Litigants before the Civil Courts of Nova Scotia, 1749–1801," *Histoire Sociale / Social History* 36, no. 72 (2003): 340–41.

65. *Watson v. Proud*, C/21, RG 37, NSA.

66. Ibid. For more on writs of certiorari (i.e., definitions and uses), see William Blackstone, *Commentaries on the Laws of England*, 4 vols. (Oxford: Clarendon Press, 1765–69), 4:xxiv.

67. Note that the earliest extant record of the continuous series dates to 1155–56. Elsa de Haas, *Antiquities of Bail: Origin and Historical Development in Criminal Cases to the Year 1275* (New York: Columbia University Press, 1940), 62; Christopher Coredon, *A Dictionary of Medieval Terms & Phrases* (Woodbridge: D. S. Brewer, 2004), 219.

68. Blackstone, *Commentaries*, 3:129; see also Joseph Harrison, *The Practice of the Court of Chancery*, 2 vols. (London: A. Strahan, 1796), 1:164–66.

69. Maxwell Cohen, "Some Considerations on the Origin of Habeas Corpus," *Canadian Bar Review* 16 (1938): 92, 96, 97; Phineas Pemberton Morris, *Practical Treatise on the Law of Replevin in the United States; with an Appendix of Forms, and a Digest of Statutes* (Philadelphia: Kay & Brother, 1878), 255–65. For more on the writ de nativo habendo, see Blackstone, *Commentaries*, 1:26.

70. Bryan A. Garner, ed., *Black's Law Dictionary*, 9th ed. (Eagan, Minn.: West, 2009), s.v. "De Homine Replegiando."

71. "Some Defects in the Law of Habeas Corpus," *Law Review and Quarterly Journal of British and Foreign Jurisprudence* 22 (1855): 149–68; James Kent, *Commentaries on American Law*, 4 vols. (Philadelphia: Blackstone Publishing Co., 1889), 26–33.

72. See Wynn, "A Province Too Much Dependent"; McLaughlin, "New England Planters." For more on the history of jury trials in Canada specifically, see Re-

gina Schuller and Neil Vidmar, "The Canadian Criminal Jury," *Chicago-Kent Law Review* 86, no. 2 (2011): 497–535; R. Blake Brown, *A Trying Question: The Jury in Nineteenth-Century Canada* (Toronto: University of Toronto Press, 2009).

73. The language in the following account has been adapted slightly from the original deposition in order to retain clarity. *Watson v. Proud*, C/21, RG 37, NSA.

74. The reasons for this are unknown.

75. *Watson v. Proud*, C/21, RG 37, NSA.

76. The reenslavement of free and allegedly free Black people became all too common in the wake of the Loyalist diaspora. The relative lack of surviving sources pertaining to reenslavement in the Maritimes reveals a need for historians to look elsewhere for analogous historical processes. Alongside Nova Scotia, the Bahamas had the highest incidence of wrongful reenslavement in the Loyalist diaspora. There the practice became pervasive enough that Governor Lord Dunmore established a succession of courts dedicated solely to hearing evidence to the legal freedom of Black people. The means of reenslavement in the Bahamas mirrored those often seen in Nova Scotia: destruction of freedom papers, followed by sale to the West Indies. See Carole Watterson Troxler, "Uses of the Bahamas by Southern Loyalist Exiles," in *The Loyal Atlantic: Remaking the British Atlantic in the Revolutionary Era*, ed. Jerry Bannister and Liam Riordan (Toronto: University of Toronto Press, 2012), 185–208, esp. 194–95, 199–200.

77. See, for example, the story of Sam Ives, in Book of Negroes, Guy Carleton, 1st Baron Dorchester: Papers, National Archives, Kew (PRO 30/55/100) 10427, p. 19; Thomas Clarkson, "Some Account of the New Colony at Sierra Leone," *American Museum; or Universal Magazine*, May 1792, 229–30; Complaint of Mertilla Dixon, file M97, RG 34-321, NSA; C. B. Fergusson, ed., *Clarkson's Mission to America, 1791–1792* (Halifax: Public Archives of Nova Scotia, 1971), 90; also see also Carole Watterson Troxler, "Re-enslavement of Black Loyalists: Mary Postell in South Carolina, East Florida, and Nova Scotia," *Acadiensis* 37, no. 2 (2008): 70–85; Troxler, "Uses of the Bahamas." For an attempted measure to curb the incidence of Black kidnappings in Nova Scotia, see "Unpassed Bills: 'A Bill Intituled an Act for the Regulation and Relief of the Free Negroes within the Province of Nova Scotia,' 1789," NSA.

78. Complaint of Mertilla Dixon, file M97, RG 34-321, NSA.

79. Cumberland County Census 1785, doc. 37, vol. 443, RG 1, NSA; Cumberland County Census 1791, doc. 1, vol. 444, RG 1, NSA; Fergusson, *Clarkson's Mission*, 90.

80. Fergusson, *Clarkson's Mission*, 90.

81. See Troxler, "Re-enslavement of Black Loyalists."

82. General Sessions at Shelburne, Nova Scotia, July 8, 1791, Shelburne Records, vol. 141, MG 4, NSA; King v. Jesse Gray, November 9, 1786, Shelburne, doc. 27.2, vol. 27, RG 60, NSA.

83. General Sessions at Shelburne, Nova Scotia, April 10, 1786, Shelburne Records, vol. 141, MG 4, NSA.

84. Troxler, "Re-enslavement of Black Loyalists," 77.

85. General Sessions at Shelburne, Nova Scotia, April 5, 1791, Shelburne Records, vol. 141, MG 4, NSA.

86. Troxler, "Re-enslavement of Black Loyalists," 84.

87. She could not have been too far along in her pregnancy. She told Marshall she was pregnant eight days before the beating, and it is unlikely she would have told him unless it was necessary. This points to the physical changes characteristic of pregnancy becoming too pronounced to hide, leading to an estimate that Watson may have been twenty-one weeks pregnant at most. Even with modern medicine, a preterm birth at this stage of pregnancy is not considered viable. See Barbara J. Stoll et al., "Causes and Timing of Death in Extremely Premature Infants from 2000 through 2011," *New England Journal of Medicine* 372 (2015): 331–40.

88. "Index Sheet 66," Halifax County Land Grants, Department of Lands and Forests, Crown Land Information Management Centre, Nova Scotia; G. L. Saunders, *Trees of Nova Scotia: A Guide to the Native and Exotic Species* (Halifax, N.S.: Department of Lands and Forests, 1973), 1–37.

89. As prominent archaeologist Charles E. Orser Jr. wrote, "Only archaeology has the power to resurrect the daily lives and cultural patterns of the invisible men and women of the past. By piecing together the often-scant evidence left behind by a people in their artifacts and building remains, archaeologists can construct pictures of the past that are unique, insightful, and intimately human" (*Images of the Recent Past: Readings in Historical Archaeology* [Walnut Creek, Calif.: Altamira Press, 1996], 10). For more on historical archaeology and what land can tell historians about the people who lived in it, see Heather Macleod-Leslie, "Archaeology and Atlantic Canada's African Diaspora," *Acadiensis* 43, no. 1 (2014): 137–45; Cottreau-Robbins, "Searching for the Enslaved," 129–31; Alexandra A. Chan, *Slavery in the Age of Reason: Archaeology at a New England Farm* (Knoxville: University of Tennessee Press, 2007); James Deetz, *In Small Things Forgotten: The Archaeology of Early American Life* (New York: Anchor Press, 1977).

CHAPTER 2

A Scheme to Desert
The Louisiana Purchase and Freedom Seekers in the Louisiana-Texas Borderlands, 1804–1806

MEKALA AUDAIN

Around dusk on October 16, 1804, a large group of enslaved people from at least two plantations or ranches in Natchitoches Parish, Louisiana, escaped. Their plan was to "desert to Nacogdoches" in Spanish Texas.[1] A group of nine raided a local house and stole guns and lead powder. Another group, whose members had heard about the plan to run away, joined the nine at the house and fled with them into the night. Using whistles to communicate among themselves during their escape, the men, women, and children who likely made up this group entered the Kisatchie Forest.

The freedom seekers had not traveled far into the dense forest when patrols, alerted by the whistling, fired at them. Though they were unable to capture all of the fugitives from slavery, the patrols' arrival disrupted the momentum of the escape and separated one member from the rest of the group. Unable to rejoin those who were fleeing slavery and unwilling to continue the journey to freedom alone, he voluntarily returned to Natchitoches. Upon his arrival to the Louisiana post, Capt. Edward D. Turner, who was in charge of monitoring the border between Louisiana and Spanish territory, and other Natchitoches officials captured and questioned him.[2]

The recaptured fugitive's interrogation yielded several insights into the origins of the planned escape. In a letter to William C. C. Claiborne, governor of then Territorial Louisiana, Turner surmised that, based on the pace in which the group traveled, the fugitives from slavery had stolen twenty horses. He also revealed that the former freedom seeker had "turned informer," and his testimony had "already implicated thirty" people in the escape attempt. The former fugitive named a Spaniard living in Nacogdoches as the instigator of this act of resistance. The Spaniard had reportedly informed group members that "if they went to the Spanish Country they would be made free." To corroborate the information Turner received, Natchitoches officials consulted a local Indigenous community. A Native American boy who was a member of the Caddo Nation revealed that the group had been among them the previous night. Members of the Caddo community had advised the freedom seekers to be "firm and determined."[3]

One year after the Louisiana Purchase, enslaved people who escaped from Natchitoches, Louisiana, did not associate freedom with the northern United States, the Ohio River valley, or Canada; instead, they looked to the U.S. western frontier to find freedom. On the recommendation of local Spaniards, they used El Camino Real (the King's Highway or Royal Road), more than a one-hundred-mile section of which was a trading route connecting Natchitoches to Nacogdoches, to reach Spanish Texas. They not only repurposed El Camino Real but also sought temporary refuge and created alliances with a local Indigenous community. These acts of resistance contributed to increasingly fraught political and diplomatic relations in the region. Capitalizing on the shifting international boundaries after the Louisiana Purchase and a subsequent border dispute between Louisiana and Spanish Texas, enslaved Black people and fugitives from slavery—with help from Spaniards and the Caddo—created alternate avenues to freedom in the Louisiana-Texas borderlands as part of the Underground Railroad.

This chapter builds on existing scholarship about those who fled from slavery by decentering the North as a site of freedom. The most recent scholarly monographs about the Underground Railroad, such as Eric Foner's *Gateway to Freedom* (2015) and Manisha Sinha's *The Slave's Cause* (2016), feature escape routes leading north and spaces of freedom in that region during the antebellum period.[4] However, not all freedom seekers were able to reach the northeastern United States, the Ohio River valley, or Canada. Examining the experiences of fugitives from slavery on the early nineteenth-century Louisiana-Texas frontier not only alters the chronological and geographical scopes of the Underground Railroad but also pivots historical discourse away from well-established routes in the antebellum northern United States and the Ohio River valley. Taking this approach investigates the ways in which enslaved Black people thought about and executed their escapes in the absence of an established antislavery activist community to assist them. Moreover, it includes the region's racial and ethnic demographics to discuss the historical actors who participated in these journeys to freedom. Lastly, this perspective moves beyond the idea of southern slavery and northern freedom to take into account how enslaved people adapted their plans and routes to freedom as U.S. westward expansion placed them farther south.

This work also contributes to existing scholarship about the Louisiana Purchase and Louisiana during its territorial period.[5] There has been limited scholarly attention about the Underground Railroad in the Louisiana-Texas borderlands. Many scholarly monographs address the social and political consequences of the Louisiana Purchase, Louisiana's transition from European to U.S. rule, and the link between U.S. expansion and slavery. Articles that examine fugitives from slavery who escaped to Nacogdoches situate freedom seekers as just one of many groups of people who crossed the Louisiana-Texas border during this time period, trace the history of El Camino Real as a route to freedom, or highlight the diplomatic consequences of these escapes to Texas.[6] This chapter expands these works by uncovering the intellectual nature of planning and executing escapes and linking the Louisiana Purchase to enslaved resistance. By reimagining U.S. westward expansion in the Deep South, this work considers how the Louisiana Purchase shaped escape routes and informed the process in which enslaved people planned their escapes.

Formation and Operation of the Underground Railroad in the Louisiana-Texas Borderlands

Enslaved Louisianans who were able to take advantage of the global and political implications of the Louisiana Purchase transformed the physical landscape of freedom. When enslaved people attempted to self-emancipate by escaping from Spanish Louisiana to Spanish Texas in the late eighteenth century, Texas officials typically returned them to their Louisiana enslavers.[7] However, in April 1789 a Spanish royal decree permitted fugitives from slavery who escaped from colonies not controlled by Spain to find freedom in Spanish territory. Once Louisiana was under U.S. rule beginning in 1803, this royal decree applied to men and women in bondage who fled to Texas, creating another option to freedom for the territory's enslaved population.[8]

The increased number of destinations for freedom seekers helped fuel the existing culture of resistance in the region. Enslaved Louisianans had sometimes used grand marronage (long-term or permanent escape in nearby swamps or forests) to become free. By the summer of 1804, however, local government officials in northern Louisiana had targeted Maroon communities, aiming to arrest and reenslave their members.[9] To curtail the number of fugitives from slavery who escaped to Texas, Turner ordered more local white residents to patrol the banks of the Sabine River, which freedom seekers crossed to enter Texas, to "keep the Negroes within their respective boundaries."[10] These changes required men and women enslaved in Louisiana who thought about running away to find a place where they believed they could have a more permanent freedom. Under the recommendation of Spaniards who frequently traveled to Natchitoches to trade goods, Nacogdoches became a destination for freedom seekers likely because they imagined Louisiana officials would not be able to easily capture them there.[11] These ideas about refuge outside of the United States were not the first time that enslaved Black people viewed Spanish territory as a haven.

Fugitives from slavery who escaped from Natchitoches were part of a long history of freedom seekers who sought freedom and protection in the Spanish-speaking world. Spanish Florida, which was south of the British-controlled North American colonies, became a space of freedom as early as 1687, when enslaved Black people from colonial Carolina fled there. From its Spanish colonial period through the U.S. Civil War Florida remained a place of refuge for enslaved people who self-emancipated.[12] While U.S. expansion allowed slavery to spread farther south and eventually west, enslaved people in northern Louisiana used help from local Spaniards to identify Spanish-controlled areas as havens and forged new routes to freedom to arrive to Texas.

By escaping west to Texas, freedom seekers helped create a nineteenth-century Underground Railroad in the Louisiana–Texas borderlands. Foner describes the operation of the Underground Railroad in antebellum New York as "an umbrella term for local groups that employed numerous methods to assist fugitives, some public and entirely legal, some flagrant violations of the law," while Sinha explains the network as "distinct sites of activist interracial abolitionism and anti-slavery politics."[13] In contrast, the U.S. National Park Service defines the Underground Railroad as the "efforts of enslaved African Americans to gain their freedom by escaping bondage," including those who journeyed to freedom without assistance and others who were able to connect to a well-organized network of antislavery activists.[14] Escapes to Nacogdoches were more aligned with the National Park Service's definition of the Underground Railroad. In the Louisiana-Texas borderlands, there were few if any local organized groups or distinct sites of antislavery work aimed at assisting fugitives from slavery. The group of freedom seekers that ran away in early October received some assistance from

Spaniards and members of the Caddo; used an escape route that included at least one "stop," even though it was not a designated one; and arrived to a destination where they expected the residents would offer them freedom and protection from U.S. enslavers and people employed to kidnap and capture fugitives from slavery. However, a physical network of routes did not yet exist in the region. Instead, there was an informal communication network among enslaved Black people in and around Natchitoches Parish that spread information about freedom in Spanish territory.

Enslaved people thinking about escape on the Louisiana-Texas frontier received information about freedom from local Spaniards. Through Spaniards' frequent visits to northern Louisiana, Black people in bondage heard news and rumors about the freedom that existed in the neighboring Texas community.[15] While Spaniards' motives to undermine slavery were unclear, there is no evidence that suggests there was a religious rationale or a commitment to abolition guiding their efforts. Spaniards' roles in these escapes depart from the current historical understanding of the Underground Railroad. Their actions reframe the work of assisting Black people who fled slavery outside of religious obligation and away from a growing regional antislavery movement to consider the possibility of individual gain or the state of regional or international politics as reasons to aid freedom seekers. Spaniards were not the only people on the Louisiana–Texas frontier willing to assist enslaved Louisianans.

Fugitives from slavery could also rely on securing a temporary refuge with members of the Caddo Nation during their escapes. Enslaved people who fled from Natchitoches and encountered the Caddo, apparently viewed this Indigenous community as a source of assistance and a safe place to stop and perhaps gather additional supplies. Moreover, Capt. Turner's first inclination to seek confirmation from the Caddo about the early October escape suggests that there was a positive relationship—the degree to which is unclear—between enslaved Black people and the local Indigenous group. The Caddo did not actively hinder Black people from reaching freedom, nor did they provide extensive information about the group of freedom seekers when Natchitoches officials questioned them. This decision likely bolstered enslaved people's ideas about safety within the community.[16] The work of the local Indigenous community to subvert U.S. slavery by aiding freedom seekers moves beyond a Black/white racial binary when understanding who participated in enslaved Black people's journeys to self-emancipate. Although the Caddo's actions and assistance from Spaniards helped enslaved Louisianans run away, men and women in bondage still faced the burden of planning the logistics of their escapes, such as determining who should accompany them and the items that they should take when escaping to Texas.

The Freedom Seeker Experience on the Louisiana-Texas Frontier

Fugitives from slavery from northern Louisiana used their own communication networks and ethnic backgrounds to visualize their pathways to freedom in distinct ways from those who escaped north. Because firsthand accounts of escapes to Spanish Texas in the early nineteenth century are not yet available, correspondence from Louisiana and Texas officials provides information about what freedom seekers in the region prioritized at the beginning of their escapes. Securing weapons and ammunition in addition to convincing other enslaved people to accompany them were important parts of their plan. The demographics of the group and the detailed plans of their escape were not included in the correspondence. However, based on other escapes in this region and time period, this group was likely made up of enslaved men, women, and children. Their decision to run away as a large group indicates that Africans probably had a central role in this act of resistance because African freedom seekers typically fled in groups, while African American fugitives from slavery ran away as an individual or in pairs. Though Africans who ran away assumed greater risk by electing to escape in a group, this choice highlights that they valued maintaining their kinship and community ties while they absconded from slavery and once they became free.[17] These decisions were part of the ways in which enslaved people who escaped from northern Louisiana envisioned their lives as freed people differently from those who fled to the North in the later antebellum era, and they prepared for their escapes to reflect their goals.

Fugitives from slavery deviated from the secrecy and stealth associated with the Underground Railroad leading north to reach freedom in Spanish Texas. People in bondage who fled from the South to the North during the antebellum era often employed clandestine measures such as using disguises, traveling at night, and excluding children to avoid detection. However, freedom seekers from Natchitoches did not share these same concerns about discovery. The group of fugitives described in the opening of this chapter created whistles and whistle codes to communicate during the escape despite knowing that patrols, militiamen, and local white residents would be able to hear them. They also used guns to defend themselves and horses to reach their destination faster. The noise generated from gunfire and horse hooves alerted others of their presence. The shorter distance to freedom and the ability to protect themselves from danger could explain the differences in strategies between those who fled west and those who absconded north. Traveling on or near an established trade route while armed and on horseback perhaps allowed those who escaped from slavery to take a bolder approach to their journeys to freedom. These choices, in addition to them electing to flee in groups, reflect the marked ways in which they understood the process of escape differently from those who sought freedom in the North.

The characteristics of slavery and frontier culture in early nineteenth-century northern Louisiana informed the ways in which fugitives from slavery thought about escape and aided them during their search for freedom. First, there were not as many mobility restrictions and laws prohibiting access to weapons in the Natchitoches region as there were in the antebellum Cotton South. For example, some Louisiana enslavers assigned selected enslaved men to hunt animals likely to feed the enslaver's family and supplement the enslaved population's food rations. While there were a number of rules to regulate this type of work, some enslaved Louisianans' access to weapons, ammunition, and horses allowed them to obtain a better understanding of the physical landscape outside of the ranch or plantation and become adept in using and handling guns.[18] As a result, those who escaped from northern Louisiana tailored their escape strategies to include elements from their experiences as enslaved people that would aid them in evading capture, not detection. By prioritizing defense, speed, and strength in numbers, freedom seekers probably believed that they had the best chance of successfully reaching Nacogdoches. However, once they fled their ranch or plantation another obstacle awaited them. Their plans to run away to Texas also had to include how to traverse the landscapes of Louisiana and East Texas.

Even though fugitives from slavery received assistance from Spaniards and Native Americans, the difficult topography of northern Louisiana in some areas made the over one-hundred-mile journey to freedom more burdensome. While navigating the hilly, piney-wooded terrain of northern Louisiana, those who escaped endured heavily forested areas, a lack of fresh water, and a dwindling food supply. In addition to piney hills, bayous and marshes characterized the Natchitoches Parish landscape. Traveling through this terrain required a degree of physicality that added to the hardship of escape. Once freedom seekers reached El Camino Real or its surrounding area, the most significant concern was securing fresh water and food. There were a number of salt springs (ground deposits of salt) in the area that made finding enough fresh water for a large group especially challenging. Moreover, areas that had fresh water attracted white residents who obtained their water from these places, increasing the danger for fugitives from slavery. The forest provided wild turkeys and boar that freedom seekers could hunt, and pecans from nearby trees could also be added to their diets.[19] As they escaped west and crossed the Sabine River, they entered eastern Spanish Texas, a region also characterized by piney woods. From there, they had to travel nearly seventy-five miles to reach Nacogdoches. Once they arrived to Spanish Texas's easternmost frontier post, they had to depend on the commandant and local residents to protect them and help them maintain their freedom.

Although local Spaniards informed potential fugitives from slavery about freedom, the commandant of Nacogdoches did not actively encourage enslaved people to escape to the frontier post. José Joaquín Ugarte became the military commandant of Nacogdoches in 1803. Scarcely more than a year later, he had become an enemy of northern Louisiana enslavers and Governor Claiborne. White Natchitoches residents blamed him not only for offering freedom to those who ran away but also for the general insubordination of the enslaved population. Claiborne agreed with these accusations. Ugarte noted that the "complaints of the governor are destroying me, making me the author of the insurrection" of enslaved people in Louisiana.[20] These allegations against Ugarte made him solely responsible for the creation of Nacogdoches as a location on the Underground Railroad to Spanish Texas. According to Louisiana enslavers, enslaved Louisianans had escaped not because of the harsh conditions of slavery but because news of freedom in Texas had enticed them. Moreover, they claimed that local Spaniards lured enslaved people away from their plantations and ranches not only by telling them about freedom and sometimes even accompanying them on their journeys but also by ensuring that Nacogdoches was a safe haven that protected freedom seekers once they arrived. As Ugarte unintentionally and unwillingly became a central figure in El Camino Real's transformation into a route to freedom, enslaved communities in Louisiana continued to believe that Texas was a space of refuge.

The International Implications of U.S. Fugitives from Slavery in Spanish Texas

Despite the objections of the commandant at Nacogdoches, the frontier post remained a destination for fugitives from slavery in the region. A second group of freedom seekers escaped in October 1804. Seven adult enslaved Louisianans ran away during the harvest season likely to avoid the higher production quotas and additional workload. Harvest season also meant that there would be ripened crops to supplement the meager rations they would be able to steal before running away. Included in the group of freedom seekers were four Black men, two mulatto men, a Black woman, and a two-year-old child. Determined to be free, the fugitives from slavery not only carried their belongings but also traveled with "eleven horses, some merchandise, five guns, about thirty pounds of powder, and about one hundred pounds of bullets," all of which they had stolen from their plantations or ranches for their escape.[21] For more than a week, the group attempted to make their way to Nacogdoches. While the ammunition and weapons helped ensure their safety, these supplies also slowed their pace. Nine days after they had escaped, the enslaver of four of the freedom seekers arrived in Nacogdoches to retrieve them. Alexis Cloutier had not traveled alone to the Spanish Texas frontier town to recover his property. Five militiamen, two mulatto men, and a free Black man accompanied him to help him capture and deliver those who had escaped back to slavery.[22]

Similar to the group of fugitives from slavery who had escaped earlier in October, this group of freedom seekers did not search for freedom quietly. Patrols and nearby white residents were able to hear horse hooves and perhaps the cry of a child, but the freedom seekers were prepared to defend themselves. This group of fugitives from slavery also fled west to Nacogdoches, signaling that enslaved people in the region understood El Camino Real as the route to freedom they should use. They had learned about freedom in Texas from two local Spaniards who had traveled to Natchitoches. One Spaniard even accompanied them to make sure that they reached their destination.[23] Many aspects of this escape closely resembled the one featured at the beginning of the chapter, which suggests that enslaved Louisianans maintained the local communication network that disseminated ideas about how to run away. Despite the existence of a network that relayed important information about escape, the limited number of spaces of freedom on the Louisiana–Texas frontier meant that enslavers like Cloutier also knew about Texas as a haven and were able to track the freedom seekers to Nacogdoches in a matter of days.

Once Louisiana enslavers located freedom seekers in Texas, they had difficulty retrieving fugitives from slavery across international boundaries. The Fugitive Slave Act of 1793 did not make any provisions for enslavers trying to reclaim enslaved people who escaped beyond U.S. borders. To recover freedom seekers who fled to Texas, Louisiana enslavers could seek assistance from Governor Claiborne. In an effort to address the complaints of Louisiana enslavers who wrote to him about their property escaping to Nacogdoches, Claiborne wrote to Ugarte; Sebastián Nicolás de Bari Calvo de la Puerta, the Marqués de Casa Calvo, the Spanish boundary commissioner; and Nemesio Salcedo, the commandant general of the Provincias Internas (Interior Provinces), asking them to locate fugitives from slavery and facilitate their deliveries to their U.S. enslavers. However, because of the unreliable postal service in Texas, weeks or even months passed before officials received and responded to these requests. Because using official channels to ensure the return of those who escaped slavery was often a lengthy process that resulted in further delay, some enslavers tracked freedom seekers on their own or traveled to Nacogdoches to directly negotiate with the commandant. Consequently, the frontier town's status as a place for fugitives from slavery fueled resentment between white Natchitoches residents and enslavers and local Spaniards who assisted enslaved Louisianans.

Even though only a few Spaniards had helped enslaved Black people run away, their willingness to offer this aid put Nacogdoches residents at risk. Viewing the Spanish Texas frontier post as a haven for freedom seekers, many northern Louisiana enslavers implicated the town's residents in harboring fugitives from slavery. After one group of enslaved people escaped from Natchitoches, Capt. Turner believed that angry white residents would "go to Nacogdoches and lay it in waste."[24] The relationship between enslaved Louisianans, fugitives from slavery, and Spaniards incited threats of violence from white Louisiana residents because Nacogdoches had become a central part of remaking the geography of freedom in the aftermath of the Louisiana Purchase. However, Black people's and Spaniards' acts of resistance also had far-reaching consequences beyond slavery and freedom. Nacogdoches's position as a destination on the Underground Railroad contributed to regional tension between Spanish and Louisiana officials about the boundaries of their respective territories.

While fugitives from slavery searched for freedom in Texas and their enslavers attempted to retrieve them, the U.S. and Spanish governments had differing ideas about the location of Louisiana's western border. President Thomas Jefferson used eighteenth-century maps of French Louisiana to argue that the U.S. territory's western boundary extended as far southwest as the Rio Grande. U.S. Secretary of State James Monroe and U.S. Minister to France Robert Livingston agreed with Jefferson and included Texas as part of the United States. After an exploration mission in eastern Spanish Texas and northern Louisiana, the Marqués de Casa Calvo identified the Sabine

River as the boundary between the two nations.²⁵ Establishing this boundary also clearly marked where slavery ended and freedom began for freedom seekers. Yet, these border claims did little to improve diplomatic relations in the region. The territory near the Sabine River remained disputed because of distrust between Louisiana and Texas officials.

Although the Spanish boundary commissioner recognized the Sabine River as the border, Spanish Texas officials were wary of the United States' proximity because there were no assurances that the U.S. government would not encroach on Spanish land. In 1805 Texas authorities disregarded Casa Calvo's recommendation and stationed troops near Los Adaes, a former Spanish mission founded in 1716 that was located east of the Sabine River. By the end of that year, there were 700 troops in Texas, 141 of them in Nacogdoches.²⁶ Concerns about the prospect of war increased in Louisiana. In a letter to Claiborne, Dr. John Sibley, a Natchitoches resident and the Indian agent for territorial Louisiana, wrote that 220 Spanish troops had been in Nacogdoches since July 14, 1805. Unconvinced that the French and Spanish residents of Louisiana would side with the United States, Claiborne moved troops to Pointe Coupee, which was approximately 150 miles southeast of Natchitoches, to protect Louisiana and, more importantly, New Orleans.²⁷ As tension between the two nations heightened, both U.S. and Spanish officials viewed this dispute as a way to assert dominance and secure control and authority in the region. Meanwhile, enslaved people thinking about running away used this conflict to change how the Underground Railroad operated to better help them navigate their journeys through contested territory.

The conflict over the boundaries of U.S. and Spanish territory did not deter enslaved Louisianans from running away; instead, it forced them to adapt their plans of escape. In May 1806 three enslaved brothers and an enslaved woman escaped from Opelousas, Louisiana. Three children also accompanied them. Because of the ongoing disagreement between the United States and Spain about borders, all travelers had to have a passport to enter Spanish Texas or to enter Louisiana. While the freedom seekers had secured a passport prior to running away, Spanish officials in Nacogdoches discovered the travel document to be a forgery soon after the fugitives from slavery arrived.²⁸ The preparation needed to obtain or create this document was one way that the dispute over imperial control in the region reshaped how enslaved Louisianans escaped slavery. In addition to securing information, food, and other materials for their journeys, potential freedom seekers had to make arrangements to secure forged documentation that appeared authentic enough to allow them to cross the border. It is unknown what process these fugitives from slavery used to acquire these documents, but their preparedness highlights that the communication network among enslaved people in Louisiana had become as valuable as the physical routes to freedom. Updated information about the status of the Louisiana-Texas border and how to cross it permeated the communication network, allowing freedom seekers to adapt to these changes and continue their plans for freedom. Enslaved Louisianans not only expanded their communication networks to include details about the border but also created a new point of origin for their pathways to freedom.

In the midst of the militarization of the Louisiana-Texas border, enslaved people planning to escape developed more routes to freedom that led them to Texas. Enslaved people in Opelousas, which was nearly 150 miles south of Natchitoches, devised their own communication network that included local information and information from northern Louisiana. They paired their knowledge about the surrounding area and news about freedom in Texas with escape strategies that northern Louisianans used to create new routes to freedom. These routes led them to Natchitoches first; freedom seekers then used El Camino Real to reach Nacogdoches. They likely had no one to guide them, and the presence of troops probably limited the roles that Spaniards and members of the Caddo Nation could have in an escape. Even though these realities added more uncertainty while traveling, enslaved Black people farther south in Louisiana used this route to reach Texas. This escape shows that enslaved Louisianans controlled the expansion of physical routes on the Underground Railroad within Louisiana. Men and women in bondage in Opelousas were able to gather pertinent information about what fugitives from slavery needed for their escapes, dictated where routes would form, and maintained control of these routes without the efforts of free Black people and white men and women from the United States.

Conclusion

The Louisiana Purchase ushered in political and diplomatic changes that allowed freedom seekers from Louisiana to consider the Spanish-speaking world as a haven. Casting these wider geographical and chronological parameters of the Underground Railroad not only traces how routes formed in Louisiana, but also considers the different approaches fugitives from slavery used to plan and execute their escapes. While Spaniards informed enslaved people about freedom nearby and how to arrive there, fugitives from slavery had to create avenues to freedom and adjust them during their journeys to account for a number of factors: the proximity of patrols tasked with capturing freedom seekers, U.S. militia members, and Spanish soldiers; the willingness of local Indigenous communities to protect those who fled slavery during their escapes; the availability of other spaces for rest and securing food; and any detours or delays that arose as they searched for freedom. While fugitives from slavery did not have clear knowledge of what to expect once they arrived in Spanish Texas, their escapes signaled that they understood that permanent freedom was not in the United States. Their acts of resistance exposed and critiqued a growing paradox of slavery and freedom in the United States: gradual abolition efforts in the North at the same time that U.S. slavery expanded farther south and west. In pursuing an international route to freedom on the western frontier, these escapes rejected the notion of freedom for Black people being primarily available in the antebellum North or Canada.

NOTES

I would like to thank Zakiya Adair, Winnifred Brown-Glaude, Emahunn Campbell, Melissa Cooper, Janet Gray, Cassandra Jackson, Craig Hollander, Melissa Rogers, and Piper Williams for their helpful suggestions and feedback. Also, thank you to Keilah Michal Spann for allowing me to interview her for this work. Spann is a preservationist and cultural resource management strategist. From 2014 to 2016 she was the director of programming for the Cane River National Heritage Area in Natchitoches, Louisiana.

    1. H. Sophie Burton and F. Todd Smith, *Colonial Natchitoches: A Creole Community on the Louisiana-Texas Frontier* (College Station: Texas A&M University Press, 2008), 141, 151, 156; Edward D. Turner to William C. C. Claiborne, October 16, 1804, in *Official Letter Books of William C. C. Claiborne, 1801–1816*, ed. Dunbar Rowland, 6 vols. (Jackson, Miss.: State Department of Archives and History, 1917), 2:387.

    2. Turner to Claiborne, October 16, 1804, in Rowland, *Official Letter Books*, 2:387; Keilah Michal Spann, telephone interview with the author, July 2, 2017. Enslaved Louisianans refers to enslaved men, women, and children who were born in Louisiana before and after Louisiana's transition to U.S. rule and those who arrived in Louisiana before and after its transition to U.S. rule.

    3. Turner to Claiborne, October 16, 1804, in Rowland, *Official Letter Books*, 2:387.

    4. For more about the Underground Railroad, see Larry Gara, *The Liberty Line: The Legend of the Underground Railroad* (Lexington: University of Kentucky Press, 1961); Keith P. Griffler, *Front Line of Freedom: African Americans and the Forging of the Underground Railroad in the Ohio Valley* (Lexington: University Press of Ken-

tucky, 2004); Fergus Bordewich, *Bound for Canaan: The Epic Story of the Underground Railroad, America's First Civil Rights Movement* (New York: Amistad, 2006); Cheryl Janifer LaRoche, *Free Black Communities and the Underground Railroad: The Geography of Resistance* (Urbana: University of Illinois Press, 2013); R. J. M. Blackett, *Making Freedom: The Underground Railroad and the Politics of Slavery* (Chapel Hill: University of North Carolina Press, 2013); Matthew Salafia, *Slavery's Borderland: Freedom and Bondage along the Ohio River* (Philadelphia: University of Pennsylvania Press, 2013); Robert H. Churchill, *The Underground Railroad and the Geography of Violence in Antebellum America* (New York: Oxford University Press, 2020). The study of freedom seekers in the nineteenth-century U.S.-Mexico borderlands is an emerging field. See Sean Kelley, "'Mexico in His Head': Slavery and the Texas-Mexico Border, 1810–1860," *Journal of Social History* 37, no. 3 (2004): 709–23; Sarah Cornell, "Citizens of Nowhere: Fugitive Slaves and Free African Americans in Mexico, 1833–1857," *Journal of American History* 100, no. 2 (2013): 351–74; James David Nichols, *The Limits of Liberty: Mobility and the Making of the Eastern U.S.-Mexico Border* (Lincoln: University of Nebraska Press, 2018); Mekala Audain, "'Design His Course to Mexico': The Fugitive Slave Experience in the Texas-Mexico Borderlands, 1850–1853," in *Fugitive Slaves and Spaces of Freedom in North American*, ed. Damian Alan Pargas (Gainesville: University Press of Florida, 2018), 232–50; Gerardo Gurza-Lavalle, "Against Slave Power? Slavery and Runaway Slaves in Mexico–United States Relations, 1821–1857," *Mexican Studies / Estudios Mexicanos* 35, no. 2 (2019): 143–70; and Alice L. Baumgartner, *South to Freedom: Runaway Slaves to Mexico and the Road to the Civil War* (New York: Basic Books, 2020).

5. The term "Louisiana" in this work refers to the Territory of Orleans (1803–12). Louisiana became a U.S. state in 1812. This chapter uses the terms "Louisiana" and "territorial Louisiana" to describe events that happened within the current geographical boundaries of Louisiana.

6. See Peter J. Kastor, *The Nation's Crucible: The Louisiana Purchase and the Creation of America* (New Haven, Conn.: Yale University Press, 2004); Adam Rothman, *Slave Country: American Expansion and the Origins of the Deep South* (Cambridge, Mass.: Harvard University Press, 2005); John Craig Hammond, *Slavery, Freedom, and Expansion in the Early American West* (Charlottesville: University of Virginia Press, 2007); Lance R. Blyth, "Fugitives from Servitude: American Deserters and Runaway Slaves in Spanish Nacogdoches, 1803–1808," *East Texas Historical Journal* 38, no. 2 (2000): 3–14; Rolanda Teal, "Underground Railroad Route along El Camino Real de las Tejas," U.S. National Park Service (2010), https://www.nps.gov/elte/learn/historyculture/trailwide-research.htm; Eric Herschthal, "Slaves, Spaniards, and Subversion in Early Louisiana: The Persistent Fears of Black Revolt and Spanish Collusion in Territorial Louisiana, 1803–1812," *Journal of the Early Republic* 36, no. 2 (2016): 283–311.

7. José Joaquín Ugarte to Juan Bautista Elguézabal, December 4, 1804, box 2S79, Bexar Archives, Dolph Briscoe Center for American History, University of Texas

at Austin (hereafter Briscoe Center). All translations are mine unless otherwise noted. In the eighteenth century, fugitives from slavery from Louisiana also escaped to Los Adaes, a Spanish military post. See Gwendolyn Midlo Hall, *Africans in Colonial Louisiana: The Development of Afro-Creole Culture in the Eighteenth Century* (Baton Rouge: LSU Press, 1995).

8. Aurelia Martín Casares and Margarita García Barranco, "Legislation on Free Soil in Nineteenth-Century Spain: The Case of the Slave Rufino and Its Consequences, 1858–1879," *Slavery & Abolition: A Journal of Slave and Post-slave Studies* 32, no. 3 (2011): 465.

9. Jean Baptiste Grappe, "Policies on Slavery," July 30, 1804, translated by Dr. James J. Baran, folder 3, Hazel K. Carter Collection, Northwestern State University, Cammie G. Henry Research Center, Natchitoches, Louisiana. For more about marronage, see Sylviane A. Diouf, *Slavery's Exiles: The Story of the American Maroons* (New York: New York University Press, 2014).

10. Edward D. Turner to Governor Claiborne, July 30, 1804, in *The Territorial Papers of the United States, Volume 9: The Territory of Orleans, 1803–1812*, ed. Clarence Edwin Carter (Washington, D.C.: U.S. Government Printing Office, 1940), 272.

11. Under Spanish law, colonial Mexican residents could only purchase and trade with goods that first arrived at Veracruz, located over a thousand miles away from Nacogdoches. See Vito Alessio Robles, *Coahuila y Texas en la época colonial* (Mexico City: Editorial Cultura, 1938), 608, 612.

12. Jane Landers, *Black Society in Spanish Florida* (Urbana: University of Illinois Press, 1999), 24–25, 29–35; Matthew J. Clavin, *Aiming for Pensacola: Fugitive Slaves on the Atlantic and Southern Frontiers* (Cambridge, Mass.: Harvard University Press, 2015), 1, 2, 6.

13. Eric Foner, *Gateway to Freedom: The Hidden History of the Underground Railroad* (New York: W. W. Norton & Company, 2015), 15; Manisha Sinha, *The Slave's Cause: A History of Abolition* (New Haven, Conn.: Yale University Press, 2016), 400.

14. "What Is the Underground Railroad?," https://www.nps.gov/subjects/undergroundrailroad/what-is-the-underground-railroad.htm; Deanda Johnson, interview with the author, November 5, 2019. Johnson is the Midwest regional program manager for the National Park Service's Network to Freedom program, which preserves historical sites associated with the Underground Railroad and educates national audiences about the Underground Railroad.

15. Turner to Claiborne, October 17, 1804, in Rowland, *Official Letter Books*, 2:386; Robles, *Coahuila y Texas*, 608, 612. For more about white Louisiana residents' fears of enslaved people and Spaniards working together, see Herschthal, "Slaves, Spaniards, and Subversion."

16. For more about Indigenous communities in the U.S. Southwest borderlands, see F. Todd Smith, *The Caddo Indians: Tribes at the Convergence of Empires, 1542–1854* (College Station: Texas A&M University Press, 1995); Juliana Barr, *Peace Came in the Form of a Woman: Indians and Spaniards in the Texas Borderlands* (Chapel Hill: University of North Carolina Press, 2007); Pekka Hämäläinen, *Comanche Em-*

pire (New Haven, Conn.: Yale University Press, 2008); Brian DeLay, *War of a Thousand Deserts: Indian Raids and the U.S.-Mexican War* (New Haven, Conn.: Yale University Press, 2008). In the U.S. southern borderlands, Indigenous populations worked to uphold the institution of slavery and sometimes also aligned with enslaved and free Black people. In the eighteenth century, members of Indigenous groups worked in Carolina and the Lower Mississippi valley as slave catchers. Fugitive slaves who escaped to Florida and free Black people who moved to Florida joined the Seminoles in the early decades of the nineteenth century. During the Seminole Wars, they helped defend their adopted communities. See Peter Wood, *Black Majority: Negroes in Colonial South Carolina from 1670 through the Stono Rebellion* (New York: W. W. Norton & Company, 1974); Daniel H. Usner, *Indians, Settlers, and Slaves in a Frontier Exchange Economy: The Lower Mississippi Valley before 1783* (Chapel Hill: University of North Carolina Press, 1992); Hall, *Africans in Colonial Louisiana*; Kevin Mulroy, *Freedom on the Border: The Seminole Maroons in Florida, the Indian Territory, Coahuila, and Texas* (Lubbock: Texas Tech University Press, 2003); Barbara Krauthamer, *Black Slaves, Indian Masters: Slavery, Emancipation, and Citizenship in the Native American South* (Chapel Hill: University of North Carolina Press, 2015).

17. Gerald W. Mullin, *Flight and Rebellion: Slave Resistance in Eighteenth-Century Virginia* (New York: Oxford University Press, 1974), 43–44; John Hope Franklin and Loren Schweninger, *Runaway Slaves: Rebels on the Plantation* (New York: Oxford University Press, 1999), 229. Family obligations and childrearing expectations often prevented enslaved women from escaping at the same rates as men, but some fugitive slave women and mothers who fled from U.S. borderlands communities escaped with other women and their children. See Deborah Gray White, *Ar'n't I a Woman? Female Slaves in the Plantation South*, rev. ed. (New York: W. W. Norton & Company, 1999), 70–74; Jennifer L. Morgan, *Laboring Women: Reproduction and Gender in New World Slavery* (Philadelphia: University of Pennsylvania Press, 2004), 50–68. For more about African and African American escape patterns, see Diouf, *Slavery's Exiles*.

18. Grappe, "Policies on Slavery," July 30, 1804, translated by Dr. James J. Baran, folder 3, Hazel K. Carter Collection, Cammie G. Henry Center, Northwestern State University, Natchitoches, Louisiana.

19. Spann, interview, July 2, 2017.

20. José Joaquín Ugarte to Nemesio Salcedo, December 26, 1804, Provincias Internas, vol. 200, Archivo General de la Nación, Mexico City, Mexico.

21. Ugarte to Elguézabal, October 25, 1804, box 2S79, Bexar Archives, Briscoe Center.

22. Ugarte to Elguézabal, October 25, 1804, December 4, 1804, box 2S79, Bexar Archives, Briscoe Center.

23. Ibid.

24. Turner to Claiborne, October 16, 1804, in Rowland, *Official Letter Books*, 2:386.

25. The Marqués de Casa Calvo declared that territory east of the Sabine River

would be under U.S. jurisdiction, while land west of the river would belong to Spain. See Gilbert C. Din, *An Extraordinary Atlantic Life: Sebastián Nicolás Calvo de la Puerta y O'Farrill, Marqués de Casa-Calvo* (Lafayette: University of Louisiana at Lafayette Press, 2016), 236, 253, 255–57.

26. Donald E. Chipman and Harriet Denise Joseph, *Spanish Texas, 1519–1821*, 2nd ed. (Austin: University of Texas Press, 2010), 238; Din, *An Extraordinary Atlantic Life*, 254.

27. Claiborne to James Madison, November 5, 1805, in Rowland, *Official Letter Books*, 3:225–27.

28. Nemesio Salcedo to Governor Claiborne, September 18, 1806, Spanish Materials from Various Sources, vol. 10, Dolph Briscoe Center for American History, University of Texas at Austin.

CHAPTER 3

Looking for Freedom in the Borderlands
U.S. Black Refugees from Slavery in Early Independent Mexico, 1821–1836

THOMAS MAREITE

During one of his several trips to Mexican Texas to promote Black emigration from the United States to Mexico, abolitionist Benjamin Lundy arrived at San Antonio de Béxar in August 1833 and recognized a man named Mathieu Thomas, whom Lundy had met the previous summer in Nacogdoches. Lundy knew Thomas as a free Black who was originally from North Carolina and had been brought to the region as an enslaved person in the 1820s before being manumitted. Employed as a blacksmith in San Antonio, Thomas appeared to be doing well for himself, and he enthusiastically asserted that "the Mexicans pay him the same respect as to other labouring people," regardless of the color of his skin. Lundy was apparently not aware that Mathieu Thomas was in fact not a free Black man at all but rather a fugitive from slavery.[1] His apparent success in Mexico, in line with Lundy's goal of presenting Mexico as a haven of racial equality, moreover, obscured a series of challenges the blacksmith had to overcome to secure his own freedom in the years before the Texas Revolution, as we will see.

Escaping mostly from Louisiana, Arkansas, and Mississippi but also from the new colonies founded in Texas from 1821 onward, countless fugitive slaves settled in the northeast of Mexico prior to Texas independence in 1836. However, a thorough analysis of their experiences upon arrival, such as those of Mathieu Thomas, is largely lacking in the scholarly literature. Indeed, the growing historiography on the flight of Black people in the U.S.-Mexico borderlands has predominantly focused on the twenty-five years spanning Texas independence in 1836 to the outbreak of the U.S. Civil War in 1861.[2] By contrast, fugitive slaves who fled to the northeast of Mexico before 1836, lured by independent Mexico's gradual abolition of slavery and the evolution of its asylum policy regarding foreign escaped slaves, have received far less scholarly attention.[3]

This chapter examines fugitive slaves' settlement experiences and the (geo)political repercussions of Black flight to northeastern Mexico between 1821 and 1836. How did escaped bondspeople experience settlement in Mexico? To what extent were they free? And how were their freedoms acquired? How did Mexican authorities, local and federal, respond to the arrival of U.S. fugitive slaves, and to what extent were official policies really enforced? How did Black flight to Mexico affect relations between borderland communities and state governments?

This chapter is divided into four sections. The first introduces the intertwined and contradicting federal policies that led to the abolition of slavery, on the one hand, and the expansion of foreign colonization based on slavery in Mexico's northeastern fringes, on the other. The second delves into failed diplomatic negotiations between the U.S. and Mexican governments over the restitution of runaways and the development of free-soil policy in early independent Mexico. The third sheds light on fugitive slaves' strategies of formal and informal settlement in the northeast of Mexico. The final section underlines the extent to which Black freedom was precarious and contextual in the U.S.-Mexico borderlands.

Slavery and Colonization in Early Independent Mexico

As Agustín de Iturbide's Plan de Iguala (March 1, 1821) marked the definitive formation of an independent Mexican state, a national discourse emerged to challenge the existence of slavery in the new republic. With about three thousand enslaved people remaining in Mexico, the institution had eroded to near economic and social insignificance. Its legal eradication seemed only a matter of time. Since preserving African slavery involved almost no practical advantage, given that other forms of free and unfree labor had largely replaced it, a general emancipation would hardly entail substantial economic readjustments for *hacendados* (large landholders), and its social and political effects could easily be contained.[4] The Plan de Iguala pledged equality among Mexicans regardless of race, although it did not explicitly mention slavery. In its wake, the Junta Provisional Gubernativa, the first provisional national government, formed the Comisión de Esclavos (Slaves Committee) under the aegis of lawyer Juan Francisco Azcarate y Lezama.

In October 1821 the committee proposed to abolish slavery and slave trafficking in exchange for an indemnity to slaveholders and to protect foreign fugitives willing to stay in Mexico with a "law of asylum."[5]

This early abolitionist proposal was never implemented. However, antislavery sentiment continued to grow in Mexico, finding expression in newspaper editorials and in popular and political culture. In September 1825 the *Gaceta Diaria de México* included a short antislavery pamphlet in which the author argued that "anyone who justifies such an obnoxious system deserves contempt from the philosopher and vengeance from the black."[6] The same year, Mexican writer José Joaquín Lizardi published a theater play entitled *El negro sensible*. In this drama, set in a sugar plantation somewhere in the Spanish Caribbean, Lizardi displayed the violence of slavery as an institution and implicitly legitimized Black resistance. The term *negro sensible* (sensitive Negro) referred to Catul, an enslaved man running away to reunite with his wife, Bunga, after their former slaveholder had separated them.[7] In the context of increasingly strained relations with the United States, Mexican opposition to slavery represented a clear expression of the young nation's moral superiority to its northern neighbor. The construction of a distinct sense of *mexicanidad* (Mexicanness) through antislavery rhetoric deliberately contrasted with the proslavery ideology of the U.S. South. Gen. José María Tornel y Mendivil, a staunch abolitionist, condemned the contradiction between the ideals of 1776 and the preservation of slavery in the United States, calling it hypocritical.[8] Mexican slaveholders emancipated their bondspeople as an act of patriotism. Symbolic manumissions were carried out every year on September 15 in commemoration of Hidalgo's Grito de Dolores, further consolidating the myth of the new nation's indifference to color. In 1826 President Guadalupe Victoria promised to raise a fund aimed at manumitting the last enslaved people in Mexico. Tornel proposed an abolition bill in 1827. The Cámara de Diputados began discussing the abolition of slavery in January 1828 with no substantial disagreements on the subject, except on explicitly granting freedom to enslaved people from foreign lands who were merely passing through Mexico. Making use of temporary extraordinary powers, President Vicente Guerrero unconditionally banned slavery in Mexico on September 15, 1829, despite protests by slaveholders in Córdoba (Veracruz) and Texas, which was later exempted from the decree.[9]

Furthermore, Mexican officials often expressed support for African American immigration to Mexico. Vice President Gómez Farías supported it in the hope of using the new settlers as a demographic and military buffer against Comanche attacks and U.S. westward expansion, while the Secretaría de Estado promised land and instruments for cultivation to the newcomers.[10] Discretion was nonetheless recommended to the Mexican chargé d'affaires in the United States, Joaquín María del Castillo, when advertising Mexico's official support for Black colonization for fear of antagonizing the northern republic.[11] As a result of these policies, abolitionists in the United States increasingly saw independent Mexico as a promised land for Black people.

Benjamin Lundy, editor of the *Genius of Universal Emancipation*, made three trips to Mexico in the first half of the 1830s, hoping to establish a Black colony. Observing the relative prosperity that free Black people enjoyed in Mexico, he declared that Mexico's "native inhabitants are almost to a man, opposed to slavery." At the 1833 National Colored Convention held in Philadelphia as part of the national free Black movement of the nineteenth century, organizers contemplated establishing colonies in Mexican Texas.[12] With slavery abolished and a relative openness toward free Black immigration to Mexico, Mexican officials became more willing to welcome U.S. fugitive slaves as well. Senator Francisco Manuel Sánchez de Tagle, an ex-integrant of the Comisión de Esclavos in 1821, argued that by openly welcoming U.S. fugitive slaves, Mexico would win new subjects loyal to the republic and willing to help defend it against the United States or Native Americans.[13] By the eve of Texas independence, ship captain and Massachusetts-born abolitionist Jonathan W. Walker even projected establishing a colony of escaped slaves in part of Lundy's grant, which he had eventually obtained in 1835.[14] The horizon would have thus been clear for enslaved people willing to abscond from the U.S. South to northeastern Mexico had it not been for one very influential development: the European American colonization of Texas.[15]

During a journey to Texas to retrieve four enslaved people who had absconded from his estate and a neighbor's plantation in western Louisiana, slaveholder Jacob Kirkham met a Connecticut-born pioneer named Moses Austin. Both men traveled together to San Antonio, along with a native of Virginia named James Forsythe, with distinct yet to some extent related objectives in mind. As he made clear in December 1820 when he was interrogated by the Spanish authorities, Austin's goal was not to secure runaways but instead to obtain a large land grant for colonization and the cultivation of cotton and sugar. Governor Martínez, initially reluctant to contemplate Austin's scheme, soon admitted that all past plans to bring settlers to northeastern Mexico had failed. A decade-long economic and demographic devastation of the province, the presence of hundreds of squatters illegally occupying land in Texas, and the threat posed by Native Americans to undermilitarized settlements all convinced Martínez of the benefits of foreign colonization as a means to secure the region for New Spain.[16] Moses Austin, who had originally settled in Spanish Louisiana in 1797, was thus granted two hundred thousand acres of land for the settlement of three hundred Catholic families on the Brazos and Colorado Rivers. Yet the old man died in June 1821 while visiting Missouri, where he owned a mine, to recruit settlers. On his deathbed, Moses expressed his last will: his son Stephen was to pursue his project in Texas. A new phase in the (geo)political landscape of slavery and freedom in the U.S.-Mexico borderlands began, one that dramatically shaped the experiences of U.S. fugitive slaves across the border.

Stephen F. Austin's efforts to carry out his father's wishes succeeded, and the first settlers had arrived by the end of 1821, many of them driven away from the United States by the financial panic of 1819. Yet colonization underwent an early setback with the advent of an independent Mexican government as prospective settlers began to worry that property rights in enslaved people, which lay at the very core of Austin's enterprise, would no longer be guaranteed. Over the following years, fierce discussions broke out in the Mexican Congress about whether to allow slavery in the northeastern colony and under which terms foreign colonization should be allowed. For Mexican political leaders, Austin's plan was riddled with moral and practical dilemmas. While they regarded the northern frontier's colonization by U.S. settlers as a potential geopolitical threat, Mexican officials also favored the prospect of a large-scale migration to Texas that would create a demographic and economic buffer against *indios bárbaros* and foreign adventurers. As the Spanish Empire abandoned to Mexico a problem it had never solved (securing its northeastern border in Texas), Austin's project represented a unique opportunity to populate and develop the northeastern part of the nation. However, it also clashed with rising antislavery voices. Despite the instability of early Mexican political leadership, Stephen F. Austin actively defended his colony, ensuring its survival and development though at times facing unequivocal adversity.[17] From November 1823 onward, a new Congreso General Constituyente that was formed to draft a federal constitution discussed a ban on the slave trade in Mexican territory. After heated debates, the decree issued on July 13, 1824, finally outlawed both the domestic and foreign slave trades, with a six-month exception for the Isthmus of Tehuantepec. Smugglers would be imprisoned for a year and their cargo confiscated. Additionally, enslaved people "introduced" into Mexico were considered free simply by entering its territory.[18]

Yet the ban's consequences were not entirely clear, due to the ambiguities underlying the term "introduction." Did the decree apply only to slave traders? Or did it also include individuals traveling with their enslaved people? This ambivalence played in favor of foreign colonization in northeastern Mexico, and new colonists kept arriving along with their enslaved men and women. Subsequent legislation only added to these ambiguities. The federal colonization law of August 18, 1824, and the federal constitution enforced shortly thereafter both left the matter of slavery to the discretion of the individual states of the republic. This meant that despite an amenability to the manumission of enslaved people, the immediate and unconditional abolition of the slave trade, and the passing of free-womb laws, the outcome of this Mexican progressiveness was decidedly mixed. Thus, while in northeastern Mexico the state of Tamaulipas de facto abolished slavery in 1825 by declaring all of its residents (including enslaved people) free and equal, Nuevo León simultaneously issued a free-womb law and prohibited slave introduction without outlawing slavery altogether.[19]

It was in this climate of uncertainty about the future of slavery in Texas that Coahuila y Tejas's constitutional congress began to draft its state constitution in August 1824. The process was to last almost three years. Two parties soon took shape. On the one hand, the Tejano faction of the state legislature, along with the Coahuilenses Viesca brothers, advocated the legal support of slavery in the new constitution. On the other, an antislavery faction led by Manuel Carrillo and Dionisio Elizondo from Coahuila sought to achieve full abolition. Yet by contrast with Tamaulipas, Coahuila y Tejas could not afford a general emancipation that would imply a large financial compensation to the slaveholding population of Texas. Nor could it free enslaved people unconditionally without provoking the wrath of its increasingly influential European American planters. A middle ground between the two parties was therefore reached. The state constitution of March 11, 1827, ruled that enslaved men and women already in Texas would retain this status until their death. However, all children born to enslaved parents would be free, and the introduction of enslaved people was prohibited starting six months after the publication of the constitution (article 13). The constitution also underlined the "imprescriptible rights of liberty, security, property, and equality" for its inhabitants, including those in transit, although enslaved people were not explicitly mentioned in it (article 11). New settlers in Texas largely ignored the provision after its implementation, and at the initiative of San Felipe de Austin's *ayuntamiento* (municipality), a decree permitting the introduction of indentured servants (March 5, 1828) effectively nullified the constitutional prohibition. U.S. enslaved people were brought to Texas under the disingenuous title of indebted laborers, with service contracts of up to ninety-nine years.[20]

In the midst of these political developments, colonists and enslaved people kept arriving in Texas. Austin secured three more contracts after he met the terms of his initial contract in 1825, and his colony, developed around San Felipe de Austin, seemed the most attractive for prospective settlers. Other European American colonies blossomed, economically connected to Atlantic capitalist markets through Louisiana. According to Graham Davis, between 1823 and 1835 no fewer than forty-one land contracts were signed between *empresarios*, most of them foreigners, and the Mexican state. Most of these entrepreneurs failed to develop their colonies, although exceptions included Green DeWitt, who founded his colony in 1825 around the town of Gonzales, along the Guadalupe and Lavaca Rivers. At the close of the 1820s, the foreign-born colonists had settled mostly east of the Colorado River in small slave societies and had developed a fast-expanding plantation economy, mostly producing cotton for Atlantic markets. By contrast, the Tejano and Mexican population of Texas lived mostly in the old settlements of San Antonio, Goliad (previously known as La Bahía), and Nacogdoches, with the exception of De León colony (around Victoria).

Extradition or Free Soil?

From the beginning of his colony in Texas, Austin strove to institute laws regulating slavery and fugitive slaves. "Criminal regulations" passed in January 1824 formalized proceedings for the arrest of escaped slaves from inside and outside Austin's colony. The settlement of U.S. escaped slaves in Texas was clearly at odds with the development of such a slave society, with potentially disruptive effects on the flourishing yet still fledgling colony. As early as December 1824, Austin expressed concern to the legislature of Coahuila y Tejas about self-emancipated slaves arriving from Louisiana and beyond and requested (in vain) formal instructions on how to react. Austin's view was clear: "If the runaway remains here, he is a nuisance to the Country—if his owner claims him and he is not given up it will destroy all harmony between the Citizens of that State [the United States] and this."[21] In August 1825 Benjamin Rush Milam bitterly underlined that "the Stait of

Louisianna have lost a grait maney slaives that have taken refuge in this Republick of Mexico," urging U.S. minister in Mexico Joel R. Poinsett to conclude an extradition agreement with its government.[22] Dutch-born Philip Hendrik Nering Bögel, who passed himself off under the moniker Baron de Bastrop, the Texas representative at the Congress of Coahuila y Tejas, also began pressing for extradition from 1824, apart from attempting to secure a legal sanction for slavery in Texas. Even U.S. secretary of state Henry Clay grew concerned by enslaved people escaping to "the adjacent territories of Mexico." In March 1825, when Clay sent Poinsett instructions for the negotiation of a treaty of "amity, commerce, navigation and neighbourhood" with Mexico, he underlined the necessity of inserting a provision "for the regular apprehension and surrender [of fugitive slaves] to their respective proprietors, or their lawful agents."[23]

By the end of September 1825, U.S. and Mexican officials had reached an agreement regarding mutual restitution (article 33). The final treaty was concluded on July 10, 1826, with a period of eight months for its ratification by both parties. Yet despite an initial agreement on article 33, the Mexican House of Representatives' Foreign Relations Committee advised rejection of article 33 in April 1827 on both practical and ideological grounds. To begin with, the notion of Mexican enslaved people fleeing to the United States was absurd, and therefore the clause of "mutual restitution" was of little real use to the young republic, while protecting U.S. fugitive slaves would undermine foreign influence over Texas. In addition, the committee underscored the need to protect a fugitive slave's "inalienable right" to freedom, while Mexican secretary of state Sebastián Camacho stressed that restitution would represent a "violent collision with the feelings of the Mexican people." This sentiment was echoed outside the parliamentary arena in Mariano Arevalo's *Diálogo entre un barbero y su marchante* (Dialogue between a barber and his client), which expressed indignation at slavery and openly criticized Poinsett's efforts to secure restitution.[24] Delays in the ratification finally prompted both administrations to drop the treaty in 1827. After new negotiations, another treaty was concluded in the first weeks of 1828, again providing for the restitution of fugitive slaves. Yet again Mexican representatives expressed uneasiness with some articles, including the new article 33, on the grounds that it directly contradicted the federal ban on the slave trade (1824). The House of Representatives once again rejected the article, compelling Poinsett to use "very strong language" to push the cause of restitution, which he considered essential "to the future understanding between the two nations." Nonetheless, the Mexican Senate eventually supported the deputies in their opposition, and the treaty failed once more to be ratified.[25]

Poinsett's failure to secure a restitution agreement with Mexico did not discourage his successor Anthony Butler. On April 5, 1831, a treaty of "amity, commerce and navigation" formalized the mutual return of fugitive slaves, provided that they had reached Mexico less than a year before their extradition (original article 34). Once more, the implied reciprocity was fictional: slavery had already been *formally* abolished in Mexico (except in Texas), and escape attempts across the border were entirely one-directional. Once again, Mexican representatives in the Cámara de Diputados soon objected to restitution and eventually rejected article 34, though by a majority of only one vote, in October 1831. By contrast with previous negotiations, however, the Senate's Comisión de Relaciones Exteriores insisted on including the article to prevent border tensions, fearing private slaving raids from the United States to Mexico, as well as out of respect for private property. Yet the Cámara de Diputados sustained its decision against the Senate by a constitutionally required majority of more than two-thirds of its members. By the end of the year, Butler had grudgingly agreed to omit article 34, as it was delaying and jeopardizing the treaty's ratification (effective in April 1832). To President Andrew Jackson, Butler nevertheless defiantly underscored that "the rejection impairs no right nor will it interpose any restraint in the employment of all such means as may become necessary for enforcing these rights should the evil resulting from the loss of slaves to our Citizens by then seeking refuge in the Mexican Territory ever grow into such magnitude as to require the interposition of the Government."[26]

U.S. abolitionists retrospectively condemned the federal government's attempts to extract restitution from Mexico. Gerrit Smith, for instance, termed it a "heaven-defying crime."[27] David Lee Child, editor of the *Anti-Slavery Herald*, stressed in 1843, as controversies on Texas were raging, that Mexico had been "bullied into a surrender of one of the clearest of a sovereign and independent people, by threats of violating that right by force and invasion." During the U.S.-Mexican War (1846–48), which followed the U.S. annexation of Texas in 1845, Loring Moody from the Massachusetts Anti-Slavery Society vehemently criticized the U.S. government's pressure on Mexico "to act the part of watchdogs to the plantations of the South-Western slave-holding states."[28] Similarly, just after the conflict, the jurist William Jay of the American Anti-Slavery Society published an essay exposing the war's proslavery origins. It was the failure to secure the Mexicans' agreement on restitution, Jay claimed, that had reinvigorated "the efforts of slaveholders to possess themselves of Texas."[29]

In addition to the fact that negotiations on extradition repeatedly resulted in deadlock, Mexican free-soil policy toward foreign escaped slaves acquired momentum in the wake of the 1824 federalist constitution. While the slave trade ban passed in July 1824 formally provided for the freedom of smuggled bondspeople, some states chose to enforce provisions freeing self-liberated slaves from outside the states' jurisdictions. For instance, in 1825 the states of Tamaulipas and Occidente granted "unalienable rights of freedom, safety, property, and equality" to all their citizens, as well as to outsiders "in the quality of transient," theoretically protecting runaways from outside the two states. Likewise, in August 1827 San Luis Potosí's governor, Ildefonso Díaz de León, openly granted freedom to any escaped bondsperson from adjacent states from September 16, 1827, onward while also abolishing slavery within his jurisdiction as a tribute to Hidalgo's Grito de Dolores. San Luis Potosí's sanctuary policy was rooted in a liberal and anti-imperialist tradition that had emerged during the Mexican wars for independence. Protection provided to escaped slaves was unconditional and tied to inalienable rights inspired by progressive ideals: unlike the late colonial period, freedom granted to runaways was detached from the observance of Catholicism. As a result, enslaved people from neighboring states such as Coahuila y Tejas and Nuevo León escaped to San Luis Potosí in an attempt to secure formal freedom. For instance, in January 1828 Cosme Cervantes and Francisco Nuñez, two bondspeople fleeing from Santa Rosa de Muzquiz (Coahuila), addressed the Comisión de Peticiones (Petition Committee) of San Luis Potosí's state legislature. The two men solicited *amparo* (protection) from what they termed the "great Mexican Republic." Introducing themselves as part of a "disgraced class," Cosme and Francisco (successfully) requested *cartas de libertad* (freedom papers) from the state legislature.

Such free-soil policy at the state level prefigured the development of federal free-soil policy; the latter slowly emerged from the second half of the 1820s, reaching full fruition in the 1830s.[30] This was to be seen in the Mexican state's response to a request from Louisiana for the restitution of escaped slaves. Although the Mexican consul in New Orleans favored acquiescing to Louisiana's request, citing the growing frequency of escape attempts and the danger of further straining relations with the United States as reasons, the new liberal government formed in early 1833 declined the proposition.[31] Instead it asserted its staunch commitment to free-soil policy, and all subsequent efforts by Louisiana representatives, such as Edward Douglass White, to conclude an accord failed.[32]

Formal and Informal Settlement(s)

From 1821 onward, U.S. planters migrating westward in the hope of making a fortune through cotton brought to Texas an ever-increasing number of enslaved people. As the Mexican government grew wary of European American immigration after the release of Gen. Manuel de Mier y Terán's alarmist report on Coahuila y Tejas in 1828, a new colonization law (April 6, 1830) outlawed the further introduction into Texas of U.S. settlers and enslaved people. Yet by May 1834, when this formal prohibition was dropped, the total number of U.S. migrants and bondspeople in Texas had nearly doubled, with the latter composing a tenth of nearly twenty thousand inhabitants. Two years later, bondspeople numbered at least five thousand, while the general population was estimated at about thirty thousand individuals.[33] U.S. migration to Texas was part of a larger trend. From the 1790s onward, thousands of planters left the Atlantic seaboard for territorial Mississippi (1798) and territorial Louisiana (1803), drawn by the possibilities for the production of sugar, corn, indigo, and, most importantly, cotton. As a result, Louisiana's and Mississippi's combined population (including enslaved people) more than tripled between 1810 and 1830, reaching slightly fewer than 350,000 inhabitants, a number ten times higher than the population of Texas at the time.[34] Because of this long southward and westward extension of slavery, and because bondspeople in the U.S. South and Texas grew increasingly aware of Mexico's rising antislavery stance, the ranks of fugitive slaves looking for freedom in Mexico swelled. For instance, abolitionist Benjamin Lundy recalled that all the enslaved people belonging to a Francis Berry from Virginia, who had settled at Gonzales (Texas), had absconded "to the Spaniards" and that for this reason the planter did not wish to acquire others.[35] When escaping from the U.S. South and the European American colonies in Texas, runaways used two main strategies to achieve freedom. First, they looked for informal (or de facto) freedom by settling in Mexico without seeking the recognition of the Mexican state. Second, they sought formal (or de jure) freedom through Mexico's acknowledgment of their legal status as "free."[36] This second option was the most popular.

Some enslaved freedom seekers settled deep in the Mexican interior in the hope of escaping deportation by Mexican officials, abduction by slave hunters, and attacks by Native Americans. In 1825 a man named Jack Yaczon escaped from Opelousas (Louisiana) to Monterrey (Nuevo León). A year later, Maryland-born slave trader and Yaczon's slaveholder, Alexander Robb, dispatched an associate to lobby Monterrey's *alcalde segundo* (deputy mayor) Nicanor Martínez, to return Jack, an enterprise that seemingly succeeded despite the legal defense provided for Yaczon by local resident José de Garay. Another enslaved man, named Andrés Dortola, fled to Mexico in 1823. Instead of settling in Texas, the man pursued his escape until reaching Guadalajara (Jalisco), where he requested freedom: since he had converted to Catholicism, Andrés expected to be protected by a *real cédula* (royal decree) passed in 1750 that granted freedom to foreign Catholic enslaved people.[37]

Yet most bondspeople fleeing to Mexico settled in its immediate territorial and maritime borderlands. Runaways regularly reached civilian settlements or military posts, looking for formally recognized freedom. As during the late colonial period, Nacogdoches represented the main gateway to freedom for runaways, though the freedom they acquired in eastern Texas was extremely precarious. According to a local folktale, "a handsome young gentleman in good style" reached the town in 1827. The distinguished traveler introduced himself as Claud[e] Riviere from Baton Rouge, "the son of a wealthy sugar planter, seeking investments here," while in fact he was an escaped slave. He joined a local ball and became "the leader, popular partner for the beauties of the ball-room." Soon enough, though, Tennessee-born Rezin P. Bowie, James Bowie's brother (both of them famous land speculators and slave smugglers), "walked across the floor to Riviere, and touched him on the shoulder." Bowie promptly carried Claude back as an enslaved man to Louisiana.[38]

Escaped slaves increasingly viewed San Antonio, along with Nacogdoches, as an attractive beacon of freedom before 1836. The *Indianola Bulletin* reminisced in 1854 that fugitive slaves occasionally "found their way to that city of blood, chivalry and greasers," where "the population was numerous, isolated and disposed to protect them."[39] Free Black people were already a common sight among its multiracial population in the early 1820s.[40] While the *ayuntamiento* often took a proslavery approach, the federal government's representatives in San Antonio seemed more sympathetic to the plight of enslaved people, whether fugitives or not. For example, in January 1823 Governor José Felix Trespalacios granted freedom to thirty-year-old enslaved man Phil as a reward for denouncing his slaveholder's attempt to steal cattle.[41]

Furthermore, fugitive slaves could and did embark on commercial vessels sailing to Mexican ports either clandestinely or as crew. In 1834 a man was found in Matamoros (Tamaulipas) hidden aboard the *Juxpeña*, arriving from New Orleans.[42] By the early 1830s, the growing port city on the Rio Grande delta hosted an expanding population of free Black people (natives mostly of Louisiana and Haiti) and U.S. fugitive slaves, a by-product of the liberalization of its maritime trade with New Orleans during the 1820s. Matamoros was attractive for its relative commercial prosperity, in addition to being more sheltered from Comanche incursions than other towns on the upper river such as Laredo, a border town frequently attacked by Native Americans, economically depressed and demographically stagnating.[43] Along the Caribbean coast, Tampico, Veracruz, and Minatitlán increasingly welcomed U.S. runaways as a result of an increased maritime interconnection with U.S. southern ports after 1821. Veracruz's strong connection to the Black Atlantic dated back to the early colonial period, as enslaved people introduced in New Spain transited through the port. In the 1820s foreign travelers frequently evoked the presence of African Americans (free or otherwise) in Veracruz, where "crowds of Negro porters [we]re in constant motion, discharging and carrying the cargoes of boats to the Custom-house within the gates, where a noisy concourse of cart-men are scrambling and quarrelling for the chance of employment."[44] Farther south, in January 1831 Mexican authorities at Minatitlán freed three bondspeople arriving from the United States with their enslaver, Charles C. River. One of them, Elia Green, was a laundress and dressmaker. Another, a man named Anthony Collins, was sent to work on maize *milpas* (crop-growing areas) in the hills surrounding the town, likely with the third liberated bondsman, eighteen-year-old Isaac.[45]

Yet even after slavery definitively ceased to exist in Mexico, not all fugitive slaves presented themselves to Mexican civilian and military settlements. Instead of negotiating their status as formally free refugees with the Mexican authorities, some runaways attempted to gain freedom informally by remaining out of the reach of the federal state. For instance, some sought shelter with settlers in Texas, even in European American colonies, where some planters hired them in the interest of acquiring cheap labor. This is suggested by Lundy, for instance, who told of a planter from Louisiana who attempted in August 1834 to retrieve some of his enslaved people from Texas, where they were being kept by a planter named Nathaniel Robbins.[46] Additionally, some fugitive slaves looked for refuge among Native Americans, in particular among the Comanches who had de facto sovereignty over areas extending from the Rio Grande to the Colorado River. As underscored by Sean M. Kelley, the naturalist and physician Gideon Lincecum noted the presence of numerous self-emancipated slaves in the Comanchería during the early 1830s. Tawélash groups along the Red River also welcomed runaways.[47]

Finally, escaped slaves in Mexican Texas often deliberately remained in forests and swamps. As an example of the "borderland" Maroons described by Sylviane Diouf, Stafford Point's settler Dilue Rose Harris reminisced that in 1834 an escaped "African negro" was wandering along the Navidad River at the fringes of local plantations.[48] Likewise, while traveling through Texas during the winter of 1834–35, traveler Andrew Parker met an enslaved man "chained in a baggage wagon, for the purpose of carrying him home to his master." The fugitive had "run away from [him] three months previous, and had all that time lived in the woods, and obtained his food by hunting."[49] Such wilderness marronage still represented a realistic solution for fugitive slaves before 1836. Most of the new planters had settled with their enslaved people along the fertile banks of the Colorado and Brazos Rivers, the original location of Austin's colony. Population density outside of this plantation-centered region remained fairly low, and lands peripheral to it had not yet been cleared for cotton, sugar, and tobacco production. The social, political, and environmental hegemony of European American settlers was still limited to their immediate surroundings before the plantation economy (and slavery) dramatically expanded in postindependence Texas.[50]

Precarious and Contextual Freedom(s)

Mexican civilian and military officials in Texas did not receive clear instructions on how to treat escaped slaves, except for the ambiguous federal slave trade ban of 1824 and article 11 of the 1827 state constitution. As a result, they often had to make their own decisions. In September 1827 Encarnación Chirino, *alcalde* at Nacogdoches, solicited orders from José Antonio Saucedo, Bexar department's *jefe político* (political chief), on how to deal with a Black bondsperson and two army deserters from Louisiana who had just reached the town. Waiting for instructions, Chirino decided to protect the runaway in exchange for his work. Coahuila y Tejas's state government forwarded Chirino's request to the federal government in vain, and whether or not the enslaved person was returned to Louisiana remains unknown. In May 1829 Juan Ignacio Ibarbo, Chirino's successor, similarly requested instructions on the issue from Bexar department's *jefe político*, Ramón Múzquiz. Ibarbo reiterated his demand for some months, yet not receiving any reply, he eventually chose to deliver the runaways to their identified slaveholders.⁵¹ Requests for formal instructions originating from Coahuila y Tejas's government went up to the federal Consejo de Gobierno (Government Council), but all were left unanswered.⁵² Thus, when three U.S. escaped slaves reached Nacogdoches in January 1832, Chirino, once more *alcalde*, again expressed his indecision. The enslaver of one of the escapees, an enslaved woman, had journeyed to the town, intending to retrieve her, but the department's Jefatura Política (Political Head Office) instructed Chirino not to deliver the woman before receiving orders from Saltillo. They came in March 1832: the three runaways were to be returned, unless they and their enslavers had settled in Coahuila y Tejas after September 11, 1827 (six months after the publication of the state constitution of 1827).⁵³

The treatment of self-liberated slaves by civilian and military officials proved inconsistent, since it was usually based on a personal interpretation of the laws. As Tawakoni and Waco natives attacked San Antonio in August 1830, Mexican military forces swiftly retaliated. The First Permanent Company of Tamaulipas soon launched a large punitive expedition. By mid-September 1830 the party had reached a Tawakoni settlement on the San Gabriel River. The company killed eight Tawakonis during the ensuing assault, and an enslaved man originally from Austin's colony was seized along with four Native American children, who were sent to Monterrey. While the bondsperson was being transferred to Lavaca, Manuel de Mier y Terán, the general commandant and inspector of the eastern Internal Provinces, instructed commandant Antonio Elosua "to locate his owner" using newspaper advertisements, likely reasoning that the fugitive could not benefit from Mexico's protection due to Texas's exemption from the abolition of slavery in December 1829.⁵⁴

Restitution occurred especially when willingness to maintain friendly relationships with the U.S. government and the European American colonists prevailed over the Mexican state's need to assert its exclusive sovereignty over the province. Decision-making on fugitive slaves was to a large extent shaped by diverging visions of foreign settlement in Texas, considered alternatively as a threat or an opportunity for Mexico. Officials who viewed European American colonization positively as a source of economic development and safety against Native Americans showed more eagerness to deliver escaped slaves to their European American slaveholders. In September 1831 a refugee from slavery reached Fort Tenoxtitlan (along the old Camino Real between San Antonio and Nacogdoches), one of the two posts (with Lavaca) where free Black emigrants were officially supposed to settle, and sought the protection of Tejano lieutenant colonel José Francisco Ruíz.

Tenoxtitlan had been established in 1830 as part of an attempt to "Mexicanize" Texas following Mier y Terán's alarming report in 1828 and to protect civilian settlements from Native Americans. No translator was present at the fort, and communication between Ruíz and the fugitive was not easy. Ruíz wrote to Samuel May Williams, secretary at San Felipe de Austin's *ayuntamiento*, that "according to what [he had] been able to understand," the enslaved man was claiming to have escaped from the United States. Yet Ruíz was skeptical about this account, convinced instead that the asylum seeker had in fact "run away from some inhabitant of this department" and was attempting to evade restitution by strategically claiming to have absconded from beyond the Sabine River. The officer therefore decided to send the runaway to Austin's colony, where he maintained friendly contacts: to him, this ad hoc restitution was a show of goodwill to maintain amicable relations between the planters and the Mexican state in Texas.[55]

While some officials like Ruíz actively pursued and delivered enslaved freedom seekers to their slaveholders, others nonetheless sheltered them even at the risk of heated conflicts with planters. In August 1831 two escaped slaves from Louisiana solicited the protection of Virginia-born John Davis Bradburn, the military commandant for Mexico at the fort of Anahuac, on the northeast side of Galveston Bay on the delta of the Trinity River. Bradburn welcomed the two men and enlisted them in the ranks. In exchange, the refugees were employed as brickmakers and construction workers, building part of the fortress and some houses for the officers. When their owner, William M. Logan, personally requested their restitution, Bradburn relied upon a personal interpretation of an ambiguous set of laws and refused to comply. The officer assumed that Texas's exemption from the abolition of slavery applied exclusively to the European American colonies of Texas, not to Texas as a whole, an interpretation advocated by the planters. The European American population on the Trinity River quickly viewed Bradburn's refusal to deliver the two men as a serious casus belli. Retrospectively, Bradburn underscored that protecting the two men had become "a circumstance that kept damaging [him] a lot and attracting [him] the hate of the colonists."[56]

A mob of resentful planters soon surrounded Anahuac, pressing for the return of the enslaved men to Logan. Mier y Terán advised Bradburn to argue that claims on runaways should be addressed directly to the Mexican government through U.S. ministers in Mexico, not to local officers like him. The general commandant thereby sought to deflect pressure from European American settlers in Texas and the United States to the federal level in the hope of locally safeguarding peace and sovereignty on the republic's northern fringes. However, this response did not please local planters, and the discrepancy of interpretations between Bradburn and the mob quickly escalated into an open conflict. Settlers rose in rebellion against the military authorities of Anahuac after some men who had plotted to illegally retrieve the two enslaved men were detained. Against the backdrop of increasingly frequent regionalist rebellions in 1830s Mexico, this particular controversy soon culminated in a pledge of allegiance to Santa Anna by the planters in support of federalism and local autonomy against a perceived trend toward centralization under conservative president Anastasio Bustamante. With slavery at its very roots, the resulting months-long conflict (remembered as the "Anahuac disturbances") further divided the Mexican state and the European American colonists in Texas, Margaret S. Henson even describing Anahuac as "the cradle of the Texas Revolution."[57]

Mexico's lack of legal and moral support for institutionalized slavery on its northeastern periphery constituted a constant source of annoyance for slaveholders in Texas. The intervention of state officials into the realm of slavery conflicted with the new colonists' sense of liberty, deeply embedded in attributes and performances of whiteness, masculinity, and household mastery. It also clashed with a common preference by U.S. settlers for minimal interference by central governments.[58] While the Mexican state increasingly strived to reassert its authority over Texas and rejected extradition, legal strategies gradually lost popularity among European American slaveholders." In a climate of rising defiance inaugurated by the Fredonian Rebellion, led by *empresario* Haden Edwards in eastern Texas (1826), they began to illegally retrieve their "property."

In April 1832 Peter and his son Tom escaped from the plantation of Alexander Thompson on the Brazos River to San Antonio, where they successfully requested *amparo* from the town's civil court. The two men had been brought to Texas as enslaved people less than two years before their flight. In March 1832, in relation to another case, the state authorities had affirmed the freedom of enslaved people who had been introduced in Texas after September 11, 1827 (six months after the publication of the 1827 state constitution). As such, Peter and Tom were indeed eligible for such protection. As the court was financially unable to maintain the refugees, it temporarily sent them to John William Smith's house to be employed as domestic servants in exchange for food and a small salary. Yet one night in May 1832, Smith "maliciously" delivered them (for a bounty) to several *norteamericanos* led by Henry Stevenson Brown. According to a contemporary, the renowned slave hunter "understood the Spanish language and was well acquainted in and around San Antonio." A settler on the Red River had also commissioned Brown's crew to retrieve five of his bondspeople from San Antonio, where they had "received countenance and protection from the authorities and population generally." One of the mercenaries, Basil Durbin, found out that while "one of the negroes was making shingles on the Medina [River], the others were employed about the city." Brown's men came down from their camp "in the hills above the city" and abducted the man working on the Medina "after a brief struggle." Later, the mercenaries kidnapped "another [runaway] hauling wood between the powder house and town" after a fierce conflict. A third runaway was arrested while the first two abducted men were "hurried off to Gonzales." Then, Brown's party quickly retreated.

This filibustering expedition infuriated most of San Antonio's Tejanos. Ramón Múzquiz, the *jefe político*, termed it "atrocious": the affair "[was] so serious as to [have provoked] the attention of the people of the City regarding the outrage that [had been] committed against the legally constituted laws and authorities." Military expeditions were launched to arrest the kidnappers. Lt. Pedro Rodríguez was sent to the former Spanish mission of San José y San Miguel de Aguayo, some miles south of San Antonio, where some of the raiders were thought to have escaped. The troops found and fired at Basil Durbin before jailing him at San Antonio. His accomplices had seemingly sought refuge in Gonzales, on the Guadalupe River, in DeWitt's colony. Múzquiz therefore instructed Capt. Gaspar Flores to head to Gonzales, where he would arrest Brown's crew at whatever cost ("up to the point of being dead men in case they are obstinate"). Commanding a force of thirty-two men, Flores reached Gonzales and began negotiating with *comisario* (commissioner) Ezekiel Williams and *empresario* Green DeWitt for the arrest of the raiders and the recovery of the abducted slave refugees. However, the search proved to be unsuccessful. The self-liberated men had seemingly been sent away from Gonzales. Only one of the mercenaries, Benjamin Duncan, was arrested and transferred to San Antonio's *calabozo* (dungeon), where he waited "to have his case more fully investigated." Captain Flores soon became aware of the complacency of the new municipality of Gonzales, which was controlled by European American settlers, toward Brown and his men. Despite pledges of goodwill, town leaders demonstrated no intention to actively look for the abducted slave refugees. Williams and DeWitt argued in favor of Duncan, who, according to them, "[had] conducted himself in this Colony honestly." Both men told

Flores that they had seen Brown heading to Austin's colony just before the Mexican officer's arrival at Gonzales and that Peter and Tom had expressed willingness to return to Thompson. In San Antonio, however, this version of events was contradicted by the testimony of a man of color named Jon, who himself had narrowly escaped abduction and who asserted that the raiders were very likely still lurking in DeWitt's colony, although no further evidence could be found on the subject.

The state of Coahuila y Tejas ordered the prosecution of John William Smith, intending to make the case into a show of firmness against the increasingly rebellious European American population. Yet all the prisoners connected to the case were bailed out, and in the midst of Múzquiz's vain attempts to arrest the other culprits, Williams even openly acknowledged having participated in Peter and Tom's forced return to Alexander Thompson. The *ayuntamientos* of Gonzales, San Felipe de Austin, Brazoria, and Nacogdoches eventually terminated their pretense of cooperation to the point of not even replying to letters sent from San Antonio on the issue. The state authorities finally dropped the case in August 1833, concerned that, under the "current political circumstances," any further prosecution would affect the "tranquility of the department" and trigger serious conflicts between the Mexican state and the European American settlers, as in Anahuac. Although a criminal case against two participants in the expedition was held dormant on the shelves of *licenciado* (lawyer) José Maria Aguirre in Saltillo, no further attempt to prosecute the raiders was made. Peter and Tom's case illustrates the adoption of more aggressive tactics by slaveholders to retrieve self-liberated slaves. The Mexican state's powerlessness to convict the mercenaries along with the complicity of proslavery municipal authorities influenced by European American planters sheds light on how independently from Mexico slaveholders acted during the years leading up to the Texas Revolution.[59] Tensions regarding runaways in the Louisiana-Texas borderlands also took more global expressions. In March 1834 rumors that the United States intended to occupy Texas as far as the Nueces River in retaliation for the escape of criminals, deserters, and enslaved people across the border began alarming the Mexican government.[60]

In addition to fugitive slaves, Mexican and American free Black people in Texas were frequent collateral victims of slaving raids. In October 1823 an official at Nacogdoches reported that "some Englishmen" had crossed the border and captured a "mulatto" who had been living in the town for four years and "was known here as free" on the false charge of being a runaway.[61] In this context, fugitive slaves in the borderlands faced an almost constant threat of reenslavement, especially given the occasional collusion between some local agents and slaveholders. In January 1831 Manuel de los Santos Coy, *alcalde* at Nacogdoches, wrote to Col. José de las Piedras regarding instructions issued to local Indigenous communities by Col. Peter Ellis Bean, who was born in Tennessee and who was Mexico's appointed agent for Native Americans in eastern Texas, to extralegally return to him any fugitive slave "found in the countryside." Two runaways had already been returned to their enslaver following these instructions. Bean first denied the accusations before arguing that such restitutions had already been practiced elsewhere in the borderlands.[62] Unsurprisingly, then, freedom for slave refugees in Nacogdoches proved fragile. In October 1831 San Antonio's *alcalde* requested information from Santos Coy regarding the legal status of a Black man named Anderson, who had resided for two years in Nacogdoches before settling in San Antonio. Santos Coy replied that, although "it is sure that until now no one [has] claimed him," he believed Anderson had arrived in Texas "fleeing from the United States of the North." After two relatively safe years at Nacogdoches, Anderson suddenly had to flee along with another self-emancipated slave who was arrested at San Felipe de Austin after failing to present evidence of his freedom. Though the exact motives for his second flight remain unclear, Anderson's story sheds light on the precariousness of self-emancipated slaves' freedom in Texas, of which Mathieu (or "Matthew") Thomas's case below offers another striking illustration.[63]

Mathieu Thomas, born enslaved in 1780, arrived east of Nacogdoches (near San Augustine) in 1824 from the U.S. South along with his enslaver, Robert Callier. In 1826 members of the Yokum Gang, a group of thieves and slave stealers active in the Louisiana-Texas borderlands, murdered Callier because he had rejected Matthew Yokum's demand to marry Callier's daughter Susan. In February 1828 Susan Callier sold her deceased father's bondspeople, Sally (age forty), Luisa (age two), and Thomas, to settler Elijah Lloyd at Nacogdoches for one thousand pesos. Soon afterward, Lloyd was convicted of murder and imprisoned. He promised Thomas unconditional freedom in exchange for his help in escaping from the municipal jail of Nacogdoches, to which Thomas consented. Lloyd fled from the Mexican authorities riding a horse to Louisiana, where he subsequently died, leaving the promise unfulfilled. Fearing that Lloyd's heir(s) would attempt to nullify the informal agreement between the two men, Thomas ran to Nacogdoches in May 1830, seeking the *amparo* of local administrators.

In his petition to *alcalde* Vicente Córdova, Thomas sought to appeal to antislavery ideals and justified assisting his slaveholder to escape as "the only means of liberating [him]self from the slavery to which [he] was reduced by account of [his] color, and to which death is preferable." Thomas based his request on a state decree issued on September 15, 1827, providing for the emancipation of enslaved people whose deceased slaveholder had no natural heirs (*herederos forzosos*). State authorities in Saltillo nonetheless rejected it in October 1830, arguing that such an article only applied to slaveholders "naturally dead," not to ones who had disappeared. Despite this verdict, Thomas obtained freedom papers from Colonel de las Piedras in June 1831 and worked as a domestic servant in exchange for his protection. As the private and the public realms overlapped on *amparo*, Thomas lost his protector and prospects of freedom with de las Piedras's fall from grace and eviction in August 1832. Fearing reenslavement, Thomas headed to San Antonio, where he eventually settled, unaware that his difficulties were not over yet.

In October 1832 Elijah Lloyd's only heir and nephew, a native of Tennessee named William M. Lloyd, who had been in Texas since 1828, arrived and claimed Thomas as his "property," presenting evidence of the transaction made at Nacogdoches in 1828. San Antonio's *alcalde*, José Antonio de la Garza, expressed his confusion, as Thomas had previously showed him his *carta de libertad* (certificate of freedom). With two conflicting documents in his hands, de la Garza flipped the burden of proof by requiring Lloyd to prove that Thomas was effectively his enslaved man. A month later, Lloyd returned from Nacogdoches and San Felipe de Austin after collecting several testimonies supporting his cause. However, he failed to convince José Antonio de la Garza. Despite the fact that Lloyd could have qualified as a natural heir as defined by law, Mathieu Thomas was eventually freed from custody. He met Lundy for the second time some months later, now a free man.[64]

Conclusion

As this chapter has demonstrated, although the principle and practice of unconditional free-soil policy took root during the years leading up to the Texas Revolution, freedom for self-emancipated slaves in northeastern Mexico between 1821 and 1836 remained highly conditional upon local decision making, unstable balances of power, and the prevalence of grassroots administration in the borderlands. Flight represented a risk-laden decision, with often-unpredictable consequences for enslaved absconders such as Mathieu Thomas. The shared story of Mexican administrators and escaped slaves from the U.S. South and the new colonies in Texas was first and foremost a tale of convergence (or divergence) of interests between both sets of actors. The fate of runaways was always dependent on the responses of officials to larger borderlands dynamics and geopolitical developments. Local civilian and military administrators regularly ignored, dismissed, or disobeyed complex and sometimes contradictory instructions on free-soil policy or simply devised their own policies on the settlement of foreign fugitive slaves when clear orders from above were wanting. In contrast with the religion-based asylum policy that characterized the late colonial period, the ideal and practice of unconditional free-soil policy for foreign self-liberated slaves, inspired by the liberal doctrine of transcendental human rights, emerged during the first decade of Mexico's independence. In the midst of the gradual abolition of slavery and the slave trade (with the ambiguous exception of Texas), Mexican governments repeatedly refused to return U.S. slave refugees from 1825 onward. Independent Mexico's growing intransigency over slavery, including an increasingly consistent enforcement of free-soil policy, eventually prompted many European American planters to take illegal action themselves. As a result, the threat of abduction by armed raiders constantly jeopardized slave refugees' bids for freedom in northeastern Mexico, especially from the early 1830s onward. While the massive expansion of slavery generated by the European American colonization of Texas progressively strained the relationship between the Mexican state and the new colonists, the independence of Texas in 1836 reinforced Mexico's emerging antislavery commitment and shaped an even more binary political landscape of slavery and freedom in its northeastern borderlands.

NOTES

I would like to thank Girija Joshi and Damian A. Pargas for their comments on earlier versions of this chapter.

1. Thomas Earle, *The Life, Travels and Opinions of Benjamin Lundy, Including His Journeys to Texas and Mexico, with a Sketch of Contemporary Events, and a Notice of the Revolution in Hayti* (Philadelphia: W. D. Parrish, 1847), 48.

2. Ronnie C. Tyler, "Fugitive Slaves in Mexico," *Journal of Negro History* 57, no. 1 (1972): 1–12; Rosalie Schwartz, *Across the Rio to Freedom: U.S. Negroes in Mexico* (El Paso: Texas Western Press, 1975); Sean M. Kelley, "Mexico in His Head: Slavery and the Texas-Mexican Border, 1810–1860," *Journal of Social History* 37, no. 3 (2004): 709–23; James D. Nichols, "The Line of Liberty: Runaway Slaves and Fugitive Peons in the Texas-Mexico Borderlands," *Western Historical Quarterly* 44, no. 4 (2013): 713–33; Sarah E. Cornell, "Citizens of Nowhere: Fugitive Slaves and Free Afri-

can Americans in Mexico, 1833–1857," *Journal of American History* 100, no. 2 (2013): 351–74.

3. Exceptions include especially James Harrison, "The Failure of Spain in East Texas: The Occupation and Abandonment of Nacogdoches, 1779–1821" (PhD diss., University of Nebraska, 1980); Lance Blyth, "Fugitives from Servitude: American Deserters and Runaway Slaves in Spanish Nacogdoches, 1803–1808," *East Texas Historical Journal* 38, no. 2 (2000): 3–14.

4. Kelley, "Mexico in His Head," 709.

5. Juan Francisco de Azcarate, *Dictamen de la Comisión de Esclavos* (Mexico City: Imprenta Imperial de Alejandro Valdés, 1821); Archivo General de la Nación (AGN), Mexico City, Gobernación Sin Sección 11, folder 15 (December 1821); Salvador Méndez Reyes, "Hacia la abolición de la esclavitud en México: El dictamen de la comisión de esclavos de 1821," in *De la libertad y abolición: Africanos y afrodescendientes en Iberoamérica*, ed. Juan Manuel de la Serna (Mexico City: Centro de Estudios Mexicanos y Centroamericanos, 2010), 179–93.

6. *Gaceta Diaria de Mexico* (Mexico City), September 16, 1825 (accessed through Hemeroteca Digital, Biblioteca Nacional de España); *El Fénix de la Libertad* (Mexico City), January 23, 1834. All translations are mine.

7. José Joaquín Lizardi, *El negro sensible* (Mexico City: Ontiveros, 1825); Catherine Raffi-Béroud, *En torno al teatro de Fernández de Lizardi* (Amsterdam: Rodopi, 1998), 152–64.

8. José María Tornel y Mendivil, *Breve reseña de los acontecimientos mas notables de la Nación Mexicana, desde el año de 1821 hasta nuestros días* (Mexico City: Cumplido, 1852).

9. *El Sol* (Mexico City), January 31, 1828; AGN, Gobernación Sin Sección 116, folder 16, Decreto de Vicente Guerrero a José María de Bocanegra, September 15, 1829; AGN, Justicia y Negocios Eclesiásticos 48, folder 34, fols. 306–7; María Camila Díaz Casas, "¿De esclavos a ciudadanos? Matices sobre la 'integración' y 'asimilación' de la población de origen africano en la sociedad nacional mexicana, 1810–1850," in *Negros y morenos en Iberoamérica: Adaptación y conflict*, ed. Juan Manuel de la Serna (Mexico City: UNAM, 2015), 273–303; Raúl A. Ramos, *Beyond the Alamo: Forging Mexican Ethnicity in San Antonio, 1821–1861* (Chapel Hill: University of North Carolina Press, 2008), 117; Andrew J. Torget, *Seeds of Empire: Cotton, Slavery and the Transformation of the Texas Borderlands, 1800–1850* (Chapel Hill: University of North Carolina Press, 2015), 144; Schwartz, *Across the Rio*, 6–7, 15–16; Kelley, "Mexico in His Head," 714–15.

10. Archivo Histórico de la Secretaria de Relaciones Exteriores (SRE), Mexico City, Legajo Encuadernado (LE) 1075, Exposición de Víctor Blanco, December 5, 1822, and Blanco to López, December 9, 1822; SRE, LE 1057, fols. 73–74, Agustín J. de Iturbide y Huarte to Secretario de Relaciones Exteriores, May 19, 1833; SRE, Archivo de la Embajada Mexicana en los Estados Unidos de América (AEMEUA) 21, folder 2, fol. 114, Secretaria de Estado to Encargado de Negocios (de los E.U. Mexicanos), 20 August 1833; SRE, AEMEUA 21, folder 2, fols. 80–85, Gómez Farías to

Joaquín María del Castillo, October 26, 1833; SRE, AEMEUA 23, folder 8, Lombardo to Castillo de Lanzas, January 17, 1834; Cornell, "Citizens of Nowhere," 357; Schwartz, *Across the Rio*, 21–22.

11. SRE, AEMEUA, 23, folder 8, fol. 167, Lombardo to Encargado de Negocios, January 17, 1834.

12. *Genius of Universal Emancipation* (Baltimore) 12 (October 1831): 87, and 12 (December 1831): 114; *The Liberator* (Boston), February 4, 1832; *L'Abeille* (New Orleans), May 15, 1833; *Niles Weekly Register* (Baltimore), May 18, 1833; SRE, LE 1057, fol. 56, Webb to Legación Mexicana, March 31, 1832; Carlos Bosch Garcia, *Documentos de la relación de México con los Estados Unidos (31 de diciembre de 1829–29 de mayo de 1836) II—Butler en persecución de la provincia de Texas* (Mexico City: UNAM, 1983), 1:299–300; Benjamin Lundy, *The War in Texas: A Review of Facts and Circumstances, Showing That This Contest Is a Crusade against Mexico* (Philadelphia: Merrihew and Gunn, 1837), 5; Earle, *The Life*, 54, 63, 116, 142–43; E. S. Abdy, *Journal of a Residence and Tour in the United States of North America, from April 1833 to October 1834* (1835; New York: Negro Universities Press, 1969), 12; Library of Congress, Washington, D.C., Benjamin Lundy Papers, 1814–1906, Lundy to his father Joseph, Mouth of the Mississippi, April 13, 1835. According to Virginia-born manumitted slave James C. Brown, Lundy had contemplated establishing a Black colony in Texas since at least 1819. Benjamin Drew, *A North-Side View of Slavery. The Refugee: or, The Narratives of Fugitive Slaves in Canada. Related by Themselves, with an Account of the History and Condition of the Colored Population of Upper Canada* (Boston: J. P. Lewett and Co.; New York: Lamport and Blakeman, 1856), 241.

13. Schwartz, *Across the Rio*, 18–19.

14. Jonathan Walker, *Trial and Imprisonment of Jonathan Walker, at Pensacola, Florida, for Aiding Slaves to Escape from Bondage. With an Appendix, Containing a Sketch of His Life* (Boston: Anti-slavery Office, 1845), 108–10; Frank Edward Kittredge, *The Man with the Branded Hand: An Authentic Sketch of the Life and Services of Capt. Jonathan Walker Rochester* (New York: Frank Edward Kittredge, 1899), 12–14; Julius A. Laack, "Captain Jonathan Walker, Abolitionist," *Wisconsin Magazine of History* 32, no. 3 (1949): 313; Alvin F. Oickle, *The Man with the Branded Hand: The Life of Jonathan Walker, Abolitionist* (Yardley, Pa.: Westhome Publishing, 2011), 26–33.

15. By contrast with "Anglo-American," "Anglo" or "American," "European American" accounts for the diversity of foreign colonizers in Mexican Texas by including non-Anglophones more directly. See Pekka Hämäläinen, *The Comanche Empire* (New Haven, Conn.: Yale University Press, 2008), 2.

16. Graham Davis, *Land! Irish Pioneers in Mexican and Revolutionary Texas* (College Station: Texas A&M University Press, 2002), 21.

17. Randolph Campbell, *An Empire for Slavery: The Peculiar Institution in Texas, 1821–1865* (Baton Rouge: Louisiana State University Press, 1989), 10–34; Ramos, *Beyond the Alamo*, 27–110; Torget, *Seeds of Empire*.

18. Joaquín Ramírez y Sesma, *Colección de decretos, ordenes y circulares expedidas por*

los Gobiernos Nacionales de la federación mexicana, desde el año de 1821 hasta el de 1826 (Mexico City: Martín Rivera, 1827), 177.

19. On state-by-state slavery-related constitutional provisions, see Jaime Olveda Legaspi, "La abolición de la esclavitud en México, 1810–1917," *Signos Históricos* 29 (January–June 2013): 22–25; Díaz Casas, "¿De esclavos a ciudadanos?," 292.

20. On slavery in early independent Mexico, see Torget, *Seeds of Empire*; Campbell, *An Empire for Slavery*, 10–34. On article 13 and its de facto nullification, see J. P. Kimball, *Laws and Decrees of the State of Coahuila and Texas* (Houston: Telegraph Power Press, 1839), 78–79, 314; David Woodman Jr., *Guide to Texas Emigrants* (Boston: M. Hawes, 1835), 25, 145; William Hooker Fiske, *A Visit to Texas, Being the Journal of a Traveller through Those Parts Most Interesting to American Settlers* (New York: Goodrich and Wiley, 1834), 10.

21. Eugene G. Barker, "The Government of Austin's Colony, 1821–1831," *Southwestern Historical Quarterly* 21 (1918): 229; Eugene Barker, ed., *Annual Report of the American Historical Association for the Year 1919: The Austin Papers* (Washington, D.C.: Government Printing Office, 1924), 1:996–1002, Austin to Legislature of Coahuila y Texas, December 22, 1824.

22. George R. Nielsen, "Ben Milam and United States and Mexican Relations," *Southwestern Historical Quarterly* 73, no. 3 (1970): 393–95; Jeffrey R. Kerr-Ritchie, *Freedom Seekers: Essays on Comparative Emancipation* (Baton Rouge: Louisiana State University Press, 2014), 23; Schwartz, *Across the Rio*, 8–9.

23. James Franklin Hopkins, ed., *The Papers of Henry Clay* (Lexington: University of Kentucky, 1959), 4:166–77, Clay to Poinsett, Washington, March 26, 1825.

24. Mariano Arévalo, *Diálogo entre un barbero y su marchante* (Mexico City: Imprenta de Galván, 1828), 5 ("¿no es este aquel pueblo que vio con horror la esclavitud, el mismo a cuyo nombre se pretende exigir de nosotros que devolvamos los esclavos que busquen asilo entre nosotros, y que se cree con derecho para disponer de mas de un millón de infelices como si fuesen bestias de carga, y sobre los que ninguno puede tener dominio?").

25. Benson Latin American Collection (BLAC), University of Texas at Austin, "Despatches from U.S. Ministers in Mexico" (microfilm edition), reel 4, U.S. Legation in Mexico to Clay, March 18, 1828; William R. Manning, ed., *Early Diplomatic Relations between the United States and Mexico* (Baltimore, Md.: Johns Hopkins University Press, 1916), 227–31, 240–45; Schwartz, *Across the Rio*, 10–14; Carlos Bosch García, *Problemas diplomáticos del México independiente* (Mexico City: Fondo de Cultura Económica, 1947), 30, 282–94; Carlos Bosch García, *Historia de las relaciones entre México y los Estados Unidos: 1819–1848* (Mexico City: Secretaría de Relaciones Exteriores, 1985), 31–36.

26. SRE, AEMEUA 23, folder 5, fols. 25–29, Comisión de Relaciones, December 2, 1831, and fols. 18–22, Comisión de Relaciones, December 14, 1831; Dolph Briscoe Center for American History (hereafter Briscoe), University of Texas at Austin, Anthony Butler Papers, 2B179 and 2B180, Butler to Van Buren, May 26, 1831, Butler to Livingston, October 25, 1831, and December 15, 1831; BLAC, "Despatches from

U.S. Ministers in Mexico," reel 6, Hall of the Committee of Senate, October 21, 1831, Butler to Livingston, July 22, 1831, November 23, 1831, December 6, 1831, and December 24, 1831, Butler to Jackson, May 25, 1831, and December 23, 1831; Manning, *Early Diplomatic Relations*, 251; William R. Manning, ed., *Diplomatic Correspondence of the United States: Inter-American Affairs, 1831–1860 (Mexico, 1831–1848)* (Washington, D.C.: Carnegie Endowment for International Peace, 1937), 8:269; David M. Hunter, ed., *Treaties and Other International Acts of the United States of America* (Washington, D.C.: Government Printing Office, 1931–48), 3:633–34, 638–39; Carlos Bosch García, ed., *Documentos de la relación de México con los Estados Unidos* (Mexico City: UNAM, 1983), 2:70–72; Schwartz, *Across the Rio*, 7–18; Irene Zea Prado, *Gestión diplomática de Anthony Butler en México, 1829–1836* (Mexico City: Secretaría de Relaciones Exteriores, 1982), 31.

27. Gerrit Smith, *Substance of the Speech Made by Gerrit Smith, in the Capitol of the State of New York, March 11th and 12th, 1850* (Syracuse, N.Y.: V. W. Smith and Co. Printers, 1850), 23, in Samuel J. May Anti-slavery Collection (SJMASC), Cornell University Library, Division of Rare and Manuscript Collections.

28. David Lee Child, *Texas Revolution: Republished with Additions from the "Northampton (Massachusetts) Gazette," to Which Is Added a Letter from Washington on the Annexation of Texas, and the Late Outrage in California* (Washington, D.C.: J. and G. S. Gideon Printers, 1843), 67–68, SJMASC; Loring Moody, *Facts for the People: Showing the Relations of the United States Government to Slavery* (Boston: Antislavery Office, 1847), 33–34.

29. William Jay, *Review of the Causes and Consequences of the Mexican War* (Boston: Benjamin B. Mussey and Co.; Philadelphia: Uriah Hunt and Co.; New York: M. W. Dodd, 1849), 15, SJMASC.

30. Yale University (YU), Sterling Memorial Library, Mexico Collection, reel 13, box 51, folder 874, and box 52, folder 898; Manuel Muro, *Historia de San Luis Potosí, desde 1810 hasta nuestros días* (San Luis Potosí: Esquivel y Cía., 1910), 1:460–67; Centro de Estudios de Historia de México, XLIX-2 serie 1-1, box 17, "San Luis Potosí, agosto 31 de 1827, José Eulogio de Esnaurrizar, Gobernador [...] se dará libertad a los esclavos que residan en el Estado de San Luis Potosí."

31. SRE, AEMEUA 20, folder 9, fol. 51, Pizarro Martínez to Encargado de Negocios, April 7, 1832. On Pizarro Martínez's complaints about the increase of white settlers and "people of color" illegally entering Texas, see SRE, AEMEUA 18, folder 7, fol. 18, Pizarro Martínez to José Maria Tornel, February 10, 1831; SRE, AEMEUA 22, folder 14, fols. 34–35, Pizarro Martínez to Encargado de Negocios, February 24, 1834.

32. American Memory (Library of Congress), A Century of Lawmaking for a New Nation: U.S. Congressional Documents and Debates, 1774–1875, *Journal of the House of Representatives of the United States, 1833–1834*, Wednesday, March 5, 1834, 385; *American State Papers, House of Representatives, 23rd Congress, 1st Session, Public Lands* (Washington, D.C.: Gales and Seaton, 1860), 6:950; Cornell, "Citizens of Nowhere," 353, 356–57.

33. For an extensive economic, demographic, natural, and topographical contem-

porary account of early 1830s Texas, see Mary Austin Holley, *Texas: Observations, Historical, Geographical and Descriptive. In a Series of Letters Written during a Visit to Austin's Colony, with a View to a Permanent Settlement in That Country, in the Autumn of 1831* (Baltimore, Md.: Armstrong and Plaskitt, 1833), 133–40. On the process above described, see Davis, *Land*, 112; Alwyn Barr, "Freedom and Slavery in the Republic: African American Experiences in the Republic of Texas," in *Single Star of the West: The Republic of Texas, 1836–1845*, ed. Kenneth W. Howell and Charles Swanlund (Denton: University of North Texas Press, 2017), 423–36.

34. Third and Fifth U.S. Federal Census, Population Schedule, Louisiana (1810 and 1830).

35. Harold Schoen, "The Free Negro in the Republic of Texas, I," *Southwestern Historical Quarterly* 39, no. 4 (1936): 298.

36. The terms "de facto" and "de jure" are used in Bram Hoonhout, "The West Indian Web: Improvising Colonial Survival in Essequibo and Demerara, 1750–1800" (PhD diss., European University Institute, 2017), 117.

37. AGN, Gobernación Sin Sección, box 58, folder 12, fols. 28–29, Solicitud de Andrés Dortola a Sección de Gobierno, February 8, 1823; James D. Nichols, "The Limits of Liberty: African Americans, Indians, and Peons in the Texas-Mexico Borderlands, 1820–1860" (PhD diss., State University of New York at Stony Brook, 2012), 27–28; Archivo Histórico de Monterrey, Capital del Estado, Colección Correspondencia 17, folder 67, fol. 1, Poder a favor de Diego de Lachica, January 5, 1826, and 137, folder 16, fol. 10, Reclamo por ser esclavo, 1826. On Robb, see Bryan Prince, *A Shadow on the Household: One Enslaved Family's Incredible Struggle for Freedom* (Toronto: McClelland & Stewart, 2010), 24–25.

38. Robert Bruce Blake Collection (Blake), Nacogdoches Archives (NA), 45:339–41.

39. "Reminiscences of Western Texas—No. XII. First Abolition Movements in Texas—Adventures among Runaway Slaves in San Antonio, 1833," *Indianola (Tex.) Bulletin*, April 26, 1854.

40. Jesús F. de la Teja and John Wheat, "Bexar, Profile of a Tejano Community, 1820–1832," *Southwestern Historical Quarterly* 89, no. 1 (1985): 7–34.

41. Briscoe, Bexar Archives (hereafter BA), microfilm edition, reel 73, frame 994, "Trespalacios' affidavit of the emancipation of American negro Phil, January 8, 1823"; Ramos, *Beyond the Alamo*, 92, 116–23.

42. SRE, AEMEUA 22, folder 14, fols. 144–46, Pizarro Martínez to Encargado de Negocios, December 8, 1834, and Pizarro Martínez to Secretario de Estado y del Despacho de Relaciones, December 6, 1834; SRE, AEMEUA 25, folder 1, fol. 11, Pizarro Martínez to Encargado de Negocios, January 15, 1835.

43. Stanley C. Green, *The Mexican Republic: the First Decade, 1823–1837* (Pittsburgh: University of Pittsburgh Press, 1987), 119; Vito Alessio Robles, *Coahuila y Tejas, desde la consumación de la independencia hasta el tratado de paz de Guadalupe Hidalgo* (Mexico City: Porrua, 1979), 1:242; Gilberto Miguel Hinojosa, *A Borderlands Town in Transition: Laredo, 1755–1870* (College Station: Texas A&M University Press, 1983); Omar Valerio Jiménez, "Although We Were the Last Soldiers:

Citizenship, Ideology and Tejano Unionism," in *Lone Star Unionism, Dissent and Resistance*, ed. Jesús F. de la Teja (Norman: University of Oklahoma Press, 2016), 129–32.

44. William Bullock, *Six Months' Residence and Travels in Mexico* (London: J. Murray, 1824), 493; Henry George Ward, *Mexico in 1827* (London: Henry Colburn, 1828), 29; Josiah Conder, *Mexico and Guatemala* (London: James Duncan, 1830), 1:212; George Francis Lyon, *Journal of a Residence and Tour in the Republic of Mexico in the Year 1826* (London: J. Murray, 1828), 2:214, 225.

45. AGN, Movimiento Marítimo, Fondo Pasaportes 32, fols. 84–86.

46. Schoen, "The Free Negro," 297.

47. Kenneth W. Porter, "Negroes and Indians on the Texas Frontier, 1831–1876," *Journal of Negro History* 41, no. 3 (1956): 191–97; Kelley, "Mexico in His Head," 712.

48. Dilue Harris, "The Reminiscences of Mrs. Dilue Harris. I," *Quarterly of the Texas State Historical Association* 4, no. 2 (1900): 105–8. On "borderland Maroons" (understood as fugitives settled at the fringes of plantations and farms), see Sylviane Diouf, *Slavery's Exiles: The Story of the American Maroons* (New York: New York University Press, 2014), 72–96.

49. Andrew A. Parker, *Trip to the West and Texas* (Concord, N.H.: W. White; Boston: B. M. Mussey, 1836), 242.

50. On landscape, slavery, and slave flight, see Walter Johnson, *River of Dark Dreams: Slavery and Empire in the Cotton Kingdom* (Cambridge, Mass.: Harvard University Press, 2013).

51. Blake, NA 21:19, September 17, 1827; BA, reel 108, frame 946, José Maria Viesca to Jefe Politico del Departamento de Bexar, November 3, 1827; Blake, NA 21:204–5, May 12, 1829; BA, reel 122, frames 384–95, Ibarbo to Múzquiz, May 12, 1829; BA, reel 125, frames 270–73, Ibarbo to Múzquiz, August 31, 1829; Blake, NA 12:134, September 17, 1829; NA, 12:147, November 26, 1829. On Ramón Múzquiz, see Andrés Reséndez, "Ramón Múzquiz. The Ultimate Insider," in *Tejano Leadership in Mexican Revolutionary Texas*, ed. Jesús F. de la Teja (College Station: Texas A&M University Press, 2010), 128–45.

52. Archivo General del Estado de Coahuila (Saltillo), Siglo XIX, box 5, folder 9, file 2, José María Letona, Gobierno del Estado de Coahuila y Texas, a Consejo de Gobierno, May 19, 1831.

53. BA, reel 147, frame 438, Chirino to Ramón Múzquiz, January 17, 1832; BA, reel 147, frames 756–62, Ramón Múzquiz to José Maria Letona, January 30, 1832; BA, reel 148, frame 362, from Leona Vicario to Jefe Politico del Departamento de Bexar, March 3, 1832; BA, reel 148, frame 885, Jefe Político de Bexar to Leona Vicario, March 24, 1832.

54. Malcolm McLean, ed., *Papers Concerning Robertson's Colony* (Arlington: University of Texas at Arlington, 1974–93), 5:59–60, 65–67, 4:483–84, 498–523. On the expedition, see Foster Todd Smith, *From Dominance to Disappearance: The Indians of Texas and the Near Southwest, 1786–1859* (Lincoln: University of Nebraska Press, 2005), 141–42.

55. McLean, *Papers Concerning Robertson's Colony*, 6:414; Ramos, *Beyond the Al-*

amo, 121–22. On Tenoxtitlan and Lavaca as places of settlement, see SRE, AEMEUA 18, folder 7, fol. 39, Pizarro Martínez to Mier y Terán, April 4, 1831; SRE, AEMEUA 20, folder 9, fol. 16, Pizarro Martínez to Encargado de Negocios, February 2, 1832; *Marine Journal* (New Orleans), February 2, 1832.

56. Beinecke Rare Book and Manuscript Library, Yale University (hereafter BRBML), Henry Raup Wagner Collection of Texas Manuscripts, box 3, folder 86, Bradburn to Comandante General, Estados Internos de Oriente, Anahuac, Texas, February 2, 1832, and box 3, folder 91, Bradburn, Report to the Comandante General, Estados Internos de Oriente, report of events in Anahuac, 1832 (quote).

57. Winnie Allen and Katherine Elliott, eds., *The Papers of Mirabeau Buonaparte Lamar* (Austin: Pemberton Press, 1968), 1:91; BRBML, Thomas W. Streeter Collection of Texas Manuscripts, box 1, folder 19, Austin to Múzquiz, June 26, 1832; BRBML, "Communications forwarded from San Felipe de Austin relative to late events in Texas," MS Zc52832co; SRE, AEMEUA 20, folder 9, Pizarro Martinez to Encargado de Negocios, June 14, 1832; Margaret S. Henson, *Juan Davis Bradburn: A Reappraisal of the Mexican Commander of Anahuac* (College Station: Texas A&M University Press, 1982); Nichols, "The Limits of Liberty," 28; Paul D. Lack, "Slavery and the Texas Revolution," *Southwestern Historical Quarterly* 89 (1985): 184. On federalist uprisings in the 1830s, see David J. Weber, *The Mexican Frontier, 1821–1846* (Albuquerque: University of New Mexico Press, 1982), 245–53; Timothy Anna, *Forging Mexico, 1821–1835* (Lincoln: University of Nebraska Press, 2001), 34–41.

58. William Harris Wharton, one of the leaders of the Texas Revolution, directly linked the intervention of the Mexican government in slavery-related matters and the conflict of 1835–36, arguing that "with a sickly philanthropy worthy of the abolitionists of these United States, they have, contrary to justice, and to law, intermeddled with our slave population, and have even impotently threatened in the war now pending, to emancipate them, and induce them to turn their arms against their masters" (Campbell, *An Empire for Slavery*, 42).

59. BA, reel 150, frame 203, José Antonio de la Garza to Múzquiz, May 23, 1832; BA, reel 150, frames 218–22, Múzquiz to Alcaldes of Goliad and Austin, May 24, 1832; BA, reel 150, frame 249, Antonio Elozua to Alejandro Treviño, May 26, 1832; BA, reel 150, frames 262–71, "papers relating to Brown and other Americans on the subject of their having stolen negros—1832"; BA, reel 150, frame 339, Williams and De Witt to Múzquiz, May 30, 1832; BA, reel 150, frame 452–56, Múzquiz to José Antonio de la Garza, June 1, 1832; BA, reel 150, frames 608–14, Múzquiz to Alcalde of Austin, June 6, 1832, and Múzquiz to Chief of Police of Gonzales, June 6, 1832; BA, reel 150, frames 719–25, Williams to Múzquiz, June 12, 1832, and Miguel Arciniega to Múzquiz, June 12, 1832; BA, reel 151, frames 355–56, "Chisman's affidavit of Brown's delivery of two negroes to Thompson, July 4, 1832"; BA, reel 151, frames 769–71, Juan José Ruiz to José Antonio de la Garza, July 21, 1832; BA, reel 152, frame 250, Santiago del Valle to Jefe Politico del departamento de Béjar, August 3, 1832; BA, reel 152, frame 489, Williams to Múzquiz, August 10, 1832; BA, reel 156, frames 416–22, Seguin to Jefe Político interino del departamento de Béjar, May 17, 1833; BA, reel 156, frames 493–95, Manuel Jimenez to Juan A. Seguin, May 23, 1833; BA,

reel 157, frame 773, Ayuntamiento's acknowledgment of decrees, Bexar, August 4, 1833; BRBML, Luis Alberto Guajardo Papers on the History of Coahuila, box 4, "Notes for the apuntes 1833–1849"; *State Gazette* (Austin), August 16, 1856; Torget, *Seeds of Empire*, 160; Andrés Reséndez, *Changing National Identities at the Frontier: Texas and New Mexico, 1800–1850* (New York: Cambridge University Press, 2004), 162.

60. SRE, AEMEUA 23, folder 8, fol. 36, Lombardo to Joaquín María del Castillo, March 1, 1834; SRE, LE 1057, fol. 109.

61. BA, reel 75, frame 675, Juan Seguin to Luciano Garcia, October 12, 1823; Blake, BA, supplement volume 8:341.

62. Blake, NA 52:36–38, Santos to Piedras, January 13, 1831, and Piedras to Santos, January 13, 1831; Jack Johnson, *Indian Agent: Peter Ellis Bean in Mexican Texas* (College Station: Texas A&M University Press, 2005), 149; Torget, *Seeds of Empire*, 97–98. In July 1826 Bean, anticipating a ban on slavery, had suggested to Austin that they should classify slaves as indebted laborers, an idea put into practice following the issuance of Coahuila y Tejas's constitution.

63. BA, reel 145, frame 851, Manuel de los Santos Coy to alcalde de Béxar, November 8, 1831.

64. BA, reel 153, frame 738, De la Garza to alcalde of Nacogdoches, October 25, 1832; BA, reel 154, frame 70, "Investigation of Elias Loid's claim for runaway slaves, October 20, 1832"; Blake, NA 16:395–99, Petition of Matthew Thomas, May 15, 1830; *Laws and Decrees of the State of Coahuila and Texas* (Houston: Telegraph Power Press, 1839), 79 (decree no. 19, article 5, September 15, 1827). In his request, Mathieu Thomas mistakenly based his argument on "the law no 18 of the 19th of September, 1827."

PART 2

Africa

CHAPTER 4

The International Migration of South Carolinian Free People of Color, 1780–1865

LAWRENCE AJE

During the 1790s, in the wake of the Revolution of Saint-Domingue, South Carolina sought to prevent the immigration of free West Indians of color by adopting its first major restrictive immigration legislation. In a similar effort to curtail the growth of the free population of color, an 1820 law prohibited the ingress of all free people of color, including those who had left the state and who wished to return. An 1820 law also provided for the mandatory deportation of manumitted slaves. Two years later, in the aftermath of the Denmark Vesey plot, a law provided for the temporary incarceration of free seamen of color during the length of time their vessel remained in port. In the face of growing oppression, free South Carolinians of color initially left the state to settle in the North. However, starting in the 1820s, some chose to emigrate to Sierra Leone, Liberia, Haiti, and Canada. Quite surprisingly, despite the implementation of strict migratory laws, a number of migrants managed to return to the state. However, the enslavement crisis of 1860 marked a turning point in the history of the state's outward migration, as droves of free people of color who feared reenslavement fled South Carolina.

Scholars, including Archibald Alexander, P. J. Staudenraus, and Eric Burin, have produced numerous remarkable full-length studies that offer a thorough and longitudinal approach to the question of African American migration and the colonizationist and emigrationist movements, while others, such as Ousmane Power-Greene, have analyzed the debates these movements generated.[1] This chapter adds to the body of localized studies that were conducted on North Carolina, Virginia, and Pennsylvania by scholars such as Claude Clegg, Beverly C. Tomek, and Marie Tyler-McGraw.[2] Although Horace Fitchett in his landmark 1950 study analyzed the profile and motivations of South Carolinians who migrated to Liberia by providing valuable data, he failed to historicize the phenomenon and to examine it against the backdrop of other competing destinations.[3]

Drawing from various archival records, this chapter aims at quantifying and historicizing the out-migration and international circulation of South Carolinians of color between 1820 and 1865. It argues that factors such as the racial makeup, the gender balance, and the mean age of the free Black population, as well as testimonies from other migrants who had already left or returned, played a significant influence in a prospective migrant's decision to migrate and in their choice of destination. By adopting a longitudinal approach to the international out-migration of South Carolinians of color, this chapter analyzes the evolution of the push-and-pull factors and argues that this emigration started in the 1830s and not in the 1850s, as it has commonly been acknowledged.

South Carolina and Colonization

During the antebellum period, the main drive behind the migration of free African Americans, regardless of their geographic origin, was to escape racially oppressive laws. Before the creation of the American Colonization Society (ACS) in 1816, South Carolinians had already expressed some interest in settling in West Africa. South Carolinians such as John Kizell and Boston King were among the 7,163 Black people who were evacuated by the British forces in Charleston in 1782 and were subsequently sent to Nova Scotia.[4] These evacuees formed a significant share of the 1,200 Black Loyalists who were later relocated to Freetown, in Sierra Leone, in 1792.[5] John Kizell, a native-born West African of the region of Sherbro who was enslaved around 1769 and sent to Charleston, played a role, along with Paul Cuffe, in the project of establishing the colony in Sherbro, an island off the Sierra Leonean coast.[6]

After the creation of the ACS, there was a resurgence of interest in emigration to West Africa among free South Carolinians of color. In 1819 William Meade, an Episcopal minister and agent of the ACS, carried out a promotional and fund-raising tour of the southern states. In Charleston he met James Creighton, an elderly free man of color, and his son in law, Samuel Holman. They both informed Meade of their intention to relocate to West Africa and the preparatory plans they had already undertaken to that effect. Holman was the mixed-race son of an Englishman who had married his African bondswoman and settled in South Carolina along the Santee River. His two sons, John and Samuel Holman, were both born enslaved. After being emancipated and sent to England to be educated, they both engaged in the slave-trading business. Samuel Holman, who was familiar with West Africa, particularly with Sherbro, had met, "within the last eight months," the settlers Paul Cuffe had transported on board the *Traveller* in 1816. Holman expressed his desire to relocate to Sierra Leone, where he wished to settle as a merchant.[7] Holman acted as an ambassador to some extent and had already been corresponding with the governor of the colony, Charles MacCarthy, to organize the practical modalities of his move along with some forty other free Black people.[8] During his stay, Meade was also approached by three free people of color who were disposed to emigrate as "servants of God."[9]

The Liberian colonization project initially received support in South Carolina. During his tour, Meade managed to secure multiple fifty-dollar pledges from elite donors in Charleston, such as Senator William Smith and diplomatist Joel Poinsett.[10] Similarly, during his service as a local agent of the colonization society, Reverend Christopher Gadsen, the rector of St. Philip's and later bishop of South Carolina, collected over $500 from leading Charleston citizens, including statesman and diplomat Charles C. Pinckney.[11]

Interestingly enough, the first South Carolinian expedition to West Africa was financed by the free Black man Meade had met in 1819, James Creighton, and not by the ACS.[12] In 1821 Creighton, a seventy-year-old former barber who was born in Congo country in the 1760s, bought a vessel, the *Calypso*, and, accompanied by his relatives and other free people of color, fled the "oppressive laws" of South Carolina to settle in Sierra Leone. Creighton was the owner of several bondspeople, to whom he offered the choice either to accompany him in his expedition and have their freedom or to remain enslaved in South Carolina. Only one enslaved man chose to follow him.[13] Since legislative acts regulating coastal and foreign trade did not legally qualify people of color to command ships, Creighton resorted to hire Captain Duncan, a white man, to be the skipper of the *Calypso* for the voyage.[14]

Not all Black emigration to the West African coast in the first days of settlement of Liberia was voluntary. After being tried for their involvement in the 1822 Denmark Vesey conspiracy, Charles Drayton, a bondsman, and three free men of color, Saby Gaillard, Prince Graham, and Quash Harleston, were banished from the state.[15] The three free men of color chose to migrate to Liberia.[16] In October 1822 the banished men, some of whom were accompanied by their families, arrived in Freetown, Sierra Leone, on board the *Dolphin*. The vessel had not been chartered by the ACS.[17]

Between 1820 and 1830 the state of South Carolina deported twenty-six manumitted bondspeople to Liberia. This number pales in comparison with South Carolina's upper southern neighbors, Virginia, North Carolina, and Maryland, which respectively sent 703, 340, and 197 migrants to the West African colony.[18] This lack of momentum in the colonizationist movement in South Carolina can be attributed to the growing resistance to the project in the state. In the late 1820s the ACS's attempt to secure federal funding for its colonization plan sparked indignation in South Carolina. This resulted in the withdrawal of the support the society had hitherto benefited from among the leading citizens of the state.[19] A major reason for this shift in public opinion stemmed from the fact that the society was believed to be covertly serving an abolitionist agenda.[20] The ACS was accused of disseminating through its journal, the *African Repository and Colonial Journal*, "sentiments which are to make the slave dissatisfied with his condition, and the master doubtful, whether he ought to hold in subjection his slave."[21] The state voiced its opposition to the ACS in the local press, with the *Charleston Mercury* publishing a series of essays signed "Brutus" that vilified the society as being "murderous in its principles." Brutus also questioned whether Congress would become complicit by becoming "an instrument in the hands of fanaticism."[22] In 1827 these essays, which would later be found to have been authored by lawyer, planter, writer, and South Carolinian politician Robert James Turnbull, were published in pamphlet form under the self-explanatory title *The Crisis: Or, Essays on the Usurpations of the Federal Government*. Turnbull's voice was given national resonance when Senator Robert Y. Hayne of South Carolina argued before the Senate the unconstitutionality of a congressional appropriation to fund the colonization project.[23]

When the ACS sought to allay the fear of southern slaveholders by refraining to openly condemn slavery as a moral issue, it raised the suspicion of free Black people and abolitionists. In 1817 opposition to the ACS first originated in the free Black community of Virginia before climaxing with a massive public protest in Philadelphia, when three thousand Black people, led by James Forten and Richard Allen, both of whom had been initially in favor of voluntary migration to Africa, condemned the project.[24] In 1830 the First National Colored Convention signed a resolution opposing the actions of the American Colonization Society.[25] Among Black people, suspicion about the ACS's genuine intentions primarily stemmed from the fact that many believed that this white-sponsored program was in reality seeking to rid the United States of its free Black population through deportation. In the 1830s immediatist abolitionists took up the cause and publicized it by criticizing the ACS for condoning race prejudice, upholding slavery, and disparaging free people of color.[26]

Despite the growing opposition to the ACS, the society still received some support in South Carolina. In 1828 the ACS counted as life members, after a contribution of thirty dollars and upward to the funds of the institution, a number of leading Charlestonians, many of whom were members of the clergy.[27] During the 1840s free Charlestonians of color such as Captain Williamson, Richard Holloway, the Weston brothers, Richard Murray, and Isaac Johnson financially supported the ACS by giving donations that ranged from five to thirty dollars.[28] Some of these donors belonged to the mulatto elite. As a result of the general opposition to the ACS, no state or auxiliary colonization society was ever formed in South Carolina.[29] Yet between the 1830s and the 1850s, agents of the society toured the state, as exemplified by Robert S. Finley, William McLain, and George W. S. Hall, who in 1832, 1842, and 1852 respectively visited Charleston and informed prospective emigrants.[30] In the same vein, up until the 1850s, the ACS still rallied some assistance in South Carolina through subscriptions to the *African Repository and Colonial Journal*.[31]

Emigration Tides to Liberia

The aggravation of sectional tensions led to a degradation of the status of free people of color. They consequently lent an attentive ear to the arguments of ACS agents and started to reconsider the perspective of relocating to Liberia. During the late 1820s, the expansion of white male suffrage in South Carolina led to the formulation of political demands by the laboring class. White mechanics expressed open hostility against free Black and hired-out enslaved labor, which they perceived as unfair competition.[32] Thus, starting in the 1830s, free people of color organized preparatory meetings, like the one held in Titus Gregorie's house in December 1831, to plan out the practical modalities of this emigration.[33] Before making their final decision to leave South Carolina and return to "Africa, the land of [their] fathers," the group sent Charles Snetter as a delegate to Liberia on an exploratory

TABLE 4.1 Number of Emigrants from South Carolina Sent to Liberia by the American Colonization Society, 1820–1859

DECADE	NUMBER OF EMIGRANTS
1820–29	26
1830–39	191
1840–49	141
1850–59	125
TOTAL	483

Source: Data compiled from *African Repository and Colonial Journal* 10 (1834): 292; *African Repository* 33 (1857): 152–55; *Forty-Second Annual Report of the American Colonization Society, with Minutes of the Annual Meeting and of the Board of Directors, January 18, 1859* (Washington, D.C.: C. Alexander Printer, 1859), 9; *Forty-Third Annual Report of the American Colonization Society, with Minutes of the Annual Meeting and of the Board of Directors, January 17, 1860* (Washington, D.C.: C. Alexander Printer, 1860), 8; *African Repository* 36 (1860): 142–43.

journey.[34] His mission was to confirm if the reports in circulation concerning the colony were true. Snetter arrived in Liberia in July 1832 and then returned to Charleston, where he reported favorably about what he had seen.[35]

A year after the 1831 preparatory meeting was held, several leading free Charlestonians of color were determined to leave the state with their families. Thomas S. Grimke, a white attorney and brother of abolitionist sisters Angelina and Sarah Grimke, made the application for their passage and aided them in making arrangements. Grimke also "bore unqualified testimony to their sobriety, industry, intelligence and integrity." In December 1832 a record number of South Carolinians—155, the majority of whom were Charlestonians (92.9 percent)—proceeded to Savannah, Georgia, where they embarked on the final leg of their journey to Liberia on the *Hercules*.[36] South Carolina did not allow ACS chartered vessels in the state. Therefore, as exemplified by the expedition of the *Hercules*, emigrants had to first travel out of the state to Savannah, Baltimore, Norfolk, or New Orleans before boarding the ship that would take them across the Atlantic Ocean.[37]

As table 4.1 shows, despite a peak in the early 1830s, the emigration of South Carolinians to Liberia was quite evenly distributed throughout the three decades between 1830 and 1860, with anywhere between 141 and 191 migrants leaving every decade. However, on closer inspection, these departures tended to be concentrated around specific years of these decades. During the 1830s, all the emigrants left in 1832 and 1833. These years coincide with the Nullification Crisis and the repeated attacks from white mechanics who called for the passage of restrictive legislation against hired-out bondspeople and free Black artisans. These departures also occurred in the wake of Nat Turner's Rebellion, which led to a deterioration of the condition of free people of color. In the United States as a whole, whereas there had formerly been some reluctance on the part of free Black people to emigrate, six vessels sailed to Liberia in 1832.[38] That year alone, 749 free people of color and 247 manumitted bondspeople left the United States for Liberia.[39] South Carolinian emigrants, the majority of whom were free people of color from Charleston, represented 25.2 percent of the total.

Between 1833 and 1848 only twenty South Carolinian migrants settled in Liberia.[40] This sharp decrease was probably due to negative and widely publicized reports by former Charlestonians about Liberia, such as those of Thomas Givens and Thomas C. Brown.[41]

During the 1840s, 85 percent of all departures occurred between 1848 and 1849.[42] These departures did not illustrate the pessimism free people of color may have felt regarding the inevitability of the spread of slavery in the territories recently open to settlement after the Mexican-American War and the rejection of the Wilmot Proviso by the Senate. They seem to have concerned disillusioned free Charlestonians of color who had returned from the North due to a lack of economic opportunities.[43] Charlestonians represented 85.1 percent of all South Carolinian migrants between 1848 and 1849.[44] The resurgence in emigration after 1840 may also have been the result of other factors, such as increasing taxation targeting free people of color, their relegation to churches reserved for the enslaved that had been built in the 1840s, and the loss of religious duties they had previously exercised. The fact that Liberia became independent in 1847 and thereafter not only Black-governed but also recognized by international powers such as Great Britain and France may have favorably impressed prospective migrants.[45] The increasing interest in Liberia is evidenced by the fact that requests for copies of the country's constitution were made in Charleston.[46] Moreover, favorable reports from people who had recently emigrated to the colony also convinced the hesitant to leave.[47]

Finally, during the 1850s, 80 percent of all departures occurred between 1850 and 1852 in the aftermath of Governor Whitemarsh Seabrook's December 1850 address before the South Carolina Assembly. Seabrook vehemently called for the expulsion of "free negroes, mulattoes and mestizoes" who did not own real estate or enslaved property. He justified this measure on the grounds that in "every community, where the institution of slavery is interwoven with its social system, the public tranquility and safety demand the toleration of only two classes, white men and colored slaves."[48] At the close of the decade, reiterated appeals were made to expel or enslave free people of color, as well as to limit their economic rights. These attacks, which started in the backcountry districts before spreading throughout the state, seemed to have convinced only eighteen South Carolinians to board a vessel headed to Liberia.[49] Yet the fierce hostility free people of color were subjected to in the backcountry is illustrated by the fact that, whereas between 1820 and 1840, two-thirds of the migrants to Liberia originated from Charleston, between February 1850 and May 1860, they only represented 42.1 percent of all migrants.[50] During the 1850s, emigrants from the interior of South Carolina went from representing half to being the majority of certain expeditions.[51]

In the late 1840s the indebtedness of the ACS may explain the decrease in the overall number of emigrants to Liberia. Until the 1850s, the colonization societies in Liberia proposed to "send out all proper applicants for emigration free of charge, to furnish them with a house or house-room, provisions, medicine, nursing, &c., for six months after their arrival in Liberia without compensation." Emigrants were also entitled to five acres of land in the public domain on the condition that after a period of two years they had enclosed and built "a comfortable house" on it. Should the need arise, "in case of misfortune" the colonization society would extend the supply of rations and provide assistance in the building of the house and enclosing of the lot.[52] These provisions were so liberal that as early as 1846 the managers of the ACS insisted that the society relieve itself from its debt. This was all the more urgent because the ACS was unable to meet the numerous applications for emigration it received.[53] In 1852, despite the ACS's insistence that it would not refuse to transport emigrants who could not pay in full or in part the average amount of sixty dollars for their transportation and first six months of subsistence, the cost proved prohibitive to many.[54] In 1859 the ACS deplored the fact that it could not meet the demands, as its funds were exhausted.[55]

The Profile of South Carolinian Migrants to Liberia

In 1866 the ACS estimated that, during the forty-nine years of its existence till November 1865, it had sent a total of 11,288 emigrants, 460 of whom came from South Carolina.[56] This is an undercount. My calculations give me a total number of 509 migrants between 1828 and April 1860.[57] Despite its slight inaccuracies in the total counts, the ACS stated that 40.49 percent of the emigrants were born free, 3.09 percent had purchased their freedom, and 53.5 percent were manumitted to go to Liberia.[58]

Emigrant lists became more detailed during the late 1840s, thus allowing us to establish a finer profile of those who migrated to Liberia. As a general rule, migrants, whether freeborn or manumitted for the purpose of relocation, moved as families and rarely as individuals.[59] The typical migrant was on average thirty. Yet in some cases, expeditions comprised individuals whose ages ranged from seventy-five years old to a few months old.[60]

The legal status of South Carolinian emigrants to Liberia varied over time. The first contingent of settlers was comprised of twenty-six Georgetown bondspeople who had been freed.[61] In May 1832 the ACS's second consignment was made up of fourteen manumitted bondspeople from Marlborough County accompanied by thirty-four free passengers.[62] However, that same year, 163 out of the 168 migrants who traveled on the *Hercules* in December 1832 were free people of color who had been born free.[63] Until the 1850s freeborn Charlestonians, added to those who had purchased their freedom, made up the majority of the migrants. Out of a sample of forty-one Charlestonian emigrants who left the state between 1850 and 1851, sixteen had purchased their freedom themselves or had been purchased by a relative.[64]

Chris Dixon's analysis stating that the majority of the forty-five hundred African Americans who migrated to Liberia during the 1850s were recently manumitted enslaved persons who had been freed on the condition that they would be deported is confirmed by the profile of the South Carolinian migrants in those years.[65] In 1849, out of the sixty-five South Carolinian passengers who boarded the *Huma*, fifteen were freeborn migrants from Hamburg. The remaining fifty came from Charleston and were nearly equally distributed between freeborn and born enslaved. Out of the twenty-two migrants who were born enslaved, twenty-one had been manumitted to be deported to Liberia by three different slaveholders.[66] In 1859, out of the fifteen migrants who settled in Liberia, ten had been born enslaved.[67] After 1850 the share of migrants from the backcountry increased. Whereas all the twenty-six South Carolinians who migrated to Liberia in 1860 were freeborn, only two came from Charleston. The rest were from Newberry District.[68]

If we exclude recently manumitted bondspeople whose professions were rarely mentioned, the great majority of antebellum emigrants were skilled mechanics. The range of professional occupation did not significantly vary over time. The 1833 *Hercules* expedition, which shipped the highest number

TABLE 4.2 Occupational Data of the Emigrants of the 1833 *Hercules* Expedition

TRADE	NUMBER	TRADE	NUMBER
Seamstresses and mantua-makers	25	Pastry cooks	3
Carpenters	16	Shoemakers	3
Washers and ironers	14	Sawyers	1
Farmers	6	Cabinetmaker	1
Tailors	4	Mason	1
Nurses	4	Tinner	1
House servants	4	Painter	1
Wheelwrights	4	Schoolmaster	1
Millwrights	3	Drayman	1

Source: *Sixteenth Annual Report*, 65; *African Repository and Colonial Journal* 8 (1833): 128; *African Repository* 27 (1851): 154–55.

of migrants to Liberia, provides useful occupational data on ninety-three emigrants from Charleston (see table 4.2).

Given the range of professional activities the emigrants on the *Hercules* engaged in, the majority of whom were artisans, it is no wonder that they were wooed by ACS agents who believed that settlers of this type could make a valuable addition to the colony by contributing to its material development. In an 1834 public meeting of the ACS that was held in Philadelphia, the society's agent, Robert S. Finley, who had toured South Carolina in 1832, acknowledged that the free population of color of Charleston and New Orleans were "far superior to their brethren of the northern cities." He added that "very many of them are wealthy and respected." Given that the free people of color of the South were "better educated than at the north, although laws have been passed to prevent the slaves from being taught to read," Finley concluded that it was in the South that the ACS should "go to select well informed and temperate people of color, to send to the colony of Liberia; because those of the north are not sufficiently competent."[69] An analysis of the emigrant lists does indicate that the literacy rate among emigrants was relatively high. Interestingly enough, many enslaved persons who had been manumitted to be deported mastered reading, which was not prohibited by South Carolina law until 1834.[70]

In addition to fleeing from racially oppressive laws and seeking full enjoyment of civil rights, former South Carolinians who settled in Sierra Leone (Boston King, James Creighton, and freeborn Edward Jones) and many others who settled in Liberia (James Eden and Francis Devany) were also motivated by the desire to evangelize their African brethren.[71] By ranking order, South Carolinian emigrants belonged to the Methodist, the Baptist, and the Presbyterian religious denominations.[72] The absence of members of the Episcopalian Church among the migrants is evidence that members of the free elite of color chose not to emigrate to Liberia.

Emigrating sometimes entailed a professional adjustment. The 1833 "respectable" Charlestonian migrants who owned property initially set up shops in Monrovia. Over time they "wisely resolved to devote themselves to agriculture" and "formed themselves into a company, that they may prosecute it with the more energy and success."[73] In 1850 the migrants from Charleston and Savannah who settled in Greenville, the capital of Sinoe County, were said to have "erected many substantial houses, and cleared gardens and farms for cultivation" shortly after their arrival.[74] The settlers set out to cultivate coffee, which they hoped could be exported in a couple of years.[75]

As the Brown and Givens examples show, African American nineteenth-century migration to Liberia was also characterized by the return of disillusioned migrants. Although the extent of the phenomenon of return from Africa cannot be numerically assessed with accuracy from the creation of the ACS to 1865, its importance until 1843 was not as significant as abolitionist propaganda made it appear. Between 1820 and 1843, 11.6 percent of the 4,454 emigrants who were sent out by the ACS to Liberia left the colony. It is interesting to note that all the migrants from the United States who chose to leave the Liberian colony resettled, by ranking order of preference, to Sierra Leone, Cape Palmas, and the United States.[76] For instance, thirteen emigrants from the 1832 *Hercules* expedition returned to the United States, while twenty-four chose to relocate to Sierra Leone or Cape Palmas, which was part of Maryland in Africa, the settlement founded by the Maryland State Colonization Society.[77]

Competing Destinations

Whereas Liberia has received a lot of attention in the study of antebellum African American out-migration, a variety of other destinations sparked the interest of prospective South Carolinian migrants of color. Indeed, as exemplified by the Holman brothers, there were a few rare instances of free South Carolinian people of color who temporarily lived in Europe. In the late 1820s Francis Huger indicated having sojourned in England. On his way back to the United States he lost many of his belongings, as well as his money, which placed him in an uncomfortable economic situation. Huger, who in 1829 resided in New York, complained of the lack of job opportunities in the city and contemplated relocating to New Orleans.[78] Three decades later, in 1858, after having spent three years in New York, Francis Cardozo left the United States to study ministry at the University of Glasgow and then in London. In 1864 he returned to New Haven, Connecticut, where he remained until his return to South Carolina after the Civil War.[79] The aforementioned migratory trajectories were personal and atypical.

A few years after the settlement of Liberia, the ACS had to compete with other rival resettlement projects that would prove to be appealing to free Black people for mass emigration. The West Indies and Canada attracted a growing number of migrants, as these locations were geographically closer to the United States. These destinations also gained traction among African Americans because they were Black-led emigration plans.

Haiti as a "Place of Refuge"

South Carolinians may have turned an attentive ear to the arguments put forward in the debate between African colonization and free emigration to Haiti in the 1820s. Haiti was described as having the same climate and type of government as the United States. Emigrants would be granted full citizenship and religious freedom.[80] The five-year payment exemption of a patent (license) for mechanics and artisans must have proven appealing to Charlestonians.[81] Indeed, after the Denmark Vesey plot in 1822, free Charlestonian artisans of color were subjected to increasing professional taxation. By 1826 six thousand African Americans had responded to Haitian president Jean Pierre Boyer's 1824 invitation to migrate to Haiti.[82] By the end of the decade, between eight thousand and thirteen thousand African Americans had followed suit.[83] However, many of these emigrants returned.[84] In the late 1850s the emigration project was revived under President Fabre Geffrard. Emigrants would have their transportation costs defrayed and would be provided for during the first eight days after their arrival. Settlers were promised sixteen acres of land, exemption from military service, naturalization, and religious freedom on the condition that they work the land and remain on the island for at least three years.[85]

There is no conclusive evidence to ascertain the exact number of free South Carolinians of color who migrated to Haiti. It seems that many elements acted as deterrents for their migration to the island. Since its independence, Haiti had experienced several episodes of political upheaval, which made the island unstable. In comparison with Liberia, the island lacked economic and social opportunities. In the 1820s and 1860s the emigration scheme was primarily aimed at alleviating the shortage of agricultural laborers.[86] Given the urban profile of the free population of color of South Carolina and its specialization in skilled trades, engaging in agriculture may not have been very appealing. If some did migrate, they may have been among the settlers who received land in the mountains, where government land lay, but after finding it hard to adjust due in part to hostile Haitian neighbors, some settlers preferred to remain in towns.[87]

Benjamin Hunt, who visited the island in the late 1850s, reported that the best immigrants from the 1824 emigration wave to the island had returned to the United States.[88] Except for a few successful American immigrants, the majority were day laborers who were rather poor. Hunt's description of aged Philadelphians who monopolized the rag-picking activity in Port-au-Prince and Cap-Haïtien must have been shocking to readers.[89] Emigrants also struggled with the language barrier and the Catholic religion.[90] Even though a few emigrants carried out missionary activity in Haiti and by 1829 had gained native converts, their efforts paled in comparison with the scope of the evangelization project that Black South Carolinians could engage in should they choose to migrate to Liberia.[91]

In 1850 mulattoes, some of whom were very light skinned, represented three-quarters of the total South Carolinian free population of color.[92] The repeated intraracial tensions between Black people and mulattoes in Haiti seemed to have been of great concern to prospective emigrants.[93]

The growing disillusionment of free African Americans in the late 1850s in the wake of the *Dred Scott* decision and the passage of legislation calling for either their enslavement or their expulsion may nevertheless account for the fact that, for the year 1859 alone, around six hundred emigrants from the United States settled in Haiti.[94] The following year, the enslavement crisis, which threatened to reenslave South Carolinians of color who failed to comply with the 1820 law providing that free people of color born before that date should have proof of their freedom by birth or by manumission, led to hundreds fleeing the state.[95] These migrants were described as, for the most part, quadroons and mulattoes.[96]

Under the supervision of James Redpath, agents of the Haitian Bureau of Emigration organized several meetings at the close of 1860 in Philadelphia to promote the benefits for free people of color to migrate to the island. Shortly after their arrival in Philadelphia, in November 1860 the hundreds of refugees who had fled South Carolina as a result of the 1860 enslavement crisis received the visit of one of these agents, Reverend Theodore Hollins. A portion of the refugees obtained passage in Boston and New York for Haiti.[97] Others chose to emigrate to the West Indies and to Africa, presumably Liberia.[98] In December 1860 the majority of the free people of color who remained in Charleston expressed favorable views at the idea of emigrating to Haiti.[99] In 1861 societies promoting emigration to Haiti were created in Philadelphia, Boston, and Charleston.[100] By 1861 three thousand migrants had left the United States for Haiti.[101]

The Canadian Haven

It is difficult to assess the number of South Carolinians who crossed the border to settle in Canada prior to the Civil War. The migrants we can trace were mostly free people of color who were born free or had been legally manumitted. A few South Carolinian fugitive bondspeople also managed to seek refuge in the province. These migrants settled in Upper Canada, specifically in Toronto, Chatham, and Windsor.

In 1853, after having lived in Pennsylvania for eight years, the Hanscomes and the Gardens, who belonged to Charleston's aristocracy of color, moved to Toronto, where they would later be joined by another Charlestonian and relative named Thomas Inglis.[102] Upon arriving in Canada, these migrants could interact with other fellow Charlestonians who had relocated there as early as the 1840s, such as Richard Holloway Clark.[103] By the end of the 1850s, Charlestonians who belonged to the mulatto elite were able to form a small community in Toronto.[104]

The adoption of the Fugitive Slave Act in 1850 led to a massive exodus of Black northerners to Canada. William L. Humbert, a South Carolinian fugitive bondsman, fled from Charleston in September 1853 and, after having lived some months in the free states, crossed the border to settle in Windsor to avoid being captured by the "ten dollar commissioner."[105] For some South Carolinians, the paths to Canada were sometimes winding. In 1858 T. A. Pinckney, a free Black Methodist reverend from Charleston who had been a missionary in Liberia, "remained some time" in England and then migrated to Canada, where he acted as a Methodist preacher, traveling agent promoting emigration, and teacher in Chatham.[106] Finally, a large contingent of South Carolinian migrants of color, some of whom had been illegally emancipated in violation of the 1820 law prohibiting private manumission, moved to Canada in the wake of the 1860 enslavement crisis.[107]

A deterrent to long-term settlement by South Carolinians in Canada was, according to Edward Holloway, a free Charlestonian of color who settled in New York in the 1850s, the "very severe coldness of the winters," which made it an "unpleasant abode for persons from a southern clime."[108] Discrimination also existed and increased with the growing number of settlers of color after the 1850s. However, in Canada, Black people enjoyed the same civil rights as whites. After a three-year period of residence, they could claim citizenship.

Jamaica: The Promised Land?

Given the high proportion of mulattoes in the free population of color of South Carolina the latter were not very receptive to Pan-Africanist rhetoric. In the 1850s the resurgence of emigrationist discourse, advocated by leading figures such as Martin R. Delany, who deplored the impossibility for African Americans to ever achieve full racial integration, found a supportive audience among South Carolinians who had already left the state.

Starting in the late 1850s, Jamaica became a competing destination for Haiti in the West Indies. The former British colony had abolished slavery after 1838 and was envisaged as a possible destination for relocation, as it offered political stability and was Protestant.[109] Writing from New York in 1857, Edward Holloway, a free person of color and former resident of Charleston, lauded the benefits of migrating to Jamaica, which he described as a "promised land" where he hoped to achieve "political, intellectual and physical manhood," as well as "social equality."[110] Interestingly enough, he held this information from his father-in-law, Thomas C. Brown, who after having returned from Liberia and lived in Philadelphia, relocated in Jamaica.[111] Unfortunately, we cannot ascertain the exact number of migrants from South Carolina who chose to settle on the island. Yet, just as with Haiti, it seems that the light-skinned complexion of some free Black South Carolinians may have played a determining role in their reluctance to emigrate to Jamaica. After leaving Stateburg, South Carolina, in 1843 and living for two years in Liberia, where he "completely failed," Jack Thomas moved with his relatives to Panama. Thomas, his brother, and his father worked as overseers for the Panama Railroad Company. Thomas moved to Jamaica in the late 1850s.[112] In an 1860 letter Thomas sent to his friends who had remained in South Carolina, the deep-seated prejudice some light-skinned free South Carolinians of color harbored for darker-skinned Black people transpired. Describing the island to his friends, Thomas made the following statement: "Now I suppose you all would like to know what sort of a place Jamaica is. Well in the first place, if you like Negro Company, you may go."[113]

Conclusion

With the outbreak of the Civil War, the emigration and colonization movement came to a halt. Between 1860 and 1865 only twenty-six emigrants, all freeborn, from South Carolina relocated to Liberia.[114] Whereas some free people of color who had left the state in the late 1850s elected to return definitively, such as Francis L. Cardozo, or temporarily, others, such as the Hanscomes and the Gardens, chose to remain in Canada after the Civil War, where their light skin enabled them to pass as white.[115]

As this chapter has sought to show, the receptivity of South Carolinians of color to the colonizationist and emigrationist discourse depended on numerous variables but was first and foremost deeply influenced by the historical contexts in the United States and in the host countries, contexts that included a number of push-and-pull factors.

The forced Atlantic migration of Africans to the Americas during the transatlantic slave trade has become the hegemonic theoretical framework in Black diaspora studies. However, as the migration of free South Carolinians of color shows, the international circulation of free African Americans in the nineteenth century constituted a specific diasporic paradigm that was determined by a combination of historical, social, and racial factors.

NOTES

1. Archibald Alexander, *A History of Colonization on the Western Coast of Africa* (Philadelphia: William S. Martein, 1846); P. J. Staudenraus, *The African Colonization Movement, 1816–1865* (New York: Columbia University Press, 1961); Eric Burin, *Slavery and the Peculiar Solution: A History of the American Colonization Society* (Gainesville: University Press of Florida, 2005); Ousmane Power-Greene, *Against Wind and Tide: The African American Struggle against the Colonization Movement* (New York: New York University Press, 2014).

2. Claude Clegg, *The Price of Liberty: African Americans and the Making of Liberia* (Chapel Hill: University of North Carolina Press, 2004); Beverly C. Tomek, *Colonization and Its Discontents: Emancipation, Emigration, and Antislavery in Antebellum Pennsylvania* (New York: New York University Press, 2010); Marie Tyler-McGraw, *An African Republic: Black & White Virginians in the Making of Liberia* (Chapel Hill: University of North Carolina Press, 2007).

3. Horace Fitchett, "The Free Negro in Charleston, South Carolina" (PhD diss., University of Chicago, 1950).

4. Robin W. Winks, *Blacks in Canada: A History* (Montreal: McGill-Queen's University Press, 1997), 32; Susanna Ashton, "Memoirs of the Life of Boston King, a Black Preacher," in *I Belong to South Carolina: South Carolina Slave Narratives*, ed. Susanna Ashton (Columbia: University of South Carolina Press, 2010), 18.

5. Nemata Blyden, "'This Na True Story of Our History': South Carolina in Sierra Leone's Historical Memory," *Atlantic Studies* 12 (2015): 357–58.

6. Kevin Lowther, *The African American Odyssey of John Kizell: A South Carolina Slave Returns to Fight the Slave Trade in His African Homeland* (Columbia: University of South Carolina Press, 2011), xiv–xv; Blyden, "'This Na True Story,'" 358; James Sidbury, *Becoming African in America: Race and Nation in the Early Black Atlantic* (New York: Oxford University Press, 2007), 13.

7. *Southern Evangelical Intelligencer*, July 31, 1819.

8. *Second Annual Report of the American Society for the Colonizing of Free People of Color in the United States, with an Appendix*, 2nd ed. (Washington, D.C.: Printed by Davis and Force, Pennsylvania Avenue, 1819), 145–46.

9. Ibid., 145.

10. Meade spent some time in Georgetown and in the hinterland (Camden and Columbia). Ibid., 146–47.

11. *African Repository and Colonial Journal* 6 (1831): 195.

12. Indeed, with the passage of the 1820 law, the enslaved could only be manumitted by a legislative act. *The Sun*, November 7, 1821.

13. *Spectator*, October 30, 1821; Lowther, *African American Odyssey*, 226–27.

14. William Robert Emmons, *Establishing African Homelands for Black Americans* (Los Angeles: Johnson, Pace, Simmons & Fennell Publishers, 1992), 245.

15. Petition of the Members of the Zion African Methodist Episcopal Church, ca. 1817, ND #1893, Records of the General Assembly, South Carolina Department of Archives and History, Columbia; Lionel H. Kennedy and Thomas Parker, *An Official Report of the Trials of Sundry Negroes Charged with an Attempt to Raise an Insurrection in the State of South Carolina* (Charleston: James R. Schenk, 1822), 185–86.

16. Douglas R. Egerton, *He Shall Go Out Free: The Lives of Denmark Vesey* (Lanham, Md.: Rowman & Littlefield, 2004), 201.

17. *British and Foreign State Papers, 1823–1824* (London: James Ridgway and Sons, Piccadilly, 1843), 11:427–31; Lowther, *African American Odyssey*, 275.

18. Data compiled from *Tables Showing the Number of Emigrants and Recaptured Africans Sent to the Colony of Liberia by the Government of the United States: Also, the Number of Emigrants Free Born, Number That Purchased Their Freedom, Number Emancipated, &c.; Together with a Census of the Colony, and a Report of Its Commerce, &c. September, 1843* (Washington, D.C., 1845), 300.

19. Staudenraus, *African Colonization Movement*, 69.

20. Lawrence Aje, "'Africa, the Land of Our Fathers': The Emigration of

Charlestonians to Liberia in the Nineteenth Century," in *Pan-Africanism, Citizenship and Identity*, ed. Toyin Falola and Kwame Essien (New York: Routledge, 2013), 28–41; *Colonizationist and Journal of Freedom* (Boston) (1834): 40–41.

21. Brutus (Robert James Turnbull), *The Crisis or Essays on the Usurpations of the Federal Government* (Charleston: A. E. Miller, 1827), 64, 124; *African Repository and Colonial Journal* 4 (1829): 58–59.

22. Alexander, *A History of Colonization*, 349.

23. Staudenraus, *African Colonization Movement*, 184.

24. "Sentiments of the People of Color," in *Thoughts on African Colonization: Or an Impartial Exhibition of the Doctrines, Principles and Purposes of the American Colonization Society. Together with the Resolutions, Addresses and Remonstrances of the Free People of Color*, by William Lloyd Garrison (Boston: Garrison and Knapp, 1832), 8; Wilson Jeremiah Moses, ed., *Liberian Dreams: Back-to-Africa Narratives from the 1850s* (University Park: Pennsylvania State University Press, 1998), xviii–xix.

25. James Forten, John T. Hilton, and William Wells Brown, "Early Manuscript Letters Written by Negroes," *Journal of Negro History* 24, no. 2 (1939): 202.

26. Garrison, *Thoughts on African Colonization*.

27. *Fifteenth Annual Report of the American Society for Colonizing of the Free People of Colour of the United States, with an Appendix* (Washington, D.C.: James C. Dunn, 1832), 55.

28. *African Repository and Colonial Journal* 16 (1840): 239; *African Repository and Colonial Journal* 19 (1843): 290.

29. The same was true of Alabama and Georgia. Claude Andrew Clegg, *The Price of Liberty: African Americans and the Making of Liberia* (Chapel Hill: University of North Carolina Press, 2004), 150.

30. *African Repository and Colonial Journal* 8 (1833): 123–24; William McLain to James L. Petigru, February 28, 1854, 1169.03.01, James Louis Petigru Papers, 1816–63, South Carolina Historical Society, Charleston.

31. *African Repository* 27 (1851): 94. The title of the journal was shortened to *African Repository* in 1850, three years after the independence of Liberia, in 1847.

32. See, for instance, "Petition of One Hundred Eleven Sundry Mechanics of the City of Charleston," ca. 1828, ND #1811, #48, 280–83, Records of the General Assembly. See also meetings of the Mechanic's Society of Charleston, *City Gazette*, September 17, 24, 29, 1830.

33. *African Repository and Colonial Journal* 8 (1833): 74–77.

34. Ibid., 75.

35. Ibid., 210.

36. South Carolinians, who represented 86.6 percent of this expedition, were accompanied by twenty-four emigrants from Florida and Georgia. *Sixteenth Annual Report of the American Society for Colonizing of the Free People of Colour of the United States, with an Appendix* (Washington, D.C.: James C. Dunn, 1833), 13.

37. Ibid., 13, 34.

38. Charles I. Foster, "The Colonization of Free Negroes, in Liberia, 1816–1835," *Journal of Negro History* 38, no. 1 (1953): 56, 60.

39. Dorothy Porter, ed., *Early Negro Writing, 1760–1837* (Boston: Beacon Press, 1971), 252–53.

40. *African Repository* 33 (1857): 153–54.

41. *Examination of Thomas C. Brown, A Free Colored Citizen of South Carolina as to the Actual State of Things in Liberia in the Years 1833 and 1834 at the Chatham Street Chapel, May 9th and 10th 1834* (New York: S. W. Benedict & Co. Printers, 1834); *Liberator*, February 22, 1834.

42. Namely, 108 out of 126.

43. *African Repository and Colonial Journal* 23 (1847): 190.

44. *African Repository and Colonial Journal* 24 (1848): 162, 189–90; *African Repository and Colonial Journal* 25 (1849): 221–22; 316; *Thirty-Third Annual Report of the American Colonization Society, with Minutes of the Annual Meeting and of the Board of Directors, January 15, 1850* (Washington, D.C.: C. Alexander Printer, 1850), 7.

45. *African Repository and Colonial Journal* 25 (1849): 7–8.

46. Samuel Phil Sigler, "The Attitudes of Free Blacks towards Emigration to Liberia" (PhD diss., Boston University, 1969), 87–88.

47. Ibid., 133.

48. *Journal of the House of Representatives of the State of South Carolina Being the Annual Session of 1850* (Columbia, S.C.: Steam-Power Press of I. C. Morgan, State Printer, 1850), 23–24. The address was published in the press. See *Daily National Intelligencer*, December 2, 1850.

49. See, for instance, the petition of the eighty-four Sumter District residents, ca. 1858, ND #1873; petition of forty residents of Horry District, ca. 1859, ND #1801; and petition of the South Carolina Mechanics Association, November 16, 1858, ND #1858, #25, all in Records of the General Assembly. On the hostile atmosphere against free people of color in Charleston during the 1859 municipal election, see Charleston Mercury, November 2, 1859. On the Assembly debates that followed the different proposals that targeted the free population of color, see Journal of the House of Representatives of the State of South Carolina Being the Session of 1859 (Columbia, S.C.: Gibbes R. W., State Printer, 1859), 160–61.

50. African Repository 26 (1850): 110, 247; African Repository 27 (1851): 24, 154–55; African Repository 28 (1852): 379; African Repository 29 (1853): 25–26.

51. These emigrants came from Abbeville District, Orangeburg, Beaufort, Hamburg, Lancaster, Camden, and Greenville. African Repository 27 (1851): 154–55; African Repository 29 (1853): 25–26; African Repository 36 (1860): 142–43; African Repository 30 (1854): 55.

52. African Repository 26 (1850): 335.

53. Twenty-Ninth Annual Report of the American Colonization Society: With the Proceedings of the Board of Directors and of the Society: January 20, 1846 (Washington, D.C.: C. Alexander Printer, 1846), 17.

54. Information about Going to Liberia with Things Which Every Emigrant Ought to Know: Report of Messrs. Fuller and Janifer: Sketch of the History of Liberia: and, the Constitution of the Republic of Liberia (Washington, D.C.: C. Alexander Printer, 1852), 3–5.

55. *Pittsfield Sun*, March 10, 1859.

56. This total number included 172 "freedmen" who were manumitted during the Civil War and 346 migrants from Barbados. In addition, 5,722 liberated or recaptured Africans were sent to Liberia by the U.S. government. *African Repository* 42 (1866): 223.

57. Between 1820 and 1856, the ACS records give a total of 415 migrants from South Carolina. However, they fail to consider the twenty-six migrants who boarded the *Randolph* in December 1828 and the fifteen migrants from Hamburg who were part of the 1849 *Huma* expedition. The 1843 Census of Liberia also wrongly attributes the origin of the *Randolph* migrants as Georgia. However, an 1828 account providing "items of intelligence" from Liberia mentions that the *Randolph* arrived "with 26 passengers from Georgetown, South Carolina," and the "emigrants from South Carolina ... enjoyed almost universal and perfect health" (*African Repository and Colonial Journal* 4 [1828]: 82). The percentages are calculated with a total number of 11,116 migrants (i.e., 11,288 minus the 172 freedmen). *African Repository* 42 (1866): 223; *African Repository* 33 (1857): 152–55; *Forty-Second Annual Report*, 10; *Forty-Third Annual Report*, 8; *African Repository* 36 (1860): 36–37, 115, 142–43.

58. *African Repository* 42 (1866): 222.

59. *African Repository and Colonial Journal* 25 (1849): 221–22; *African Repository* 27 (1851): 24. For enslaved families who had been manumitted, see *African Repository* 26 (1850): 107–9.

60. *African Repository* 26 (1850): 247; *African Repository* 27 (1851): 154–55.

61. *African Repository and Colonial Journal* 4 (1828): 82.

62. Alexander, *A History of Colonization*, 349.

63. Twenty-two Georgians were part of this expedition, which counted five enslaved persons who had been manumitted to go to Liberia. *Tables Showing*, 304.

64. *African Repository* 26 (1850): 110, 247; *African Repository* 27 (1851): 154–55.

65. Chris Dixon, *African Americans and Haiti: Emigration and Black Nationalism in the Nineteenth Century* (Westport, Conn.: Greenwood Press, 2000), 92.

66. *African Repository and Colonial Journal* 25 (1849): 220–22; Fitchett, "The Free Negro," 239–41. Of the migrants who embarked on the *Colonel Howard* in May 1848, 24.4 percent were bondspeople who were liberated to be deported to Liberia. *African Repository and Colonial Journal* 24 (1849): 189–90.

67. *Forty-Third Annual Report*, 8.

68. *African Repository* 36 (1860): 142–43.

69. *The Colonizationist*, 285, 287.

70. David J. McCord, *Statutes at Large of South Carolina* (Columbia, S.C.: A. S. Johnson, 1840), 7:468–69. See, for example, the list of emigrants of the *Huma* in 1849 in *African Repository and Colonial Journal* 25 (1849): 221–22.

71. Blyden, "'This Na True Story,'" 358, 360; *African Repository and Colonial Journal* 8 (1833): 242.

72. *African Repository and Colonial Journal* 9 (1834): 128; *African Repository* 27 (1851): 24.

73. *African Repository and Colonial Journal* 8 (1833): 128, 348; *African Repository and Colonial Journal* 9 (1834): 8.

74. *African Repository* 26 (1850): 195.

75. Ibid., 235–36.

76. Of the 4,454 emigrants who were sent out by the ACS, 11.6 percent left the colony between 1820 and 1843. *Tables Showing*, 306.

77. Unfortunately, as the South Carolinian contingent did not form the bulk of other expeditions between 1820 and 1843, it is difficult to ascertain precisely the number who left the colony. Ibid., 304.

78. Francis Huger to James W. Holloway, September 1, 1829, Holloway Scrapbook, Avery Research Center, Charleston.

79. Wallace Bertram Korn, "Jews and Negro Slavery in the Old South 1789–1865," in *Strangers & Neighbors: Relations between Blacks & Jews in the United States*, ed. Marianne Adams and John Bracey (Amherst: University of Massachusetts Press, 1999), 165.

80. Loring Daniel Dewey, *Correspondence Relative to the Emigration to Hayti* (New York: Mahlon Day, 1824), 7–8, 10. "Place of refuge" appears on 7.

81. Ibid., 9.

82. Dixon, *African Americans and Haiti*, 16.

83. James Oliver Horton and Lois E. Horton, *In Hope of Liberty: Culture, Community, and Protest among Northern Free Blacks, 1700–1860* (New York: Oxford University Press, 1997), 194; John Edward Baur, "Mulatto Machiavelli, Jean Pierre Boyer, and the Haiti of His Day," *Journal of Negro History* 32, no. 3 (1947): 327.

84. Benjamin Hunt, *Remarks on Hayti as a Place of Settlement for Afric-Americans; and on the Mulatto as a Race for the Tropics* (Philadelphia: T. B. Pugh, 1860), 10–11; *African Repository and Colonial Journal* 5 (1829–30): 185.

85. James Redpath, *A Guide to Hayti* (Boston: Haytian Bureau of Emigration, 1861), 105; *Charleston Mercury*, October 12, 1859.

86. Dewey, *Correspondence*, 23; Dixon, *African Americans*, 34.

87. *African Repository and Colonial Journal* 5 (1829–30): 184; Hunt, *Remarks on Hayti*, 11.

88. Hunt, *Remarks on Hayti*, 11.

89. Ibid., 12, 14.

90. Baur, "Mulatto Machiavelli," 327; Leslie M. Alexander, "The Black Republic: The Influence of the Haitian Revolution on Northern Black Political Consciousness, 1816–1862," in *African Americans and the Haitian Revolution, Selected Essays and Historical Documents*, ed. Maurice Jackson and Jacqueline Bacon (New York: Routledge, 2010), 62; Dixon, *African Americans*, 41.

91. Baur, "Mulatto Machiavelli," 327; Alexander, "The Black Republic," 62; Dixon, *African Americans*, 41.

92. *The Seventh Census of the United States: 1850* (Washington, D.C.: Robert Armstrong, 1853), 339–40.

93. Hunt, *Remarks on Hayti*, 13, 20, 31; Dixon, *African Americans*, 199–200;

Friendly Moralist Society Papers, June 11, 1848, Avery Research Center, Charleston; *Revue des Deux Mondes* 29, no. 23 (1859): 348, 350; Matthew J. Smith, *Liberty, Fraternity, Exile: Haiti and Jamaica after Emancipation* (Chapel Hill: University of North Carolina Press, 2014), 82.

94. In 1859 Arkansas enacted legislation calling for the expulsion of free Black people. Florida and Missouri passed expulsion bills that were eventually vetoed by their governors. Tennessee and nine other states debated the possibility of expelling their free population of color. Alexandre Bonneau, *Haïti: Ses progrès, son avenir* (Paris: E. Dentu, 1862), 105; Jonathan M. Atkins, "Party Politics and the Debate over the Tennessee Free Negro Bill, 1859–1860," *Journal of Southern History* 71, no. 2 (2005): 245.

95. Many free people of color could not prove their free status due to inadequate documentation or as a result of having been manumitted in trust and granted a nominally enslaved status. From eight hundred to a thousand South Carolinians of color fled the state by land or by sea between August and November 1860. For a remarkable and detailed analysis of the enslavement crisis, see chapter 7, "Masters or Slaves," in *Black Masters: A Free Family of Color in the Old South*, by Michael P. Johnson and James L. Roark (New York: Norton, 1984), 233–87; *Farmers' Cabinet*, November 16, 1860.

96. *Liberator*, November 16, 1860.

97. *Farmers' Cabinet*, November 16, 1860; Johnson and Roark, *Black Masters*, 292; *Philadelphia Inquirer*, March 6, 1861; John R. McKivigan, *Forgotten Firebrand: James Redpath and the Making of Nineteenth-Century America* (Ithaca, N.Y.: Cornell University Press, 2008), 76.

98. *Daily Ohio State Journal*, November 15, 1860; *Philadelphia Inquirer*, March 6, 1861.

99. James D. Johnson to Henry Ellison, December 19, 1860, Ellison Family Papers, South Caroliniana Library, University of South Carolina, Columbia.

100. *African Repository* 37 (1861): 94.

101. Alexander, "The Black Republic," 74.

102. Julie Winch, *A Gentleman of Color: The Life of James Forten* (New York: Oxford University Press, 2002), 343.

103. Richard Holloway Clark to Grandmother Elizabeth Holloway, December 1, 1857, Holloway Family Scrapbook.

104. Johnson and Roark, *Black Masters*, 232–36.

105. This was in reference to the fee that commissioners who captured a fugitive slave would receive. Benjamin Drew, *A North-Side View of Slavery. The Refugee: Or the Narratives of Fugitive Slaves in Canada. Related by Themselves, with an Account of the History and Condition of the Colored Population of Upper Canada* (Boston: John P. Jewett & Company, 1856), 333.

106. Winks, *Blacks in Canada*, 230; *Mission to Fugitive Slaves in Canada: Being a Branch of the Operations of the Colonial Church and School Society: Report for the Year 1858–9* (London, 1859), 31.

107. *Farmers' Cabinet*, November 16, 1860; *Philadelphia Inquirer*, March 6, 1861.
108. Edward Holloway to Charles Holloway, March 16, 1857, Holloway Scrapbook.
109. On the promotional efforts in Canada to channel immigration to Jamaica at the expense of Haiti in the early 1860s, see McKivigan, *Forgotten Firebrand*, 74–75; Winks, *Blacks in Canada*, 164–65.
110. Holloway to Holloway, March 16, 1857, Holloway Scrapbook.
111. Ibid.
112. Johnson and Roark, *Black Masters*, 220.
113. Ibid.
114. *African Repository* 37 (1861): 67.
115. Johnson and Roark, *Black Masters*, 336; Winch, *Gentleman of Color*, 343.

CHAPTER 5

Liberia as a Theater
Performance, Race-Making, and the Liberian Nationality

CAREE A. BANTON

In 1664 members of the Lower House of the State of Maryland requested that their counterparts in the Upper House draw up legislation "obliging negroes to serve *durante vita* [for life]" so as to lessen the damage incurred by slaveholders when enslaved people "pretended to be Christened," thereafter declaring, "And soe pleade the lawe of England."[1] Acting and pretense as pathways to freedom underscored a significant aspect of an Atlantic world in which emerging racist ideology revolved around Black people overcoming their supposed innate depravities. Even as the law eroded the freedom of the enslaved, the same measures would prove inadequate in its restoration. Overt suggestions and undercurrents in everyday life questioned Black presence in spaces and conditions supposedly reserved for whites. As white supremacists increasingly embedded racial surveillance throughout society and as freedom through law was often foreclosed, performance provided the grounds upon which Black people would be recognized as human beings deserving of basic rights.

If a successful escape could have guaranteed the full benefits accorded to those who experienced liberty as a natural right, then perhaps such pretenses would not have persisted. By the nineteenth century, the specter of runaways would come to define what Manisha Sinha described in her book of the same title as *The Slave's Cause*.[2] In a burgeoning abolitionist movement, the drama surrounding the enslaved unveiling of their scars of bondage would come to serve as a kind of cultural touchstone for thinking through the vagaries of Black performativity and freedom. As running away in a white supremacist society specifically necessitated certain kinds of performances, it produced new possibilities as it pushed against the limitations placed upon the enslaved. It inadvertently created a form of theater in which Black escapees attempted to subvert race and gender as they publicly performed a false identity that would be widely assumed to be that of a freed person.

Slave narratives and other writings in the nineteenth century largely were replete with Black people performing these contrived visions of freedom. C. Riley Snorton in *Black on Both Sides* notes instances that specifically involved fugitives undertaking cross-gender escape.[3] For instance, in *The Underground Railroad* (1872), William Still illustrated the nature of Black performativity through the various ways runaways enacted a future freedom as they fled enslavement.[4] Snorton focused on Still's exploration of the escape of Clarissa Davis in 1854, the escape of Maria Ann Weems of the District of Columbia in 1855, and the famous transatlantic escape of Ellen Craft, who at first went by the alias William Johnson and then William Craft of Georgia in 1848 to point how gender obfuscation undergirded performance during the fugitive passage. Even Harriet Tubman, who came to embody fugitivity of the Underground Railroad, once "disguised a Black man as a bonneted woman in order to obstruct his arrest and re-enslavement by Northern deputies."[5] Harriet Jacobs described her own escape in 1842 in *Incidents in the Life of a Slave Girl* (1862), noting: "I wore my sailor's clothes, and had blackened my face with charcoal. I passed several people whom I knew. The father of my children came so near that I brushed against his arm; but he had no idea who *it* was."[6] Thus, fugitives who achieved freedom through subterfuge would be forced to make continued pretensions.

Through the proliferation of slave narratives, the spectacle of the performing fugitive Black body would also structure antislavery activism. In her widely acclaimed work, *Scenes of Subjection* (1997), Saidiya Hartman positioned Jacobs's narrative as part theatrical performance by showing how she was forced to dramatize her story in a way that was useful to her efforts to lobby the white readers whose support she counted on in freedom. Hartman suggests that Jacobs necessarily had to obliterate the very nature of the condition under which she existed, performing a palatable version of slavery so as to make her story understandable to whites.[7] Viewing Black life as a theater and using the framing of "scenes," Hartman showed how terror and violence infiltrated various areas of Black life in ways that produced constraints, delimited possibilities, and curtailed freedom. To that end, Hartman, in rethinking scenes generally viewed as areas of "Negro enjoyment," "jollity," or "simulated contentment" free from the enslaver's control and co-opted by historians as areas of slave agency, argues rather that they were merely a part of the far-reaching theatrics that characterized the everyday terror that Black people experienced.[8] Thus, Hartman concludes that scenes of enjoyment where the enslaved were forced to dance, play musical instruments such as the fiddle, and laugh on command in the presence of their slaveholders were characteristic renewals of the initial act that enslavers had used to convert Africans into slaves in the first place.

Performance ultimately pervaded all aspects of Black life. Planters often stressed the centrality and significance of its social rituals to the smooth running of the plantation as a means of reinforcing the dynamics of power. Thus, the emergence of minstrelsy in the mid- to late nineteenth century as a new kind of performance in which whites in blackface caricatured and lampooned Black people was no surprise. The proliferation of images of the happy, carefree slave, the "Negro" musician, and the efforts of free Black people toward respectability by "putting on airs" fortified the primacy of minstrel shows. With resisting slaves, roving abolitionists, and minstrel shows, the nineteenth century teemed with theatrical drama.

If the world ordered by racial capitalism and enslavement demanded performances of freedom-seeking Black people, migration away from the United States would not eliminate such expectations. Instead, as Black people migrated or were colonized to places such as Liberia, the legacy of racism continued to not only curtail the promises of freedom but also structure the expectations placed upon them. The theatrics around running away and minstrelsy that had circumscribed Black freedom became a part of a larger transatlantic racial theater. The very fugitive performances that had encapsulated the escape from enslavement would also define Liberia's efforts as it navigated freedom on the global landscape.[9] Such considerations were not outside the diplomatic and economic maneuvers that defined treaty-worthiness; instead, they proved central to its meaning. Thus, the lens of fugitive performativity served to unmask what the guise of "freedom" ignored by unveiling the process by which Liberia transformed from colony and emigration destination to treaty-worthy republic.

The ways that legitimate diplomacy was configured for white nationalities during and after slavery left Black nationalities like Liberia outside of the dominant "diplomatic grammar." Thus, across the Atlantic, Black migrants were forced to negotiate not only their individual citizenship but also Liberia's sovereignty. The republic thus became a space not only that produced performances but also where the witnessing of other spectacles exposed spectatorship as a corporeal practice, social act, structured ritual, and contingent event. As Jacques exclaimed to Duke Senior in act 2, scene 7 of Shakespeare's play *As You Like It*, "All the world's a stage; and all the men and women merely players."[10] Given the nature of nineteenth-century circumstances, Liberia invites us to see the ways in which it became embroiled in the theatrics of the era and served as the theater of Black people enacting the various dramas in which they and the republic became embroiled.

The relationship between the body and politics has long been a central concern of political thought. The "body politic" and the "person of the state" are key metaphors of political theory. Through the "theater state," a formulation created by the anthropologist Clifford Geertz, political entities became places where religion and ritual acted to bind together a multiethnic polity.[11] Because ritual performances became essential not out of coercion but because members wanted to be a part of the drama, it served to foster "a grand cultural experiment unlike anything seen before or after in their world."[12] Such understandings of the body have been used to define and restrict the arena and range of political action, distinguish legitimate from illegitimate relations, and exclude others through constructions of race, gender, and class. Michel Foucault's *History of Sexuality* (1978), for instance, influentially redrew the relationship between the body, power, and politics by interpreting the history of modern states through "biopolitics."[13] Achille Mbembe, drawing on Orlando Patterson's "social death," defines "necropolitics" as death while living under biopolitics.[14] Theorists and historians alike, such as Ann Stoler in her work *Race and the Education of Desire* (1995), further meditated on the connections between the exercise of state and imperial power and gendered and racial constructions of the body.[15] With Black bodies largely muted in transatlantic political thought, positioning nineteenth-century Liberia as a theatrical space might help to recover this lost view.

Current scholarship on race has been centered on the ways in which it implicates a set of social relationships and hierarchies, as well as a set of embodied practices that is carried out within these relationships. The framework of performance and theater allows us to imagine anew the study of race in transatlantic history and to account for the ruptures. If Blackness, the not accidental formation of the transatlantic slave trade, became deeply embedded in global processes, by necessity it should be accorded central consideration in thinking about Liberia's political relationality as it became a theater of freedom and a Black nationalist project, particularly the requisite performances so clearly required in the republic's diplomatic relations. Within the contexts of embodied practices, the Liberian "theaters" in which the performance of race was carried out provide a rich avenue for a different kind of political and diplomatic exploration. The juxtaposition of race, performativity, and Liberia signals a whole spectrum of views on Blackness and freedom, bringing into view the multiple regard in which Liberia was held. The variety of ways in which Liberia as a Black republic came to stand in for the racialized Black body and what this body did in its quotidian and staged performances begs numerous questions. How were Black individuals and the Black nation implicated in the theatrics of the nineteenth century? What kinds of performances did political signification of Liberia carry? What kinds of white supremacist registers were required to perform and signal civilization to the white world? How would Liberia stage itself even as it struggled economically and sociopolitically?

This chapter brings together the study of race, freedom, and performance into an inquiry into the ways in which they were inextricably entangled in ideas of Liberia as an emigration destination, colony, and republic. Centering Blackness and the performative Black body in imaginative, theatrical, literary, and diplomatic relations surrounding Liberia necessarily expands the idea of the theater even as performance and theater offer a multilayered approach to the study of race. Using the frameworks of performance and play, I attempt to understand freedom across the global nineteenth century not only on an individual level but also on the national level. By exploring the rituals and ceremonies of Black freedom, I examine how fugitivity embedded in Black racial identity making served as the imaginative venue and precursor for negotiating Black national sovereignty. The chapter thus concludes that the complex relations between the Black body and diplomacy in which the social performative context of Blackness and Liberia existed constrained its political and diplomatic goals.

Liberia and Literary Imaginative Performances of Freedom

Throughout the nineteenth century, as racial subjectivity circumscribed and marked freedom, it also rendered the Black body captive to all kinds of observers. Given that the semiotics of Blackness were contained implicitly within the body, Black existence drew the kind of scrutiny that created spectacle. In the diaspora, where Black people existed in conditions of bondage, the free Black community, which represented an aberration, stood out as if on full display. Free Black people were required to perform in ways that would contradict what was believed to be their natural savage and depraved state. Carrying out such demands, free Black people created communities and institutions ranging from churches to Freemasonry. Given all the theatrical performance requirements, staging and transformation became significant aspects of Black life.

As reform emerged in the late eighteenth and early nineteenth centuries, the free Black community became a target. Many reformists had grown alarmed that the increasing numbers of free Blacks would create an unmanageable population.[16] Like the idea of Indian reservations, the idea of colonizing Black people to Africa emerged. Black people had long petitioned and sought arrangements to remove themselves to Africa. They yearned for a homeland that would transcend their statelessness and where inclusion would not depend upon performance. Without this achievement, it appeared that their liberty might never be protected and that true citizenship would forever elude them. Time and again, Black people returned to a reality structured by the absence of an Afrotopia and the fantasy of the all-inclusive tribe. Yet, like some acts of fugitive performativity, Black statehood also seemed predestined to fail.

In the reform era, however, it was the American Colonization Society (ACS) that formalized ideas of colonizing Black people in Africa in 1816. It would play a key role in Liberia's formal beginnings in the 1820s, ultimately bringing to a white vision of the nation Black people desired. Historians have debated the founding of the colonization movement. While Douglas Egerton has argued that colonizationists were driven by views that slavery and unfree labor were both ruinous to society, Eric Burin has noted that manumitters as a particular class of people were variously motivated by convenience, control, profit, humanitarianism, and Christian sensibilities.[17] By showing the effects of their actions on slavery, Burin has argued that the movement should be viewed as a conservative approach to emancipation.[18] Ultimately, as white philanthropists carried out performative partnerships and slaveholders sought to shield their enslaved property from free Black people, colonization came to suit both of their needs. With both racism and benevolence birthing the emergence of Liberia, the colony emerged within a theater of contradictions.[19] By creating the scion of an unbroken line of colonization and imperialism under the veil of benevolence, colonizationists had fabricated the absolution they would come to hide behind. As their benefactor, the ACS undeniably helped to shape the ideology surrounding Black freedom in Liberia.

ACS documents articulate yet another dimension of the transitivity of racial performance in which Blackness took on new meanings in light of concerns over a Liberian modernity through which free Black people could prove their civilization by projecting behaviors deserving of equal treatment to whites.[20] Given the circulation of the *African Repository and Colonial Journal* and roving speakers, these ideas found their own stage, as well as their own hugely enthusiastic global audience. The ACS as Liberia's patron came with a wide cast, including Black migrants, missionaries, diplomats, and colonial spectators.

On June 20, 1874, at the fifty-seventh anniversary of the American Colonization Society, Reverend Thomas H. Pearne, secretary, referenced a speech entitled "The Future of the African Race." Delivered in recent months by Wendell Phillips, an abolitionist crusader from Boston whose speeches invigorated the antislavery cause in the years leading up to the American Civil War, the speech echoed many of the views outlined by the ACS. He noted that "whatever that race may have been at an early period, they have not in modern times lifted themselves into greatness and renown by any grand, heroic achievement; that it is vain for them to claim equal consideration with others until they prove themselves to deserve it by doing something which shall lift them to a level with the highest and the greatest." Phillips outlined that Black people required performances and visual displays that would convey their civilization to the world. Indeed, with underlying assumptions surrounding Black failure to realize certain markers of civilization, he pointed out that they must "achieve something in art, or science, or discovery, or commerce, or government, which will make the race historic and give to it immortality." Hence, as their actions formed a spectacle to be consumed, the different disciplines also became props for Black people to demonstrate their attainment of certain milestones. Phillips recognized the many opportunities that freedmen had used to "make for themselves an honorable name and a worthy record," and he celebrated their many successes. He pointed out that they "have won admiration by their efforts at self-improvement and education; by their industry, order, and thrift; by examples among themselves of eminent positions honorably reached and worthily maintained. All this is well. Let the good work go on. But all must admit that the competition is a sharp one, that the struggle is unequal, and that they suffer under many disadvantages."[21] Consequently, Black migrants, rather than being entirely self-generated, came to be considered as the constructed elite artifacts of colonizationists.

Through the ACS, many others in the nineteenth century, such as Horace Greeley, joined in the chorus of colonization ideology that suggested that Black people needed to prove themselves outside of the nation before they could aim to seek citizenship rights in the United States.[22] Liberia served a belief that at a distance, in their new theater of freedom, Black people would be "a free, happy, prosperous people; in a climate natural to them, and where they can walk erect among equals, and say of the soil, and of the improvements, and of the government—*these are our own*."[23] These ideas structured the terms under which Black people operated under the white gaze, aiming to perform some aspect of whiteness to make up for an ostensible racial deficit.

Black migrants themselves variously came to view the colony as a hopeful Black nationalist experiment, a civilizing opportunity, as well as a place where, according to Claude Clegg, malaria threatened any prospects of liberty.[24] While the different ideological dynamics that undergirded abolitionism and colonizationism shaped Black ideas and interest in Liberia, they also outlined the necessary transatlantic dimensions of nineteenth-century Black freedom and the necessity for Black people to "perform" in order to prove themselves. In Liberia, Black people who were ostensibly "free" of the shackles of Blackness and no longer supposed to be passing for free remained trapped in a variety of ways. As they helped to imaginatively curate Liberia and the kinds of performances that were required of Black freedom there, these views further helped to establish a durative white supremacist presence in Liberia.

Colonizationists were keen to warn Black people to properly use the stage space. On January 20, 1874, at the same address delivered at the fifty-seventh-anniversary celebrations of the ACS in Washington, D.C., Reverend Thomas H. Pearne further outlined the expected performances of Black people as they were moved to the new theater of freedom in Liberia. Pearne declared that the ACS as a society had afforded the Black race not only an opportunity but also an "occasion, the theater and the motive for a grand achievement; an achievement which, for its beauty and moral grandeur, will take rank with the greatest and the noblest in past ages."[25] He emphasized the kind of chance afforded through Liberian colonization that charged nothing while supplying the means of survival for six months after migrants arrived. Environment became an additional player, as Liberia was believed to be the perfect place for upliftment because of its kind nature, productive soil, and pleasant climate. With such blessings, a subsistence living that would provide food and sustenance could be achieved virtually without much effort, leaving the mind and body free to be used in other endeavors.

At the core of benevolent colonization ideology was an effort to place Black people in favorable circumstances in a country where they could pursue their freedom and ostensibly be redeemed by their own agency and national pretensions of the freedom they would conjure up. In this instance, parodying whites as a way of demonstrating Blacks' civilization defined expected performances. Liberia thus became more than just a new country and new surroundings. To the ACS, the new opportunity was also a new stage that invited spectatorship. It afforded and entrusted Black people with the responsibilities of building up, maintaining, and developing in the "presence of the whole world, and especially of the one hundred and fifty million Africans, a free, Christian Government." As they pointed out, "The theater is provided: there is not only the soil of Liberia, with its area of fifty or sixty thousand square miles and its population of six hundred thousand," but there is also the possibility of indefinite expansion into the interior. The ACS imagined the whole continent as a stage, noting that the colonized Black people "may have there really the range of the whole continent of barbarism to traverse and to redeem. And it is their's [sic] upon this theater, to make themselves felt as a mighty power of reformation and regeneration; a civilizing and restoring power." The ACS opined that "others, with far less opportunity, with greatly inferior occasions, with a more contracted theater, and with motives of much less magnitude, have wrought wonders, and have placed themselves on high, as among earth's greatest heroes."[26] Many in the ACS believed that their motive was most certainly glorious, given the possibilities Liberia presented. They believed it would awaken the drive and incite the determination of the most indifferent, dull, and unconcerned Black migrant.

With the Civil War, colonization once again came to occupy a significant place in the political discourse. On August 14, 1862, President Abraham Lincoln met a group of colored men at the White House. According to E. M. Thomas, chairman of the delegation of colored men, "They were there by invitation to hear what the Executive had to say to them about the Scheme of Colonization."[27] The Reverend J. Mitchell, commissioner of emigration, introduced the guests. After they were all seated, "the President, after a few preliminary observations, begun to speak with the group."[28] He first informed them that Congress had provided a portion of money, which he had reserved for the colonization effort of at least a portion of those of African descent to a different country. Lincoln noted that "it had for a long time been his inclination, to favor that cause."[29] The president thereafter sought to defend his position on why colonization was a good and necessary endeavor.

In laying out the reasons why he believed that Black people should become colonists, Lincoln reflected the ways in which race had seeped into his understanding of the American body politic. Against an ideological screen that provided a seemingly perfect contrast, Lincoln pointed out that "you and we are different races. We have between us a broader difference than exists between almost any other two races."[30] The meeting between the group of colored men and Lincoln exemplified the rigid boundaries of American democracy, but it also illustrated the changing meaning and rationalization of colonization. Rather than contemplate the prospects of giving citizenship and equality to the more than four million African Americans who would be released from slavery after the Civil War, Lincoln embraced colonization as political compromise. The gravity of his thoughts on colonization rested on the prospects for equality, which he argued could not be achieved if both races were to remain in the same space. He was explicit in expressing his view that Negroes were as capable as whites to progress intellectually, economically, and politically. However, the implementation of a colony was the only medium through which the races would enjoy "equal but separate" progress. One can only imagine the specter of the spectacled Lincoln, the great emancipator, hailing colonization as the scheme that would level the playing field between the races. Having become even more explicit in this interesting meeting, the notion of separate but equal occupied a significant part of colonization discourse and ultimately would be used as a catchphrase to entice Black people—both African Americans and those from the West Indies—to emigrate to various colonization destinations.

Liberia Onstage

Liberia appeared on stages beyond those created by the American Colonization Society throughout the nineteenth century. In places where Black people gathered to discuss freedom, Liberia would have been part of the imaginative possibilities put forward. One such venue was the very popular colored conventions, where Black people gathered to discuss political matters and to organize on state and national levels. Speeches and poems but especially the songs that were often sung at colored conventions became a space in which to stage the debate over Black liberty. Liberty songs sung at the antislavery meetings such as the 1843 Michigan state convention included "I Am a Friend of Liberty," "Freedom's Gathering," and "I Dream of All Things Free." Liberia of course emerged within this discussion of liberty, but rather than express an interest in emigration, conferencegoers belted out "Liberia Is Not a Place for Me" at the 1851 Ohio state convention and

"Come Join the Friends of Liberty" at the 1858 Massachusetts convention.[31] At the 1859 New England convention, the Black abolitionist William Wells Brown even penned his own song, which was sung by conference attendees.

Early literature revealed the interplay of ideas between Black and white people, abolitionists and colonizationists, and the extensive transatlantic debate surrounding expectations of the would-be free Black people. As a "new theater of freedom," Liberia would be cemented in the antislavery imagination through a series of literary and minstrel performances. As the colored conventions gained steam, Harriet Beecher Stowe's *Uncle Tom's Cabin* also became integral to the transnational creation of Liberia as a space of Black freedom and a body politic. Liberia occupied a defining space in Stowe's novel, which had been largely directed toward whites. The novel originated in the midst of abolitionist discussions during the perilous 1850s, and Stowe's intent was to embolden white citizens who were being legally obligated by the Fugitive Slave Law to be the long arms of the southern plantation owners and defy the Fugitive Slave Law, which she believed was unchristian.[32] Rather than focusing directly on the resistance of the enslaved, Stowe created the Black body to stimulate white feelings as they witnessed Black suffering. Stowe aimed to stir the hearts of white parents to empathize with their enslaved counterparts who were separated from their children by relating whites' own experience of having lost children themselves. Having read the book alongside the stipulations of the new law, whites would have to make a decision about whether or not to help a fugitive slave if one showed up at their doorstep.

Stowe's *Uncle Tom's Cabin* shaped not only Black personhood but also Black nationality through the role of Christianity in Liberian colonialism. Christianity directed Black interests in and relationships with Liberia while also circumscribing Blackness and Liberia in the global arena. However, it primarily featured as a prop that would be used as a tool of repair. Such notions manifested themselves primarily through the character of George Harris and his imagination of freedom and nationhood: "To fill up Liberia with an ignorant, inexperienced, half-barbarized race, just escaped from the chains of slavery, would be only to prolong, for ages, the period of struggle and conflict which attends the inception of new enterprises."[33] Many advocates of creating the colony of Liberia pressed for churches' support based on ideas that Black people were depraved heathens. This resulted in Stowe's request to "Let the church of the north receive these poor sufferers in the spirit of Christ; receive them to the educating advantages of Christian republican society and schools, until they have attained to somewhat of a moral and intellectual maturity, and then assist them in their passage to those shores, where they may put in practice the lessons they have learned in America."[34] Stowe's religious sentiments represent how nineteenth-century philanthropic and Christian efforts to resolve the conflicts inherent in American freedom in which Liberia became entangled took on a transnational dimension.

More than anything else, *Uncle Tom's Cabin* fueled the creation of ideas of Black freedom on the Liberian stage. Several of Stowe's characters who were freed ended up in Liberia. But before their migration, their views illustrated not only the vigorous nature of the colonization debate but also how Liberia lived and performed in the transatlantic imagination. Sending the Black characters to Liberia rested on Stowe's belief that racial homogeneity created stable political communities. Jason Richards argues that "four black characters, Uncle Tom, Black Sam, Adolph, and George Harris, employ blackface and colonial mimicry simultaneously to resist and conform to various aspects of national identity, while they test racial barriers to self-making and actualize differing degrees of self-hood."[35] Arthur Riss and other scholars contend that Stowe's decision to send several Black characters to Liberia at the end of the novel revealed her own desires for a racialized nationalism. For them, George Harris and George Shelby, who in name and character both resembled the first president, symbolized Stowe's push for racial homogeneity contained within a Black nationality. Riss highlights that George Harris evoked Washington in his use of revolutionary rhetoric and a New World vision of freedom and empire in Liberia. George Shelby, on the other hand, by manumitting his slaves, is configured into a character who reflects a black parody of Washington, who attempted to embody democratic ideals. Riss concludes that Stowe makes the two Georges over in George Washington's image and then places them in separate nationalities as a way of creating a racial solution for the United States.[36]

This further emerged as a solution to the national contradictions that the Black fictional presidential characters embodied. George Harris's letter toward the end of Stowe's novel was particularly demonstrative of the place Liberia had come to occupy in state and diplomatic discourse. Stowe used the Black character of Harris to make certain points. Harris explained: "But, you will tell me, our race have [sic] equal rights to mingle in the American republic as the Irishman, the German, the Swede. Granted, they have. We ought to be free to meet and mingle, to rise by our individual worth, without any consideration of caste or color; and they who deny us this right are false to their own professed principles of human equality."[37] Harris pointed out the racism at play with the exclusion of Black people from America that seemingly informed his view: "We ought, in particular, to be allowed here. We have more than the rights of common men;—we have the claim of an injured race for reparation. But, then, I do not want it; I want a country, a nation, of my own."[38] The views of Harris's character helped to shape the debate over Liberia, allowing a masculinist African diasporic politics to animate and anchor the migrants' colonizationist and civilizationist mission.

Stowe's novel later evolved into theatrical stage dramas called "Tom Shows." While Stowe's novel stoked imagination about the possibilities and limits of Black freedom, performances that accompanied "Tom mania" proved significant in the theatrical creation of a visual economy of Blackness for whites to continue to consume and exploit. Theatrical performances of the book eventually made it to the stage in New York at the National Theater.[39] Reports were that there was "not one dry eye" when one fugitive slave in her quest to escape eventually made it to the other side of the Ohio River to freedom. *Uncle Tom's Cabin* came to highlight the truly transnational discussion that defined efforts to negotiate Black freedom. The performance of the theatrical version of *Uncle Tom's Cabin* as far away as Brazil, Mexico City, and other Latin American countries innovated upon blackface performances that had originated in the United States.[40] Like the minstrel show, these performances caricatured and limited African American abilities and reinscribed boundaries around Black identity. Tom mania and its associated minstrel shows played a key role in staging and articulating the meaning of Liberia and Black freedom. Stowe's novel instantiated contrived forms of Black performances. With actors and actresses who emerged in theatrical performances of *Uncle Tom's Cabin* as "Tommers," minstrelsy suggested something else about the performativity of Black freedom. It carried with it the idea that Black freedom and Blackness itself were nothing but parodies. Black people could only mimic whites because they had not yet achieved the level of civilization to know and enjoy freedom on their own terms.

Though Stowe's *Uncle Tom's Cabin* was intended for a white audience, Black people would intervene in a debate that sought to exclude them. Their instinctive reactions to minstrel shows aimed at poking fun at Black people came quickly to counteract the images that were being created. Early adversaries of the performances included Frederick Douglass and Martin Delany, who were outspoken critics of minstrelsy.[41] Both were outraged by what they saw as the continued degradation of Black people on the minstrel stage. Douglass's attacks began in an often-cited passage that first appeared on October 27, 1848, in his newspaper, the *North Star*. Douglass condemned blackface performers as "the filthy scum of white society, who have stolen from [Black people] a complexion denied to them by nature, in which to make money, and pander to the corrupt taste of their white fellow-citizens."[42]

Delany, who worked with Douglass on his newspaper, channeled his disgust into *Blake* (1860), a novel seemingly written in direct response to Harriet Beecher Stowe's minstrel-driven work.[43] Delany satirically attacked Stowe's transformation of Black life into a passive, grotesque, and emasculated existence. Delany's writing shifted from utopias in Africa to horror scenarios in the diaspora where he could write characters strong enough to face seemingly insurmountable odds. Delany found solace in novels where the real-life horrors he feared most could be confronted or even vanquished. Taking on a fundamentally different tone and outcome, Delany revised Stowe's freedom narrative offered through *Uncle Tom's Cabin* by creating a story about the fictional escape of Henry Blake from a plantation in the South. Literary scholars suggest that Blake is himself a revision of George Harris, or rather a revision of Stowe's notion of a Black rebel.[44] Unlike George, who performs whiteface, Blake is unambiguously Black and is committed to slave rebellion, which he first organizes at home, not on the distant shores of Liberia, where George imagines his revolution. Following his escape, Blake travels through the United States, Canada, Africa (possibly Liberia), and Cuba on a transnational undertaking to bring together Black people from around the Atlantic to struggle for their freedom. Delany's counternarrative dismantled racist stereotyping while hinting at the possibility of the violent overthrow of slavery.

Race, Liberia, and Diplomatic Performances

Once migrants arrived in Liberia, the nation came to serve as a display case. The same violence that had pushed them to emigrate was the same that had created Liberia. Yet Liberian migrants believed they possessed the ability to remake the world and cast it anew by demonstrating their abilities. Each new migrant group imbued the republic with a frenetic sense that all things are possible. With a script created by the ACS running up against their own desires, the expectation was for the emigrants to assemble to carry out their orders and expectations and create a stencil through which to carve other performances. Such demands brought together individual and national freedom in ways that caused the migrants to become an embodiment of the nationality. The new nomenclature for the migrants, Americo-Liberian, produced as part of the nation-building process, provided the lexicon that secured the union. The hyphen at first glance denotes the clear points of the migrants' places of origin and arrival, the ways in which Americanness would contribute to the cultivation of a civilized Black nationality, but it also demonstrates the inherent contradictory relations of power. The ways in which Liberia was abundantly discussed as it unfolded and in the half-century after arrival reflected one set of ideas that stood opposite to how Black people performed their identity as they sought to unclasp the grasp of the ACS and reposition Liberia on the global stage.

Eventually, however, migrants realized that for their performances to be legitimized they would have to be brought into the realm of diplomacy. However, Blackness represented a unique positionality that was viewed as adversarial to what it meant to be not only a citizen but also a civilized nation. A note to the ACS from a British minister in Liberia in 1843 outlined the problems that Liberia's status as an unrecognized American colony would create. British traders in particular were keen to note that Liberia did not possess an internationally recognizable diplomatic status to prohibit trading activities within the colony. The British insisted that "in order to avert future serious trouble and contention in that quarter, her majesty's government should be accurately informed what degree of official patronage and protection, if any, the United States government extend to the colony of Liberia."[45] Similarly, British diplomats were also keen to find out "how far, if at all, the United States Government recognized the colony of Liberia as a national establishment."[46] The rhetoric of a lack of recognition became one of the many criticisms made by the British. Operating based on its established colonial relationship with neighboring Sierra Leone, Britain regarded Liberia and the ACS as "private persons not entitled to exercise sovereignty especially in the levying and collecting of customs duties."[47] Border disputes, as well as certain laws, further created friction between Liberia and European powers. With this kind of play, Liberia was forced to enter into a diplomatic drama that would secure its territorial integrity. To assuage political threats and to solve some of these diplomatic issues, the colony needed to become independent.[48]

The lack of recognition was a dual indictment for Liberia as a Black community and a colony without sovereignty. A kind of racism lurked in the shadows that was buried behind the legitimate complaint about sovereignty. Still, the debacle surrounding sovereignty had forced Liberia to come to grips with the unsettled questions of the nature of the political relationship between the indigenes and the state. Such debates surrounding Liberian emigration, colonization, and diplomacy, like fugitivity, would also inform the embodied practices of racial Blackness. The natives entered onto the Liberian stage in more serious and deliberate ways, as their territory now proved indispensable in important matters of trade, territorial boundaries, sovereignty, and diplomatic recognition. British merchants had often complained that the Liberian government "have shown a disposition to enlarge very considerably the limits of their territories; assuming to all appearance quite unjustifiably, the right of monopolizing the trade with the native inhabitants along a considerable line of coast, where the trade had hitherto been free."[49] British capital operated in a variety of ways across different spaces and temporalities to exert dominance. Whereas land and labor were contested in other periods, boundaries were the new target of this time. In this instance, it created a new enclosure for domination and sought to subsume markets in new ways as the abolition of the slave trade freed the Atlantic coast from slavery. As European imperialism appeared in new guises, it created new forms of subordination for Black people who had sought to escape its reach.

Joseph Jenkins Roberts, who had become governor of the Liberia commonwealth, highlighted how race shaped his pursuit of independence. The decision to become independent, according to Roberts, was a direct result of the "embarrassment we labor under with respect to the encroachments of foreigners, and the objections urged by Great Britain in regard to our sovereignty."[50] Other more pressing reasons ultimately drove Liberia to regularize its status in accordance with modern international law. Because Liberia was "neither a sovereign power nor a bona fide colony of any sovereign nation," British and French traders often refused to pay coastal trading taxes, which created a deficit in the national budget. The ways in which this affected the nation's revenue and commercial ventures and the fact that Liberia had no navy or gunboats to protect the coastline or trade thus drove the need to proceed with formalizing independence.[51]

This deficit created by trade and economic instability in Liberia was in many ways similar to the lack many saw in the enslaved. In similar fashion, the deficit would play a significant role in Liberia's exclusion from the family of nations. Indeed, much like abolitionists' investment in respectability politics that demanded Harriet Jacobs to render a palatable story, the ACS through its journal, the *African Repository and Colonial Journal,* noted, "Was that Republic to be formally received into the family of nations, a treaty of amity and commerce had to be negotiated, a postal arrangement effected, or a correspondence on its behalf to be conducted."[52] As race extended across the Atlantic, it carried with it a series of consents that entertained certain possibilities and injunctions that served to limit others. Given this, racial performances were expected of erstwhile free Black people in an ostensibly free colony so as to enable them to join the larger family of nations.

Liberia's independence from colony to nation ultimately came on July 26, 1847. Beyond independence, recognition among other nations was a diplomatic staple that would come to depend on the insurmountable nature of Blackness in the republic. One of the major challenges thereafter was turning into a tangible reality the recently proclaimed formal independence into national equality under international law. The Liberian republic's quest to be accepted as a "treaty-worthy" nation by Europe's colonial powers shaped thinking about an array of issues, including borders, ethnic groups, and ideas of Blackness. The social differences, the tensions, and the ambiguous nature of the place of the indigenes had begun to manifest themselves in territorial, political, economic, and diplomatic challenges within and outside the republic. The nation's independence had elevated the existing territorial boundary disputes and tensions between settlers, European colonizing powers, and indigenes into a higher theater. Alongside these challenges, the question of who was a part of the nation came to the fore, limiting and informing who could perform on such a stage. According to Saidiya Hartman, "Blackness incorporates subjects normatively as black, the relations among blacks, whites, and others, and the practices that produce racial difference."[53] Thus, despite their efforts to flee Western hegemony, Black peoples and their nationalities' sense of worth, respectability, and legitimacy depended on formal recognition by other countries.

Race continued to structure the kinds of postindependence performances necessary for Liberia's incorporation into the family of sovereign nations. As had been necessary for new nations like the United States in the postrevolutionary era, diplomatic and trade relationships with other nations had to be established, but with the added barrier of race.[54] Eliga Gould shows that as early as 1776, John Adams had begun to work on "a plan of treaties to guide the new nation in its relations with other governments."[55] Treaty-worthiness informed the operation of trade during peacetime and laid out the beginnings of a foreign policy that sought to bring infant republics into the fold of nations. On the other hand, Black nationalities were depicted globally in diplomatic talks with race as the ground upon and against which their treaty-worthiness would be defined. When Haiti gained independence, Jean-Jacques Dessalines declared it a nation of Black people. After decades of defeating recolonization efforts and the loss of almost half their population and resources, Haitian leaders came to the realization that their declared independence of 1804 was insufficient. Consequently, the top priorities after the revolution was having the country's independence recognized by the international community. Alexandre Pétion's focused efforts on the independent South American countries proved largely fruitless, as he was unable to get recognition from their leaders. By 1825 recognition by France would come with an onerous indemnity debt. Though Haiti's revolution had produced freedom, debt payment served to transform the island into France's commercial colony, which served as a new form of enslavement.[56] With such political, economic, psychological, and performative costs to the process of gaining international recognition for Black republics in the nineteenth century, the work of recognition became a significant source of anxiety.

Similar to recognition of the individual, recognition by other nations became analogous to the conception of Liberia's sovereign citizenship. This recognition was not only diplomatically imperative but also critical for Liberia's economic survival. The desire for inclusion created an inadequate set of criteria to which the national project aspired. Independence, having grown out of a need to project Black people's civilization to the outside world, became a means of commanding respect. Treaty-worthiness was Liberia's attempt to gain acceptability from white gatekeepers in much the same way that fugitives performed freedom for white spectators. Liberia's relationship with the wider white world was primarily one of reflecting Black people's humanity, civility, and modernity and substantiating abolitionists' and Pan-Africanists' belief in African capabilities. Though the claim of treaty-worthiness relied on the idea of sovereignty and mutual respect among equal nations, it functioned in a manner similar to baptism and conversion to produce freedom and citizenship. Establishing treaty-worthiness through the diplomatic recognition of other civilized white nations became the mirror against which Liberia could symbolically project a sense of modernity as a newly independent Black nation. The impulse to do so, which animated efforts to integrate Liberia into the wider body of nations, itself reflected the nation's otherness.

Given these issues, freedom within the language of national sovereignty enabled very little for Liberia. By bringing together Black transatlantic freedom movements that gave new meanings to and expressions of Blackness, the nation metaphor obscured the fact that as one of the most critical political representatives of emigration and colonization movements within the

African diaspora in the nineteenth century, Black people continued to live a kind of fugitive life. As Hartman outlined, "The language of freedom no longer becomes that which rescues the slave from his or her former condition, but the site of the re-elaboration of that condition, rather than its transformation."[57] Africa's place as the progenitor of Blackness as abject, degraded, and uncivilized served as one reason for the continued demand for Black performances of freedom.[58] Liberia and Liberians quickly realized its limits and possibilities based on ideas about Black subjection. With the heightened tension brought about by independence, Black freedom could be possibly curtailed by Liberia's exclusion from the family of nations based on the same grounds that humanity had been denied during enslavement.

Joseph Roberts, Liberia's first president, who had migrated from Virginia, would become its primary diplomatic architect. The presence of the Black body in certain spheres often served as a source of disruption and resistance. But free Black people in Liberia influenced not only abolition but also transatlantic policy considerations. Indeed, even as they were demanding public recognition as citizens, free Black people became principal diplomatic actors, playing a key role during Liberia's quest for independence and recognition. With the nation often metaphorically standing in for the person in the nineteenth century, historical explorations of these kinds of bodies and legal and artificial persons reveal the complex interactions between race, freedom, sovereignty, and authority. The use of the metaphor of the nation as a person ascribed an outsized amount of agency to Black people by allowing them to view the state as themselves and its actions as their own. The free Black body advocating for individual and national citizenship highlights the nature of performativity as Liberia sought inclusion and citizenship into the family of nations. Consequently, the history of freedom and diplomacy would be directly tied to an account of Black identity.

In 1849 Roberts secured an invitation to the Peace Congress held in Brussels. These kinds of political theater functioned to cover up the grotesque ways in which European nations violently restrained Black freedom. Nonetheless, Roberts addressed the congress and signed treaties with the English, French, and Belgians.[59] The demands of freedom also transformed spaces in which diplomatic policies were being negotiated on behalf of the republic into a theater. Through talks at the negotiating table and observations, diplomacy on an individual or national level became a matter of performances. As racism operated on visceral and affective registers, those like Roberts who desired to be included had to perform accordingly. In the end, Roberts's speech was considered to be "of excellent good sense and judgment, appropriate, mannerful, and the assembly made it the speech of the Congress." Roberts's presence in this crowd was not only diplomatically significant but also necessary for the respect and recognition that Black people desired from whites. Operating within and through the established strictures of established diplomatic procedures exposed white supremacy's system of governance, which sought to curtail and confine Black sovereignty. Following this appearance in Brussels, many would look at "Gentleman Roberts and the new African republic with much hope for the future."[60] The English and French governments' recognition of Liberia's sovereignty highlighted the intersections of the nation-building process with abolition and colonization. The French government gave orders to their naval officers on the African coast to put "two to three ships at Roberts' disposal when he needed to go on expeditions to destroy barracoons, break up slave trading parties, and otherwise promote the interest of humanity on the African Coast."[61] Their recognition became indicative of Liberia's efforts toward development, modernization, and respectability.

Treaty-worthiness and such kinds of diplomatic tasks served to epistemologically erase Black personhood. It inscribed race at its initial scene through an act of negation of Blackness through the construction of a binary opposition between Black and white. Given the implications of Roberts's Black body and Black republic, the ACS elected to use the white Philadelphia colonizationist Gerard Ralston to serve as the consul general for Liberia for the purpose of negotiating treaties and diplomatic ties. Ralston moderated the diplomatic negotiations that transformed Liberia from a colony to an independent republic. According to the ACS, "Mr. Ralston promptly appeared and ably acted, and he probably signed more documents of this public and important character, as the representative of Liberia, than any of the distinguished men with whom he was thus brought in contact."[62] In Ralston's view, political and economic independence was elemental to Black progress. He considered diplomatic recognition to be the hallmark of Black progress and the most sustainable objective of the Liberian colonization scheme. In subsequent years, Ralston secured European diplomatic recognition of Liberia's independence. Even the hesitant United States wavered under pressure from Ralston and eventually recognized the sovereignty of its stepchild by signing a treaty agreement that still shapes the contentious relationship of power, domination, political development, and dependence between the two nations.

Ralston further negotiated treaties that criminalized the slave trade and secured commercial agreements relevant to Liberia's economic development. On May 21, 1862, in London in a paper read before the Society for the Encouragement of Arts, Manufactures, and Commerce entitled "On the Republic of Liberia, Its Products and Resources," Ralston outlined Liberia's economic viability by marketing the nation's agricultural and manufactured products.[63] The editor of the *Merchants' Magazine and Commercial Review* stated that the "commercial importance to the United States of a close friendship with Liberia cannot be over-estimated." Referring to how Liberian commodities factored into European trade, the editor noted that "even the trifling article of ground nuts has become an important object of commerce for France, and it will doubtless henceforth prove very valuable to England for the manufacture of soap and also for oil for burning and for lubricating machinery." Ralston anticipated that America would soon "reap a portion of the great harvest which is already ripe in Africa to those who seek it. We know of no good reason why she should not reach forth her hand and pluck the rich and good fruit there awaiting her."[64]

The border area remained the one troublesome area that demanded even more careful diplomatic resolution. Liberia remained under the gaze of the British and French governments. The British and the French went about their piecemeal absorption of Liberian territory in a few ways. Liberia's territorial claims were based on negotiations with indigenous chiefs; thus, Europeans tried to acquire Liberian territories by making their own treaties with the chiefs or by questioning the validity of Liberia's treaties. In 1886 Secretary of State E. J. Barclay wrote to an Americo-Liberian agent regarding contested territory between the French and Americo-Liberians. Barclay noted, "[There] is said to be a treaty concluded on the 4th February 1868, between France and the Chiefs of Besiby for the recognition of French sovereignty over that portion of our Republic, concerning which I need only repeat what you have observed in your above cited dispatch, viz: 'that these territories have formed a portion of the Republic of Liberia long before the date of the so-called treaty.'"[65] Although the French claimed rights to a segment of Liberian territory on the grounds of an 1868 treaty, Barclay maintained that "Liberia's claims predated those of the French."[66] In these diplomatic performances, maneuvering race across different temporalities sometimes functioned to level the playing field.

Visualizing Blackness in Liberia

If certain aspects of race required performance, then the nation certainly became a theater. Migrant Black people had based their sense of liberatory achievements on their formation of a community to carry out their civilizing and Christianizing missions and their abilities to return to Africa to build a nation. Liberia's social, legal, political, and economic spheres highlighted the state's efforts to assert its modernity as a qualification for treaty-worthiness and citizenship among other nations. These instances illuminated the ways in which white supremacy through the white gaze continued to affect ideas of Blackness via efforts to create and project Black nationhood within a modernist idiom that would gain respectability for the nation.

Indeed, the transnational drama would be diplomatically embedded in Liberian political culture through the performances that freedom and Blackness demanded. Beyond a literal "theater of freedom" where Liberia denoted Black freedom, the figurative use of the term "theater" also begs questions about associated performances. Liberia's cultural struggle to set the criteria for a modern, civilized Black identity affected how the state related to different migrant groups. Given the nature of Blackness, migrants were locked in a state of everyday dis-ease that seemingly collapsed space and stopped time. Black people's own internalization of the idea of their depravity created different performances. According to an American physician who toured the settlements in 1858, "One source of friction was the assumption of an air of superiority on the part of emigrants from Virginia." Migrants from Virginia who were mostly mulattoes drew cultural capital from their mixed-race origins. He further noted that some of the colonists "complained of caste and say that the Virginians are mostly too high-headed and are all the time claiming that they are the quality of Liberia."[67] Joseph Jenkins Roberts, who became the first president of Liberia, was one such migrant from Virginia; he was largely viewed as nearly white and parlayed his social status into economic and political prosperity. Conversely, "pure blacks," who often came from other states, were not viewed in the same way. On June 2, 1834, a Samson Caesar noted in a letter: "There have come a great many from North Carolina who are dregs in this place." Seasoned migrants like John Brown Russwurm noted that new migrants were refusing to earn their stay.[68] As they had between "saltwater" slaves and creoles on American plantations, conflicts again developed between established migrants and new arrivals.[69]

Beyond the different groups of migrants, Liberia's native population further magnified the need for performativity. Liberia as a didactic theater was designed to civilize natives and to teach African receptives to behave and act appropriately. In this quest, civilized migrants censored natives and recaptives. These cultivated efforts, designed to show them how to act, sharpened conceptions of the racial body of the nation-state. On this ground, the culture of the diaspora was granted far more prominence in the political rendering of Liberia's identity as a nation and, counterintuitively, so too were the behaviors of the natives, but in an inverse fashion. The willingness to denigrate African practices in the fashioning of the law and through civilizing practices revealed a disturbing readiness to replace one kind of exclusionary representation with another.

New efforts to visualize Liberia for the purposes of exploitation and accumulation became a counterpoint to the racist diplomatic rhetoric. The ACS circulated imagery such as daguerreotypes to create cultural ideas about Liberia. In 1853 Augustus Washington, a daguerreotypist, emigrated to Liberia. Deborah Willis in *Reflections in Black: A History of Black Photographers, 1840 to the Present* argues that Black photographers were concerned about the representation of Black people in popular visual culture in the United States. Consequently, their photographs and the Black subjects in them aimed to amend this damaging portrayal. Among the first images that Washington created were images of Liberia's first president, Joseph Jenkins Roberts. When Washington's images of Roberts were circulated in the United States, newspapers such as the *Public Ledger* complimented Roberts as representative of the advancement of the republic. As the article in the *Public Ledger* pointed out, "Science and Art are taking hold in long benighted Africa. The Liberian Republic is gradually and permanently spreading its powerful influence for good."[70] The *Public Ledger*'s reference to Liberia's science and art suggested that the image was received as suggestive of the rise to progress and Black people's capacity for civilization.

Washington circulated images of both Roberts and his wife. As Dahlia Scruggs observed, "Roberts' intense gaze beams out from under a slightly lowered brow and closed fists rest on his lap but do not entirely relax. First Lady Jane Roberts inhabits a more plaintive pose. A languid gaze is matched with sloping shoulders and slightly hunched back. Her hands, in lace gloves, rest on her lap while gently curled fingers cradle a fan. Both sitters posed in three-quarter view." The performance conveyed by the Liberian president and First Lady was not unlike that in portraits of other leaders. However, with the discourse around race, their "marshaled pose, dress and countenance to convey identity, construct self according to bourgeois criteria" would be interpreted through a different set of lenses.[71] By pointing to Black migrants in Liberia partaking in various acts, images served to invert the minstrel performance and racist caricature that had defined life in the United States and aimed to parody the aesthetic of southern plantations. As Penelope Byrde observes, "By presenting themselves as respectable middle-class subjects, the Robertses refuted negative stereotypes that pervaded the portrayal of African Americans in nineteenth-century visual culture."[72]

The presentation of Roberts, his dress, and his home was burdened with performing not only Roberts's status but also that of the republic. As noted by some Liberian emigrants in Bell Wiley's *Slaves No More: Letters from Liberia, 1833–1869*, "for official functions, top hats and tails were de rigueur, no matter that they were hardly appropriate in ninety-degree weather with an equally high humidity."[73] Such adornments functioned to highlight the level of civilization that Black migrants had achieved in Liberia by serving to distinguish the elites from the lower class in Liberian society. For new Black migrants in Liberia who were stunned by what they regarded as some natives' lack of civilization, evidenced through little to no dress, the minimal clothing and possessions of even the most recently arrived deprived Black migrants separated them from those who were perceived to be the heathen uncivilized indigenes. For the indigenes, clothing also marked Black migrants. Indigenes often viewed the clothes and performances of the Black migrants as a reflection of whiteness. Indigenes viewed whiteness as related to cultural performances such as clothing, writing, and religion as opposed to color. Given the social, cultural, and material meanings associated with civilization, clothes functioned as a significant symbol of social difference. Following the circulation of the image, African Americans coveted the chance to have their portrait taken without racist bias.

In Edward Clay's series *Life in Philadelphia*, which offered an image of Black people through wood engravings, he highlighted the bourgeois dress and manners to deride Blacks' ambitions in order to show an inability to overcome the trappings of racial difference, which had rendered them socially inferior to whites. The presence of the Liberia "presidential mansion" in the image aimed to show Black people's efforts to parody and occupy roles and take on performances characteristically associated with whites. Like the emergence of Liberia across the Atlantic, holding those two views together depended upon a level of discord concerning the alleged depraved position of Black people in the United States and the sophistication and ceremony of the undertakings represented in order to convey how Black people could achieve upward mobility in Liberia. Given the markings of race that were trapping and trailing them, many believed that "their thoughts [were] someone else's opinions, their lives a mimicry, their passions, a quotation."[74] In his work *The Negro Family in the United States* (1966), E. Franklin

Frazier suggested that Black people, bereft of culture, attempted to escape the animal-like trappings to which they were reduced in slavery through a kind of slavish copying of white bourgeois habits.[75] Zora Neale Hurston also pointed out that "the Negro's universal tendency towards mimicry is not so much a thing in itself as an evidence of something that permeates his entire self."[76] However, Hurston viewed Black people's inclination toward mimicry as being significant to their negotiation of white supremacy.

Liberians had an opportunity to perform an image in the Chicago World's Fair in 1893. The Liberian display at the fair highlighted the advances of the Liberian nation and announced a shift that projected its posture as it advanced toward the turn of the century. The display created an understanding of the migrants' association with the natives, who were present through their ethnology and objects. The display, even if it did not always enact it, marked migrants' desire to be contrary to natives. It aimed to depict not only the progress that had been made in civilizing the natives through the introduction of agricultural production but also the migrants' advancement relative to the natives' primitivism. The visual mosaic of Monrovia oriented people toward the kinds of products and iconography that projected the vistas and architecture of Monrovia in contrast to the hinterlands and represented the iconographies of capitalism and Christianity as opposed to primitivism. Liberians displayed natives and architecturally complex buildings as testaments of their advancements. From the periphery, the city looked civilized and modern. Many of the exhibitions complicated accounts of migrants' interactions with the natives represented in our broader social discourse. As they staged ideas of Blackness alongside their views of indigenes, Black migrants projected meanings of race from the vantage point of the Liberian nation-building project.[77]

Conclusion

Liberia as an idea and a place became a theater in which the performance of race was carried out. Given the significance of the racialized body in modern political thought, Black migration to Liberia and the republic's diplomatic efforts open up new avenues to consider the multifaceted ways in which the Black body can be read into and through. It also invites us to consider what spaces outside the traditional venues might be called a theater. On the one hand, the study of race, theater, and performance allows for historical inquiry into the ways in which Blackness has been represented onstage and how theatrical performances provided physical and imaginative venues for the negotiation of ideas of race. On the other hand, performance and theater move such negotiations outside of the physical theater itself to posit the wider society as a space in which race is embodied, practiced, performed, and negotiated. The use of the concepts of performance and theater proffers a nuanced and layered approach to the historical study of race and race-making. Liberia might have been deemed politically fruitless, but it was nonetheless enlivening to observe. Liberia's precarious place among the family of nations moved diplomatic deliberations into peculiar global spaces and areas in which race was negotiated and performed. By implicating a wider array of communities and involving particular kinds of performances from Black people, recognition of Black nationalities further highlighted the vagaries of Black internationalism in the nineteenth century.

Given the circumstances under which Liberia came into being, its diplomacy presented a paradox. Quotidian performances, diplomatic dialogues, and other kinds of mundane negotiations occurring in the public realm created circumstances where the ACS, Black migrants, missionaries, and the nation became both part of the spectacle and spectators. In significant ways, spectatorship proved to be agential and reciprocal rather than passive. From Roberts to Ralston to Douglass, white abolitionists, colonizationists, Black abolitionists, Black nationalists, diplomats, and migrants in Liberia all created the interplay of performances that framed the issue of Blackness, Black freedom, and Liberia's sovereignty as a Black republic. During these transformed theatrical moments, Black people of different genders, ages, ethnicities, nationalities, races, and classes constructed and inhabited certain kinds of subject positions; as a consequence, their acts and performances were able to negotiate, influence, and augment the ideas and experience of freedom to varying degrees. Though the agendas of these various actors might have varied widely, many reinforced "ready-made categories" of power and domination that were grounded in nineteenth-century notions of race that newly influenced freedom.[78]

NOTES

1. State Convention of the Colored Citizens of Ohio (Columbus, Ohio, 1851), "Minutes of the State Convention of the Colored Citizens of Ohio, Convened at Columbus, Jan. 15th, 16th, 17th and 18, 1851," Colored Conventions Project Digital Records, https://omeka.coloredconventions.org/items/show/249.

2. Manisha Sinha, *The Slave's Cause: A History of Abolition* (New Haven, Conn.: Yale University Press, 2016).

3. C. Riley Snorton in his recent book pointed out how male fugitives had a ten-

dency to disguise themselves in women's clothing, while women often "dressed in the garb of men" (*Black on Both Sides: A Racial History of Trans Identity* [Minneapolis: University of Minnesota Press, 2017], 57).

4. See George Hendrick and Willene Hendrick, eds., *Fleeing for Freedom: Stories of the Underground Railroad* (Chicago: Ivan R. Dee, 2004).

5. Barbara McCaskill, *Love, Liberation, and Escaping Slavery: William and Ellen Craft in Cultural Memory* (Athens: University of Georgia Press, 2015); McCaskill, "Multiple Oppressions, Multiple Consciousness, and the Spirit of Harriet Tubman in Sapphire's *Push*," in *Sapphire's Literary Breakthrough: Feminist Pedagogies, Erotic Literacies, Environmental Justice Perspectives*, ed. Elizabeth McNeil, Neal Lester, DoVeanna Fulton Minor, and Lynette Myles (New York: Palgrave Macmillan, 2012), 47–66.

6. Harriet A. Jacobs, *Incidents in the Life of a Slave Girl: Written by Herself, 1813–1897*, ed. L. Maria Child (London: Hodson and Son, 1862).

7. Saidiya V. Hartman, *Scenes of Subjection: Terror, Slavery, and Self-Making in Nineteenth-Century America* (New York: Oxford University Press, 1997), 102.

8. Anita Patterson, review of *Scenes of Subjection: Terror, Slavery, and Self-Making in Nineteenth-Century America*, *African American Review* 33, no. 4 (1999): 684.

9. Lauren Heintz, "Fugitive Performance: Negotiating Biopower and the Law in U.S. Chattel Slavery," *American Quarterly* 71, no. 3 (September 2019): 675–95.

10. William Shakespeare, *As You Like It*, ed. Horace Howard Furness (New York: Dover Publications, 1963).

11. Clifford Geertz, *Negara: The Theatre State in Nineteenth-Century Bali* (Princeton, N.J.: Princeton University Press, 1980).

12. Julie Zimmermann Holt in Matthew Wills, "The Mysterious Pre-Columbian Settlement of Cahokia," https://daily.jstor.org/the-mysterious-pre-columbian-settlement-of-cahokia/.

13. Michel Foucault, *The History of Sexuality*, 3 vols. (New York: Pantheon Books, 1978).

14. Achille Mbembe, "Necropolitics," trans. Libby Meintjes, *Public Culture* 15, no. 1 (2003): 21.

15. Ann Laura Stoler, *Race and the Education of Desire: Foucault's "History of Sexuality" and the Colonial Order of Things* (Durham, N.C.: Duke University Press, 1995).

16. Beverly C. Tomek, *Colonization and Its Discontents: Emancipation, Emigration, and Antislavery in Antebellum Pennsylvania* (New York: New York University Press, 2011), 6.

17. Douglas R. Egerton, "'Its Origin Is Not a Little Curious': A New Look at the American Colonization Society," *Journal of the Early Republic* 5, no. 4 (1985): 463–80; Eric Burin, *Slavery and the Peculiar Solution: A History of the American Colonization Society* (Gainesville: University Press of Florida, 2005).

18. Burin, *Slavery and the Peculiar Solution*, 16.

19. Tom W. Shick, *Behold the Promised Land: A History of Afro-American Settler Society in Nineteenth-Century Liberia* (Baltimore, Md.: Johns Hopkins University

Press, 1980); Marie Tyler-McGraw, *An African Republic: Black & White Virginians in the Making of Liberia* (Chapel Hill: University of North Carolina Press, 2007).

20. Nicholas Guyatt, *Bind Us Apart: How Enlightened Americans Invented Racial Segregation* (New York: Basic Books, 2016), 4.

21. Ibid., 140.

22. Robert M. Entman and Andrew Rojecki, *The Black Image in the White Mind: Media and Race in America* (Chicago: University of Chicago Press, 2000), 147.

23. *African Repository* 29 (1853): 93. The title of the journal was shortened in 1850.

24. Claude Andrew Clegg, *The Price of Liberty: African Americans and the Making of Liberia* (Chapel Hill: University of North Carolina Press, 2004); Kenneth C. Barnes, *Journey of Hope: The Back-to-Africa Movement in Arkansas in the Late 1800s* (Chapel Hill: University of North Carolina Press, 2004).

25. *African Repository and Colonial Journal* 50 (1874): 141.

26. Ibid.

27. "The Scheme of Colonization—Interview between the President and a Committee of Colored Men—Remarks of the President, Washington, August 14th," recorded in the *Christian Recorder*, August 23, 1862.

28. Ibid.

29. Ibid.

30. "Address on Colonization to a Deputation of Negroes," August 14, 1862, in *Collected Works of Abraham Lincoln*, 5:371.

31. State Convention "Minutes of the State Convention."

32. Harriet Beecher Stowe, *Uncle Tom's Cabin* (Boston: Charles E. Brown & Co., 1852).

33. Ibid., 521.

34. Ibid., 319.

35. Jason Richards, "Imitation Nation: Blackface Minstrelsy and the Making of African American Selfhood in *Uncle Tom's Cabin*," *NOVEL: A Forum on Fiction*, special issue, "Postcolonial Disjunctions," 39, no. 2 (2006): 204–20.

36. Arthur Riss, "Racial Essentialism and Family Values in *Uncle Tom's Cabin*," *American Quarterly* 46, no. 4 (1994): 513–44.

37. Stowe, *Uncle Tom's Cabin*, 310.

38. Ibid.

39. John Frick, *"Uncle Tom's Cabin" on the American Stage and Screen* (New York: Palgrave Macmillan, 2012), 29–70.

40. Celso Castilho, *Slave Emancipation and Transformations in Brazilian Political Citizenship* (Pittsburgh: University of Pittsburgh Press, 2016).

41. Robert S. Levine, *Martin Delany, Frederick Douglass, and the Politics of Representative Identity* (Chapel Hill: University of North Carolina Press, 1997).

42. Frederick Douglass, *North Star*, October 27, 1848, quoted in Eric Lott, "'The Seeming Counterfeit': Racial Politics and Early Blackface Minstrelsy," *American Quarterly* 43, no. 2 (1991): 223–54.

43. Martin Delany, *Blake, or the Huts of America: A Corrected Edition* (Cambridge, Mass.: Harvard University Press, 2017).
44. Jeffory Clymer, "Martin Delany's Blake and the Transnational Politics of Property," *American Literary History* 15, no. 4 (2003): 709–31.
45. United States Congressional Serial Set, vol. 442, doc. no. 162, p. 7.
46. *American Journal of International Law* 4, no. 3, supplement (1910): 214.
47. *African Repository and Colonial Journal* 31 (1845): 20.
48. Ibid.
49. Raymond Leslie Buell, *The Native Problem in Africa* (New York: Macmillan, 1928), 707.
50. Elwood D. Dunn, Amos J. Beyan, and Carl Patrick Burrowes. *Historical Dictionary of Liberia*, 2nd ed. (Lanham, Md.: Scarecrow Press, 2001), 84.
51. *African Repository and Colonial Journal* 31 (1845): 20.
52. *African Repository* 49 (1873): 190.
53. Hartman, *Scenes of Subjection*, 56–57.
54. See Eliga H. Gould, *Among the Powers of the Earth: The American Revolution and the Making of a New World Empire* (Cambridge, Mass.: Harvard University Press, 2012), 3.
55. Ibid., 1.
56. Charles H. Wesley, "The Struggle for the Recognition of Haiti and Liberia as Independent Republics," *Journal of Negro History* 2, no. 4 (1917): 369–83.
57. Saidiya Hartman, interview with Frank B. Wilderson III, "The Position of the Unthought," *Qui Parle* 13, no. 2 (2003): 185.
58. Richard Wright, *Native Son* (New York: Harper Perennial Modern Classics, 1993).
59. *Treaty of Friendship and Commerce between Her Majesty and the Republic of Liberia. Signed at London, November 1848. Presented to Both Houses of Parliament by Command and Her Majesty, 1850* (London: Harrison and Son), 4.
60. Ibid.
61. Teah Wulah, *Back to Africa: A Liberian Tragedy* (Bloomington, Ind.: Author House, 2009), 281.
62. *African Repository* 49 (1873): 190.
63. Gerard Ralston, "On the Republic of Liberia, Its Products and Resources" (1862), paper read before the Society for the Encouragement of Arts, Manufactures, and Commerce, May 21, 1862.
64. *Merchants' Magazine and Commercial Review*, 1853, 200.
65. E. J. Barclay to M. Leopold Carrance, December 29, 1886, box 1, LGA I, Holsoe Collection.
66. Ibid.
67. Bell Irvin Wiley, *Slaves No More: Letters from Liberia, 1833–1869* (Lexington: University Press of Kentucky, 1980), 6.
68. Ibid.

69. Ira Berlin, *The Making of African America: The Four Great Migrations* (New York: Viking, 2010), 8.

70. "Daguerre in Africa," *Public Ledger*, May 13, 1854.

71. Dahlia Scruggs, "'Photographs to Answer Our Purposes': Representations of the Liberian Landscape in Colonization Print Culture," in *Early African American Print Culture*, ed. Lara Langer Cohen and Jordan Alexander Stein (Philadelphia: University of Pennsylvania Press, 2012).

72. Penelope Byrde, *Nineteenth Century Fashion* (London: B. T. Batsford Limited, 1992), 55.

73. Wiley, *Slaves No More*, 6.

74. Oscar Wilde quoted in Clemmont E. Vontress, "The Negro Personality Reconsidered," *Journal of Negro Education* 35, no. 3 (1966): 210–17.

75. See E. Franklin Frazier, *The Negro Family in the United States* (Chicago: Phoenix Books, 1966).

76. Zora Neale Hurston, "Characteristics of Negro Expression," in *Negro: An Anthology*, 1969, 39–61.

77. Caree Banton, *More Auspicious Shores: Barbadian Migration to Liberia, Blackness and the Making of an African Republic* (New York: Cambridge University Press, 2019), 278.

78. Marlene Daut, *Tropics of Haiti: Race and the Literary History of the Haitian Revolution in the Atlantic World, 1789–1865* (Liverpool: University of Liverpool Press, 2015).

CHAPTER 6

The Making of a Pan-Africanist
George Henry Jackson and the Lukunga Mission in the Congo Free State

MARCUS BRUCE

> In those somber forests of his strivings his own soul rose before him, and he saw himself,—darkly as through a veil; and yet he saw in himself some faint revelation of his power, of his mission. He began to have a dim feeling that, to attain his place in the world, he must be himself, and not another.
>
> —W. E. B. DU BOIS, *The Souls of Black Folk*

> Do you now live so that you are conscious of yourself as an individual; that in each of your relations in which you come into touch with the outside world, you are conscious of yourself, and that at the same time you are related to yourself as an individual? Even in these relations which we men so beautifully style the most intimate of all, do you remember that you have a still more intimate relation, namely, that in which you as an individual are related to yourself before God?
>
> —SØREN KIERKEGAARD, *Purity of Heart Is to Will One Thing*

In 1893 George Henry Jackson (1863–1943), a thirty-year-old African American Baptist minister and doctor, set out for Africa to work as a medical missionary for the American Baptist Missionary Union (ABMU) to the Lukunga Mission in the Congo Free State. A member of the wave of college and university students who set themselves the mission "to evangelize the world in this generation," the Reverend Doctor Jackson sought to fulfill a pledge he had made as a newly converted twenty-one-year-old man who believed that "some responsibility was mine" in both the redemption of Africa and conversion of the world.[1] Leaving his wife and two small children behind in London, Jackson, along with his brother, Stephen, sailed first for Belgium and then along the coast of France and Africa until they reached the Congo. Upon his arrival in Africa, Jackson worked alongside other African American, Anglo-American, and British missionaries at the Lukunga Mission, evangelized among the Congolese people, created schools and churches, and provided medical care and surgery for the Congolese people and his fellow missionaries. Jackson also supplemented his income in the Congo by accepting a salaried position as a doctor and surgeon for the Congo Free State at the Lukunga Station, a posting that gave him an unchecked and unobstructed view of the daily administration, inner workings, and abuses of King Leopold II's colonial government. Jackson arrived in the Congo just as the exploitation, abuses, and violence of Leopold's colonial government, becoming more widespread, gained international exposure. The African American journalist George Washington Williams's "Open Letter to His Serene Majesty Leopold II, King of the Belgians and Sovereign of the Independent State of Congo" of 1890 ignited what scholar Adam Hochschild has called one of the first human rights campaigns.[2]

Over the course of an eighteen-month period before his agonized decision to leave the mission field, Jackson documented his Congo work in a private journal and monthly correspondence with the ABMU. He recorded his struggle to define the nature of his responsibility to his family, his institutional sponsors, the ABMU, the Congolese people, the local colonial government, and himself. Jackson's writings—his recently discovered Congo journal, correspondence, articles written for the *Baptist Missionary Magazine* and the *Yale Medical Journal*, and documented comments on the Congo—offer a new historical perspective on one African American living and working in King Leopold's Congo. In the case of African Americans, the missionary or messianic destiny was to advance the enlightenment of Africa and ultimately the elevation of all humanity. They believed that they were descendants of "the woeful nation, Ethiopia, whose rising on mighty wings was foretold in Scripture."[3] Many African American missionaries, an estimated total of 116 by one scholarly account, set out for Africa between 1877 and 1900, "68 in Liberia, 20 in the Congo, 13 in Sierra Leone, 6 in South Africa, 3 in Nigeria, 3 in Mozambique, and 1 each in Cameroons, Angola and Rhodesia."[4]

Jackson was neither the first person of African descent nor the first African American to work at the ABMU's Lukunga Mission, a historic mission site initially created in honor of the pioneering medical missionary David Livingston, the famed Scottish missionary, physician, and explorer. When

Jackson arrived in the Congo, there was already a small community of African American women, members of the women's mission society and graduates of Spelman College, a historically Black institution of higher learning for African American women, working as teachers and missionaries in Lukunga. Clara Howard (1866–1935) and Nora Gordon (1866–1901) were delighted by the arrival of Jackson, who served as their advocate in the acquisition of funds necessary for building a school for their Congolese students, provided them with the sanitary housing in which they could live, and, in the case of Howard, used his status with the colonial government to facilitate her adoption of a Congolese child. While there have been a number of historical, biographical, and autobiographical accounts of American and African American missionaries working in the Congo, Jackson's writings offer the unusual perspective of one missionary's struggle to define the nature and extent of his responsibility, what Michel Foucault has described as the cultivation and formation of the self, in relation to Africa in his written accounts.[5]

In "Self Writing," Foucault argues that individuals can constitute themselves as selves, subjects, and souls through writing. The writing of a journal and even letter writing can be used as "techniques" by which an individual can record, review, chart, and draw strength from their own practices and exercises of the self for their own spiritual progress and development. Written accounts can then become an individual's means of cultivating and sustaining a "conscience" and a sense of responsibility.[6] Using excerpts and materials from Jackson's previously unpublished private journal, correspondence, and published articles, this essay will examine how Jackson used written documents to "write the self," that is, cultivate, examine, and constitute a conscience, by (1) recording the techniques and strategies he used to sustain himself (reading, exercising, writing, learning a new language, praying and singing with other missionaries, conducting scientific research, and building houses for fellow missionaries in the Congo); (2) struggling to reconcile what he had been told to expect with what he actually experienced; (3) and taking stock of and giving an account of his own conscience and sense of responsibility in the disorienting, violent, and dehumanizing context of King Leopold's Congo Free State. The texts and the content of Jackson's recorded memories of the Congo offer us a rare glimpse of the complex interior life of one person of African descent, but they also demonstrate the use of writing in "constituting a certain way of manifesting oneself to oneself and to others." Jackson's Congo writings, in the words of Foucault, offer us "a history of the cultivation of self."[7]

"Some Responsibility Was Mine"

Long before Jackson had arrived in Africa, he had declared, in one written account after another, the connection between his personal destiny and mission work in Africa. Born on February 28, 1863, in Natick, Massachusetts, where one of colonial America's first missionaries, John Eliot, had met with great success evangelizing among Native Americans, or "praying Indians," Jackson came into the world one month after the Emancipation Proclamation. He represented what Abraham Lincoln would call later that same year "a new birth of freedom." Jackson embodied a new and yet to be defined freedom, and like so many other African Americans in the years that followed the Emancipation Proclamation, he would spend the remainder of his life exploring, practicing, and defining precisely what that freedom meant. The eldest son born to James Jackson, an African American tailor who would later become a Civil War veteran, and Mary Avilda Roberts Jackson, of Native American and Welsh descent, Jackson was a tall, light-skinned young man with an athletic build who distinguished himself as one of the first colored American students to graduate with distinction from Natick High School.

Mindful of the auspicious date upon which their son had been born, Jackson's parents employed a local phrenologist to read his skull and predict his future. The result was a prediction that their son would be a person of some importance, a governor in their state's administration. Jackson would later write that these "signs" of his specialness would make his mother "indefatigable" in her efforts to make sure that he became "something." Mary Avilda would be present on the night Jackson received his call or vocation to pursue missionary work in Africa. The occasion offers some insight into his eventual decision to become a missionary.

In an essay written for his application to become a missionary for the ABMU, Jackson recalls the specific occasion, in the presence of his mother, when he received the conviction that he was being called to the mission field. "I felt called to the work," Jackson wrote, "while reading Matthew 26 one evening to my mother. The needs of the field also made me feel that some responsibility was mine in the conversion of the world."[8] The brief account marks the birthplace of Jackson's conviction that some responsibility was his in the conversion and salvation of Africa and the world, yet the specific means for achieving these tasks came from a number of different sources, sources that reveal the discursive practices that shaped Jackson's unique and distinctive practice of the self.

Prior to his solemn pledge before his mother to become a missionary, Jackson records that in 1881 he had been "convicted" of his own personal need for salvation while attending Sunday evening services at the Boston YMCA led by Reverend Deming, an evangelical who transformed the YMCA's brand of muscular Christianity into an evangelical mission. Yet it was not until Jackson's conversion and baptism on March 2, 1884, by the local minister at the First Baptist Church of Natick, Reverend F. P. Sutherland, that the twenty-one-year-old Jackson began to see possibilities for his own life. Sutherland, a recent graduate of Hamilton Theological Seminary, was preparing to become a medical missionary to Burma, and through his influence Jackson began to see a way to give voice and expression to his ambition.[9]

The year 1884 marked another significant event that would have a direct impact not only on Jackson's life and vocation but also on the continent of Africa and the entire world. Just eight months after Jackson's conversion to Christianity and call to missionary work, fifteen European nations with colonial holdings in Africa gathered at the West African Conference at Berlin in November 1884 to negotiate and formalize the division of Africa into colonial possessions, leaving the bulk of central Africa, from the Congo basin to the Tigre River, to the Belgian king Leopold II's International African Association. The association, created at the Brussels Geographic Conference of 1876, created the Congo Free State, an imperial and economic mad scramble for African resources initially disguised as an internationally neutral, philanthropic, benevolent, and religious endeavor with the sole charge of civilizing and Christianizing the people of the Congo. Little more than five years after the Berlin conference ended in February 1885, King Leopold's promise that the Congo Free State would be a neutral zone free of trade, slavery, and alcohol was exposed as a sham by George Washington Williams's famous open letter denouncing King Leopold's duplicity, violence against the Congolese people, and exploitation of their land and natural resources. Was Jackson aware of this aspect of the Congo before he went? Did he read Williams's letter? How much Jackson knew of this history remains a question.[10]

Over the course of the next nine years, following his conversion and pledge to become a missionary, Jackson prepared himself to work as a medical missionary in the Congo, attending Hamilton Theological Seminary from 1884 to 1887; pastoring Immanuel Baptist Church, an African American church in New Haven, Connecticut, from 1887 to 1892; attending and receiving degrees from both Yale Divinity School and Yale Medical School from 1889 to 1892; and honing and practicing his skills as a home missionary in the state of Connecticut by creating new churches in Stamford, Norwalk, Bridgeport, Milford, Ansonia, Hartford, New London, and Putnam. Each of these churches would support Jackson both financially and spiritually in his commitment to missionary work in Africa. The written accounts of this period reveal Jackson's tenacious and single-minded commitment to fulfilling his pledge and achieving his stated goal of missionary work in Africa. Two documented examples are illuminating.

Jackson frequently declared his commitment to missionary work in Africa. In 1886, while a student at Hamilton Theological Seminary, in training to become an ordained minister, Jackson was selected as a student leader to attend the seventh annual convention of the American Inter-Seminary Missionary Alliance in Oberlin, Ohio, an interdenominational gathering of professors, missionaries, and seminary students committed to missionary work throughout the world. In the discussion following an address entitled "Missions in Africa," Jackson is recorded as publicly declaring that "he looked forward with pleasure to the time when he should enter the field. The climate of Africa is not so unhealthy as it is reported to be. He would rather give five years of his life in Africa and see one soul converted than give fifty years in America." Four years later, in a letter written on November 22, 1889, Jackson, now a pastor at Immanuel Baptist Church and an 1889 alumni of Yale Divinity School, recorded his reason and purpose for his further study at Yale. "Last October," he wrote, "I entered the Yale Medical School and am now pursuing the full medical course in connection with my pastoral work and practice of medicine ... in Africa."[11] Again, Jackson had affirmed his commitment to missionary work in Africa.

Jackson's ambition and plans to do missionary work in Africa were also well known among the clergy in New Haven. In a letter of recommendation supporting Jackson's application to the ABMU, one clergyman remarked that the conviction with which the vocation to missionary work in Africa had overtaken him surprised even Jackson. Jackson's zeal for missionary work in Africa was so pronounced and highly regarded that it led the historically Black college Shaw University in 1892 to award him an honorary degree before he had even set foot in Africa. More importantly, Jackson's pledge and commitment to missionary work in Africa gave him a sense of mission, direction, and destination for his life that also provided him with standing in the world, training to develop his considerable talents, and a measure for determining the extent and degree of his achievement. He would, in his own words, claim and fulfill his responsibility in the "conversion of the world." The challenge he would face in the mission field, something he anticipated and wrote about, would be to determine the form that commitment and responsibility should take.

In addition to his pledge to work as a medical missionary in Africa, Jackson took on two additional responsibilities in his life. In 1888 Jackson married Grace Lillie, a young Anglo-American woman he had met in rural New York while studying at Hamilton Theological Seminary. Grace joined him in New Haven and assisted Jackson in his duties as pastor of the active and growing congregation of Immanuel Baptist Church. Within three years they had their first child, Donald Fancher, and just a few months before the family's departure for England, they welcomed a second child, Dorothy. While Jackson worked in Africa, he settled his family in a house in London. Yet their well-being and financial needs and his responsibilities as a husband and father would remain matters of ongoing concern frequently referenced in his Congo writings.

At every stage of his career, Jackson embraced a new set of discursive practices that expanded and defined his conception of self and what he could and might accomplish in the larger world: the muscular Christianity of the Boston YMCA, the missionary zeal and goal of the Inter-Seminary Alliance, the Yale University tradition of sending educated missionaries throughout the world, and the African American religious ideal of redeeming Africa. Through his embrace and adoption of each new form of religious discourse and principles, Jackson appeared to be searching for the one that would allow him to better define his sense of responsibilities. Yet what is clear is that each new religious discourse with its accompanying set of discursive practices gave him a vision of himself beyond the confines and limitations of American discourses on race, especially those regarding African Americans and what they were capable of doing and achieving. From this collection of principles and practices regarding the self and conscience, Jackson forged a new conception and practice of the self specifically designed to articulate his evolving sense of responsibility. The Congo would play a large role in this process.

Prior to his arrival in Africa, precisely what his commitment and responsibility might mean, entail, or cost him remained unclear and, beyond his desire to save souls, a mystery in many of the accounts that Jackson left behind. In this respect, Jackson was not unlike many other young men of his generation who envisioned and committed themselves to a task that they neither fully understood nor were equipped or even capable of achieving. What did it mean to "save" Africa? What did it mean to be responsible for "the conversion of the world"? Africa, at best, for Jackson and so many others, was an idea, a mission, and a destination without real content or substance, more a reflection of their own ideas, aspirations, hopes, and dreams. This was certainly the case with Jackson, who would come to contrast American misconceptions about Africa with its harsh and "deadly" realities. In his Congo writings, Jackson would "write the self," that is, bear witness to what he said and did in the Congo and the manner in which he charted and corrected his developing sense of responsibility, duty, and conscience.

Writing the Self

In "Self Writing," an essay that formed a portion of a much larger work entitled *The Hermeneutics of the Subject*, Foucault uses the practice of writing to trace the history of subjectivity, the formation of the self, and the arts of oneself in the Hellenistic, Roman, and early Christian cultures. Foucault identifies two forms of writing, hupomnemata and correspondence, among others, that played important roles in different cultures in the definition and cultivation of the self. Hupomnemata were "account books, public registers, or individual notebooks serving as memory aids" and "constituted a material record of things read, heard, or thought thus offering them up as a kind of accumulated treasure for subsequent rereading and meditation." Correspondence, or letter writing between individuals, was a second form of writing the self that revealed not only a variety of practices of the self—how to train and discipline oneself, a regime for self-formation, and lessons learned—but also, most important of all, the opportunity and occasion "to show oneself, to project oneself into view."[12]

Of Jackson's Congo writings—his private journal, correspondence with the ABMU, reports and articles written for the *Baptist Missionary Magazine*, and scholarly articles for the *Yale Medical Journal*—his private journal and correspondence clearly fall into these two forms of self writing. One can literally chart in these two forms of writing, between his application to the ABMU and his eventual resignation, the manner in which Jackson used writing to cultivate a sense of responsibility and self.

Jackson's Congo journal offers a rich example of hupomnemata, "an account of the self through an account of the day," and his daily life, ongoing work, and sojourn in the Congo. It forms and serves as the notes, details, statistics, and historical documentation for a history that has yet to be written. Yet its more immediate role for Jackson was to provide a record and an account of the manner in which he fulfilled his pledge and responsibility "to convert the world" by working in Lukunga, Congo, as a doctor, a teacher, a preacher, a fellow Christian, a husband, and a father. From the first entry of the journal on May 12, 1893, just as Jackson and his family were departing from Boston for England, until January 10, 1895, when he and his brother Stephen made their way back from the Congo, Jackson made over 156 entries of varying lengths and detail, recording his impressions, which ranged from his first sighting of Africa to the kinds of medical issues he addressed to the numbers of new Congolese converts, young people at his Sunday school meetings, and members of his choir.

The first entry in Jackson's Congo journal gives some clue of how he viewed his mission to the Congo. "At last," he muses, "the promised hour approaches for which I have prayed, worked and prepared ... our mission to shed abroad the light that has shined in our own hearts."[13] Africa and the Congo were not only the goal for which he had prepared but also the appointed or promised hour, not unlike that of Jesus in the Garden of Gethsemane, where Jackson's pledge and commitment would be tested.

Jackson recorded his first euphoric sighting of Africa and recalled the biblical reference to Ethiopia in Psalm 68:31, a favorite citation for both missionaries and African Americans seeking the redemption of Africa. Jackson's comments evoked his sense of the high calling and vocation to which he had pledged himself. "This afternoon late," he wrote, "for the first time my eyes beheld the dim and cloudlike outline of the African coast. I thanked God for the privilege ... a regenerated Ethiopia lifting up her hands unto thee."[14]

Jackson even transformed his first bout of fever into an occasion of character building, refining him for the work and commitment the Congo would require of him. "I staid for 8 days constantly burning but only the Lord by burning fever," he reasoned, "was refining my character, consuming the dross that I might present to him a living sacrifice, wholly acceptable unto God, a reasonable service."[15]

Jackson used his journal writing for more than noting his impressions, fears, and aspirations. Writing was also a regular exercise and form of documentation designed to note his progress toward the fulfillment of his pledge and his responsibilities as medical missionary in the Congo. On more occasions than one Jackson gives an account of how providing medical aid becomes an opportunity to speak of his faith. "I found a poor fellow nearly dead with consumption and though I told him he could not live many days when he had heard the gospel story his face brightened up." "Perhaps in glory I may see him again," Jackson prayed, "washed in the blood of the

Lamb." Jackson was eager to provide his patients with both spiritual guidance and medical care.

Jackson also took seriously his work among the young Congolese boys who attended his Sunday school meetings, choir rehearsals, and instruction in the French language. "Today has been great in many ways. I have been very busy indeed. Led the singing and choir, organized a Sunday school with 201 present and Preached at the evening service." He confessed, "I am very happy and glad to work."[16]

Still further, the Congo journal, along with Jackson's other Congo writings, offered something more: it also recorded the various "practices" of the self that Jackson used to sustain, maintain, and make progress toward an understanding of the nature of his responsibility and himself. Jackson's Congo writings offer readers an unusual opportunity to discover how one African American medical missionary used writing as a means to practice and realize a specific form of subjectivity, or self, that he defined as "responsible."

Jackson scrupulously documented his medical work in the Congo and considered each surgery and each medical examination an opportunity to evangelize among the Congolese people. He also recorded evangelizing and medical aid trips to villages within walking distance of the Lukunga Mission, the large numbers of Congolese people gathering to hear missionaries tell stories of Jesus, the mass conversions of villagers, and the gathering of young Congolese boys and men to attend his weekly Sunday school meeting, choir rehearsal, and classes in French. Jackson noted his efforts to set aside time to construct new buildings for the women missionaries in Lukunga, expand the existing structures to accommodate the mission's growth, and gather for fellowship meetings of prayer and song with the other missionaries.

Jackson's Congo journal also records a wide range of specific activities and exercises that Jackson used to care for his body, mental stability, and sense of self. In addition to his busy schedule working as a doctor, teacher, and evangelist, Jackson also found time to engage in athletic activities, read and reread his favorite novels, maintain regular correspondence with family and the ABMU, investigate blood diseases peculiar to the Congo through scientific experiments, and study the various dialects of the Congolese people. A firm believer that the body was the temple of God, Jackson exercised regularly, hunting, fishing, swimming, and playing tennis to maintain good health, resistance to the frequent bouts with fever peculiar to the Congo, and the sound body he believed necessary for a virtuous and Christian life.[17]

Jackson also read the religious and adventure novels of Charles Kingsley, most notably *Hypathia* and *Two Years Ago*. Kingsley was a Christian writer whose works Jackson found intellectually stimulating and sustaining during his time in the Congo. In addition to the correspondence he wrote to his wife and extended family, Jackson wrote over twenty letters to the ABMU, at a rate of one a month, giving a detailed account of the status and progress of the work at the Lukunga Station. With the aid of a microscope he had purchased before arriving in the Congo, Jackson conducted scientific research on the various bacteria that caused the fevers peculiar to the Congo. And, committed to speaking and preaching in the language of the Congolese people, Jackson, who spoke and read six languages—English, French, Spanish, Hebrew, Latin, and Arabic—began studying Kikongo and other indigenous languages. He also found time for photographing the African people, building mission outposts, collecting tribal weapons from the Congolese (which he later donated to the Yale Peabody Museum), and beginning work on a book about his experiences in the Congo. Jackson's consciously planned and developed regimen of physical, intellectual, and spiritual activity was a means of managing his health and anxiety, focusing his attention, and reinforcing his commitment to the mission work before him.[18]

For Jackson, "writing the self" was also a way to examine, interrogate, and give an accounting of his actions, decisions, and responsibilities. Jackson wrote frequently about the impact his extended mission in Africa was having on his wife, his children, and himself. Jackson used the pages of his Congo journal to express his feelings of loneliness and longing for his wife, Grace, and his fear that perhaps the prolonged separation might harm their marriage: "How very lonely I am tonight. I long so much to hear the dear voices of my loved ones. How long O Lord how long? Poor Grace how lonely she must feel."[19]

Jackson periodically agonized over how to effectively be a father and representative of masculinity to a son, his eldest child, Donald Fancher, who was so far away. The morning of his departure for Africa, Jackson recalled parting from his "blue-eyed boy" and worrying over his extended absence and the loss of "influence which I would exert toward shaping his character." Still later he expressed fondness for his children and prayed as a worried father that God would guide his son to "manhood."[20]

Finally, Jackson was equally concerned about the state of his spiritual life in the Congo. Periodically haunted by his own fears and disturbing dreams, worried about the poor and unsanitary living conditions in the Congo, unsettled by the occasional outbreak of violence and conflicts, more critically and medically aware of the prevalence of disease and death among both the Belgian soldiers and the Congolese people, and mindful of his own growing frustration regarding the management of the Lukunga Mission, Jackson began to realize that neither a well-planned regimen nor a prolonged stay in the Congo was advisable for missionaries. In his journal Jackson wrote openly of leaving the Congo: "Am heartily sick of the whole thing here. I am sure my spiritual life is shocked severely at the condition of things here and it will take a long time to regain what I have lost. I want to do his work and accomplish something in the little time that is left of life."[21] In his letters to the ABMU he expressed the same concern regarding the impact of the Congo on other missionaries and himself: "The missionaries generally do not like to seem to complain yet they live under circumstances very dangerous to life. Yes the Congo is costly but infinitely more to the missionaries than the brethren who at home give their hard earned dollars to support it."[22]

Jackson's written accounts of the impact of the Congo on himself, the other missionaries, the Congolese people, and the Belgian soldiers also served as the occasion for a new understanding of his responsibility and his mission. What, for Jackson, had been primarily a mission to provide medical care and the gospel to the Congolese people now became something more, a desire to share the reality and the truth of life in the Congo. In Jackson's letters to the ABMU he revealed a new understanding of himself, his responsibility, and his mission.

Cultivating a Conscience

"To write," argues Foucault, "is thus to 'show oneself,' to project oneself into view, to make one's own face appear in the other's presence."[23] For George Henry Jackson, writing was more than an exercise or a record of exercises used to practice and correct, or "right," the self. It was also a way to declare and reveal the self and the conscience he had been nurturing and developing since his conversion. Jackson's letters to the ABMU chronicle his distinctive practice of conscience, which led him to "the promised hour," the moment of revelation he had been anticipating since the initial night of his epiphany while reading Matthew 26, the account of Jesus's hour of crisis, decision, and conscience in the Garden of Gethsemane.

Over the course of the eighteen months Jackson spent in the Congo, he penned monthly letters to the ABMU's governing secretary, Samuel Duncan, giving periodic updates on the status and progress of the missionaries and an account of his own work. This too was a way of giving his impressions of the mission. Duncan had advised Jackson to write and provide information on the Lukunga Mission. Duncan specifically placed Jackson in charge of the African correspondence in a letter written before Jackson's departure: "I shall follow you with the deepest interest, and I trust that you will at all times communicate with me freely and fully, as having now the charge of African correspondence."[24] With diligence, professionalism, and insight, Jackson took this charge seriously, writing over twenty lengthy, detailed, and informative letters outlining the status of the mission, the health of the eight missionaries living and working at the station, their progress in evangelizing and providing medical care among the Congolese people, and the budgetary issues and constraints of the mission. Yet here too, as in his other Congo writings, Jackson's practice of the self is evident. The letters not only represent a fulfillment of the responsibility Duncan had laid upon Jackson's shoulders but also reveal numerous points of divergence between Jackson and the ABMU administration and the places where Jackson began to develop his own distinctive vision of the work that needed to be done in the Congo. These letters also represent a redefinition and a new clarity about his "responsibility" where the Congo and the mission field were concerned.

Upon his arrival at the Lukunga Mission, Jackson quickly surmised that the state of the mission and its management were not as they had been reported. Jackson's initial days at the mission were a startling revelation that left him wondering if the ABMU board knew the state of things at their primary mission station. Jackson's first alarm was the unsanitary conditions in which the missionaries, including Jackson as the mission doctor and his brother Stephen, were expected to live and work. "There are many things about Lukunga," Jackson confessed, "which I am sure the board ought to know." There was not suitable or sanitary housing for any of the missionaries working in the field. There were, Jackson continued, no adequate facilities for a doctor to work, and, as a consequence, "I am obliged to turn away people with cancers or tumors or gangrenous extremities which should be removed but there is no place in which to do it."[25]

Jackson grew more concerned as he discovered the manner in which mission funds were be dispensed, funds Jackson had helped to raise by speaking to African American churches that were eager to support his efforts to provide medical care and the gospel message for the redemption of Africa. A repeated refrain throughout Jackson's Congo writings, both the journal and the letters, is whether the ABMU, American churches, or the world at large actually knew and understood what was taking place in the Congo. Jackson's letters grew more urgent and frank in his description of the state of mission stations in the Congo: "I wish a representative of the Union could inspect the field for I believe that much money has been unwisely appropriated, and some needed things neglected." He offered his professional assessment of the mission: "In my own judgment no station on Congo or in the tropics on the west coast will make the health station that the board desires to have."[26]

Though the ABMU had been initially generous in the funds it provided Jackson for the care of his family, his outfitting for the Congo, his regular salary, and his medical work, it quickly became clear that the funds were insufficient to cover all of these needs or the incidentals that emerged in the unstable environment of the Congo. King Leopold II's colonial government was not averse to taxing the ABMU and its staff of missionaries for every conceivable item necessary for survival in the Congo, and this included not only the basics of food and materials for constructing housing but also the employment of local Congolese men on a regular basis for the transportation of materials and people. Remedying the problem required extra expenditures and reallocation of funds that needed the approval of both the ABMU board and the veteran missionary in the field, Theodore Hoste, with whom Jackson developed a strained and often volatile relationship. To provide the additional funds for building materials and the Congolese carriers to transport the items, Jackson took a part-time position working as a doctor and surgeon for the colonial government. The unusual position—the employment of an African American doctor and missionary by King Leopold's colonial government—afforded Jackson a view of the abuses, exploitation, and violence of Leopold's colonial government and would leave an indelible imprint on him. Yet the medical care Jackson was able to provide to weary, diseased, and disoriented colonial soldiers at colonial stations provided him with the additional funds necessary to increase the household budget of his wife in London and reimburse the ABMU for any extra cost that he had incurred in buying more building materials, purchasing medical supplies, or employing additional carriers. Yet Jackson's resourcefulness and independence seemed only to further exacerbate and increase the differences that existed in his relationship with the ABMU board and Hoste.

Jackson's strongly stated ideas and recommendations in the ABMU letters are important because they signal his recognition of the distinctive voice, views, and conscience he had been seeking and practicing. In a letter dated May 14, 1894, the same letter that carried his resignation, Jackson defended himself and his views of the Lukunga Mission against the charge that perhaps he had become "prejudiced" against the ABMU board's policy and the management style of the senior British missionary at the Lukunga Mission.

When the mission board questioned Jackson's experience, judgment, and professional opinion, he forcefully and articulately responded with a newfound confidence in his own sense of what he was witnessing in the Congo. Responding to the charge of prejudice, Jackson insisted, "If I have become prejudiced my mind has unconsciously become so because of what my *eyes* have *seen* and my *ears* have *heard*, not from a home office 10,000 miles away but right upon the very spot of which I speak."[27]

Much later in the same letter, Jackson argued that his strongly stated and worded position was a matter of conscience. "You mention," Jackson observes, "that younger missionaries should take the advice of those longer in the field.... That there are many things in my experience I have yet to learn I most heartily confess but *one* of them is that I must against every scruple and better judgment fall in, silently, with what I deem abuses."[28]

In another letter to the ABMU, Jackson offered a more pointed critique that marked the emergence of a new confidence in himself, his experience, and his judgment. Jackson argued that the mission board, rather than trusting in his judgment, had "tied his hands" and questioned his professional accounts of the state of affairs in the Congo. "It was the greatest disappointment," Jackson confessed, "in my life after nine hard years of patient training in theory and practice to find myself forced to return. It seemed to me that the board assumed that the missionaries which they had chosen after special preparation were incapable of exercising judgment in matters pertaining to their own work at Lukunga."[29]

In both the Congo journal and his correspondence with the ABMU Jackson agonized over whether he should remain in the Congo or officially resign his position as the medical missionary for the Lukunga Mission. After he had submitted his resignation to the ABMU he speculated over whether he might continue to work for the ABMU in some other capacity or work with another denominational group in the Congo or South Africa. Yet Jackson always returned to what was now a more clearly defined set of "responsibilities." On May 14, 1894, Jackson submitted his letter of resignation, at once a declaration of conscience and the unveiling of the self he had nurtured, cultivated, disciplined, and examined since the night of his epiphany in Natick. After listing the reasons that compelled him to resign—the lack of sufficient financial support from the mission board for his mission work, the ongoing conflict with both the ABMU and more senior British missionaries in the field, and the board's disregard for and lack of confidence in his professional judgment—the Reverend Doctor George Henry Jackson submitted his resignation as a missionary of the ABMU effective January 1,

1895.[30] This was the appointed time, the promised hour, and the revelation he had sought in trying to understand and know the nature and extent of his responsibility in the conversion of the world. With a clarity and sharpness that had been absent before, Jackson declared his conscience and, in doing so, revealed himself.

Jackson's Congo writings document the process by which he practiced care of the self and, more specifically, the cultivation of a conscience. In many respects, he had arrived at—or returned to—the place where he had begun on the night he had read Matthew 26 and discovered that "some responsibility was mine in the conversion of the world." For the nine years that followed his epiphany he had trained and prepared for Africa and the Congo with that sense of responsibility before him. Once in Africa he had practiced medicine, preached the gospel, and taught among the Congolese people in fulfillment of that pledge of responsibility. Now Jackson's written resignation and the agonized struggle that produced it revealed the self, the conscience, and the man he had become.

The Pan-Africanist

George Henry Jackson left the Lukunga Mission in the Congo Free State in January 1895. After rejoining his family in London, Jackson returned to the United States, where he worked for two years as a physician in New Haven, Connecticut, before accepting a position with President William McKinley's administration as the American consul to Cognac and La Rochelle, France, from 1897 to 1914. During these years Jackson represented the United States in every area of national, international, and business relations with France. He also gained a respected name and reputation among the prominent citizens of the busy port city of La Rochelle. And he nurtured the educational and athletic development of local youth and his son by creating a rugby club that brought together local businessmen, politicians, and the French and U.S. militaries in organized matches, which he hosted on a playing field financed with his own money. Jackson became an international businessman after his diplomatic service and remained in Paris until 1936, when he returned to the United States, this time settling in Los Angeles, California, where, in his retirement, he again began to pursue a ministry among young people and the incarcerated. Jackson died in 1943 in Los Angeles, yet he never lost sight of his belief that he had some responsibility for addressing the problems and troubles of the world.

Jackson also never forgot his time as a missionary in the Congo. The religious conscience he had discovered, nurtured, and declared in the Congo became the source of a political conscience that manifested itself in Pan-Africanism. Over twenty-five years after his resignation from his missionary work and departure from the Congo, George Henry Jackson was once again confronted with the challenge of deciding and defining his "responsibility" to Africa. Whereas his initial commitment had been based upon a religious vision of Africa and its needs, Jackson would discover the various ways in which his personal experiences and time in Africa informed how he viewed not only himself and other people of African descent but also, more importantly, Africa and its people.

In 1918 Jackson, while working as an international businessman in Paris, offered his assistance to W. E. B. Du Bois, one of the original participants in the First Pan-African Conference of 1900 and the organizer of three Pan-African Congresses. Jackson aided Du Bois in enlisting the interest and support of Senator Blaise Diagne, the first Black African elected to the French Chamber of Deputies and a prominent figure who was widely respected among Francophone politicians and intellectuals. Du Bois planned to hold the Pan-African Congress in Paris in February 1919 to coincide with the Paris Peace Conference at Versailles, and he was eager to win the support and endorsement of Diagne.

Jackson possessed the requisite linguistic and diplomatic skills for carrying out the challenge of inviting and persuading many of the French and African delegates, in particular Diagne, to attend the meeting. He proved particularly successful at helping French African and African American delegates to "understand" each other. In this respect Jackson's credentials were impeccable. He had not only lived and worked in Africa as a missionary and a doctor for over a year and a half but also worked in the U.S. diplomatic corps for sixteen years conducting complex negotiations between the U.S. and French governments, the U.S. military, and international businessmen in the cities of Cognac and La Rochelle.

More importantly, Jackson had now defined what he considered to be his responsibility and mission to Africa. As a young missionary and doctor in 1892 setting out for the Congo and eventually serving for eighteen months there, Jackson had been unsure of himself and how to navigate and express himself amid the shifting and competing demands and challenges of the Congo. In the Congo he had confronted himself, his commitments, and his own ambitious ideas about himself and his relationship with Africa. He had set out to redeem Africa and the world, and while he had failed at both tasks, he had discovered and learned how to save and value himself. Now, twenty-five years later, he knew his limitations, and, more importantly for the Pan-African Congress of 1919, he knew what he had been able to do and what he could and could not accomplish in Africa, specifically in the Congo. He was one of the few African Americans present and seated at the congress who had actually lived and worked in Africa and was acquainted with the more ambitious and boastful claims of African Americans who nurtured dreams of "redeeming" Africa.

Jackson's role as a Pan-Africanist was subtle, behind the scenes, and focused as always on the practical, all of which were a consequence of his brief time in the Congo. He would use his French skills to interpret and translate the disparate and often conflicting views of Africa espoused by delegates who represented many different parts of the African diaspora and now emerging and organizing the Pan-African world. Jackson would be among the delegates who would propose that African countries be provided with educational opportunities and resources. His proposal would be rooted again in what he had learned while creating schools for the Congolese people. He knew that the educational opportunities he proposed for African nations would also be the occasion, as they had been for him, for the members of the Pan-African Congress and African nations to discover and learn the real needs, concerns, and shared values of the wider African diaspora in England, France, Haiti, and the United States.

Jackson's most important contributions to the Pan-African Congress of 1919 and the subsequent congress of 1921 was what he had discovered about himself while living and working in the Congo. To each congress he brought something that many of the delegates, especially those from the United States, may not have clearly understood. His conception of Africa—and himself, for that matter—had been profoundly shaped by his time in the Congo. He had arrived with a particular set of assumptions and ideas and left the Congo with new ways of seeing and imagining himself and Africa. The challenge and the promise of Pan-Africanism, as far as George Henry Jackson was concerned, would be for the delegates of the Pan-African Congresses to see, imagine, and cultivate new ways for the world to see Africa and the African diaspora.

NOTES

1. George Henry Jackson, unpublished Congo journal and letters, courtesy John W. Jackson Family.
2. See Adam Hochschild, *King Leopold's Ghost: A Story of Greed, Terror, and Heroism in Colonial Africa* (New York: Pan Macmillan, 1998).

3. Wilson Jeremiah Moses, *The Wings of Ethiopia: Studies in African-American Life and Letters* (Ames: Iowa State University Press, 1990), 143–44.

4. Laurie Maffly-Kipp, *Setting Down the Sacred Past: African-American Race Histories* (Cambridge, Mass.: Belknap Press, 2010), 175.

5. Most notably in the work of George Washington Williams and William Sheppard. Several important explorations into this history include Sylvia Jacobs, *Black Americans and the Missionary Movement in Africa* (Westport, Conn.: Greenwood Press, 1982); George Henry Jackson, *The Medicinal Value of French Brandy* (Montreal: Thérien Frères, 1928); Sandy D. Martin, *Black Baptists and African Missions: The Origins of a Movement, 1880–1915* (Macon, Ga.: Mercer University Press, 1990); Edmund Merrian, *The American Baptist Missionary Union and Its Missions* (Boston: American Baptist Missionary Union, 1897).

6. Michel Foucault, "Self Writing," in *The Hermeneutics of the Subject: Lectures at the College de France, 1981–1982* (New York: Palgrave Macmillan, 2017). See also Foucault, *Ethics: Subjectivity and Truth*, vol. 1 of Essential Works of Foucault, 1954–1984 (New York: New Press, 1998); Foucault, *Technologies of the Self: A Seminar with Michel Foucault* (Amherst: University of Massachusetts Press, 1988), 5.

7. Foucault, "Self Writing," 213.

8. George Henry Jackson, application essay, Jackson, George Henry (1863–1943), 1893–1932, International Ministries—Missionary Correspondence, Group 1, Series 1, American Baptist Historical Society (ABHS), Mercer University Atlanta, Atlanta, Georgia.

9. Edmund Merrian, *The American Baptist Missionary Union and Its Missions* (Boston: American Baptist Missionary Union, 1897).

10. See George Washington Williams, "Open Letter to His Serene Majesty King Leopold II," in *Congo Love Song: African American Culture and the Crisis of the Colonial State*, ed. Ira Dwokan (Chapel Hill: University of North Carolina Press, 2017).

11. Alumni report, November 22, 1889, Yale University Manuscripts and Archives Digital Library.

12. Foucault, "Self Writing," 216.

13. Jackson, journal, May 12, 1893.

14. Ibid., August 20, 1893.

15. Ibid., October 16, 1893.

16. Ibid., July 15, 1893.

17. For more on this connection, see Clifford Putney, *Muscular Christianity: Manhood and Sports in Protestant America, 1880–1920* (Cambridge, Mass.: Harvard University Press, 2001).

18. Jackson, *Medicinal Value*.

19. Jackson, journal, August 25, 1894.

20. Ibid., August 4, 1893.

21. Ibid., August 28, 1894.

22. Ibid., October 3, 1893.

23. Foucault, "Self Writing," 5.
24. Samuel Duncan to George Henry Jackson, July 20, 1893, ABHS, Duncan, Sam Wayne (1940–), 1968–1979, International Ministries—Missionary Correspondence, Group 1, Series 1, ABHS, https://imageserver.library.yale.edu/digcoll:4350238/guest8b9a336748334987bbcd235720b09c92@yaleguest.edu/pwwFzJpy8lgJjBcIVFM-odrIeYw/1500.jpe?authroot=findit.library.yale.edu&parentfolder=digcoll:4350238&ip=172.101.16.29.
25. Jackson, journal, October 23, 1893.
26. Ibid.
27. George Henry Jackson to Samuel Duncan, May 14, 1894, ABHS, Jackson, George Henry (1863–1943), 1893–1932, International Ministries—Missionary Correspondence, Group 1, Series 1, ABHS.
28. Ibid.
29. George Henry Jackson to Henry Clay Mabie of the American Baptist Missionary Union, July 17, 1895.
30. Jackson to Duncan, May 14, 1894.

PART 3

Caribbean

CHAPTER 7

The British Emigration Scheme and the African American Emigration Movement to the Caribbean

DEXTER J. GABRIEL

In April 1840 two Black Baltimoreans, Nathaniel Peck and Thomas S. Price, returned to the city from a three-month tour of Trinidad and British Guiana. Their expedition to the English Caribbean had been "to ascertain the character of the climate, soil, natural production, and the political and social condition of the coloured inhabitants" and to further determine whether it was justifiable or warranted for the free Black population of Baltimore and Maryland to "emigrate tither." The two envoys turned their findings into a meticulous twenty-five-page pamphlet, painting a favorable picture of Guiana and Trinidad, where fertile land, labor, and social equality awaited African Americans and success could be attained "without regard to colour." Part travel narrative and part ethnographic study, Peck and Price's report utilized themes that spoke directly to a nineteenth-century free Black audience eager to find work and freedom beyond the national boundaries of America.[1]

In the late 1830s, planters in the British Caribbean were on a search for labor. Emancipation had lifted some eight hundred thousand men, women, and children from slavery in the Anglo-Caribbean in 1834, ending a two-century-old institution dependent on their involuntary servitude. Reformers and abolitionists maintained that freedom would arrive with little change to the agricultural production that sustained the colonial economies. The more ambitious minded claimed that output would increase. The substitution of "wages" for "the whip," the English nonconformist Josiah Conder wrote, would prove the superiority of free over enslaved labor, settling the question of what was then termed the "mighty experiment." But the transition to freedom was fraught with discontent. Formerly enslaved people balked at the newly instituted apprenticeship system, under which the majority of their labor remained under the control of plantation owners. Work stoppages, fugitivity, small-scale riots, and other acts of resistance disrupted production, and by 1838 the apprenticeship system had been abandoned and replaced with full emancipation.[2]

Planters in the less developed colonies of British Guiana and Trinidad especially complained of dire labor problems. In 1836 William Burnley, one of the largest sugar plantation owners in Trinidad and a bitter opponent of emancipation, argued before a parliamentary select committee that he "was under great alarm" as to the reliability of the then apprentices as cultivators. If the current labor issues continued, he warned that whites would eventually abandon the colonies, leaving the formerly enslaved to revert to subsistence farming and, worse, economic dependence on England's taxpayers. The only solution to avert impending ruin, Burnley maintained, was to import laborers from overseas markets. This was not a new strategy. Since emancipation in 1834, planters and colonial governments in Trinidad and Guiana had experimented with a mix of solutions to their labor problems: emigrants from more populous colonies; Africans liberated from slave ships by the British navy; and, briefly, indentured workers from South Asia. Burnley, however, argued that the most appealing laborers could be found on the North American mainland, among the free Black communities of the United States. African Americans, he contended, represented a perfect racial caste: a servile class of nonwhites who were also acculturated to Western society and industry.[3]

An American by birth, Burnley considered himself well versed in the social and political climate of his former country. Referencing the American Colonization Society, he told the select committee that whites in the United States were "very anxious at the present moment to get rid of their free coloured population" and "would be glad to see some foreign colony opened up" toward this end. Furthermore, he claimed that African Americans would be more than amenable to the colonies as "a sure asylum" where, as free laborers, they "could be comfortably located, and furnished with profitable employment." Burnley assured the committee that given proper inducements, "a very large number [of free Black people] would voluntarily emigrate." In what was perhaps an appeal to reform-minded members of the committee, he predicted that the option presented by the British Caribbean would spur greater manumission among slaveholders and further the cause of antislavery in America.[4] Burnley's plan was adopted by emigration officials in both Trinidad and Jamaica. Beginning in 1838, agents from those colonies embarked on a tour of the northeastern United States. Visiting cities with large free Black populations, they set about attracting laborers to emigrate to the Caribbean.

In the United States, the end of slavery in the British Caribbean had been closely monitored by free African Americans. Evidence of the success of emancipation permeated newspapers and pamphlets that circulated within Black communities. Annual commemorations of the passage of the British Emancipation Act, heralded as a triumph of international antislavery, on August 1 had begun as early as 1834. With the end of the apprenticeship system in 1838, the same year of the arrival of British emigration agents to America, saw the largest number of commemorations thus far: in New York and Massachusetts, spreading to Newark and Providence and westward to Cincinnati.[5] African Americans contrasted emancipation in the British colonies with the United States, where slavery appeared to be on the rise. Less than two decades previous, the Missouri Compromise had allowed the expansion of slavery into the West. Throughout the 1830s, political agitation by free African Americans and their white allies was met by mobs and riots. For two years, between 1835 and 1837, the U.S. House of Representatives instituted a gag rule over any discussion of antislavery. For many free African Americans, the emancipated British Caribbean offered both an alternative to the domestic racial and political order and a sense of hope in a renewed struggle. At a commemoration in Philadelphia in 1838, the Black abolitionist pastor William L. Douglass lauded the triumph of freedom in the British Caribbean as a beacon, declaring that if such "moral justice" could succeed there, it could as well succeed in America.[6]

It was in the midst of these events that a British Guianese planter named Edward Carbery arrived in Baltimore in September 1839. Carbery was the owner of several estates in the colony, including a coffee estate in Berbice and a sugar plantation named Thomas near the capital, Georgetown. Carbery claimed that his visit to Baltimore was coincidence, the need for a change of climate due to his wife's poor health. A few days into his stay, however, he recounted being drawn to the plight of the local free Black population. Carbery noted that many were out of work and experienced difficulties in gaining a livelihood. What was more, he witnessed the growing racial prejudice in the city, what he termed "the discomforts of various kinds to which they [free Black people] are subjected."[7] Whether Carbery's visit was as coincidental as claimed, his assessment of the dire life for free Black people in late 1830s Baltimore was hardly an exaggeration.

Like the rest of Maryland, Baltimore straddled a middle ground in antebellum America. By the 1830s the bustling port was among the top three largest cities in the United States. A mix of commercial trade, politics, and social life tied it both to nearby urban spaces in the North and to the slave-based economies that dominated the South. Baltimore's free Black population was a result of forces in play since the Revolution as the changing viability of slavery in the region shaped attitudes toward labor. Maryland had not passed gradual emancipation like its more northern neighbors. In fact, from 1790 to 1810 the state saw a sharp increase in slave ownership. But Maryland also experienced a wave of manumissions, the product of social, market, and moral factors, as well as the agency of enslaved people themselves, who filed freedom petitions or absconded. Some owners voluntarily freed those they held in bondage; in many cases, enslaved people negotiated their freedom in contracts or through self-purchase. More liberal laws allowed the increase of manumission over the ensuing decades, despite several attempts by concerned legislators to check its growth. This building wave of liberty was most evident in Baltimore, where the free Black population increased from a few hundred in 1790 to nearly fifteen thousand by the 1830s. In contrast, the city's enslaved population climaxed in 1830 at around forty-one hundred before beginning a steady decline. The number of free African Americans was continually supplemented by manumissions among Baltimore's remaining enslaved population and rural migrants from throughout the slave state who flocked to the city seeking employment and opportunity.[8]

By the early nineteenth century, the free African American population of Baltimore was well established. Like their counterparts elsewhere in the United States, free black Baltimoreans created institutions—among them schools, independent churches, and mutual aid societies—that helped sustain the burgeoning community. A small free Black elite took root, their success largely based in their ability to enter skilled trades and to become members of the clergy. Their access to higher-wage work and their ability to amass wealth never matched those of Black elites in northern cities like Philadelphia or, for that matter, southern cities like New Orleans and Charleston. Still, a distinct class structure emerged, as the economic lives of the majority of Baltimore's free Black population were significantly poorer. As enslaved labor, African Americans had been threaded throughout the city's workforce, often the property of craftsmen who employed or hired them out. While their continued presence remained vital to labor, as freed persons they were pushed mainly into more undesirable occupations.

Free Black men largely filled the roles of unskilled laborers who were often hired by the day and paid lower wages for menial tasks. African American women were mainly laundresses and domestics in white households, with a few finding jobs as cooks, midwives, and street vendors. With their reliance on such work to sustain themselves and their families, most free Black Baltimoreans lived a precarious financial existence that was vulnerable to any larger systemic shock.[9]

In the late 1830s, that shock came in the Panic of 1837. After years of economic expansion and unregulated speculation, Andrew Jackson's attempts in 1836 to rein in inflation left investors holding large debts. As banks called in loans, international institutions tightened credit. With no Federal Reserve, mismanagement by state banks, and the refusal of Martin Van Buren's administration to intercede, the panic ushered in a fiscal downturn that lasted for the next four years. The crisis stifled manufacturing throughout the nation, discouraged foreign investment, and ground shipping almost to a halt. As a port city, Baltimore faced a particularly dire situation made worse by an increase of state taxes to bolster industry. Unemployment soared, and, desperate for work, whites moved to take up even the low-paying occupations once the domain of African Americans. Joblessness among free Black households forced thousands to appeal for public relief from the city's poorhouse. Others were pushed into destitution and faced jail time for debt, vagrancy, or thefts motivated by desperation.[10]

In a city where regulations were increasingly encroaching on Black life, the economic hardships of the era only served to worsen the situation. Between 1790 and 1820, Maryland had passed a series of laws meant to restrict the mobility and rights of free African Americans. In 1801 the state constitution was amended to limit voting to "free white male citizens, and no other." Through disfranchisement and racialized laws, Maryland sought to solidify the status of free African Americans as outside the bounds of citizenship. Still, these were piecemeal efforts rather than a comprehensive strategy. As historian Martha Jones finds in her study of rights and citizenship in antebellum Baltimore, these laws often left "omissions" and "spaces" through which free African Americans might advocate for legal rights. Black Baltimoreans had long been able to depend on, if not a liberal social atmosphere, then a mostly ambivalent one greatly due to the dependence on their labor. But through the 1830s, white racial attitudes had been steadily hardening. In 1831, following Nat Turner's Rebellion in Southampton County, Virginia, which sat about a day's ride by steamboat from Baltimore, Maryland's anxious state legislature passed regulations on the growth of the free Black population. The preamble of the measure warned against "the unrestricted power of manumission" and "the evils growing out of their [free Black] connection and unrestrained association with the slaves." The law was also critical of free African Americans for "withdrawing a large portion of employment from the laboring class of the white population," citing the matter as one of "grave consideration."[11] This primacy placed on the welfare of white workers grew as emigrants from Britain, Ireland, and Germany came to Baltimore and the financial panic created greater competition. In 1838 the city, which had often skirted the more repressive state laws, now passed new legislation imposing a curfew on Black residents. The darkening mood was punctuated with racial harassment and sporadic acts of violence. In one instance, an altercation between several free Black men and a member of the city watch instigated a stone-throwing white mob of "riotous fellows," who threatened to destroy a prominent Black church.[12]

Edward Carbery's arrival in Baltimore in late 1839 coincided with this period of financial hardships and growing racial repression in the city's free Black community. The poverty, joblessness, and "discomforts of various kinds" he witnessed impressed upon him the viability of his emigration plan. Like other British Caribbean planters, Carbery couched the scheme in humanitarian language. "You are no doubt well aware," he related in an 1840 letter, "that in all the slave states the increase of free coloured populations is looked upon with dissatisfaction." Carbery believed he had a ready solution to the plight of both free Black people and the whites who disdained their presence. He claimed inspiration for his plan from similar emigration attempts being made by Trinidad based on the proposal by Burnley before the select committee years earlier in 1836. Much as Burnley had done, Carbery also tied emigration to a more passive antislavery. "I entertain no doubt," he wrote, "that I shall succeed in procuring the liberation of many slaves on condition of giving them passage to Guiana." To make this grand plan work, however, Carbery needed to convince the city's free Black populace that relocation to the British Caribbean was a viable and rewarding option.[13]

Appeals to emigration were not new to Baltimore's free Black community. An auxiliary branch affiliated with the American Colonization Society had formed in Maryland as early as 1817. In 1827 colonizationists created a more centralized state group, the Maryland State Colonization Society. The organization initially had meager success, even after a $1,000 appropriation from the state legislature to transport free Black people to the fledgling colony of Liberia. While colonizationists gained support from prominent Black leaders like the Reverend Daniel Coker, most Black Baltimoreans remained wary of white-led efforts and saw relocation to West Africa as antithetical to their citizenship claims. Nat Turner's Rebellion in 1831, however, gave the organization the public and political support it needed. The Maryland Assembly during the winter session of 1831–32 awarded the group $200,000 extended over a period of twenty years to aid in the removal to Africa "the people of color now free, and such as shall hereafter become so."[14]

As with similar schemes elsewhere in the United States at the time, attempts to promote colonization in Baltimore were often met with reproach. Agents complained of hostility and almost universal resistance from free Black residents, who made clear distinctions between voluntary emigration and compulsory acts of removal. Most free African Americans had established a sense of community in the city. Whatever repression they faced, many found it preferable to the unknown fate that awaited them in West Africa. A letter to the editor of the Boston-based abolitionist *Liberator* penned in 1831 by "a black Baltimorean" (quite likely the teacher and activist William Watkins) asserted that he "would rather die in Maryland under the pressure of unrighteous and cruel laws than be driven, like cattle . . . to Liberia."[15] Yet the Black community did not speak with one voice on the subject. With the spur in colonization following Nat Turner's Rebellion in 1831, Black Marylanders joined other migrants to Liberia, helping to double the settlement of Monrovia in eighteen months. Most were from the rural parts of the state, but a few, discontented under the emerging set of restrictive regulations, left from Baltimore as well.[16]

In the gloomy social climate of the late 1830s, free Black Baltimoreans again gave emigration a second look. However, distrust of white-led colonization efforts to faraway Africa still held sway. As had been the case with Haiti over a decade earlier, Carbery's offer of Guiana in the nearby Caribbean as a possible place of relocation appeared a reasonable alternative. Many free Black Baltimoreans were undoubtedly well-acquainted with the passage of the British Emancipation Act and its impact on the Caribbean colonies. Although antislavery literature circulated in the city less frequently by the late 1830s, Black Baltimoreans had likely read about these events in white antislavery newspapers such as the *Genius of Universal Emancipation* and *The Liberator* and the later Black-run *Colored American* out of New York. Even for those without access to such print materials, news from the nearby Caribbean regularly reached the port city, filtering to Black communities along veins of oral communication. The geographic distance to the Caribbean was far less than to West Africa, and the barriers of language and, perhaps, even custom would have appeared not insurmountable. What was more, agents like Carbery promised that in the British colonies free Black emigrants would find what they most lacked at home: jobs, greater freedom, and dignity.

Carbery found support for his scheme among local whites, including from leading antislavery organizations and local colonizationists. On the face of it, the aim of settling free African Americans in the Caribbean conflicted with groups like the Maryland State Colonization Society in building up their Liberia colony. But the end result remained the same: reducing a free Black population increasingly viewed as problematic to the white social order, decreasing a surplus workforce in a moment of scarce labor opportunities, and relieving the pressures on the city's safety net. This practice of removing unwanted members of the populace was taking place along the eastern seaboard in the wake of the financial crisis. Cities like Boston, New York, and Philadelphia all enacted or revised existing poor laws to deport hundreds of "paupers," most of them immigrant Irish. The expelling of the foreign and the poor became routine, as nativist sentiment found fertile ground in the age's economic anxiety. While colonization efforts toward Baltimore's free Black population were promoted as voluntary, at least outwardly, they worked toward similar aims.[17]

Shortly after his arrival in September, Carbery contacted members of the free Black leadership in Baltimore and presented his plan. Guiana was described as a "refuge" that had "now opened up to the free colored people of the United States." It was a place where Black Baltimoreans could be assured "a vast field of labor" and the ability to engage in various forms of enterprise. What was perhaps most appealing, Guiana was said to be "relieved from [the] weight of prejudice" that inflicted America; Guiana was a place where free Black people could "share the same moral and social advantages" and "compete with the white man" without hindrance. African Americans could remain in the United States, "confined all their lives to menial and obscure stations," or they could emigrate to Guiana, where they could possibly rise to a comfortable existence, even perhaps wealth, and enjoy "a respectable station in society."[18]

The appeal was successful enough to excite several further meetings among free Black Baltimoreans. The Baltimore Committee of Immigration was soon created, and on November 25 a public forum was held in the schoolroom of the Bethel African Methodist Episcopal Church on East Saratoga Street. Founded in 1816 after a split from the white-run Methodist Episcopal church on Sharp Street, Bethel AME Church was one of the oldest independent Black institutions in the city. It had been home to some of

Black Baltimore's most prestigious leaders, and it served as an incubator of community social and political action, including debates over colonization and emigration. A previous resolution had been passed by the Baltimore Committee of Immigration requesting that the November 25 meeting be announced the previous Sunday from pulpits throughout the city and state, inviting their congregants to attend. The purpose was to select delegates to conduct a tour first of the Caribbean colony of British Guiana and then of Trinidad. Given the mistrust of past colonization schemes, the committee had worked out with Carbery a plan to provide passage and all expenses for two individuals "to ascertain the character of the climate, soil, natural production, and the political and social condition of the coloured inhabitants." The two would function as eyewitnesses and judge for themselves the truth of Carbery's claims. Upon their return, the delegates were required to submit a written report on "all the information acquired by them."[19]

American abolitionists looking to defend the "mighty experiment" had employed fact-finding missions previously to the postemancipation British Caribbean to bolster their claims. In November 1836 the New York–based American Anti-Slavery Society sent Joseph Horace Kimball and James A. Thome on a six-month tour of the English Caribbean. The two white abolitionists divided their time between Antigua, Barbados, and Jamaica, where they observed and recorded the daily lives of the formerly enslaved and the workings of freedom. On their return, they transcribed those findings into a five-hundred-page book that circulated heavily within antislavery circles and print publications. Baltimore's Committee of Emigration was probably aware of Kimball and Thome's work, which by 1839 was being cited frequently in antislavery newspapers and literature. Here now was their chance to create something similar but without the filter of a white gaze. As a writer to the *Colored American* related, Kimball and Thome, while deserving credit, "could not consult the interests of colored men" or truly understand the plight of black laborers. If emigration to the British Caribbean was to be explored, the writer maintained that African Americans would need agents of their "own selection" and color to make the survey.[20]

The meeting to select delegates was attended by some of Baltimore's most prominent Black citizenry and chaired by the property owner Thomas Green, an immigrant from Barbados who prospered as a barber for wealthy white patrons. The selection was held by ballot, and in the end, two men emerged with the largest share of votes: Nathaniel Peck and Thomas S. Price.[21] Described in one account as self-educated, Thomas Price reportedly held several occupations, at times an ice seller, a whitewasher, and a painter.

Despite Price's humble background, those attending the meeting believed him qualified to act as an envoy on their behalf, perhaps due to his familiarity with and closeness to more common labor. Records and personal accounts list Nathaniel Peck as a wall colorer and a carpenter. A lay minister, Peck had been ordained a local deacon in 1829 and had closer affiliations with Baltimore's Black elite. This was also not his first experience with emigration. In 1820 he accompanied the founder of the Bethel AME church, the Reverend Daniel Coker, on an emigration mission to Sierra Leone, where he had praised the opportunity to tread on his "mother country." He returned to Baltimore in later years, but he remained affiliated with a local African mission and was a continued proponent of colonization.[22]

The meeting's chairman, Thomas Green, signed a written resolution to be carried by both men that "authorized, empowered, and commissioned" them to conduct their exploratory undertaking. Peck and Price also received a document of support from a notable list of white leaders: two local Baltimore court judges, a U.S. district judge, and the mayor of the city. The letter "cheerfully" praised the proceedings of the Committee of Emigration, lauding the selected delegates as "two of the most industrious, intelligent, and respectable of our coloured population." A third letter was arranged for by Carbery to be given to officials in British Guiana detailing the nature of the men's trip and its relation to the "Agricultural Interests" of the colony. Carbery's letter urged his countrymen to afford the delegation "every facility" to aid in the accomplishment of their mission: "They have consented to quit their families, and to undertake a long voyage, chiefly on the faith of my representations. . . . I cannot too strongly recommend them to your kind protection." Nearly a month later, Peck and Price embarked by train to Boston and from there, on December 21, sailed for British Guiana.[23]

The two men arrived in Georgetown, the capital, one month later, on January 21, 1840. They delivered their letters to members of the Voluntary Subscription Emigration Society, to whom Carbery had written, and by the next day had arranged a meeting with the colony's governor, Henry Light. Thomas Bagot, secretary of the emigration society, accompanied Peck and Price personally to see the governor, who offered them information on the province, as well as his protection and assistance. That same afternoon Bagot brought them before the board of directors of the emigration society, where they offered up their documented credentials. The board immediately passed resolutions supporting Carbery's plan. They further resolved to have public advertisements put up throughout the colony soliciting its inhabitants to afford Peck and Price "every assistance and kind attention in their power."

The committee also unanimously agreed to take up any expenses incurred in transporting the delegation from place to place, defraying all costs to the board. Peck and Price seemed flattered by the welcome, perhaps because such treatment from white officials would have been hard to find in Baltimore. They wrote of feeling as if they "were amongst friends" and had been offered protection and hospitality "as much so as if we were British-born subjects."[24]

The two men spent the next eleven days in Georgetown while arrangements were made for their transport. While there, they sought to become acquainted with the local affairs, manners, and customs, recording their observations with picturesque flair. The streets of Georgetown were "McAdamized," they noted, a technique of roadbuilding considered novel for its time. The principal road in the capital, Water Street, running parallel to the Demerara River, was depicted as bustling with throngs of people throughout the day. The stores were deemed attractively large and "well-fitted" with any manner of goods that "fancy may dictate." The houses lining the main street were estimated to be built twenty feet apart to allow for the proper circulation of air. Each dwelling was reportedly outfitted with galleries, balconies, and elaborate gardens filled with fruit trees, ornamental trees, shrubbery, and flowers. Water was collected by means of rain conducted by spouts into cisterns from slate roofs and was commended as "very pure, clear and pleasant" to the taste. Altogether the image painted of Georgetown was of a fairly modern space, with modern roads, businesses, and buildings: not Baltimore, certainly, but still more than the idyllic scenes of palm trees and sugarcane fields common in pictorials and narratives of the Caribbean.[25]

Peck and Price also visited the main churches in Georgetown: one Presbyterian, three Wesleyan Methodist, and one Catholic. As in Philadelphia, a large number of Black Baltimoreans were Methodists, initially drawn to the church for its comparatively liberal stance against slavery. The 1796 Methodist Christmas Conference in Baltimore had denounced the "great evil of African slavery" and stipulated rules for both officials and worshippers to move along a path of gradual emancipation. But discrimination and segregation within the church had led to a schism by the early 1800s, resulting in the exodus of members and the creation of independent Black institutions like Bethel AME Church, where Peck and Price had been formally deputized for their mission.[26] In contrast, both men found Georgetown churches of differing denominations with "persons of colour occupying pews throughout." They noted that membership appeared to be according to an individual's "standing and ability to purchase" instead of color. For Peck and Price, this was viewed as a fortunate sign of things to come. It seemed that in Guiana, they wrote, churches "had entirely abolished prejudice from the house of God, as well as everywhere else."[27]

On February 1 the delegation at last began their mission in earnest, departing Georgetown on an American steamer, the *Victoria*. They were escorted by William Jones, the son of a wealthy English absentee planter. Their destination was Leguan, an island located at the mouth of the Essequibo River that was home to a large number of sugar and coffee plantations. But production had dropped precipitously since emancipation, and it was a region that planters hoped to revive with immigrant labor.[28] Peck and Price gave their appraisal of the country as "flat, with canals running throughout." These, they explained, were designed to drain the land for sugar cultivation, to provide a boundary between estates, and to transport and ship cane. The vegetation on the island was said to grow with "the greatest luxuriance," owing to fertile soil that needed no manuring on account of the tropical climate. Oranges, limes, coconuts, pineapples, bananas, plantains, mangroves, sapodillas, guavas, and "many other fruits too tedious to mention" were all said to be in abundance. Alongside these grew vegetables such as sweet potatoes, yams, cassava, cabbage, beets, lettuce, cucumbers, tomatoes, peas, beans, and even corn. The two men assured readers that this veritable paradise of agriculture "was better imagined than described." The land in Guiana threw up such goods, they commented, "as if it were by magic."[29]

Peck and Price remained on Leguan for three days before being conveyed to the sister island of Wakenaam. A local captain afforded them passage on his schooner, which took the two to visit estates along the Essequibo River. These, it was mentioned, were located conveniently along the route of the steamship from Georgetown, providing passage to the capital four times a week. The first estate that they landed at was named the Good Intent and was owned by the very same schooner captain. From there they visited Spring Garden, whose proprietor was an American planter named Charles Benjamin. In 1832, a year before the abolition of slavery was passed, the plantation listed seventy-six enslaved people as property: thirty-one women and forty-five men. By 1836 that total number had dropped to sixty-four. Still, Benjamin had been able to claim £3,421 as compensation for the loss of his human property, as mandated by provisions in the Emancipation Act. Now the American planter was eager to acquire new labor, and he greeted the African American envoys with what they recalled as "every mark of friendship."[30]

Benjamin provided the two men with horses and accompanied them to visit several more plantations on the Arabian coast, the westernmost part of Guiana. Peck and Price described this part of the colony as "splendid," noting the "high state of cultivation," except for those fields left unworked because of the lack of laborers. This complaint of labor shortages was repeated to them frequently by their hosts, a sentiment they acknowledged "prevalent all over the colony." Both men seemed to share the assessment, painting a dismal portrait of "canes decaying for the want of persons to cut and bring them to the works." Yet Peck and Price did not rely only on the words of planters. They claimed to converse "on every occasion with the labourers" they encountered. The two spoke to them in their cottages, as they worked in the fields, and even in the buildings while they manufactured the sugar. The Black laborers reportedly expressed to them "entire satisfaction of their situation" and responded that they would welcome any amount of help in their endeavors.[31]

In actuality, the labor situation in 1840 Guiana was much more complicated. Even with the end of the apprenticeship system, former slaves in the colony resisted being placed back into submissive roles. Vagrancy laws were passed by the colonial legislature, alongside other acts of labor coercion that only exacerbated tensions. Strikes and work stoppages by freed persons were common. Many others abandoned the plantations, drifting away to peasant villages, where they formed new lives. The same governor who had greeted Peck and Price so cordially would a few years later complain of the bind in which planters found themselves: they could not "eject some twenty thousand [laborers]" from the colony, nor could they realistically coerce them. Peck and Price give no account of what the formerly enslaved people they encountered made of their presence in Guiana, nor do they seem to have pondered it enough to commit the question to their report. But given the ongoing disputes over labor and freedom in the colony, such men and women had every incentive to dissemble to two well-dressed Black men in the company of planters who owned the very land on which these workers toiled.[32]

Finishing their tour of the region, the delegation returned to Georgetown after ten days. Upon reaching the wharf they were met by Moses Benjamin, the American consul in Guiana, who offered an invitation to his home. This was not the last time Peck and Price's arrival was awaited by local white men of authority in the colony. The Voluntary Subscription Emigration Society of Georgetown had made good on its resolution to publicize the mission and advertise Peck and Price's travels in the local papers. Everywhere they went, planters and officials eagerly offered up their homes to the envoys who might procure them new laborers from America. "We were waited upon by many proprietors, as well as others," the two men wrote, "all soliciting and seeming anxious for us to pay a visit to their district first, and furnishing conveyances [in] abundance."[33]

Peck and Price spent the next week touring Berbice, located along the river of the same name in the eastern highlands. In 1764 the region had been home to one of Guiana's largest slave revolts, led by an enslaved African-born man named Cuffy against the Dutch. Now, over seventy years later, the English planters who had settled the region bitterly complained about the state of their properties. They had invested heavily on Berbice estates even after emancipation in great part based on the promise that the apprenticeship system would continue. With the abrupt end of the system in 1838, many planters now claimed their estates could not produce half the quantity they had previously. That past November, Berbice planters had written desperate pleas directly to the British Parliament, insisting that the only solution was to find new sources of labor. They petitioned Her Majesty's Government to grant them "an order to receive 500 captured Africans" seized from slave ships by the British navy to work their plantations. The request was eventually granted in March 1840. But before that time, two Black envoys from America were there to inquire on the possibilities of another source of Black labor. Eager to impress upon them the advantages of emigration, planters and colonial officials in the region received the two African Americans with open generosity.[34]

In Berbice, Peck and Price lodged at the home of a local merchant and doctor. During the day, they were ferried about by planters who steadily sent them invitations to tour their individual estates. The schedule was exhausting: the two men inspected several plantations a day before retiring in the evening and setting out again in the morning. Yet in their initial writings the delegation spoke sparingly about the condition of the estates, regaling readers instead with descriptions of the region's social conditions. The two men recounted how they "breakfasted with the gentlemanly manager" of a plantation and passed "quite an agreeable evening" at the estate of a planter and "his interesting family." Through their own experiences, Peck and Price painted an atmosphere of social equality in Berbice, where two Black men were afforded respect by members of the white planter and professional elite. They also related to readers the social lives of laborers. Writing about a settlement of East Indians, whom Peck and Price's hosts termed

"Hill-Coolies," the two men commended them as a "hardy race." But they chided the newly indentured workers for still being "in a state of ignorance" with regard to their belief in Hinduism, lamenting that "they cannot be prevailed upon to quit their idols." In contrast, visiting a local church for freed persons, Peck and Price found "250 to 300 scholars, of all ages," engaged in reading the Bible and repeating their catechism. "It was quite a gratifying sight," the two wrote, "to behold all these people seeking knowledge ... being only about 18 months since the most of them were emancipated."[35]

Among the three aforementioned groups, Peck and Price appeared to be most at ease with the planter and professional elite, men with who they presumed to share similar cultural and religious sensibilities. The freedpeople of Guiana were on the path to progress, but their proximity to slavery still left them degraded in the eyes of both men. The East Indians, meanwhile, were a people set apart completely by religion and customs. For men like Peck who had visited West Africa, these negotiations of identities were not new. The religious African mission with which he was involved still advocated many of Daniel Coker's sentiments, hoping to convert "thousands and thousands of souls ... from Paganism and Mahometanism." Nor were they new for Price. In Baltimore similar intraracial fractures occurred along social lines. The same Bethel AME Church that had sent them to find freedom in Guiana also at present allowed no leadership rights or positions to the enslaved. In their writings of fraternization and camaraderie with elite white men, Peck and Price transmitted to readers that shared commonalities of religion and education were enough in Guiana to transcend racial hierarchies.[36]

This analysis continued as they returned to Georgetown on February 18. As before, a local planter sent them an invitation and a carriage to visit his estate. On the way they stopped to inspect several plantations, dining in the company of owners and managers. The proprietor of one estate, Big Diamond, sent them an invitation to breakfast via one of his servants. Provided with a boat and provisions, they made the trip and were persuaded to visit at least two other estates. Their notes gave some description of the land and a passing assessment that the laborers they encountered had "an animated and cheerful appearance." But it was their time visiting the criminal court in Georgetown that seemed most impactful. There the two envoys marveled at seeing free Black men functioning in the roles of government. "Many of the clerks in the public offices are coloured," they wrote. "Also, tellers in the bank, &c. &c." In the court they even recounted seeing "a coloured gentleman" occupying the station of assessor. In postemancipation

Guiana, suffrage had not been granted with freedom. Voting was a privilege only granted to men who had paid a five-pound minimum in direct taxes to the colonial revenue, allowing planters to retain firm political control. Still, even with such severe restrictions in the colony, this must have been an impressive vision of freedom and citizenship to the two men.[37] In Maryland, free Black people had been unconditionally disenfranchised since 1805, and none held even low positions in government.[38] The possibility of access to even the boundaries of citizenship was enough for Peck and Price to proclaim that in Guiana, it appeared a free Black man of means could participate in civil society "without regard to colour."[39]

Over the space of nine pages, the report summarized the overall findings made in Guiana. In a brief paragraph, it gave a read on the climate of the South American colony, described as rainy due to the season but with sun "no means as oppressive" as Baltimore. Another brief paragraph determined that the soil was rich in alluvial deposits, which would make for easy agriculture. By far, the largest portion of the summary was directed to the two issues that would be foremost in the minds of prospective immigrants: the racial climate of the colony and the availability of labor. Here, Peck and Price transitioned from the style of a travel narrative to a report with information that they believed would most interest their audience, providing testimonials, observations, and relevant data to lend weight to their statements.[40]

In a section headlined "POLITICS" the report explained that in Guiana, as well as in other British dependencies, there was a law excluding all persons "not born under the British flag" from being eligible to hold office. It is uncertain how many Black migrants were expecting or seeking such an advantage. But Peck and Price followed up the remark by stating that regardless, every man stood "on an equality in the eye of the law." This may have held special pertinence to Black Baltimoreans, who often utilized the courthouse and legal avenues to put forth claims to rights and citizenship. Peck and Price referred again to the presence of officials of color in the courts as evidence and pointed out that there were no racial barriers to social and financial advancement. "The only distinction in society," they assured their readers, "is education, character and wealth, for the higher walks [of life]—then gradations down, according to condition, etc."[41]

Interestingly, the portion of the report dedicated to labor—the longest by far—was also placed under the heading "POLITICS." The conjoining of the two underscores perhaps just how closely Black Baltimoreans tied their occupational opportunities to racial discrimination, believing that, given the chance to compete freely with whites, Black people would fairly succeed.

Peck and Price gave a detailed summation of the labor prospects open to emigrants from Maryland. Agriculturists, they noted, were in greatest demand. On the estates the two men visited, they reported that each planter wanted forty to fifty workers. This would have been unsurprising to readers, as the emigration scheme had made no secret of the reasons for planters' overtures. Still, Peck and Price understood that their report would be read by men and women primarily accustomed to urban labor. To make the prospect of agricultural plantation work more palatable, they compared the field labor as "similar to working in corn-fields." Agriculturalists could complete up to four tasks a day, without fatigue, earning $33\frac{1}{3}$ cents for each. Black unskilled laborers in Baltimore, in contrast, provided work could be found, could earn maybe a dollar a day, some thirty cents less. Laborers at the wharves of Guiana, it was reported, could also earn about a dollar a day, while washerwomen could earn one dollar per dozen articles of clothing. Other women could find work in the colony as seamstresses and nurses.[42]

Peck and Price also assured prospective emigrants that more skilled jobs could be found. The plantations of Guiana were its principal economy, but their report reminded readers that these were large estates with "quite an imposing appearance." The working of sugar required the complex machinery of steam engines. Houses had to be constructed for proprietors, managers, overseers, and laborers. Buildings needed to be raised, and artisans of various crafts were essential. Carpenters were listed as "much in demand" alongside other "tradesmen." The wages were not high for the work, at only $1.00 to $1.25. But Peck and Price assured readers that as master mechanics, African American emigrants would command higher wages for their higher skillset, including bricklayers, boat builders, woodcutters, and "those who understand sawing ship-timber." Beyond these opportunities, it was expected that an influx of free Black laborers would necessitate the creation of more schools and churches, providing work for teachers and clergy, "could persons be found competent to the undertaking." In Guiana, the report pledged, "every profession is tolerated and encouraged."[43]

Peck and Price had still another proposal that they believed would entice readers, even those reluctant to take up agricultural labor. The government of Guiana, they had learned from the local papers, was putting up land for the purchasing at a reported five dollars per acre. At such low prices Peck and Price proposed that African American emigrants could buy land in shares, then cultivate it with sugarcane and other lucrative crops. The two men had paid close attention to plantation production, and their report provided information on the amount of sugar that could be harvested. They estimated that a well-cultivated acre could yield at the lowest $153 and at the highest $238 besides the further production of rum and molasses. Thirty hands, they proposed, could work some one hundred acres and amass significant financial gain.[44]

This was not a wholly far-fetched idea. Since the end of the apprenticeship, planters in Guiana had sold lots of their uncultivated estates to laborers. Edward Carbery himself in 1839 was listed among those planters transferring land to formerly apprenticed workers. Some freed persons pooled their resources and bought estates outright, forming their own villages.[45] Peck and Price envisioned the possibility of free African American entrepreneurs who brought with them the skills to prosper handsomely from such an arrangement. In order to bolster their proposal, they reprinted in full a letter from the American planter in Guiana, Charles Benjamin, who had been one of their hosts. In it, he offered some twenty thousand emigrants a chance to purchase land at ten to thirty dollars. This could be paid for with an installment of half the money, while the latter portion would be paid off in agricultural labor by the purchaser. To be clear, Peck and Price's proposal, as well as that being offered by Benjamin, amounted to sharecropping, a system that would come to represent the exploitation of Black labor in the postemancipation United States. But both men believed, perhaps naively, that in 1830s Guiana this presented an opportunity. The planters of the colony, along with the colonial government, intended free African Americans to take the place of their former slaves and apprentices. Peck and Price, however, saw the possibility of free Black emigrants becoming, through hard work, independent yeoman farmers at the least and "industrious and enterprising capitalists" at best. "A large amount of the very best land is lying idle," they related, and the possibilities were "observable to any one having the most contracted ideas of agriculture." The islands of Leguan and Wakenaam, they estimated, were capable of receiving "many thousand[s]" of emigrants. The same, they claimed, could be said of the Arabian coast, which was declared the "garden spot" of the colony and ripe for cultivation. As a region still in development, both men argued, Guiana offered free African Americans the chance to begin as laborers but, in time, become masters of the land. "It is easy to discover," they told readers, "the many advantages that this country possesses in great degree for the enterprising agriculturalist."[46]

The more practical requirements entailed in any act of migration were not lost on Peck and Price. The cost of living, housing, and other daily needs would weigh in any decision on resettlement. Anticipating such queries, the two envoys sought out information on the prices of necessary articles so that a reader might "know how to govern himself." House rent in Guiana was listed as 100 percent higher than in Baltimore. Furniture was listed as the same. Staple food goods like flour could cost eleven to thirteen dollars per barrel, while rice was fifty cents per gallon. By the pound, sugar was sixteen cents; butter, fifty to sixty cents; coffee, twenty-five to thirty cents; and tea, one to two dollars. Meat prices were not much better. Veal and mutton, being scarce, were twenty-five to thirty cents per pound; ham, sixteen to twenty cents per pound; fresh pork, twenty to twenty-five cents per pound. While beef was plentiful, it was listed at sixteen cents per pound, while a single chicken cost $1.00, a goose $2.00 to $2.50, and a turkey as much as $5.00. Vegetables were so exorbitant that they were listed simply as "very high."[47]

Compared to Baltimore, food prices were significantly higher, some approaching well over 50 percent more. Peck and Price readily admitted as much, but they pointed to other items that were much cheaper. Fuel was as low as eight cents, and the cost of clothing was almost half as much as in Baltimore. Laborers paid no rent on houses or for schooling. When placed into this context, the price of food, they argued, easily balanced out in an emigrant's favor. Furthermore, they singled out the scarcity of goods as the reason for the high food prices. The two men urged readers to see this challenge as an opportunity rather than being discouraged. African Americans who emigrated to Guiana could take up occupations as producers, supplying fruits, vegetables, meat, butter, and other items in larger quantities. This would not only be of financial benefit to any entrepreneur with such skills but at the same time drive down cost: "Let there be a sufficient number to turn their attention to furnishing those articles for market, and our word for it, they cannot fail to succeed in making money, and bringing down the prices." Once more, the two men encouraged their audience to seize the freedom offered in Guiana and use it toward their gain. "Instead of the high prices being a disadvantage," they urged, "we look upon them as a decided advantage to the enterprising producer."[48]

Of course, for Peck and Price's visions of freedom to have a semblance of possibility, they needed assurances by the white elite who governed the colony, both politically and economically. In their travels they had continually probed planters on their support for a system by which Black migrants might purchase land for cultivation. By their account, the proposal appeared to have received a warm welcome. Likely, plantation owners saw in this plan a means for greater production that would in the end yield them more labor and wealth on land that was sitting unused. However, to make certain they could convey these points to their readers, Peck and Price put a set of questions to the Voluntary Subscription Emigration Society in Georgetown in writing. They included as well the replies under the heading "Questions put to the Committee by your Delegates, and their answers," sent out on Wednesday, February 26, 1840. The questions themselves totaled six in all and can be summarized as follows: (1) Would migrants have the right to choose their employers? (2) Would the society be amiable to the plan of migrants cultivating cane fields under a sharecropping system? (3) What portion of the produced goods would migrants be able to keep as their own reward? (4) If emigrants cultivated new fields, what portion of the produced goods would they receive? (5) Were the planters willing to offer advances in money to emigrants, and under what terms? (6) What tariffs would be placed on furniture or other goods brought with emigrants into the colony?[49]

The Voluntary Subscription Emigration Society wasted little time getting back to the delegates. The following Monday, the society's board of directors held a meeting in Georgetown and drafted their answers. The minutes from the proceedings were forwarded to Peck and Price from the secretary, Thomas Bagot, and they were reprinted in their report. The board assured Peck and Price that emigrants from the United States would be free to select their employers. Each would be assigned an emigration agent to aid in negotiating a place of employment, rate of wages, nature of work, "and all other matters in which they are interested." The society further assured Peck and Price that it would pay all "passage money and expenses of maintenance" for all laborers, "whether agricultural or mechanical." Regarding the share cultivation plan envisioned by Peck and Price, the board confirmed that it had "the Society's entire approbation." While unable to give precise numbers, the board estimated that "not less than one-third" of the gross produce should be owed emigrants; on newly created fields, that number increased to one-half for the first crop and one-third of those crops thereafter. The board also found that "no difficulty would arise in procuring [monetary] advance . . . from time to time." But this would be at the discretion of individual planters and dependent on "the progress in quality and quantity" of work undertaken by the cultivator. Lastly, the board declared that beds, bedding, and cooking utensils would not be subject to duties. Furniture and some food goods would be charged a tariff, while others were free of duty. Salt fish, long a British export in the dietary maintenance of their enslaved populations and still a valuable commodity after emancipation, was listed as "prohibited altogether."[50]

Through their queries, Peck and Price sought to convince readers that they had done their due diligence in their mission. Their questions mirrored what they believed to be the primary concerns of Black Baltimoreans who might contemplate emigration. At least several of their queries were premised on the plan the two men envisioned of enterprising African American cultivators working land they would eventually settle and own. The written replies from the society affirmed Peck and Price's vision, placing their plan on a firm footing and imbuing it with an air of credible plausibility.

Their inspection of Guiana completed and the necessary data, letters, and written assurances in hand, the two delegates began their trip to the crown colony of Trinidad on March 10. After a brief stop in Grenada, they made their way on a small sloop to the eastern Caribbean island seven days later, arriving in Port of Spain on the night of March 17. The time they spent in Trinidad was brief: a total of six days, compared to over eight weeks spent in Guiana. Unsurprisingly, their report reflects this imbalance, dedicating just around three pages out of twenty-five to discussing the island. Much of this discussion followed the previous pattern: a welcome by members of the local emigration society; invitations by planters to inspect their estates, along with the requisite dinners and breakfasts; a brief physical description of the country; a short note on wages; and the prices of local goods and articles.[51]

What stands out as remarkably different in their report on Trinidad are recordings of encounters with African American migrants. Agents from the island had made the rounds in U.S. cities farther north since 1838, and some free Black people had been swayed by their offer. On their first two days in Port of Spain, Peck and Price appear to have purposefully sought out these migrants "to learn from them how they liked the island." These African Americans had arrived on the ships the *Metamora* and the *Archer*. Both had left Philadelphia that previous year, the *Archer* reportedly carrying up to 121 Black migrants and reaching Trinidad on December 27. Peck and Price met with three or four who happened to be in town. The general impression these men gave the Baltimorean delegates was fairly unfavorable. They complained that they had not been adequately paid for their labor per day, as they were accustomed to in America. What was more, their boarding was expensive, and tradesmen such as themselves were not in high demand. The report recorded the complaints for readers but also presented caveats. As the men were mechanics, it was reasoned that they had undoubtedly emigrated with unrealistic and "high-wrought expectations," and their opinions could not be relied upon.[52]

Two days later, while visiting an estate, Peck and Price encountered several more African American migrants. Here they heard similar rumblings of dissatisfaction. Some complained that after selling their furniture back in the United States for little or nothing, they were then forced to buy new furnishings at exorbitant prices. Others objected that the churches were located a good distance from where they lived and labored. The general high price of provisions was another gripe. Once more, Peck and Price dismissed these grievances and chided the emigrants for their triviality. "We endeavoured to convince [the migrants] of the necessity of undergoing some difficulty and privations," they wrote, "which is a sure attendant upon all such changes." As a counter, they pointed to two carpenters from New York, who were both satisfied and reportedly doing very well. At another plantation they found migrants whom they described as thriving. The two envoys commended them for their spirit, lauding them as people "determined to surmount all temporary difficulties, and show what can be done." They assured readers that even if Trinidad did not possess as many advantages as Guiana, it was still a place "for the industrious man of colour," who could achieve more there than in the United States.[53]

On Monday afternoon, February 23, Peck and Price left Trinidad on the sloop *Phoebe* for Saint Thomas in order to make passage to the United States. They were joined by two other African American delegates in the area who had come to inspect the island: Messrs. Smith and Shorter from Annapolis. It may have encouraged both sets of men to know that emigration was a topic of discussion throughout Maryland. Very likely the pairs exchanged notes on their observations during their week-long voyage together. However, Peck and Price make no other mention of the Annapolis delegations in their writings.[54]

The *Phoebe* reached Saint Thomas on March 31, and Peck and Price were soon bound for Philadelphia, where they arrived on April 11. The two had been gone for almost four months. Their patron, Edward Carbery, was now in Boston, busily seeking recruits for Guiana from among the city's free Black community. A pamphlet written by an anonymous "Friend to the Coloured People" had begun circulating in Boston in early 1840 citing excerpts and data by Carbery on the advantages of Guiana. It also mentioned the delegation of Peck and Price, whose arrival was reported as imminently expected. Back in Maryland, state legislators, eager at the prospect of relieving itself of its free African American population, passed an act "to encourage" emigration. Before 1844 there were no statutes placing restrictions on free Black people leaving the state. But doubts on their ability to easily return during the heightened racial climate of the late 1830s may have put off prospective emigrants. An exception had been made for trips to Liberia, providing assurances of the right to return for Black travelers in the hopes of spurring colonization. A new law in late 1839 now allowed free Black people in the state to visit Trinidad and Guiana on similar terms to ascertain "whether said places ... are suitable for the emigration and settlement of themselves or other free persons of color." The stage seemed set for emigration to the British Caribbean, and more than likely the two delegates were eager to report back on their findings. But in their absence, the emigration movement in Baltimore had moved rapidly and beyond either man's expectations.[55]

On Wednesday, April 15, Peck and Price presented their report to a 3:00 gathering at Bethel AME Church in Baltimore. A densely packed crowd filled the church and spilled outside, with some unable to reach near the doors. After an opening of singing and prayer and a formal motion, the delegates took center stage to deliver their findings. The two spoke at length, giving what one newspaper observed as a "highly encouraging and minute description" of the British Caribbean colonies. But the audience was not just there to listen. Before Peck and Price could complete their report, both men were peppered with questions, reportedly leaving them fatigued under the "laborious" interrogation. The gathering was forced to adjourn, and a follow-up meeting was agreed upon for the next day at the Methodist Episcopal church on Sharp Street. Here, Peck and Price finished their report under the scrutiny of an "anxious" audience.[56]

After providing details of their trip and their general support for emigration, the two envoys openly declared their preference for Guiana. While commending Trinidad as "a fine and beautiful island," they found it lacking in opportunities for skilled laborers and with small, undeveloped estates. In contrast, Guiana was portrayed as a more modern region "propelled by steam-engines" that lightened labor and with estates as vast as a "manufacturing village." Peck and Price's recommendation was likely also fueled by their grand vision of enterprising free Black sharecroppers who could in time become prosperous landowners in Guiana.[57] However, both men would soon learn that Black Baltimoreans had already made the decision to emigrate before even hearing Peck and Price's detailed report, and they had chosen to go not to Guiana but to Trinidad.

Even before the delegation from Baltimore left for Guiana, the local newspapers were buzzing with news of emigration to Trinidad. That past October 1839, *The Sun* newspaper of Baltimore printed news of a ship named the *Matamoras* that had recently sailed with free Black emigrants from New York for Trinidad. Advertisements in November from Philadelphia called for "Colored Emigrants to Port of Spain" to leave on the ship *Archer*. A December article made the fantastic claim that two thousand more had left Philadelphia for Trinidad: "Persons of color, of all ages and sexes ... have availed themselves of the late offer of the British government and have exchanged ... a city life for the sugar plantations of that sunny isle." A January news story wrote encouragingly of emigrants in Trinidad, where everyone had found employment and with a few even receiving $500 a year as plantation overseers. The government of Trinidad was inviting as many free African Americans as would come to the island, the paper said, promising "high wages and every advantage." The numbers of migrants and their alleged fortunes were certainly exaggerated, but the articles kept Trinidad foremost in the minds of Black Baltimoreans while Peck and Price were away on their exploratory mission.[58]

Emigration agents from the island were also making their way to the city. Just preceding Peck and Price's return, an agent for the colonial government of Trinidad, a Mr. R. S. Buchanan, had arrived in Baltimore. On Monday, April 6, he was invited to address a gathering at the Sharp Street church on the favorability of emigration to the island. Mr. Buchanan told the audience that he was prepared to make "suitable arrangements" and had secured a vessel, the *Big Northerner*, to facilitate the departure of any interested parties. He reminded them that "slavery was totally and forever abolished in the West Indies" and that Trinidad would afford them the freedom of any land that flies the British flag. "You will enjoy every privilege," he assured, "and your color will make no distinction." Instead, it was only "conduct and education" that would afford "whatever position" they could achieve as free people. Mr. Buchanan gave information on the living arrangements, free schooling, and other benefits Trinidad had to offer, which he listed from a pamphlet created by none other than William Burnley, who had first proposed the emigration scheme almost four years earlier.[59]

The colonial agent had with him an even more powerful persuasive tool: two Black men who had recently emigrated to Trinidad, a Reverend Jones and his son John Hays. Both were Baltimoreans who, heeding earlier advertisements, had left on the *Archer* out of Philadelphia. After spending four months in the colony, they returned to provide testimony "to those interested in the result of [their] visit." Jones brought news that all the emigrants who had left for Trinidad were well and prospering. His son Hays, a carpenter by trade, worked at a plantation, where he was earning good daily wages and able to cultivate and produce extra goods besides for sale. Employment was said to be open on the island for women and children, who were able to earn as much as men doing lighter work at cocoa or coffee plantations, while washerwomen could reap as much as $1.50 per dozen articles of clothing. As to the social atmosphere, Hays claimed that though he had traveled all over the world, "he never was so well treated as in Trinidad." Both father and son maintained that the only reason for their return to Baltimore was to wind up their affairs, collect their families, and resettle in the Caribbean colony.[60]

Buchanan's efforts yielded results. By the time Peck and Price arrived to give their report favoring Guiana about a week later, over a hundred Black Baltimoreans had decided on Trinidad as their destination. That same week the *Big Northerner* left with ninety-three emigrants for the colony; hundreds more were said to be awaiting passage. Throughout the year, advertisements in local papers for emigration to Guiana from Baltimore appeared almost every day of the month. But they were easily matched by those offering work in Trinidad. In the end, the majority of free Black Baltimoreans who chose to emigrate made the journey to the eastern Caribbean island, while only a scant number went to Guiana.[61]

Peck and Price must have been conflicted at this turn of events. On the one hand, emigration to the British Caribbean had become a viable alternative for African Americans in the city. On the other, most had clearly not shared their preference for Guiana. Their failure was owed in part to the more developed nature of the Trinidad emigration scheme, which preempted and overshadowed their mission. Men like Reverend Jones and his son were able to provide personal testimonials of their lived experiences as opposed to a fact-finding mission. Trinidad also had already existing communities of African Americans that arriving emigrants could join. It could also be, however, that many migrants rejected aspects of Peck and Price's vision of sharecropping. Such a system may have been unpalatable for urban men and women accustomed to greater labor independence.

Despite their inability to convince Black Baltimoreans of the efficacy of their plan, Peck and Price's report sustained a life outside the city. In May their findings were turned into a twenty-five-page pamphlet that joined an ongoing debate on free Black emigration to the British Caribbean occurring farther north.[62] This discourse had been prominently featured in the New York–based African American newspaper the *Colored American*, founded in part by the Black activist Samuel Cornish and by 1839 run by the Black Massachusetts activist Charles B. Ray. Its editorials spoke out regularly against West Indian emigration, deriding it as "nonsense" and reminding African American readers that the United States was "THE LAND OF OUR BIRTH." But the paper had been unable to contain the growing interest in the Black community, which had seen social setbacks, anti-Black sentiment, and financial hardships through the late 1830s. Even the paper's co-owner, Phillip Bell, penned an article in 1839 giving support for the possibility of emigration from America, what he derided as "this slavery-ridden, prejudice-cursed country."[63] Neither had men like Ray garnered much success rebutting the proemigration pamphlets by white colonial agents like Carbery circulating from Boston to Philadelphia. Peck and Price's report, an eyewitness account by two Black men, would make the anti-emigration efforts even more problematic.

To the *Colored American*'s fortune, aid against West Indian emigration arrived the same month Peck and Price gave their report. In April a Black migrant identified as Mr. Waugh created a pamphlet entitled *Waugh's Statement* expressing "dissatisfaction and disappointment" among emigrants to Trinidad. The *Colored American* amplified his tract, describing Waugh as a "respectable man" who perhaps "embarked with too much anticipation" but, having his "hope sunk ... became disheartened, and found he had misapprehended most things." Another article was reprinted in the paper by a Black observer from Trinidad who described work conditions on the island as "complete slavery" and claimed that many disheartened emigrants now lamented that they had been deceived. Even worse was the climate, said to be so unhealthy that many emigrants now suffered from illness; some had even died. The *Colored American* seized on these despairing accounts, and by May the paper openly pronounced "a decided stand against ... all emigration to the West Indies."[64]

That November, Ray and the *Colored American* singled out Peck and Price for condemnation, perhaps because as free African Americans their opinion carried more weight on the matter. The two envoys had hoped that displaying the cordiality they received from the white colonial elite would prove to readers the social equality in Guiana. Now the paper turned those words against them, charging that both men were in the "lap of the planters." Ray scornfully wrote that sending agents to examine the British Caribbean on emigration was useless and implied that Peck and Price had been bribed by their hosts with free passage, lodgings, food, and politeness. Any men sent on such a mission, Ray charged, "would require an unusual amount of moral courage after having been *so richly* entertained." Ray's editorial concluded with an article from the abolitionist *British and Foreign Anti-Slavery*

Reporter, which similarly denounced Peck and Price as "simple-minded men" who had been duped by white planters to see "just what they wished to see."[65]

The criticisms heaped on Peck and Price in the *Colored American* illuminate the varying experiences of Black life in antebellum America. Peck and Price were from a slave state where threats of Black removal were ubiquitous. Ray, in contrast, belonged to the Black elite of New York and New England, which faced differing challenges. It is perhaps not surprising that emigration to the British Caribbean continued longest in Baltimore, to the scorn and derision of Black activists farther north. In answer to Ray's criticism that the state of African American emigrants in the Caribbean colonies was "enough to make Angels weep," Peck and Price rejoined in rebuttal: "Turn and look to our situation in this country, particularly in the slave states.... [I]t is at least enough to make us weep."[66]

But the British emigration scheme was not to last. More migrants were returning from the colonies, Trinidad in particular, with daunting and negative stories similar to *Waugh's Statement*. Planters unwilling to offer the type of fair wage labor promised found their African American workers no easier to exploit than their former apprentices. The economic downturn in cities like Baltimore was also on the mend by 1841, creating less of an impetus for relocation. That year, white American and British abolitionists, who had taken varied stances on West Indian emigration, joined African American activists like Ray in denouncing the scheme. Interest largely waned, with only one migrant from Baltimore in 1842. Emigration to the emancipated colonies of the British Caribbean would return as a possibility for free Black people in antebellum America, usually during times of social and financial distress. But it would never regain its earlier popularity.[67]

In British Guiana and Trinidad, the planter elite would experiment with other emigration schemes to recruit for labor. Among these were West Africans, although the preferred migrants would eventually become indentured South Asians. However, in 1839, when Peck and Price made their exploratory mission, this was not yet a foregone conclusion. In Guiana, both men saw a vision of freedom, even if imperfect, that awaited African Americans willing to venture to the British colonies. They attempted to negotiate this conflict between the desires of planters and the opportunities they believed emigration presented. Though West Indian emigration paled in comparison to more prominent appeals to West African colonization, their report remains evidence of an ongoing conversation on Black migration, its possibilities, and its limits within the nineteenth-century Black Atlantic.

NOTES

1. Nathaniel Peck and Thomas S. Price, *Report of Messrs. Peck and Price, Who Were Appointed at a Meeting of the Free Colored People of Baltimore, Held on the 25th November, 1839, Delegates to Visit British Guiana, and the Island of Trinidad; for the Purpose of Ascertaining the Advantages to Be Derived by Colored People Migrating to Those Places* (Baltimore, Md.: Woods & Crane, 1840), 3, 14.

2. Gad Heuman, "Riots and Resistance in the Caribbean at the Moment of Freedom," in *After Slavery: Emancipation and Its Discontents*, ed. Howard Temperley (London: Frank Cass Publishers, 2000), 14, 143–46; William A. Green, *British Slave Emancipation: The Sugar Colonies and the Great Experiment* (New York: Oxford University Press, 1976), 153; Josiah Conder, *Wages or the Whip: An Essay on the Comparative Cost and Productiveness of Free and Slave Labour* (London: Hatchard and Son, 1833), 52.

3. Selwyn Cudjoe, *The Slave Master of Trinidad: William Hardin Burnley and the Nineteenth-Century Atlantic World* (Amherst: University of Massachusetts Press, 2018), 132–33; Green, *British Slave Emancipation*, 262–76; Madhavi Kale, *Fragments of Empire: Capital, Slavery, and Indentured Labor in the British Caribbean* (Philadelphia: University of Pennsylvania Press, 1998), 12–32, 44–47.

4. Cudjoe, *The Slave Master*, 132–33; Kale, *Fragments of Empire*, 44–47.

5. Jeffrey R. Kerr-Ritchie, *Rites of August First: Emancipation Day in the Black Atlantic World* (Baton Rouge: Louisiana State University Press, 2007), 57, 84–85. See also my forthcoming work, *Jubilee's Experiment*, which explores the debates on the success of British emancipation in African American and abolitionist activism.

6. *Colored American*, August 18, 1838; Manisha Sinha, *The Slave's Cause: A History of Abolition* (New Haven, Conn.: Yale University Press, 2016), 183–90, 251–59. On antiabolitionist riots, see David Grimsted, *American Mobbing, 1828–1861: Toward Civil War* (New York: Oxford University Press, 1998).

7. Anonymous, *Inducements to the Colored People of the United States to Emigrate to British Guiana, Compiled from Statements and Documents Furnished by Edward Carbery, Agent of the Immigration Society of British Guiana and Proprietor in That Colony* (Boston: Kidder and Wright, 1840), 15–16; despatch from Governor Light to John Russell, no. 81, June 15, 1840, in *Parliamentary Papers* 16 (1841), 138–39.

8. Barbara Jeanne Fields, *Slavery and Freedom on the Middle Ground: Maryland during the Nineteenth Century* (New Haven, Conn.: Yale University Press, 1987), 40–62; T. Stephen Whitman, *The Price of Freedom: Slavery and Manumission in Baltimore and Early National Maryland* (Lexington: University Press of Kentucky, 1997), 8–13, 63–75, 95–118; Christopher Phillips, *Freedom's Port: The African American Community of Baltimore, 1790–1860* (Urbana: University of Illinois Press, 1997), 14–16, 35–55.

9. Whitman, *Price of Freedom*, 11–31; Phillips, *Freedom's Port*, 109–12, 155–75; Jessica Millward, *Finding Charity's Folk: Enslaved and Free Black Women in Maryland* (Athens: University of Georgia Press, 2015), 41–66.

10. Phillips, *Freedom's Port*, 178–80. For more on the Panic of 1837, see Jessica M. Lepler, *The Many Panics of 1837: People, Politics, and the Creation of a Transatlantic Financial Crisis* (New York: Cambridge University Press, 2013).

11. Phillips, *Freedom's Port*, 183–92; Maryland legislature quoted in William Jay, *The American Tract Society, Withdrawal from, by Judge Jay, on the Ground of Its Alliance with the Slave Power, Proved by the Expurgation of All Anti-slavery Sentiment from Its Publication and Its Refusal to Bear Any Testimony in Opposition to the Sin of Slaveholding* (Boston: Press of Damrell and Moore, 1853), 92; Richard L. Hall, *On Afric's Shore: A History of Maryland in Liberia* (Baltimore: Maryland Historical Society, 2003), 16–17.

12. Phillips, *Freedom's Port*, 194–200; *The Liberator*, September 14, 1838.

13. Carbery quoted in *Anti-Slavery Reporter*, July 1, 1840; despatch from Governor Light to John Russell, June 15, 1840.

14. A short-lived and Black-led Haytien Emigration Society existed as well in the 1820s. Hall, *On Afric's Shore*, 15–17, 25; "An Act Relating to the People of Color in This State," Maryland Law of 1831, chap. 281 (passed March 12, 1832); Penelope Campbell, *Maryland in Africa: The Maryland State Colonization Society, 1831–1857* (Urbana: University of Illinois Press, 1971), 35–42; LeRoy Graham, *Baltimore: The Nineteenth Century Black Capital* (Lanham, Md.: University Press of America, 1982), 96.

15. Phillips, *Freedom's Port*, 212, 220–24; Campbell, *Maryland in Africa*, 39–42; Martha Jones, *Birthright Citizens: A History of Race and Rights in Antebellum America* (New York: Cambridge University Press, 2018), 37–39, 46–47; *The Liberator*, June 4, 1831. For more on African American anticolonization efforts, see Ousmane K. Power-Greene, *Against Wind and Tide: The African American Struggle against the Colonization Movement* (New York: New York University Press, 2014).

16. Hall, *On Afric's Shore*, 23; Phillips, *Freedom's Port*, 214–15.

17. Hidetaka Hirota, *Expelling the Poor: Atlantic Seaboard States and the Nineteenth-Century Origins of American Immigration Policy* (New York: Oxford University Press, 2017), 55–58.

18. Anonymous, *Inducements*, 18. These are not Carbery's words directly, but they are featured in a later pamphlet describing his appeal made as an emigration agent.

19. Peck and Price, *Report*, 3; Anonymous, *Inducements*, 16; Governor Light to John Russell, June 15, 1840; *Royal Gazette* (Guiana), January 23, 1840; Phillips, *Freedom's Port*, 133–43. The two more prominent Black Methodist churches for Afro-Baltimoreans were the Methodist Episcopal church on Sharp Street, founded in 1802, and Bethel AME Church on East Saratoga Street, founded in 1816. The former was still subject to white church authority, while the latter was fully independent and tied to the AME congregations of Philadelphia and New York. Despite their divisions, both remained central to the Black political and social life of antebellum Baltimore and saw frequent interactions. See J. Gordon Melton, "African American Methodism in the M.E. Tradition: The Case of Sharp Street," *North Star: A Journal of African American Religious History* 8, no. 2 (Spring 2005).

20. James A. Thome and J. Horace Kimball, *Emancipation in the West Indies: A Six months' Tour in Antigua, Barbadoes, and Jamaica in the Year 1837* (New York: American Anti-Slavery Society, 1838); *Colored American*, December 29, 1838.

21. Loren Schweninger, *Black Property Owners in the South, 1790–1915* (Urbana: University of Illinois Press, 1997), 122; Phillips, *Freedom's Port*, 153.

22. Price is listed as a whitewasher in local directories and Peck a wall colorer. However, both emigration officials in Guiana and church records mention other occupations. Richard J. Matchett, *Matchett's Baltimore Director[y], Corrected up to May, 1837, for 1837–8* (Baltimore, Md.: Baltimore Directory Office, 1837), 251, 258; despatch from Governor Light to John Russell, June 15, 1840; Daniel A. Payne, *History of the African Methodist Episcopal Church* (Nashville: A.M.E. Sunday School Union, 1891), 59–60; Vincent Bakpetu Thompson, *Africans of the Diaspora: The Evolution of African Consciousness and Leadership in the Americas* (Trenton, N.J.: Africa World Press, 1992), 206; Phillips, *Freedom's Port*, 215–16.

23. Peck and Price, *Report*, 4–5; *Royal Gazette*, January 23, 1840.

24. Peck and Price, *Report*, 4–6.

25. Ibid., 6. The "macadam" method was named for the Scotsman John Loudon McAdam; the technique consisted of compacted layers of small stones cemented into a hard surface through stone dust and water.

26. Ibid., 6; Phillips, *Freedom's Port*, 120–21; Donald G. Mathews, *Slavery and Methodism: A Chapter in American Morality, 1780–1845* (Princeton, N.J.: Princeton University Press, 1965), 19–21.

27. Peck and Price, *Report*, 6–7.

28. "Affairs of British Guiana," in *Parliamentary Papers* 16 (1841), 158.

29. Peck and Price, *Report*, 7.

30. Ibid., 8; "British Guiana 2282 (Spring Garden)," Legacies of British Slave-Ownership Database, http://wwwdepts-live.ucl.ac.uk/lbs/claim/view/8556.

31. Peck and Price, *Report*, 8, 9.

32. Green, *British Slave Emancipation*, 198–99. Many of the initial vagrancy laws were eventually disallowed by London for being too close in wording and spirit to the previous slave laws. See Great Britain, Parliament, House of Commons, *Accounts and Papers of the House of Commons* 45 (1848), 125–31.

33. Peck and Price, *Report*, 9.

34. Papers Relative to British Guiana, in *Parliamentary Papers* 34 (1840), 47–54; Michael Craton, *Testing the Chains: Resistance to Slavery in the British West Indies* (Ithaca, N.Y.: Cornell University Press, 1982), 270–71.

35. Peck and Price, *Report*, 10.

36. Ibid., 10–11; Daniel Coker, *Journal of Daniel Coker: A Descendant of Africa, from the Time of Leaving New York, in the Ship "Elizabeth," Capt. Sebor, on a Voyage for Sherbro, in Africa, in Company with Three Agents, and About Ninety Persons of Colour* (Baltimore, Md.: Edward J. Coale, 1820), 42–43; Phillips, *Freedom's Port*, 135.

37. Peck and Price, *Report*, 11; Allan Young, *The Approaches to Local Self-Government in British Guiana* (Kingston: University College of the West Indies, 1958), 7.

38. In 1801 the Maryland Constitution was amended to give the right to vote to "every free white male citizen of this state, and no other." See Virgil Maxcy, *The Laws of Maryland: 1692–1785* (Baltimore, Md.: Philip H. Nicklin & Co., 1811), 34.

39. Peck and Price, *Report*, 11.

40. Ibid., 13.

41. Ibid., 13–14. For Black Baltimoreans' use of the law and legal action, see Jones, *Birthright Citizens*, 59–70, 89–127.

42. Peck and Price, *Report*, 14–15; Seth Rockman, *Scraping By: Wage Labor, Slavery, and Survival in Early Baltimore* (Baltimore, Md.: Johns Hopkins University Press, 2009).

43. Peck and Price, *Report*, 14–15, 18.

44. Ibid., 14, 18.

45. Anonymous, *Inducements*, 14–15; "Affairs of British Guiana," 113.

46. Peck and Price, *Report*, 14, 18, 20–22.

47. Ibid., 18–19.

48. Ibid., 19.

49. Ibid., 15–16. These are abbreviated versions of the questions.

50. Ibid., 15–18.

51. Ibid., 22–25.

52. Ibid., 22–23; Robert Montgomery Martin, ed., *Colonial Magazine and Commercial-Maritime Journal, May to August 1840 Volume 2* (London: Fischer, Son, & Co., 1840), 119.

53. Peck and Price, *Report*, 23.

54. Ibid., 24; *The Sun* (Baltimore), January 17, 29, 1840. The passage for the Annapolis delegates appears to have been paid for by Maryland state legislators, who raised the money well into late January.

55. Anonymous, *Inducements*, 16; "An Act to Encourage the Emigration of the Free People of Colour of This State," Maryland Law of 1839, chap. 29 (passed in December Session, 1839); *The Sun*, January 22, 1840; Jones, *Birthright Citizens*, 61, 96–102.

56. *The Sun*, April 18, 1840.

57. Peck and Price, *Report*, 25.

58. *The Sun*, October 29, November 29, 30, December 6, 1839, January 15, 1840.

59. *The Sun*, April 15, 1840.

60. *The Sun*, April 4, 1840. Much of this is related through a series of letters preceding Jones and Hays's arrival, detailing what they intended to speak on in their address. The only dissatisfaction Jones and Hay related was from several barbers and waiters unaccustomed to plantation labor.

61. *The Sun*, April 17, 1840; Phillips, *Freedom's Port*, 217–18. For advertisements of passage from Baltimore, see *The Sun*, February 27, 1840, and in later editions through 1840.

62. *The Sun*, May 5, 1840.

63. *Colored American*, August 11, 1838, July 27, 1839.

64. *Colored American*, April 4, 11, 1840.

65. *Colored American*, August 1, November 7, 1840.
66. Jones, *Birthright Citizens*, 62–63; *Colored American*, May 16, 1840.
67. *Colored American*, March 20, November 13, 1841; Winch, *A Gentleman of Color*, 316–17; Phillips, *Freedom's Port*, 218–20.

CHAPTER 8

A Reinterpretation of African Americans and Haitian Emigration

BRANDON R. BYRD

In November 1895 James Theodore Holly sent his twenty-first annual report from Port-au-Prince to the Board of Missions of the Episcopal Church. Holly, who had fled from the United States to Haiti, obtained Haitian citizenship, and become the Episcopal Church's first Black bishop, mourned the death of one of the most valuable clergymen from his missionary staff and lamented the delayed work on his new church building in the Haitian capital. He promised that his Orthodox Episcopal Church of Haiti was overcoming those obstacles, though. "It will be seen," Holly concluded in an appeal for more funding, "that, notwithstanding very limited pecuniary aid from abroad, the Church in Haiti has been gradually extending its beneficent influence among the public at large ... by the ministry of its teachers, physicians, and clergy."[1]

Those physicians included Alonzo Potter Burgess Holly, a graduate of the New York Homeopathic Medical College and one of James Theodore's sons. In his missionary report, James Theodore made special mention of "a mutual relief society which Dr. Alonzo Holly organized last year among the English-speaking residents of Gonaïves," Haiti. The benevolent society of approximately fifty members charged a small entrance fee and modest monthly dues, which were then used to help sick members. It ensured that those English-speaking citizens and residents of Haiti had "nourishment and medicine" in addition to the spiritual fulfillment provided at the Episcopal services that Alonzo hosted on Sunday afternoons.[2]

Although fleeting, the reference to the Gonaïves-based mutual aid society reveals a long transnational social history of "Haitian emigration."[3] The "English-speaking residents of Gonaïves" most likely included Black men and women who, like James Theodore Holly, had moved from the United States or Canada to pursue a more meaningful freedom in Hispaniola, the island containing Haiti and the Dominican Republic, which was unified under Haitian governance from 1822 to 1844. Others probably shared the same ancestry as Alonzo Holly, a Haitian citizen born to African Americans.[4] Together, in a coastal town to which hundreds of other African Americans had migrated in previous decades, some of these first- and second-generation Haitians continued to draw on some aspects of African American culture to sustain themselves long after their initial arrival or their family's permanent settlement in Haiti. Their new social institutions, built in what had become their home, included a mutual aid society that bore a striking resemblance to those historically found in Black communities in the U.S. North.

Historians have offered a more static history of Haitian emigration. The established narrative of Haitian emigration begins in the early 1820s, when Haitian president Jean-Pierre Boyer, eager for U.S. diplomatic recognition, courted potential settlers from the United States with promises of socioeconomic opportunities provided by his government and Pan-Africanist appeals emphasizing the racial bonds between African Americans and Haitians. At least six thousand and as many as thirteen thousand responded favorably and emigrated from mainland North America to Hispaniola. Purportedly, most returned. Relying on U.S. newspapers, some of them opposed to emigration, that slowed their coverage of the Haitian movement after 1826 and scouring U.S. shipping records that provide excellent data about returns to U.S. ports but not departures from them, scholars have established a declensionist narrative in which Boyer's "migration project" not only failed but "backfired spectacularly" by contributing to Haiti's declining respect on the international stage. They have suggested that its "failure" is embodied by returnees chastened by "unforeseen hardship, disease, and a clash between reality and what they had been led to believe" and epitomized by the "diminished role" of Haiti in "African American political and economic visions" after the 1830s.[5]

In this interpretation, the 1820s movement bears only superficial relation to a subsequent wave of Haitian emigration that crested in the early 1860s. Historians have reached a consensus that a resurgence of emigrationism and Black nationalism amid the political setbacks to abolitionism in the decade before the U.S. Civil War led to the movement of approximately two thousand African Americans from the United States to Haiti under the auspices of the short-lived, Boston-based Haytian Bureau of Emigration (HBE). Relying on the archive produced by and about that organization, historians have concluded that "the Haitian emigration movement failed as large numbers of dissatisfied settlers returned to the United States."[6]

The scholarship on Haitian emigration thus obscures a great deal. Few have considered what contemporaries knew to be true: migration to Haiti persisted across the nineteenth century outside of Haiti's state-sponsored immigration projects.[7] Likewise, the failure of Haitian emigration has been accepted as fact.[8] Scholars have written its history from U.S. sources and the perspectives of its contemporary critics, who exaggerated the number of returnees and insinuated that Haiti's ostensible problems—its culture, climate, poverty, and political strife—presented insurmountable obstacles to African Americans allegedly possessed of their own pathologies and overly influenced by their U.S. identities. Their works have elided a history of permanent settlement, rendering it unthinkable.[9] With the notable exception of the scholarship on the African American immigrants to Samaná, there has been almost no consideration given to the Haitian communities produced by Haitian emigration.[10] The English-speaking residents of Gonaïves have been made invisible or illegible by the reductive idea of failure.

This chapter attempts a fuller recovery and centering of their histories. While extant scholarship has suggested a dearth of surviving evidence of permanent African American residence in Hispaniola, particularly Haiti, ample sources belie that assumption. Documents that show the consequential presence of African American immigrants and their descendants in nineteenth-century Hispaniola include ecclesiastical records from Black religious institutions established in the island, U.S. diplomatic records, U.S. and European travel narratives, and nineteenth-century Haitian histories and newspapers. By reading these underutilized documents as part of a more expansive archive of "Haitian emigration" while also reconsidering well-trod sources, this chapter pivots from a U.S.-centric framework of emigration toward a more dialogic and expansive history of immigration. It offers a dynamic retelling of movement, long-term residence, and naturalization that suggests the enduring impact of Haiti's immigration policy *and* African American immigrants on Haitian politics, culture, and society. It is a step toward a more complete picture of African American history and Hispaniola's oft-overlooked and misunderstood nineteenth century.

African Americans and the Origins of Haitian Emigration

The history of Haitian emigration begins with the Haitian Revolution. By the late eighteenth century, Saint-Domingue was the source of roughly half of the Western world's sugar and coffee. It was the "Pearl of the Antilles," the crown jewel of the French Empire. In August 1791 its enslaved population, the brutalized source of Saint-Domingue's wealth, began burning it down. The success of the slave uprising bore legislative fruit in August 1793 with the first emancipation decree in Saint-Domingue and in February 1794, when the French National Convention abolished slavery in its colonies. Word of the historic abolitionist acts stimulated by the actions of the enslaved quickly spread on the "regional network of communication—the 'common wind' which bound together the societies of Afro-America."[11] Enslaved people from the United States and across the Americas fled to freedom, to Saint-Domingue. Their daring flights, captured in myriad runaway ads, freedom suits, and court cases, reveal a hemispheric understanding of Haiti as a land of liberty even before its declaration of national independence.[12]

As Ada Ferrer has shown, those acts of self-emancipation were welcomed by local authorities in revolutionary Saint-Domingue; in fact, they encouraged the early policy making of Haiti. Shortly after issuing Haiti's Declaration of Independence, Jean-Jacques Dessalines, Haiti's first head of state, issued a decree offering to pay U.S. ship captains willing to return to Haiti people of African descent whose enslavers had stolen them from Saint-Domingue during the Haitian Revolution. He understood repopulation as a pressing need for Haiti; his successors agreed. Dessalines's assassination in October 1806 sparked a decade of civil war and regional division in the western third of Hispaniola. Haiti became two states, with Henry Christophe as king of the northern Kingdom of Haiti and Alexandre Pétion rising to the presidency of the southern Republic of Haiti.[13] The latter leader simultaneously emulated and disavowed his predecessor as he issued calls, then published in U.S. newspapers, for "men of color" to return "to the bosom of [their] native country" now that the "dreadful reigns [*sic*] of Dessalines" had ended. He then expanded that invitation to enjoy a "secure asylum" in Haiti.[14] In September 1816 Pétion issued a new constitution, whose article 44 stated that "all Africans and Indians, and the descendants of their blood, born in the colonies or in foreign countries, who come to reside in the Republic will be recognized as Haitians, but will enjoy the right of citizenship only after one year of residence."¹⁵ Article 44, Ferrer argues, "elevate[d] Haiti as a tangible source of freedom and citizenship for any black person—no matter his or her location or status—who could make it to Haitian territory." Inserted into a constitution that also banned slavery and prohibited property in human beings, the article asserted Haiti's antislavery policy and sovereignty by expanding traditional notions of free soil, asylum, and sanctuary and engaging newer ideas about freedom and universal rights in a way that responded "to initiatives and demands by black and brown people in Haiti and beyond."¹⁶

The radicalism of the 1816 constitution was clear to African Americans who saw it as the basis not just of individual emancipation from slavery but also of a more expansive and universal freedom from racism. In 1817 an African American named James Tredwell traveled from the United States to the Republic of Haiti in order "to satisfy myself and some particular friends respecting the present situation of those (once oppressed) sons and daughters of Africa."¹⁷ Tredwell likely departed from New York, the city with the largest Black population in a state that had just passed its second gradual emancipation law. Legally free, he might have possessed intimate knowledge of how racism would afflict Black New Yorkers long after emancipation. As his scant public writings show, Tredwell was motivated by a Pan-African ethos and influenced by popular understandings of Haiti, the first postslavery society in the Americas, as a singular place to assess the material and moral development of African descendant people once freed from their "cruel bondage."¹⁸ He certainly saw Haiti as a sanctuary or asylum for African Americans. In Port-au-Prince, Tredwell had "frequent interviews" with Joseph Balthazar Inginac, Pétion's secretary general. Those talks focused on one particular question from Tredwell: "What privileges people of colour might expect who should emigrate thither from America?" Before Tredwell left Haiti for the United States, Inginac gave him a letter in which he implored African Americans to "open to their eyes the Constitution of our Republic, and let them see in its 44th Article a fraternal hand opened to their distresses." Tredwell understood the letter as an "invitation to the coloured people in America to emigrate to [Haiti]."¹⁹ He subsequently published English translations of the letter, the 1816 constitution, and several other documents from Pétion's government before returning to Haiti, this time for good.

Along with the better-known Prince Saunders, Tredwell helped stimulate some piecemeal African American immigration to Haiti. Pétion published the 1816 constitution in the same year that a coalition of U.S. slaveholders and abolitionists established the American Colonization Society (ACS), an organization dedicated to the removal of free African Americans from the United States to West Africa.[20] Word of Pétion's constitution solidified Haiti's place in the heated debates about the fate of Black people in the United States.[21] Thanks to Tredwell, numerous African Americans in the U.S. North would have read or heard renditions of the 1816 constitution.[22] Many welcomed recruiting pitches from Saunders.[23] Born in New England during the era of the War for American Independence, Saunders had first traveled to the Kingdom of Haiti in 1816. He established a tenuous relationship with Christophe before returning to the United States in the spring of 1818. There, Saunders published documents showing the "enlightened systems of policy, the pacific spirit, the altogether domestic views, and liberal principles of the [Kingdom of Haiti]."[24] He solicited support for immigration to Haiti from religious leaders in Salem, Massachusetts, extolled the educational system of the Kingdom of Haiti before a large crowd of Black Philadelphians, and implored the American Convention of Abolition Societies to prioritize Haiti, not Africa, as a refuge for African Americans. While most African Americans rejected the "colonizing trick" of the ACS, some were receptive to the appeals from Haiti translated by Tredwell and Saunders. One shopkeeper in Philadelphia testified in a signed affidavit that in 1819 one of his employees, an emancipated Black man who previously worked as a porter, had expressed his intentions of immigrating to "the Republic of Hayti to which place a number of coloured persons were going."[25] Saunders corroborated this account when he returned to the Kingdom of Haiti in August 1820 with letters showing the wishes of thousands of Black Philadelphians who wanted to leave the United States too.[26]

Reconsidering the First Wave of Haitian Emigration

An uncertain number of African Americans arrived in Haiti amid political and social upheaval. Pétion died in March 1818. Boyer, his chosen successor, having retained Inginac as secretary of state, continued to recruit emigrants from the United States. He explained that African Americans could become in Haiti self-sufficient farmers within a year and predicted that their agricultural production would help strengthen commercial ties between the United States and Haiti.[27] He imagined them as key parts of a more prosperous, unified, and expanded Haiti that would be recognized by all the world's powers.[28] As Boyer's appeals to African American "cultivators" circulated in U.S. newspapers, his troops subdued Grand'Anse, a region of southern Haiti that had maintained its independence from Pétion's republic. After the suicide of Christophe, these troops then conquered the former Kingdom of Haiti. In February 1822, following his unification of the competing Haitian states, Boyer sent his soldiers into Santo Domingo. With the popular support of Spain's former colonial subjects and slaves, he declared universal emancipation across Hispaniola and united the island under the Haitian flag. His actions would open a new field for African American migrants during his presidency, a period that lasted until 1843, when Boyer, facing mass resistance to his authoritarianism, fled to exile in Jamaica.

While scholars have emphasized how and why African Americans became objects of Boyer's political interests, evidence suggests that, like Saunders and Tredwell, African American immigrants continued to be influential collaborators in Haitian state-building. In 1818, around the same time that Boyer became president of Haiti, Silvain Simonisse immigrated to Port-au-Prince. According to the nineteenth-century Haitian historians Thomas Madiou and Beaubrun Ardouin, Simonisse was born in South Carolina to an unnamed Black mother and a white father who possessed "liberal sentiments." Having received an education in England that expanded his mind and bolstered his self-confidence but that could not shield him from discrimination back in the United States, Simonisse had, along with his two brothers, adopted Haiti as his "homeland" while claiming protection under its "republican constitution."[29] In the Haitian capital, Simonisse continued to follow developments in the United States, which included the disheartening growth of the ACS. Following in the footsteps of early Haitian leaders and African American abolitionists, he proposed Haiti as an alternative home for African Americans groaning under the same oppressions that he had escaped. In 1819 or early 1820, not long after settling in Port-au-Prince and becoming a naturalized Haitian citizen, Simonisse approached Inginac with a plan to form a society for African American immigration. Inginac was, unsurprisingly, enthusiastic. Under his direction but "on the initiative" of Simonisse, the Société Philanthropique de la République d'Haïti was born in June 1820.[30]

The Philanthropic Society of Haiti established not just an institutional but also an intellectual foundation for immigration. In June 1820 the officers of the society wrote a constitution that dictated that its membership fees and the expected supplementary funds from Boyer would pay the salaries of recruiting agents sent to the United States, defray the travel costs of male laborers and their families, and provide financial support for immigrants until they became self-sufficient. The officers voiced those terms in the complementary languages of economic diplomacy and diaspora. In their founding constitution, Simonisse, Inginac, and their colleagues promised that African Americans would benefit from the fraternal altruism of Haitians, who were extending "a healing hand to their brothers in America" who faced removal to the "uncivilized" shores of Africa or continued racial oppression in the United States, while suggesting that Haiti would then profit from industrious African American immigrants. The latter would contribute to "the prosperity of the country" by adding to a population finally experiencing natural growth following the horrors of slavery, raising Haiti's export crops, and strengthening its economic ties to the United States.[31]

The society's articulation of the multiple multinational benefits of immigration soon reached its intended international audience. By May 1821 U.S. newspapers reported receiving copies of "the Constitution of a Society lately established at Port-au-Prince, with ample funds to encourage the emigration of free Africans and their descendants from the United States, and to provide for the payment of the passages of those unable to pay their own, and their support until they can find employment."[32] Those copies complemented a host of other documents from Haiti, including the Haitian Declaration of Independence and the first Haitian constitutions. Although the philanthropic society's constitution addressed legally free African Americans, it incentivized the manumission or self-emancipation of their enslaved counterparts. It promised, too, that Haiti could exercise the type of border control and extend the types of protections to migrants that would become markers of national sovereignty. The circulation and translation of the constitution thus affirmed Haitian sovereignty and allowed the Philanthropic Society of Haiti to further project Haiti's abolitionism far beyond its borders. It added to the robust archive of Black freedom and statehood that Haiti's earliest leaders projected into the Atlantic world.[33]

Although more research is needed on the society's early operations, which were suspended due to Boyer's military campaigns, the society clearly assumed an important role upon its re-formation in August 1824. In the same moment that Boyer entered into conversations with the white colonizationist Loring Dewey and sent his agent, Jonathas Granville, to the United States to promote his immigration project, Inginac resumed the presidency of the revived Philanthropic Society of Haiti.[34] The organization reportedly had as many as 240 members by its second full month of operations. Its leadership again articulated for an international audience the abolitionist and Pan-

African aspects of Haitian emigration. Echoing literature exported by the society, U.S. newspapers reported that the "chief labours of the Society ... are directed to the emancipation of the coloured population of every country from slavery and degradation, to the elevation of the African character, and to the inspiring confidence and the instilling of sentiments of virtue and benevolence into the minds of the ill-fated race."[35] They publicized the cultural function of the organization, which migrants soon experienced. According to Madiou, members of the philanthropic society formed a welcome party that delivered refreshments to the passengers of the *Charlotte Corday*, one of the first ships to arrive in Haiti under the auspices of Boyer's immigration program. They then took the migrants to the National Palace to meet Boyer. Afterward, Inginac led a reception, where he toasted his "dear brothers and friends," who could now "walk with your head held high, without fear of the insults that elsewhere follow the descendants of Africans." Simonisse then ensured that the English-speaking migrants understood the fraternal feelings expressed by his colleague. He translated the speech to his new compatriots, "who were very satisfied with it."[36]

While Haiti's first mass immigration project clearly produced a robust archive of Black internationalism, a body of sources that testify to the intellectual and affective experiences of Black collaboration across national boundaries, it also created a competing archive of abstractions, estimates, and anecdotes that historians would read as measures of its failure.[37] The Haitian government planned for the even distribution of six thousand immigrants, including the passengers of the *Charlotte Corday*, outside of Gonaïves, Port-au-Prince, Les Cayes, Cap-Haïtien, Puerto Plata, Samaná, Santo Domingo, and other towns across Hispaniola, where they would cultivate cotton, coffee, tobacco, and sugar.[38] It subsequently assessed this grand project of national and racial regeneration according to the number of potential settlers lost, not those gained. In a letter sent in April 1826 to Benjamin Lundy, a prominent Quaker abolitionist, editor, and supporter of Haitian emigration, Inginac complained that his government had "facilitated, at a great expense, the transportation hither of more than six thousand emigrants from the United States" only to see that "a portion of these emigrants (which may be estimated at about one third) elated with the idea of finding in Hayti, without labor, wealth and all the pleasures of life, have not been satisfied on their arrival in their new country." He lamented seeing "the discontented desert the country, leaving behind them but the proofs of the most cruel ingratitude."[39]

Historians have taken what Inginac called an estimate as fact. They have read his proclamation of failure, encouraged by the hopes imbued in Haitian emigration, as the evidence needed to treat similar anecdotes as data. Reading newspaper accounts of migrants' "escape" from Haiti as representative and extrapolating from passenger lists showing the arrival in U.S. ports of ships bearing African American passengers from Haiti, foundational histories of Haitian emigration during the 1820s characterize it as a short-lived failure because of the supposed disillusionment of "many" or even "most" of its participants. It is telling that the most comprehensive account of this "first wave" ends with a chapter titled "Haitian Realities and the Emigrants' Return."[40]

Yet Inginac's silent two-thirds demands our attention. Even while bemoaning the "discontented" migrants who abandoned Haiti for places unnamed, Inginac clearly suggested that some, many, or even most immigrants funded by the Haitian government remained. The implied presence of that other "portion" of immigrants begs a question that historians have answered only in passing: What happened to the African Americans who made Haiti their home?

African American Immigrants in Boyer's Haiti

A report from Lundy points toward possible answers. In August 1829 Lundy made his second trip to Haiti. The antislavery editor traveled with twelve African Americans, formerly enslaved people emancipated by their enslaver on the condition, perhaps negotiated, of their removal from Maryland to Haiti. Lundy would settle the formerly enslaved African Americans in Haiti while also assessing "the condition of the colored emigrants who were removed from the United States three or four years since." In his report back to the United States, published in the *African Repository and Colonial Journal*, the official organ of the ACS, Lundy admitted that some of the approximately six thousand African Americans "removed at the expense of the Haitian government" had "become discontented and returned" to the United States. He, however, noted that many African Americans, including those whose travel was not funded and who thus went unaccounted for by the Haitian government, had stayed. According to Lundy, Haiti's population included approximately eight thousand African Americans who had "emigrated from the United States within the past eight or nine years." Some were agricultural laborers "dissatisfied with the system of working on shares, while others are doing remarkably well." A number were even "among the most influential and respectable inhabitants" of Haiti.[41]

While Lundy had reason to exaggerate the number of African Americans living in Haiti—he was, after all, a proponent of emigration and colonization—his nuanced picture of the African American immigrant experience in Haiti cannot be dismissed. The antislavery Quaker did not ignore the reality of disillusionment, even among African Americans who remained in Haiti. The longing for home, shared by exiles, immigrants, and refugees across time and place, was real. So was discontent with the harsh material conditions that faced agricultural laborers across the slavery and postslavery societies of the Americas. Yet Lundy also pointed to the possibilities of satisfaction and fulfillment—of African Americans who, especially in Haiti's towns, found more socioeconomic opportunities and, just as importantly, respect and dignity. His narrative more seamlessly tied Haitian emigration to Haiti's domestic politics and social life.

Similar accounts from foreign residents in Haiti, including Charles Mackenzie, do the same. One year after Lundy reported his impressions of Haiti, Mackenzie, the British consul general to Port-au-Prince, published *Notes on Haiti*. In it he described the markets in the Haitian capital, where buyers could find "a respectable supply not only of tropical vegetables and fruit, but of some European kinds, which are raised by some natives, and by some of the American settlers, who have received grants of land from the government." He revealed that he had not only tasted the fruits of Haitian emigration but also observed its legacies. In his account of life in Hispaniola, Mackenzie recalled traveling "about a league" from Puerto Plata and observing "some neat cottages, surrounded with remarkably well-dressed gardens and fenced fields." He quickly "learned that they were the dwellings of some North American emigrants—the few who remained of all the first parties who had so eagerly sought the land of liberty and equality."[42]

Although Mackenzie attributed the success of African American landowners to the generous terms under which they had emigrated from the United States, he also hinted at how other African Americans were affected by Boyer's efforts to create a compliant rural workforce conducive to the rebuilding of a plantation-based economy and the political needs of his state.[43] Mackenzie recalled that, after arriving in Haiti in 1826, he had "always one labourer, generally an American emigrant, residing on my premises" two miles outside of Port-au-Prince. His lamentation that those workers tasked with maintaining his estate and growing grass for his horses rarely stayed on for extended periods suggests that temporary wage labor was one way that African American immigrants found some semblance of economic security even as they sought personal autonomy, which had become more elusive since their arrival in Haiti.[44]

In the same year that Mackenzie took up his post in Port-au-Prince, Boyer passed a new Code Rural, which affected all residents of rural Haiti, African American immigrants included. The legislation gave large landowners extensive powers and declared that any rural resident not working as a servant, employed by the government or military, or practicing a profession had to "cultivate the land." It also banned agricultural cooperatives, forbade peasants from operating their own produce stands, restricted the movement of rural residents from the countryside to towns and cities, and allowed local officials to conscript laborers for public works projects.[45] After the passage of this code, which was meant to revive sugar production, Mackenzie visited a sugar plantation outside of Les Cayes owned by a wealthy merchant and a military officer. There, he talked to the approximately sixty African Americans, "liberated" by Quakers from slavery in North Carolina, now working on the estate with the promise of receiving one-fourth of its crop. He noted that the "personal complaint, and the general grievances" of the workers "were perfectly overwhelming." Their housing was "bad, in a sort of barrack." They suffered from "want of medical attendance, and many were afflicted with ulcers in their legs." According to Mackenzie, the African Americans, effectively sharecroppers, were loudest in "their denunciations of their Haitian neighbours, whom they described as destroying their fences to admit their bullocks into their gardens, and as plundering them of their poultry and pigs." They reportedly told Mackenzie that "it was absolutely necessary to keep a regular guard at night."[46]

The conflict in Haiti's countryside, encouraged by Boyer's policies, seems to have pushed numerous African American immigrants to Haiti's cities, not back to the United States. Decades after Mackenzie published his *Notes on Haiti*, Benjamin Hunt, a white American who had lived in Haiti for more than a decade in the mid-nineteenth century, recalled that "more than one of Boyer's old immigrants ... told me that they were obliged to give up agriculture." The would-be landowners "found their fences down, or their water let off ... or evidence that cattle had been fed on their grounds over night; or the neighboring idlers ... had stolen all their plantains and sweet potatoes for the market."[47] Hunt almost certainly simplified or misidentified the cause of the possibly embellished conflict by characterizing it as "jealousy and ill-will" when it should probably be seen as another form of popular Haitian resistance to the state's attempted consolidation of land in rural Haiti.[48] Still, he presented compelling testimony about the effects of the rural conflict. Hunt reported that he knew of two African American carters "who acquired a little property" in Haiti and another "two black men and two men of color" from the U.S. North who "cultivated in a poor way, a little land which they called their own." Echoing "Boyer's old immigrants," who told him that the "annoyances" in the countryside caused them to "take to trading in towns," he implied that such examples of successful landownership were exceptions: he had not heard of any of "Boyer's thirteen thousand American immigrants . . . who, after 1836, was living on the land assigned him by [the] government on his arrival."[49]

In contrast, Hunt, like his contemporaries, had seen numerous African Americans in Haiti's cities, and he suggested how the presence of those immigrants might have amplified, not just reflected, some dynamics of class, color, and language in urban Haiti. During the mid-nineteenth-century, Haitian writers praised the African Americans who had proven themselves as "hardworking citizens" through the practice of "various trades" and "small trade" while crediting others with the ignominious start of the "rag-picking industry" in Port-au-Prince.[50] One foreign visitor noted the presence of African American women in the market in Gonaïves and recalled interviewing "Madame Johnson, an American Black, who emigrated from Philadelphia in the time of Boyer." She had found economic prosperity as the owner of a public hotel in that port town but accused less fortunate African American immigrants of being great "libertines."[51] Hunt came to similar conclusions. Some poor laborers from the urban North experienced similar misfortune as "day laborers, or worse" in urban Haiti, he asserted. Many "rag-pickers" in nineteenth-century Cap-Haïtien and Port-au-Prince were indeed "aged Philadelphians." Still, other African American immigrants, particularly those who spoke French or had some social and financial capital due to their light complexions, had prospered in Haiti's cities. Hunt cited the "successful" examples of seven merchants, four mechanics, and two lawyers, all of whom were "men of color or mulattoes" from South Carolina, Virginia, Pennsylvania, and New Orleans. He observed, too, that African American immigrants from Philadelphia, New Orleans, and elsewhere in the U.S. South operated "the best tailoring establishment," a popular bakery, and "one of the best cabinet-making establishments" in Port-au-Prince. In fact, the principal sailmakers in the Haitian capital and Cap-Haïtien were both African Americans who had apprenticed under James Forten, the famous abolitionist and sailmaker from Philadelphia.[52]

Besides becoming part of an urban poor in some cases and a petit bourgeoisie in others, African American immigrants formed an essential part of the religious life in Haiti's cities. As observed by Mark Bird, a British Wesleyan missionary who arrived in Haiti in 1841, a number of the African Americans who emigrated from the United States in the 1820s were Baptist and African Methodist Episcopal preachers. "Small churches therefore soon sprung up" across Hispaniola, and in "Port-au-Prince a neat little edifice was raised by the American colored immigrants which would accommodate some two hundred hearers." By 1869, aided by the later influx of African American immigrants and Haitian converts, the roots of Haitian Protestantism were firmly planted, as evidenced by the thousands of attendees at African Methodist Episcopal, Wesleyan Methodist, Baptist, and Episcopal services across most of Hispaniola's major towns and cities.[53]

At the same time that African American immigrants contributed to the foundations of Haitian Protestantism, they also formed abolitionist societies that collaborated with their U.S. counterparts. In March 1836 Evan Williams, a Black Virginian who moved to Haiti during the 1820s, led a small group of fellow African American immigrants and their Haitian allies in forming the Haitian Abolition Society (HAS). Williams, who ran a coeducational liberal arts school in Port-au-Prince, became its president.[54] Under his leadership, the HAS affirmed its solidarities with African Americans through correspondence with the U.S. Black press; sent abolitionist addresses given during its meetings to antislavery publications in the United States; donated barrels of sugar and bags of coffee, free produce not produced by slave labor, to the American Anti-Slavery Society and the widow of the martyred U.S. abolitionist Elijah Lovejoy; and communicated with influential U.S. politicians who were potential antislavery allies, including John Quincy Adams.[55] Its members also led Haitian celebrations of Emancipation Day in the British West Indies and hosted the U.S. abolitionists Lewis C. Gunn and Charles Burleigh on their widely publicized trip to Haiti.[56] Such efforts inspired foreign abolitionists, including William Lloyd Garrison, who celebrated the support of emancipation in the United States by "people ... who have themselves been yoked and chained in slavery."[57] They demonstrated that Haitian abolitionism was not just a legacy of the Haitian Revolution but a living politics forged out of the transnational movements, collaborations, and collective struggle of people of African descent.

Between the Waves:
The Persistent Pull of Haiti

For the members of the HAS, their fellow residents of Port-au-Prince, and the people of Haiti's other port towns and cities, the continuous nature of African American migration to Haiti was almost certainly apparent. Years after Boyer stopped financing emigration from the United States to Haiti due in part to African American immigrants' reluctance to accept the forms of rural labor preferred by his administration, African Americans continued to arrive in Haiti's ports. These migrants included sizeable parties of African Americans from the Gulf South who settled around Gonaïves in the mid-1840s and who, owing to their French surnames and assimilation to Haitian culture, would become indistinguishable from some native-born Haitian citizens within two generations.[58] Some migrants were enslaved people manumitted on the condition of their removal from the United States. This group included the dozens of African Americans who worked on the thirty-five-thousand-acre plantation established outside of Puerto Plata by Zephaniah Kingsley, a Florida slaveowner who saw the chance to profit from the strict terms of indenture that could be placed on Haitian agricultural laborers under Boyer's Code Rural.[59] Although less conspicuous than Kingsley's unfree workers, other African Americans arriving in Haiti had seized freedom on their own terms. Those migrants might have included the man who, in March 1831, fled from slavery in Randolph County, North Carolina, with the suspected goal of making "his way to Fayetteville to take water and to Wilmington and there take shipping for Hayti."[60]

As Haiti continued to attract enslaved people who viewed it as free soil, it maintained its appeal to African American professionals too. In 1832 the activist Hezekiah Grice moved from Baltimore to Port-au-Prince, where he eventually became the director of public works in the Haitian capital.[61] A few years later, Robert Douglass Jr., the accomplished painter from Philadelphia, found similar success as Boyer's court artist during his eighteen-month residence in Port-au-Prince.[62] Black abolitionist George Boyer Vashon followed in their footsteps. In 1848, having been routinely denied professional opportunities despite his intelligence and college degree, Vashon moved from New York to Port-au-Prince, where he taught Latin, Greek, and English for two years.[63]

Neither Vashon nor his predecessors were as exceptional as scholars have implied. In 1858 one doctor, a French-speaking man of color residing in Guadeloupe, argued that Haiti should embrace African American immigration again because "the men of the black and yellow race from the United States ... have very much contributed to the perfecting and extension of industry" in that country. Those "active, laborious, [and] intelligent" immigrants included not only "merchants, cultivators, [and] workers" but also preachers like Arthur Waring.[64] Around 1835 Waring, the son of a wealthy slaveowner and an enslaved Black woman, left Virginia, where he faced racial discrimination and limited socioeconomic prospects despite his legal freedom and a substantial inheritance from his father. His search for dignity, for a life without arbitrary limitations, took him across Hispaniola. He first landed in Port-au-Prince, where he joined the HAS and worked in the mercantile industry. After his business career faltered, he then moved to Puerto Plata, where he had heard of a prosperous community of immigrants from the United States and the British West Indies. That community included James Tredwell, who in 1836 reported that his fellow residents "from the States ... are, generally speaking, comfortably situated" and eagerly waiting the completion of a chapel serviced by a Methodist missionary.[65] In Puerto Plata, Waring was baptized. He grew tobacco and indigo before moving to Cap-Haïtien, where he again tried his hand at trade. His calling to become a Baptist missionary eventually came in the interior Haitian town of Dondon, and he continued in that work until his death in October 1866.[66]

By the time Waring passed, the Dominican Republic had proclaimed its independence from Haiti, but another period of Haitian state building through mass migration and transnational collaboration was on the horizon. On July 11, 1855, James Theodore Holly left New York City. The prominent Black nationalist and Episcopal deacon arrived in Port-au-Prince three weeks later, excited to begin his exploration of Haiti as a potential site of Episcopal missionary work and African American resettlement. He was aided in his exploration by Emil de Ballette, an English-educated Haitian jurist; a merchant from Charleston, South Carolina, "one of the churchmen here among the American Emigrants"; and John Hepburn, a native of Virginia who, like other African American immigrants in urban Haiti, had achieved substantial commercial success and social standing due to his ability to mediate commercial and political relationships among Haitian elites and English-speaking foreigners.[67]

With the help of Haitian informants and African American immigrants alike, Holly gained impactful meetings with prominent Haitian officials, including Faustin Soulouque. Holly asked the Haitian emperor what encouragements he might provide for African American agricultural laborers and urban professionals and suggested that immigrants should be granted a host of rights and privileges, including freedom of worship, temporary exemption from military service, relief from import duties on their personal belongings and work supplies, and a quick path to citizenship.[68] The Haitian government was noncommittal but encouraging. While Holly did not receive firm support from Soulouque or a financial commitment from the Episcopal Church, he left Haiti convinced of its value as a new homeland for African Americans. He soon published a lecture on Haiti and the Haitian Revolution that implored African Americans "to go and indentify [sic] our destiny with our heroic brethren in that independent isle of the Caribbean, carrying with us such of the arts, sciences and genius of modern civilization."[69]

The Resurgence and Generations of Haitian Emigration

The mass migration envisioned by Holly materialized under Soulouque's successor. In 1859, months after deposing Soulouque, Haitian president Fabre Geffrard confirmed the appointment of Emile Desdunes, Haiti's consul in New Orleans, as his agent of emigration. Desdunes's offer of free transportation and full social and political equality for African Americans in Haiti led to the migration of hundreds of Louisianans of African descent from May 1859 through early 1860.[70] That July, having issued a "Call for Emigration," Geffrard then launched the Haytian Bureau of Emigration. With an initial grant of $20,000 from the Haitian government, the bureau established its headquarters in Boston. Its main purpose was to facilitate the immigration of African Americans, particularly agricultural laborers who would settle in the Artibonite Valley, the fertile region that was ripe for cotton production and where the Louisianans had established themselves in the preceding months. The bureau enticed prospective settlers with generous terms of immigration, including free grants of land and guarantees that immigrants would enjoy all the civil and political rights of native Haitians.[71]

Although Geffrard appointed the Scottish abolitionist James Redpath as the head of the bureau, Holly, Henry Highland Garnet, H. Ford Douglass, William Watkins, and its other African American agents were the principal physical and intellectual forces behind the burgeoning mass movement. The agents traveled about the U.S. North and Midwest delivering lectures on Haitian emigration before audiences of prospective migrants gathered at churches, Masonic halls, and other sites of Black communal life. They not only distributed but also interpreted *A Guide to Hayti*, the pamphlet edited by Redpath that contained information on Haitian history, geography, culture, society, and politics in addition to the "laws of emigration" established by the Geffrard government. They, along with numerous local preachers and community leaders, would convince at least two thousand African Americans to accept the offer of the Haitian government and immigrate to Haiti between December 1860 and the closing of the HBE in August 1862.[72] One even joined the migration. On May 2, 1861, Holly left New Haven on the *Madeira*. Along with the nearly sixty other passengers who boarded the ship at its previous stop in Boston, he and the more than one hundred members of his "New Haven Colony" sailed to Port-au-Prince, many of them looking on the United States for the last time.[73]

While a good amount has been written about Holly as a singular Black intellectual, activist, and missionary, scholars have made insufficient use of his voluminous archive, which gives rich insights into the broader immigrant experience in late nineteenth-century Haiti.[74] During his first months in Haiti, Holly sent letters to the *Pine and Palm*, the official organ of the HBE, that downplayed the number of "deserters from our ranks" and rationalized the several deaths among his New Haven Colony, including those of his mother, then in her seventies, and his three-year-old daughter.[75] Those reports highlight the difficulties facing immigrants, particularly the very young, the infirm, and the elderly, who arrived in Port-au-Prince during the rainy season, when diseases like typhoid fever were common. They encourage a narrative, an accounting, of "failure" and return that Holly's extensive subsequent writings contradict.[76]

Despite his own travails, Holly remained in Haiti, where he became a naturalized citizen in September 1861.[77] In 1864, having organized Holy Trinity Church in Port-au-Prince, he informed Episcopal officials that its Ladies' Church Foundation Society was leading the fundraising for a church lot. It had an equal number of African American and Haitian officers. The former included his second wife, Sarah, and the wife of one of Arthur Waring's sons; the latter included the wife of John Hepburn.[78] Three years later, Holly reported that he had found the ideal place for the church lot in the heart of the Haitian capital, in full view of Haiti's National Palace.[79] He told Episcopal officials that he had the right man from among the city's "four or five American Carpenters and as many from Jamaica" to erect the new church building in the heart of the city. Since arriving in Port-au-Prince aboard the *Madeira*, William H. Jones had become the "chief government carpenter employed in that capacity by the government here." Holly knew "him to be fully capable."⁸⁰ His support of Jones reveals the bonds that migrants formed with shipmates who, in some cases, became family.⁸¹ His well-documented efforts to build a fulfilling life and a national church in Haiti highlight the elaborate connections among recent African American immigrants, naturalized and native Haitian citizens, West Indian migrants, and Haitian government officials. They show the social fabric of Port-au-Prince.

As Holly's twenty-first annual report from Port-au-Prince to the Board of Missions of the Episcopal Church suggests, these legacies of Haitian emigration were felt well outside of Haiti's capital long after its purported failure. Born in 1865 in Port-au-Prince, Alonzo Potter Burgess Holly would, in the early 1880s, open a mission school in Port-au-Prince that taught theology, geography, writing, reading, and arithmetic to the children of Haitians and African American immigrants.⁸² After obtaining his medical degree in New York, Holly facilitated the education of Haitian nurses in the United States before returning to Haiti. Back home, Holly joined the Clinique St. Jacques, the nationwide medical mission staffed by him, three of his brothers, and two other Haitian doctors. His specialties, perhaps encouraged by his family's history, were childbirth and "diseases of infants."⁸³ His field site was Gonaïves. There, Holly wrote himself into the modern history of Haitian medicine. His patients reflected the diversity of that cosmopolitan coastal town; they included "the English-speaking residents of Gonaïves."⁸⁴

Conclusion

A foundational idea associated with the purported failure and fleeting relevance of Haitian emigration—that the African Americans who remained in Hispaniola are numerically insignificant or unknowable—is unconvincing. This chapter, a step toward a more robust history of Haitian emigration inclusive of migration between the periods of state-sponsored immigration and attentive to permanent residence in Haiti, makes use of a wide range of sources, including ecclesiastical and missionary records, private correspondence, nineteenth-century Haitian histories and newspapers, U.S. diplomatic records, and U.S. and European travel writings. Along with well-trod sources such as U.S. newspapers, this more expansive archive of Haitian emigration offers important insights into the lives of African American immigrants in nineteenth-century Hispaniola.

Similar sources not explored in this essay do, too. More research is needed in civil records from nineteenth-century Hispaniola, some of which have recently been digitized and made available in the HeritageQuest database.[85] These documents, including marriage, birth, and death records, give a better sense of the number of African American immigrants and their descendants in nineteenth-century Hispaniola and, more importantly, offer insights into socioeconomic life in those immigrants' new home.[86] Historians should also make more use of oral histories and autobiographies in which African Americans and Haitians recount histories of Haitian emigration. These types of sources resist the language of failure and the temporal focus on the 1820s and the early 1860s. They force us to reckon with the enduring legacies of Haitian emigration and account for the immigrants who never returned to the United States.[87]

This research is needed for a fuller picture not just of transnational African American history but also of nineteenth-century Hispaniola, especially Haiti.[88] In "Thinking Haiti's Nineteenth Century," historian Laurent Dubois argues that "enterprising scholars" have the chance to "offer us fuller, denser pictures of Haiti's lived nineteenth century ... [through] further research into the history of migration *to* Haiti." He is correct.[89] There is an ethical and historiographical imperative to troubling the idea that Haitian emigration was a fleeting, failed experiment—to moving beyond a misconception rooted in the foundational myth of the United States as a nation of immigrants and the stereotype of Haiti as a failed state always populated by people eager to leave. A history of Haitian emigration that extends across the nineteenth century and explores the lives of immigrants can tell us a great deal about Haitian policy making and state building; the constructions of and contestations over land, autonomy, and citizenship in rural Hispaniola; the class dynamics and commercial relations in urban Hispaniola; the foundations of Haitian and Dominican Protestantism; the development of Haiti's private educational system; and the growth of several industries, including Haiti's medical field. Such a history would not just enrich our understanding of the transnational dimensions of African American history. Instead, it would also offer fresh insights into political, economic, and social life in Haiti, a country still in need of historical narratives that trouble and reject its perceived isolation and exceptionalism.

NOTES

Many thanks to Christina C. Davidson for her insightful feedback on an earlier version of this chapter.

1. James Theodore Holly, "Bishop Holly's Twenty-First Annual Report," *Spirit of Missions* 60, no. 11 (1895): 476–77, 480.

2. Ibid.

3. Nineteenth-century North Americans referred to Black North Americans' mass migration to Haiti as "Haitian emigration." I have retained that language, as have most scholars, when addressing this general movement. In other places, however, I refer more generally to "migration" or draw a distinction between "emigration from" and "immigration to." My use of immigration where relevant is intended as an intervention—as a means of centering the perspective of the Haitian state and acknowledging the long-term presence of Black North American immigrants in Haiti.

4. Still others were likely from the British Caribbean. Those intraregional streams of migration are mainly beyond the scope of this chapter but deserving of more scholarly attention.

5. Sara Fanning, *Caribbean Crossing: African Americans and the Haitian Emigration Movement* (New York: New York University Press, 2015), 116, 121–23.

6. Chris Dixon, *African America and Haiti: Emigration and Black Nationalism in the Nineteenth Century* (Westport, Conn.: Greenwood Press, 2000), 208. For scholarly treatments of both waves of Haitian emigration, see especially Floyd J. Miller, *The Search for a Black Nationality: Black Emigration and Colonization, 1787–1863* (Urbana: University of Illinois Press, 1975); and Claire Bourhis-Mariotti, *L'union fait la force: Les noirs américains et Haïti, 1804–1893* (Rennes: Presses universitaires de Rennes, 2016).

7. Thorald Burnham and Julie Winch are important exceptions. See Burnham, "Immigration and Marriage in the Making of Post-Independence Haiti" (PhD diss., York University, 2006); and Winch, "American Free Blacks and Emigration to Haiti," *Documentos de Trabajo* 33 (Centro de Investigaciones del Caribe y América Latina, Universidad Interamericana de Puerto Rico, August 1988).

8. Gerald Horne has offered productive reframing by showing how Haitian emigration and African American migrants played an integral role in the nineteenth-century political relations between Hispaniola and the United States. See Horne, *Confronting Black Jacobins: The U.S., the Haitian Revolution, and the Origins of the Dominican Republic* (New York: Monthly Review Press, 2015).

9. Burnham's work on immigration and marriage patterns in nineteenth-century Haiti is an important exception.

10. See especially Dennis Ricardo Hidalgo, "From North America to Hispaniola: First Free Black Emigration and Settlements in Hispaniola" (PhD diss., Central Michigan University, 2003); Kristen R. Fellows, "Double Consciousness and an African American Enclave: Being Black and American on Hispaniola," in *Archaeologies of Slavery and Freedom in the Caribbean: Exploring the Spaces in Between*, ed. Lynsey Bates, John Chenoweth, and James A. Delle (Gainesville: University Press of Florida, 2016), 307–28; Christopher Wilkins, "'They Had Heard of Emancipation and the Enfranchisement of Their Race': The African American Colonists of Samaná, Reconstruction, and the State of Santo Domingo," in *The Civil War as Global Conflict: Transnational Meanings of the American Civil War*, ed. David T. Gleeson and Simon Lewis (Columbia: University of South Carolina Press, 2014);

and Christina Cecelia Davidson, "Converting Spanish Hispaniola: Race, Nation, and the A.M.E. Church in Santo Domingo, 1872–1904" (PhD diss., Duke University, 2017).

11. Julius S. Scott, *The Common Wind: Afro-American Currents in the Age of the Haitian Revolution* (New York: Verso Books, 2018), 118.

12. See representative cases in Jeffrey Bolster, *Black Jacks: African American Seamen in the Age of Sail* (Cambridge, Mass.: Harvard University Press, 1997); and Ashli White, *Encountering Revolution: Haiti and the Making of the Early Republic* (Baltimore, Md.: Johns Hopkins University Press, 2010).

13. On the internal politics of postrevolutionary Haiti, see especially Mimi Sheller, *Democracy after Slavery: Black Publics and Peasant Radicalism in Haiti and Jamaica* (London: Macmillan, 2000); Matthew J. Smith, *Liberty, Fraternity, Exile: Haiti and Jamaica after Emancipation* (Chapel Hill: University of North Carolina Press, 2014); Johnhenry Gonzalez, *Maroon Nation: A History of Revolutionary Haiti* (New Haven, Conn.: Yale University Press, 2019); Jean Alix René, *Haiti après l'esclavage: Formation de l'état et culture politique Populaire (1804–1846)* (Port-au-Prince: Éditions Le Natal, 2019); and Chelsea Stieber, *Haiti's Paper War: Post-independence Writing, Civil War, and the Making of the Republic, 1804–1954* (New York: New York University Press, 2020).

14. *Boston Centinel*, May 12, 1807.

15. On the 1816 constitution and Haiti's other early constitutions, see especially Louis Joseph Janvier, *Les constitutions d'Haïti, 1801–1885* (Paris: C. Marpon and E. Flammarion, 1886); Claude Moïse, *Constitutions et luttes de pouvoir en Haïti (1804–1987)*, 2 vols. (Montreal: Éditions du CIDIHCA, 1988–90); and Julia Gaffield, "Complexities of Imagining Haiti: A Study of National Constitutions, 1801–1807," *Journal of Social History* 41, no. 1 (2007): 81–103.

16. Ada Ferrer, "Haiti, Free Soil, and Antislavery in the Revolutionary Atlantic," *American Historical Review* 117, no. 1 (2012): 47, 55.

17. James Tredwell, *The Constitution of the Republic of Hayti; To Which Is Added Documents Relating to the Correspondence of His Most Christian Majesty, with the President of Hayti; Preceded by a Proclamation to the People and the Army* (New York: James Tredwell, 1818), 3.

18. Ibid.

19. Ibid., 3–5, 7.

20. Recent histories of the American Colonization Society and colonization include Eric Burin, *Slavery and the Peculiar Solution: A History of the American Colonization Society* (Gainesville: University Press of Florida, 2005); Beverly C. Tomek, *Colonization and Its Discontents: Emancipation, Emigration, and Antislavery in Antebellum Pennsylvania* (New York: New York University Press, 2011); Nicholas Guyatt, *Bind Us Apart: How Enlightened Americans Invented Racial Segregation* (New York: Basic Books, 2016); and Tomek and Matthew J. Hetrick, eds., *New Directions in the Study of African American Recolonization* (Gainesville: University Press of Florida, 2017).

21. Recent and foundational scholarship on the Black response to colonization includes Richard J. M. Blackett, *Building an Antislavery Wall: Black Americans in the Atlantic Abolitionist Movement, 1830–1860* (Baton Rouge: Louisiana State University Press, 1983); Claude A. Clegg, *Price of Liberty: African Americans and the Making of Liberia* (Chapel Hill: University of North Carolina Press, 2004); and Ousmane K. Power-Greene, *Against Wind and Tide: The African American Struggle against the Colonization Movement* (New York: New York University Press, 2014).

22. "People of Color," *Niles Weekly Register*, October 17, 1818.

23. On Saunders's life, activism, and influence, see especially Westenley Alcenat, "'Children of Africa, Shall Be Haytians': Prince Saunders, Revolutionary Transnationalism, and the Foundations of Black Emigration, 1815–1865" (PhD diss., Columbia University, 2019).

24. Prince Saunders, *Haytian Papers: A Collection of the Very Interesting Proclamations, and Other Official Documents; Together with Some Account of the Rise, Progress, and Present State of the Kingdom of Hayti* (London: W. Reed, 1816), i.

25. Michael Nash, "Research Note: Searching for Working-Class Philadelphia in the Records of the Philadelphia Saving Fund Society," *Journal of Social History* 29, no. 3 (1996): 684.

26. Arthur D. White, "Prince Saunders: An Instance of Social Mobility among Antebellum New England Blacks," *Journal of Negro History* 55 (1975): 533.

27. *National Intelligencer*, November 19, 1819.

28. On Boyer's intertwined projects of recognition and immigration, see especially Fanning, *Caribbean Crossing*, 41–58.

29. Beaubrun Ardouin, *Études sur l'histoire d'Haïti, tome neuvième* (Paris: Dezobry et E. Magdeleine, 1860), 288. All translations mine.

30. Thomas Madiou, *Histoire d'Haïti, tome VI, 1819–1826* (Port-au-Prince: Henri Deschamps, 1988), 241.

31. Ibid.

32. "Of Hayti," *National Intelligencer*, May 8, 1821.

33. In addition to Ferrer, see Julia Gaffield, *Haitian Connections in the Atlantic World: Recognition after Revolution* (Chapel Hill: University of North Carolina Press, 2015); and Gaffield, ed., *The Haitian Declaration of Independence: Creation, Context, and Legacy* (Charlottesville: University of Virginia Press, 2016).

34. *National Gazette*, September 15, 1824.

35. "Philanthropic Society of Hayti," *Daily National Journal*, April 13, 1825.

36. Madiou, *Histoire d'Haïti*, 420–22. The *Charlotte Corday* sailed from Philadelphia in late August 1824 and arrived in Port-au-Prince about three weeks later.

37. The former archive also includes the publications produced by emigration societies founded by African Americans in eastern U.S. cities, including Baltimore, Philadelphia, and New York, and as far west as Cincinnati. See, for example, Haytian Emigration Society of Philadelphia, *Information for the People of Colour, Who Are Inclined to Emigrate to Hayti* (Philadelphia: J. H. Cunningham, 1825).

38. Loring Dewey, *Correspondence Relative to the Emigration of the Free People of*

Colour, in the United States, Together with the Instructions to the Agent Sent Out by President Boyer (New York: Mahlon Day, 1824), 12, 27.

39. "Removal of Slaves to Hayti," *Genius of Universal Emancipation*, June 3, 1826. The estimate of six thousand migrants is also found in Jonathas Granville, *Biographie de Granville, par son fils* (Paris: E. Briere, 1873), the biography of Boyer's emigration agent, written by his son.

40. Fanning, *Caribbean Crossing*, 118.

41. "From Hayti," *African Repository and Colonial Journal*, August 1829.

42. Charles Mackenzie, *Notes on Haiti, Made during a Residence in That Republic* (London: Henry Colburn and Richard Bentley, 1830), 1:13, 221.

43. For an excellent critical rereading of Boyer's immigration project, see Karen N. Salt, *The Unfinished Revolution: Haiti, Black Sovereignty and Power in the Nineteenth-Century Atlantic World* (Liverpool: Liverpool University Press, 2019), 83–112.

44. Mackenzie, *Notes on Haiti*, 36.

45. George H. Evans, *The Rural Code of Haiti, Literally Translated from a Publication by the Government Press; Together with Letters from That Country, concerning Its Present Condition, by a Southern Planter* (Granville, Middletown, N.J.: George H. Evans, 1837).

46. Mackenzie, *Notes on Haiti*, 89–90.

47. Benjamin Hunt, *Remarks on Hayti as a Place of Settlement for Afric-Americans; and on the Mulatto as a Race for the Tropics* (Philadelphia: T. B. Pugh, 1860), 10–11.

48. On peasant resistance to Boyer's authoritarian land policies, see especially Alex Dupuy, *Haiti in the World Economy: Class, Race and Underdevelopment since 1700* (New York: Routledge, 2018).

49. Hunt, *Remarks on Hayti*, 14, 11.

50. Ardouin, *Études sur l'histoire d'Haïti*, 302.

51. James Redpath, "A Visit to Hayti XII," *New York Daily Tribune*, August 1, 1859.

52. Hunt, *Remarks on Hayti*, 11, 14, 3, 6.

53. Mark Bird, *The Black Man; or, Haytian Independence* (New York: Mark Bird, 1869), 352–53, 378–81. Bird counted more than twenty-three hundred regular attendees at Protestant services. Interestingly, he also noted four hundred "Colored American Immigrants dispersed through the Republic without Pastors." On the early AME Church in Haiti, see especially Dennis C. Dickerson, *The African Methodist Episcopal Church: A History* (New York: Cambridge University Press, 2020), 17–55.

54. "Préambule et constitution de la Société d'Abolition a Haïti," *Feuille du Commerce*, September 11, 1836.

55. *Colored American*, March 11, 1837, March 15, 1838; "Address of the Haytian Abolition Society to the Haytian People," *The Liberator*, June 16, 1837; "Abolition in Hayti," *Caledonian Mercury*, November 28, 1836; "A Testimonial," *Vermont Union Whig*, July 13, 1839; and Evan Williams to John Quincy Adams, October 19, 1837,

reel 507, Adams Family Papers, Microfilm Edition, Massachusetts Historical Society, Boston.

56. "1st of August in Hayti," *The Emancipator*, September 6, 1838; "Société d'Abolition à Haïti," *Feuille du Commerce*, January 14, 1838; and "Speech of Lewis C. Gunn, Delivered before the Haytian Abolition Society, on the Evening of the 2nd of Jun., 1838," *National Enquirer and Constitutional Advocate of Universal Liberty*, February 22, 1838

57. "Abolition in Hayti," *The Liberator*, February 9, 1838.

58. Charles Miot to John B. Terres, August 11, 1899, enclosed in dispatch from William F. Powell to John Hay, August 14, 1899, in *Papers Relating to the Foreign Relations of the United States, with the Annual Message of the President Transmitted to Congress December 5, 1899* (Washington, D.C.: Government Printing Office, 1901), 397.

59. Mark J. Fleszar, "'My Laborers in Haiti Are Not Slaves': Proslavery Fictions and a Black Colonization Experiment on the Northern Coast, 1835–1846," *Journal of the Civil War Era* 2, no. 4 (2012): 478–510. In similar fashion, Boyer would settle on his own plantation one group of emancipated enslaved people from Nashoba, a utopian experiment founded by British reformer Frances Wright outside of Memphis, Tennessee. See Gail Bederman, "Revisiting Nashoba: Slavery, Utopia, and Frances Wright in America, 1818–1826," *American Literary History* 17, no. 3, symposium issue: "Race, Ethnicity, and Civic Identity in the Americas" (2005): 438–59.

60. *Carolina Observer*, June 7, 1831.

61. "Men We Have Known," *The Elevator*, August 16, 1867. On Grice, see Martha S. Jones, *Birthright Citizens: A History of Race and Rights in Antebellum America* (New York: Cambridge University Press, 2018), 35–49.

62. Douglass traveled to Haiti with Gunn and Burleigh but stayed there after they returned to the United States. On Douglass, see especially Aston Gonzalez, "The Art of Racial Politics: The Work of Robert Douglass Jr., 1833–46," *Pennsylvania Magazine of History and Biography* 138, no. 1 (2014): 5–37.

63. Vashon's thought and writing receive excellent treatment in Stephen G. Hall, *A Faithful Account of the Race: African American Historical Writing in Nineteenth-Century America* (Chapel Hill: University of North Carolina Press, 2009), 105–41.

64. David Nicholls, *From Dessalines to Duvalier: Race, Colour and National Independence in Haiti* (New York: Cambridge University Press, 1979), 277.

65. "Letter from Hayti," *Zion's Watchman*, July 20, 1836.

66. Undated questionnaire, Correspondence: Arthur Waring, 1866–67, International Mission Board Executive Records, Southern Baptist Historical Library and Archives; "The Island of Hayti," *National Baptist*, May 24, 1866; Ivah T. Heneise, *Pioneers of Light: Stories of the Baptist Witness in Haiti: 1823–1998* (Penney Farms, Fla.: International Christian Education Fund, 1999), 36–41.

67. Holly to Samuel Denison, undated [1855], Records of the Overseas Department, Haiti Mission Records, 1855–1967, Archives of the Episcopal Church. Hep-

burn would, for instance, advise Haitian president Fabre Geffrard on Mark Bird's published report on Haiti, which focused on its religious life. See Bird, *The Black Man*, iv.

68. Holly to Frank P. Blair Jr., January 30, 1858, in Blair, *The Destiny of the Races of This Continent* (Washington, D.C.: Buell & Blanchard, 1859), 36–37.

69. James Theodore Holly, *A Vindication of the Capacity of the Negro Race for Self-Government, and Civilized Progress, as Demonstrated by Historical Events of the Haytian Revolution; and the Subsequent Acts of That People Since Their National Independence* (New Haven, Conn.: William H. Stanley, 1857), 45–46.

70. Dixon, *African America and Haiti*, 138; Holly to Denison, March 19, 1860, Haiti Mission Records; *New Orleans Times Picayune*, January 15, 1860; *New Orleans Bee*, January 16, 1860. See also Mary Niall Mitchell, "'A Good and Delicious Country': Free Children of Color and How They Learned to Imagine the Atlantic World in Nineteenth-Century Louisiana," *History of Education Quarterly* 40, no. 2 (Summer 2000): 123–44.

71. James Redpath, ed., *A Guide to Hayti* (Boston: Haytian Bureau of Emigration, 1861).

72. The estimate of two thousand, since accepted by historians, comes from the *Pine and Palm*.

73. The case of the *Madeira* supports the idea that there has been some undercounting of migrants in this second wave of Haitian emigration. Most works claim that Holly sailed with 110 of his recruits. That number does not account for the approximately 59 African American passengers who boarded the *Madeira* in Boston before it picked up Holly's colony from New Haven. "Emigration to Hayti," *Weekly Anglo-African*, April 27, 1861; "Statistics of Haytian Emigration," *Pine and Palm*, October 12, 1861.

74. See especially David M. Dean, *Defender of the Race: James Theodore Holly, Black Nationalist Bishop* (Boston: Lambeth Press, 1979); Bourhis-Mariotti, "Vers l'établissement d'une 'nationalité noire'? Le rêve haïtien de James Theodore Holly," *IdeAs: Idées d'Amériques* 6 (2015): 1–16; and Felix Jean-Louis, "Double Consciousness and Missionary Work: James Theodore Holly and the Establishment of the Episcopalian Church of Haiti," in *Global Protestant Missions: Politics, Reform and Communication, 1730s–1930s*, ed. Jenna Gibbs (New York: Routledge, 2019), 111–33.

75. Letter from Holly, October 28, 1861, *Pine and Palm*, December 21, 1861. Holly's party on the *Madeira* included his mother, Jane; his wife, Charlotte; their two sons and one daughter; and an unmarried Black woman from New Haven named Almira Harris. In September 1861 Charlotte gave birth to a boy named Joseph Geffrard Holly. Mother and son both died in December 1861. By February 1862 James Theodore and his two young sons were the only Hollys in Haiti.

76. Historians have emphasized immigrants' struggles with Haiti's disease environment as a reason for the "failure" of Haitian emigration. This narrative has not adequately acknowledged that many African American immigrants were in poor health due to the effects of slavery and racial oppression. Some of them remained

in Haiti knowing that they had left a country in which their health was already imperiled and their life chances skewed.

77. "Partie officielle," *Le Moniteur Haïtien*, October 5, 1861.

78. Holly, "To the Christian and Benevolent Public," April 15, 1864; Holly to Arthur Cleveland Coxe, May 23, 1864; and "Officers of the Ladies Church Foundation Society, Port-au-Prince," undated, all in Haiti Mission Records.

79. Holly to Elwood Cooper, September 7, 1866, Haiti Mission Records.

80. William H. Jones to Holly, April 18, 1866; Holly to Denison, February 5, 1867, both in Haiti Mission Records.

81. Sarah Henley, Holly's second wife, had also traveled from New Haven to Haiti aboard the *Madeira* along with her father and mother.

82. "Report of the Mission School," undated, and "Report of the Mission School: Midsummer Term," August 5, 1884, both in Haiti Mission Records.

83. Arthur C. Holly, Clinique St. Jacques, Medical Report, July 20, 1905, Haiti Mission Records.

84. Holly, "Bishop Holly's Twenty-First Annual Report."

85. Burnham's research into Haitian marriage records is a model for this type of research.

86. See, for example, marriage license for Henry John Williamson and Jeanne Rose Elizabeth Brown, 1838; naturalization document for William H. Hill, July 19, 1862; and land concession document for Henry J. Williamson, 1866, all in Harry A. Williamson Papers, Manuscripts, Archives and Rare Books Division, Schomburg Center for Research in Black Culture, New York Public Library, http://abolition.nypl.org/texts/african_resistance/6/.

87. One example of this type of source is Theophilus Gould Steward, *Fifty Years in the Gospel Ministry* (Philadelphia: A.M.E. Book Concern, 1921). In his autobiography, Steward partially credits his desire to travel to Haiti to the memory of one of his grandmothers whom he had never met because she had immigrated to that country.

88. Here I must express my gratitude for the growing number of graduate students and junior scholars whose forthcoming research will give us a more robust history of Haitian emigration. These scholars include Westenley Alcenat, Christina C. Davidson, Bianca Dang, and Melena Sims-Laudig.

89. Laurent Dubois, "Thinking Haiti's Nineteenth Century," *Small Axe* 18, no. 2 (2014): 78–79.

CHAPTER 9

Frederick Douglass and Debates over the Annexation of the Dominican Republic

CLAIRE BOURHIS-MARIOTTI

The year 1865 marked the beginning of a new era, a postslavery era, for the entire American nation, especially for its Black population. Reconstruction, though disappointing in many ways, nevertheless had the merit of allowing a number of freedmen—some two thousand—to take up public and political positions previously closed to them.[1] Reconstruction also put an end to the African American migration projects to Haiti that had emerged in the antebellum United States, because what the Black republic offered to African Americans—freedom and citizenship—was now available in the United States.

Whereas the role of African Americans in local and national politics during the Reconstruction era has been well documented, historiography has neglected the role of African Americans in American diplomatic history. Yet African Americans were very much involved in U.S.-Caribbean diplomacy in the second half of the nineteenth century at different levels. Notably, from 1869 until the turn of the century, all the U.S. ambassadors to Haiti were Black.[2] Incidentally, by appointing Ebenezer Don Carlos Bassett as the minister resident and consul general of the United States to Haiti in 1869, Republican president Ulysses S. Grant allowed African Americans to reconnect with the Caribbean through diplomacy—the last "connection" they had had was through migration to Haiti in the early 1860s under Haitian president Fabre Nicolas Geffrard.[3]

During the Reconstruction period, the U.S. government, whose priority was to rebuild the nation and strengthen the union that had been shattered by the Civil War, focused on domestic issues rather than international ones. Thus, at the end of 1867, the House of Representatives passed a resolution to prevent any future acquisition of territory, partly because territorial expansion was still closely associated with slavery in the American collective imagination.[4] Officially, the United States no longer sought to acquire new territories. Expansion ought no longer to be territorial but economic: the United States would conquer new international markets in order to sell farm and industrial production.[5] However, the hostile attitude of Britain, France, and Spain toward the Union during the Civil War pushed the United States to seek to establish naval bases in the Caribbean in order to be able to respond rapidly in the event of an aggression by European nations from their Caribbean colonies.[6] Until then, the United States had always refused the land cessions sometimes proposed by various Haitian rulers. Negotiating with the Black republic was not an option: such a bargain would have inevitably alienated the southern states when slavery was legal in the United States, and anyway, Haiti, the Black nation that had achieved its freedom from France in the world's first successful slave revolution, had not been included in the Monroe Doctrine.[7]

Even after the recognition of Haiti by the Lincoln administration in 1862, the United States was still reluctant to do business with the small nation. But the Dominican Republic (a.k.a. Santo Domingo or Dominica), the "mulatto State" established on the eastern part of the same Caribbean island of Hispaniola, was another story.[8] When the United States officially recognized the Dominican Republic in 1866, the latter had been trying to get U.S. protection for decades, but until then, negotiations had never been successfully concluded. In the following years, the Grant administration decided to open new negotiations, first to reaffirm the Monroe Doctrine, which had been undermined by the activities of Europeans in the Caribbean islands, and second to revive foreign trade. Grant's annexationist efforts culminated in 1871, when Congress approved the nomination of a commission of inquiry whose mission was to visit the small republic established on the eastern part of Hispaniola in order to assess not only the quality of the land, its climate, and its resources but also the condition of its people and their support for annexation. Officially, the United States was not interested in annexing Haiti, and, contrary to the Dominican authorities, the Haitian government had never applied for annexation. Nevertheless, the commission's agenda included a visit to Haiti and a meeting with the Haitian president.

At the time, Frederick Douglass, who had strongly and openly campaigned for the election of Ulysses S. Grant in 1868, was hoping for a presidential appointment. Although the position of minister resident in Haiti was assigned to his friend Ebenezer Basset, Douglass's political career in the Caribbean finally took off in 1871, when he was appointed to the commission that was to go to the Dominican Republic with a view to its possible annexation. Like many other African American activists and intellectuals, Douglass felt a profound respect and admiration for the first Black republic. He had vocally defended its right to independence and praised its capacity to resist the attacks made by the slave powers ever since it had become independent in 1804: "I hold up both hands for Hayti, grateful for her humanity, rejoice in her prosperity, point to her example with pride and hope, and would smite down any hand that would fling a shadow upon the pathway of her glory."[9] Since the mid-1840s he had devoted a number of laudatory articles to Haiti in the pages of his newspapers. He regretted that Americans, particularly African Americans, knew little or nothing about this "most interesting" nation when, "considering the importance of her example ... Hayti should be an object of constant curiosity, especially to the oppressed of this country."[10]

Douglass yearned to visit Haiti and was about to do so when the Civil War started and put a halt to this "long-desired visit"—"a dream, fondly indulged, a desire, long cherished, and a purpose, long meditated." No wonder Douglass gladly agreed to join the commission of inquiry to Santo Domingo; his dream was about to come true: "We, naturally enough, desire to see, as we doubtless shall see, in the free, orderly and Independent Republic of Hayti, a refutation of the slanders and disparagements of our race." Like many other Black activists, Douglass believed Haiti could be used as a model to demand inclusion in American society. The somehow glorifying, if not utopian, vision he and other militants gave of Haiti had to serve the cause of both African Americans and Haitians: "We want to experience; the feeling of being under a Government which has been administered by a race denounced as mentally and morally incapable of self-government."[11]

Given Douglass's admiration for the Black republic and his well-known defense of the equality of Black people and their right to self-determination, one may wonder why Douglass accepted this mission to Santo Domingo. If one can perfectly understand his personal interest in visiting the island he had so long dreamed of, it is difficult to understand why he agreed to be associated with an imperialist enterprise that could eventually lead to the extinction of one or even two Black republics. This chapter will argue that this episode in Douglass's life had much to do with his support for the Republican Party and that it unveiled a little-known facet of Douglass's personality. It will also discuss what this mission to Santo Domingo reveals about the race issue in the Reconstruction era and contend that it did not augur well for the future of race relations in the United States. But first and foremost, in order to better understand the challenges of the mission entrusted to Frederick Douglass and the commission of inquiry in early 1871, one needs to understand the new interest of the United States in the small island of Hispaniola.

Renewed U.S. Interest in Hispaniola during the Reconstruction Era

Following a liberation movement that had spread throughout most of the Spanish colonies of the Americas in the 1810s, the population of the Spanish part of the island of Hispaniola rose up and proclaimed its independence on December 1, 1821.[12] A few weeks later, at the call of some insurgents, Haitian president Jean-Pierre Boyer invaded the Dominican Republic and reunified the entire island in early 1822. The Haitian occupation of the Dominican Republic lasted for twenty-two years, until the fall of Boyer in 1844, when Dominican separatists led by General Pedro Santana managed to regain the independence of the small republic. The Dominican Republic proclaimed its independence for the second time in its history on February 27, 1844. About a decade later, in June 1854, American president Franklin Pierce, who was seeking land concessions in the Dominican Republic, sent William Leslie Cazneau, a soldier during the Texas revolution and a politician, as a special agent to Hispaniola to negotiate the recognition of Santo Domingo by the United States in exchange for the cession of part of Samaná Bay, where the Americans planned to install a coaling station and a naval base. European powers that feared that the United States would settle permanently on the island of Hispaniola caused the negotiations to fail by sending consuls and consular officers to the island. Later, with the outbreak of the Civil War, the United States focused on matters at home.

As Haiti threatened to invade the Dominican Republic again, Dominican president Pedro Santana drew closer to Spain. On March 18, 1861, he publicly announced the annexation of his country by Spain, but this new Spanish occupation and its authoritarian mode of governance triggered a number of popular uprisings. Consequently, on March 3, 1865, the queen of Spain issued a decree declaring that the Kingdom of Spain abandoned its claims on Santo Domingo. A year later, Secretary of State William H. Seward, who was convinced of the strategic importance of the Caribbean island, sent an emissary to the Dominican Republic with the intent to acquire land (the Samaná Bay Isthmus) on which to build a coaling station and a naval base. This emissary, Vice Admiral David Dixon Porter, had already been sent there as a U.S. secret envoy in 1846, when President Polk, who was then worried about rumors of a Haitian invasion of Santo Domingo, had asked him to gather information about the state of the country's government and resources.[13] Twenty years after his first visit, Porter resumed negotiations with the Dominican president, General Buenaventura Báez Méndez, but this time the Dominican government turned down the American offer. The small republic had just recovered its sovereignty from Spain, and its people were not willing to be annexed by a new foreign government. The United States recognized the Dominican Republic in 1866, but the negotiations were definitively closed in 1867.[14]

When President Grant took office in March 1869, he set his imperialist gaze on the Môle-Saint-Nicolas, a small area northwest of Haiti that was of the utmost importance because it was located ninety-four miles from the Cuban coast. Grant's secretary of state, Hamilton Fish, instructed Lieutenant Commander Thomas Selfridge to carry out a confidential reconnaissance of the coasts of the Dominican Republic and Haiti with a view to establishing a naval base there.[15] Back in the United States in mid-July 1869, Selfridge depicted the situation of Sylvain Salnave, the president of Haiti, as very precarious. Salnave could easily be overthrown, so Selfridge advised the Grant administration to take advantage of this situation to ensure the lease of the Môle-Saint-Nicolas. Indeed, Salnave, who was in great difficulty in his country, intended "to retain power by defeating his adversaries, thanks to the American intervention, from which he expected money, weapons, and ammunition in exchange for the Môle-Saint-Nicolas, which he would sell or lease."[16] In September 1869, as his affairs were worsening, Salnave visited the American minister resident, Ebenezer Don Carlos Bassett, in order to obtain a loan of $2 million or $3 million from the United States, which would be "repaid from the revenues of the customs duties or by the cession of the Môle-Saint-Nicolas." But Bassett warned Secretary Fish against this offer, as he was "aware of the universal feeling of Haitians against any alienation from their territory," and the American government delayed its response to Salnave's offer.[17] In December 1869, when the Haitian legislature proposed to the United States the free use of one of its ports—none other than the Môle-Saint-Nicolas—for the installation of a coaling station and a naval base in exchange for their protection and a loan of $12 million, the Grant administration was slow to close the deal with Salnave.[18] The execution of Salnave on January 15, 1870, put a definitive end to the negotiations, initiated until then by both parties.[19] On March 19, 1870, Nissage Saget was elected president of Haiti.[20]

In the meantime, the Dominican Republic, seeking protection against a possible new Haitian invasion, was once again trying to get closer to the United States. Thus, shortly after Salnave's execution, President Báez Méndez indicated to President Grant that his people were now in favor of the annexation of their country by the United States. The Môle-Saint-Nicolas had escaped the United States, but its northeastern equivalent, the Samaná Bay, was now within reach: "As the harbor of Môle St. Nicolas on the northwestern coast of Hayti commands the 'Windward passage,' so the bay of Samaná commands the 'Mona passage,' which leads from the Atlantic Ocean (Europe and the eastern shore of the United States) to the Isthmus of Panama and the coasts of South America." From the bay and peninsula of Samaná, "the United States could reach, in a short and direct way, their objects of trade and enterprise, and keep or send out their fleets for the purpose of protection and defense."[21]

Although it sent two ships off the Dominican coast to discourage Haiti from invading the Dominican Republic in January 1870, the United States eventually rejected the annexation of Santo Domingo by a close vote of the Senate in June 1870.[22] It seems that the Senate's opposition to the annexation of the Dominican Republic, as well as the refusal of the House of Representatives to annex the island by means of a joint resolution in early 1871, prompted Grant to send an American delegation on a mission to the island.[23] Grant believed that if the United States did not acquire Santo Domingo, it would turn to Europe for political and financial support. Unlike Senator Charles Sumner, he also believed that the Dominican people wanted to be annexed to the United States and thus benefit from its democratic institutions.[24] Finally, he seemed to consider this annexation as part of the solution to the race problem in the United States, as an American Santo Domingo would serve as a haven for oppressed southern Black people.[25] Despite the rejection of his annexation project by Congress, Grant was authorized to appoint a commission whose mission consisted in going to the Dominican Republic in order to learn about the political and commercial situation of the island. Commission members would also investigate the Dominican policy regarding the allocation of land to the Americans who wished to establish a commercial activity there and, eventually, check whether the Dominican people really wished to be annexed to the United States.[26] This mission to Santo Domingo seemed all the more necessary because American public opinion was quite divided on this issue, as evidenced by the numerous newspaper articles that were then published on the subject.

In fact, most northern and Republican newspapers published articles in favor of the annexation of Santo Domingo, going so far as to claim that this annexation (and even the annexation of all the West Indies) was part of the "Manifest Destiny" of the United States: "Above all, is not this thing written as the first chapter in the West India book of 'Manifest Destiny'? And what is 'manifest destiny'? Anything in the future which we see is bound to come, as we see the annexation of St. Domingo."[27] From that moment on, not only Santo Domingo but also the entire island of Hispaniola were integrated into the expansionist scheme of the United States in the Caribbean. The island that had once been the symbol of Black freedom was now a strategic objective.

Nevertheless, proponents and opponents to this annexation project worried, among other things, that this annexation would only worsen the already complicated racial problem in the United States (the so-called Negro problem) and doubted that the United States would be able to integrate such a "mixed" people as the Dominican people—not to mention the black Haitians. Actually, the racial debate over this possible annexation did divide the nation, because it revealed the profound differences that split the (Radical) Republicans from the rest of the American population—especially southerners—at the time regarding the integration of Black people into American society. The Santo Domingo issue raised important questions about Black citizenship in the United States: contemplating the annexation of Santo Domingo (and possibly Haiti) as the thirty-eighth state of the Union inevitably raised the question of the place of people of color in the United States. Interestingly enough, newspapers presented competing representations of the Dominican people's racial composition, which depended on the pro- or antiannexation stance they wished to defend. Newspapers advocating annexation would claim that Dominicans were either white or light skinned, whereas those rejecting annexation would insist that Dominicans were not white and were therefore not assimilable into American society: "There is certainly little reason, judging from what I saw, to call Dominica a 'white republic.' The great mass of the people are negroes and mulattoes."[28] Newspapers printed testimonies of Americans who claimed they had visited Santo Domingo and gave their opinion concerning the racial composition of its population—of course, their Haitian neighbors, who were depicted as "negro," were unworthy candidates for annexation. "The character of the population of St. Domingo was also urged as an objection to [annexation] ... but on this subject the democrats do not appear to be well informed. They seem to confound Hayti with Dominica. The population of Hayti is chiefly negro, but that of Dominica has a large representation of the Spanish element in it."²⁹

The *New York Herald*, reviewing the arguments of both supporters and opponents of the proposed annexation of Santo Domingo (with the Democrats firmly opposed), concluded that the annexation would likely occur "within the next three months" and that "before the expiration of twelve months, the Republic of Haiti w[ould] follow," giving the United States "the whole island." Indeed, "the scheme of annexation covers both republics, and the authorities of Hayti ... are only awaiting the initiative of Dominica. ... With Dominica fixed, a colored commission of such men as Senator Revels, Downing the oysterman and Fred Douglass will soon settle Hayti." To sum up, "the commission means annexation."³⁰

The Mission to Santo Domingo, Frederick Douglass, and the Issue of Race

While the discussions over the "annexation-ability" of Santo Domingo and the race of its people were raging in Congress and in the newspapers, Frederick Douglass's appointment to the commission of inquiry only added controversy to this heated debate—not so much because of Douglass's race but rather because of the role he was given within this commission. Indeed, Douglass was not appointed as a *commissioner* but as an *assistant secretary*. Thus, many of his Black friends criticized the Grant administration for nominating Douglass to a position they considered as debasing and unworthy of the Sage of Anacostia. Many of Douglass's white friends also shared this view.³¹ This did not prevent Douglass from accepting this position with the three white commissioners. The president of the commission was an ex-senator and ex–president pro tempore of the U.S. Senate, Benjamin Franklin Wade, a Radical Republican. The other two commissioners were Andrew Dickson White, a historian who was Cornell University's first president, and physician and philanthropist Samuel Gridley Howe, an ex-abolitionist. The three commissioners did not travel in a small group: they were accompanied by a secretary (himself accompanied by an assistant), three other personal secretaries (one per commissioner), a messenger (Charles Remond Douglass, Frederick Douglass's youngest son), a U.S. general (General Franz Sigel, a Union major general who had embraced a parallel postbellum career as a journalist), a botanist, a geologist, several other scientists (all accompanied by assistants), and ten journalists for a total of thirty-two people. However, Frederick Douglass appears in fifth position on the official list of the "gentlemen accompanying said commission and of those authorized to accompany it" as assistant secretary, a very symbolic position of little importance, which perhaps explains why some African Americans and Sumner claimed that Douglass had been "mistreated" during the time of his mission (i.e., clearly considered as inferior to the other members) or that the president had mocked him by appointing him as a secretary.[32] The *Cincinnati Daily Gazette* corroborated these accusations: "[The commissioners] also made it so uncomfortable for Mr. Fred. Douglass to be present at their meetings that he has carefully avoided them since the first landing at the capital [Port-au-Prince]."[33] These accusations spread so far and for so long that Andrew D. White, one of the commissioners, was forced to write a letter to the Reverend J. W. Loguen, bishop of the African Methodist Episcopal Church, in which he challenged allegations of ill treatment of Frederick Douglass by the commission (especially aboard the frigate) and maintained that President Grant had given orders that "Douglass should be treated as honorably and be provided for as comfortably as the most favored persons in the expedition."[34] As will be discussed later in this chapter, the report published by the commission of inquiry may, however, be seen as supporting the rumors that pretended that Douglass had been treated unfairly or disregarded by the commission.

Even though he was only offered a position of assistant secretary, Douglass regarded this nomination as a victory not only for him but also for the entire Black community: "My selection to visit Santo Domingo with the commission sent thither, was another point indicating the difference between the old time and the *new*."[35] For Douglass, this appointment was proof of the administration's recognition of Black people's equal status. However, one cannot fail to see the paradox between Douglass's acceptance of this mission and his longtime commitment to the defense of the interests of the Black race. Frederick Douglass, the militant of the Black cause, the one who had always supported the independence of Caribbean countries—especially Haiti, the first Black republic—was in fact endorsing a mission whose ultimate goal was the suppression of at least one or even two Black republics.

Actually, Douglass may have been conscious of this paradox. Indeed, he devoted very few lines to this mission in his last autobiography, even though he considered it as "highly interesting and instructive." Douglass only gave the names of the (white) commissioners and briefly commented on the clumsy attitude of the Black waiters aboard the warship that took them to the Dominican Republic: "My presence and position seemed to trouble them for its incomprehensibility.... They were trained in the school of servility to believe that white men alone were entitled to be waited upon by colored men."[36] Douglass's biographies reveal nothing more about this mission. One of Douglass's biographers, William McFeely, indicates, however, that Douglass's participation in this expedition caused him to quarrel with his old friend Senator Charles Sumner, who fiercely opposed the annexation of the Dominican Republic and contributed to its rejection by the Senate in June 1870.[37] Douglass himself briefly mentions this dispute with Sumner in his last autobiography but assures that "it never disturbed their friendship."[38] One may wonder why Douglass alienated Sumner, a man he admired for his commitment to the Black cause, over the subject of annexation. Sumner was not alone in stressing that annexation would inevitably lead to the extinction of Black governments in the Caribbean: so did many of Douglass's (Black) friends. Thus, why was Douglass so "naïve" as to unconditionally support Grant's scheme, despite all the reservations eloquently voiced by the senator? In the absence of any satisfactory explanations on this point from Douglass himself, it is hard to answer this question without falling into speculation. However, one might venture to find the beginnings of an answer in Douglass's ambivalent and uncomfortable position in post–Civil War American society. Douglass was obviously proud of being entrusted with such a mission—a mission of international scope—but he was also plagued by his own internal conflicts, as he was both struggling to be recognized in his country (i.e., recognized by whites as their equal, and this appointment was a form of recognition) and positioning himself as an African American leader defending the interests of the Black race, which prevented him from serving his country at the expense of other Black peoples. It may have been difficult for Douglass to reconcile his allegiance to his nation and commitment to his race.

To learn more about the course of the expedition and Douglass's role in it, one may obviously rely not only on the report published by the commission of inquiry but also on the numerous articles published while the mission was in progress, between January 17, 1871, when the frigate *Tennessee* left New York, and its return to Charleston on March 26, 1871.[39] Indeed, the corps of expedition included correspondents from leading newspapers (the *Cincinnati Gazette*, the *New York World*, the *New York Herald*, the *New York Tribune*, the *New York Standard*, the *Washington Republican*, the *Cincinnati Commercial*, the *Baltimore Republican*, and the *Philadelphia Ledger and North American*). James E. Taylor, who was an artist-reporter working for *Frank*

Leslie's Illustrated Newspaper, was also part of the expedition. These "attachés" to the commissioners were supposed to give objective accounts of the commission's work to the American population by regularly publishing articles in their newspapers. Needless to say, most of these journalists were Republicans and staunch annexationists.

A resolution to form the commission was passed on January 12, 1871, by the House of Representatives. The commission would "go down to the island" of Hispaniola, particularly to Santo Domingo, to "find out there all about its history, political and social; its government and population; its debts, diplomatic engagements and financial resources; its climate and products, mineral, vegetable and marine, and so forth."[40] Part of the commission's task was to evaluate the racial composition of the country, as well as the quality of racial and social relations there, all of which were important things to be considered for a potential annexation of the country. Assessing race relations was particularly crucial should the United States consider colonizing the country, which is why visiting African American colonists who had been living in the island since the 1820s would be an important moment in the mission. Another important task entrusted to the commission was to ascertain "the desire and disposition of the people of the said republic to become annexed to, and to form part of the people of, the United States."[41]

It is thus not surprising to find in the newspaper articles of the time many details concerning not only the Dominican Republic itself (its climate, its beauty, its resources) but also the various visits of the commissioners and their companions in the Dominican Republic (they visited Samaná, Santo Domingo City, and Puerto Plata), the interviews they conducted with some of the country's inhabitants, and their talks with Dominican president Báez. The newspapers particularly insisted on the tense relations between Santo Domingo and the neighboring Republic of Haiti—tensions that seemed enough to justify annexation. For example, the *New York Daily Tribune* quoted President Báez complaining that his people "must at once prepare to defend the Dominican Republic from a Haytian invasion," their "old and often repeated source of trouble," because "the Haytians were determined to prevent, if possible, [their] alliance or union with the United States."[42]

Newspapers also widely circulated the idea that the population was clearly in favor of annexation: "The people of Dominica are for annexation and the stable government they expect from it."[43] "On the subject of annexation the people of Samaná are enthusiastic and unanimous.... [A]t the first mention of annexation they were well pleased."[44] This is of course confirmed by the long report drafted by the commission of inquiry. In its conclusions, the thirty-page-long commissioners' report devotes three pages to the "desire for annexation" and "the popular disposition" concerning their country's potential annexation to the United States. According to the report, "All classes in all parts of the republic were consulted ... and everywhere there was a general agreement in the declaration that their only hope of permanent peace and prosperity is in annexation to and becoming part of the people of the United States." Apparently, the presence of "American colonists" (i.e., African Americans who migrated to Haiti in the antebellum period and their descendants) strongly influenced "the incorporation into public sentiment of a feeling strongly favorable to annexation to the United States in preference to any other power," as confirmed by the "summary of testimony taken by F. Douglas [sic] among American colonists at Samaná." Indeed, when asked, "What are the opinions and feelings of the people concerning annexation to the United States?" the answer of the colonists was "We do not know a man here who is not in favor of it."[45]

If President Báez and most of the Dominican "witnesses" who were interviewed by the commission seemed to fear a Haitian invasion and insisted that annexation would protect them from potential Haitian attacks, such was not the case of the American colonists: "We had some such fears under Salnave, but have none now." In fact, the latter wished to be annexed to the United States because they had "no heart for exertion under their present uncertain government, for as soon as they earn a little property, some great man puts himself at the head of a revolution, and brings on war, and one side or the other plunders the people of their property. Besides, they feel that they cannot be worse off than they now are."[46] In other words, the American colonists' desire for annexation did not stem from "fear of subjugation by Hayti"; instead, it originated in their view of the Dominican government's incompetence or corruption and their experience of continued agitation and civil war in the Dominican Republic, all of which were seen as obstacles to their freedom and progress.

As expected, the issue of race—and prejudice—is omnipresent in the report of the commission of inquiry. The commissioners' report itself states that "in some parts of the interior considerable numbers of pure white race are to be found" but admits that the population of the Dominican Republic is "of mixed blood," though "generally in the mixed race the white blood predominates." However, the report also points out that "the Dominican people differ widely in this particular from the Haytian, among whom the black race is in complete ascendancy," and concludes that "Negro blood preponderates very largely in Hayti; but the pure negro of African type is not common even there. White blood preponderates largely in Dominica, but pure whites, in the popular sense of the word, are not numerous. The majority are of a mixed race much nearer white than black." The issue of race is all the more present in the final report of the commission of inquiry, as the question of race and racial prejudice was systematically raised during the many individual interviews conducted by the commissioners and other members of the expedition. Obviously, the interviewees' opinion on race rarely differed from that of the commissioners. One of the interviewees, an African American born in the United States but living in Samaná Bay, asserted that "there are very few pure whites, very few indeed. There are a great many more mulattoes than blacks." He had "never heard of any prejudice on account of color," though he had "heard entirely different from that down in Hayti." "In Hayti three-fourths are blacks. In Dominica three-fourths are mulattoes," explained George Lewis Judd, the descendant of an African American emigrant to Haiti who then lived "in exile" in the Dominican Republic. But contrary to the official statement of the commissioners, Judd affirmed that "there is a slight prejudice between mulattoes and blacks," as "mulattoes think they know more and should rule." Although several testimonies pointed in the same direction, the commissioners would write for their part that the Dominicans "seem to be practically destitute of prejudice of class, race, or color," minimizing the racial tensions that were deeply rooted in the racial composition and the history of the country.[47]

Unlike the commissioners, newspaper correspondents seemed to have been aware of the prejudice that governed race relationships in the island, particularly in Haiti. Though they were confident that the annexation of Haiti would immediately follow that of the Dominican Republic, they feared the difficult assimilation of the Haitian population. The *New York Herald* considered Haitians as unassimilable because "Haytien niggers ... have set themselves up as superior to white men." The impossibility for white people to own land in Haiti, a principle that had been included in every Haitian constitution since that of 1805, may partly explain why some American newspapers stated that Haitians "have legislated against white equality and to keep off white men."[48] The Constitution of 1867 was less explicit on this issue than the previous ones, but still, articles 4, 5, and 6 made it clear that only Haitians could own Haitian land: "No one, if he is not Haitian, may own land in Haiti, in any capacity whatsoever, or acquire any property there." It would also be harder for whites than for Black people to become Haitian citizens: "All individuals born in Haiti or in a foreign country to a Haitian are henceforth Haitian.... All Africans or Indians and their descendants qualify for becoming Haitian."⁴⁹

Racist sentiment and prejudice against the Black population of Haiti (as opposed to the "mixed" population of Santo Domingo, whose president was a "light mulatto") were pervasive in most articles. In an article about the commission's brief visit to Haiti, the *New York Daily Tribune* claimed that "even Frederick Douglass ... confesses to a feeling of sorrow and disappointment at the spectacle presented. So do Dr. Howe and Mr. Wade. They all acknowledge that the Negro Republic of Hayti is a failure" and that the "feeling of the people [in Haiti] ... is strongly against the United States."⁵⁰

While newspapers often mentioned Douglass and his supposed opinion on Dominicans and Haitians, it is difficult to know exactly what Douglass's role was and what influence—if any—he may have had on the work and conclusions of the commission. Douglass does not describe his role in his last autobiography, and the newspapers of the time did not dwell on Douglass's actions during the mission. The full report of the commission of inquiry does not help much. Apart from his being included on the list of commissioners and their "attachés," Douglass is hardly mentioned in the rest of the report. Moreover, it seems that he was absent at most of the commissioners' important meetings with Dominican and Haitian authorities. The report only states that Douglass accompanied J. S. Adam, assistant mineralogist and chemist, when the latter visited the bay of Samaná. This is not surprising, as Douglass's role was evidently restricted to making contact with the descendants of African American emigrants to Santo Domingo: on the motion of Commissioner Howe, it was decided on January 26, 1871, that "Frederick Douglass, esq., be requested to examine and report to the commission regarding the condition of the English-speaking Immigrants residing in the town of Samaná and the country adjacent." However, Douglass did not conduct all the interviews of the American colonists living in Samaná Bay, and the report only contains a "summary" of all the testimonies taken by Douglass himself.⁵¹

However, Douglass did more than visit the country and interview African Americans. Newspapers reported that Frederick Douglass gave a speech in or near Samaná on January 28, 1871, in front of approximately two hundred Black people who were the descendants of free African Americans who had voluntarily migrated to Haiti in the mid-1820s.⁵² *Frank Leslie's Illustrated Newspaper* published a picture of this event whose caption read: "Santo Domingo Commission. Address by Frederick Douglass to the negro colonizers from the United States, in the city plaza of Samaná, before the Alcalde's office. January 28th. From a sketch by James E. Taylor, our special artist accompanying the expedition." *The Sun* confirmed that Douglass "addressed a crowd of some 200 or 250 people ... for some twenty-five minutes on the many advantages which would accrue from annexation" but scathingly concluded that "his oratory ... fell on barren ground," suggesting that his audience had not understood a single word of what he had been saying.[53]

Some of the interviews published in the report of the commission confirm that this event—Douglass addressing descendants of African American emigrants while in Samana—did take place. But actually what the report indirectly reveals about Frederick Douglass's role is that he may have been confined to establishing contact with African American people and providing moral backing for the American government's initiative. Indeed, we may infer from the little place given to Douglass in the report that he (and his son) had been appointed to the commission not so much because of their qualities but because of their color and, as for Douglass, because of his international fame. This is what newspapers implied when they claimed that "the famous mulatto orator, Fred Douglass, and his son" were attached to the commission to give the latter "the complexion and all the shades, individually and politically, to serve the purpose of the administration." Their presence, they insisted, was "at once a sop to the radicals at home and a propitiation to the colored citizens of the Dominican Republic." And effectively, "How can the Dominicans refuse the embrace of the great American republic when they see one of their own race and color a dignified official and put on an equality with distinguished white men in this Commission?"[54]

Douglass's appointment can thus be seen as a simple way to cajole the Dominicans and to give them proof of the United States' lack of prejudice toward people of color. This would of course be consistent with the concerns raised by many of Douglass's friends when he was appointed to the commission and explain why he was given an insignificant position within the corps of expedition. In any case, this strategy seems to have been successful: "President Baez, a light mulatto, was in this view perfectly charmed with the equality of our mixed Commission, furnishing in its white members and members of color conclusive evidence that, as there are no distinctions of color in Dominica, so there are none in the United States."[55]

Perhaps to give a semblance of significance to Douglass's presence in Santo Domingo, the latter and the other two assistant secretaries were asked "to report to the commission the result of any observations that they may have made regarding the subjects of inquiry embraced by the resolution of Congress authorizing the appointment of this commission."[56] It is, however, impossible to know what their true contribution to this report was—other than signing at the bottom of it.

The New Douglass: From Champion of the Black Cause to Proannexation Republican

The mission took place from January to March 1871, two and a half months during which Douglass was fascinated by the beauty of the country but appalled by the poverty of her people. He came back to the United States firmly convinced that annexation would be beneficial to the Dominican people, who would become American citizens and thus benefit from the United States' democratic institutions and values. It is on this very point that Douglass and Sumner did not agree. Whereas for Sumner the annexation of the Dominican Republic meant the extinction of at least one Black republic, for Douglass, on the contrary, it meant bringing aid to a defenseless people whose nation was consumed by incessant internal quarrels and civil wars.[57]

Although Douglass asserts in his last autobiography that this dispute with Sumner over the subject of annexation did not taint their friendship, this certainly was a heated dispute, and the newspapers gleefully played upon this quarrel, which they regularly publicized in their pages: "Fred. Douglass was enthusiastic in favor of annexation. Speaking of Senator Sumner, he said: 'He is now the greatest enemy of the colored race. The arm of Democratic hate raised to strike at the liberties of our people finds its inspiration in the utterance of Senator Sumner. He has been the object of my greatest admiration, but he is now doing the work of our most implacable foe—the Democratic party.'"[58] Although it is highly unlikely that Douglass ever uttered those words, he did believe that annexation was synonymous with peace, prosperity, and stability for the Dominicans. He who had until then always admired, praised, and defended the independence of the Black republics from any interference of the white republics totally took in stride his change of heart on the matter.[59] When the United States was a slave country, "when the slave power bore rule, and a spirit of injustice and oppression animated and controlled every part of [the U.S.] government," he was indeed opposed to the expansion of the nation at the expense of the Black peoples. But since the United States had abolished slavery and since Black Americans were now free and equal, entitled to the same due protection of the law and to the same rights as their white fellow citizens, he considered that his country was enlightened enough to expand not to the detriment of Black peoples but well and truly in their interest. According to Douglass, the United States was now a democracy embracing egalitarian principles—principles and values that it aimed at disseminating in the rest of the world: "Since liberty and equality have become the law of our land, I am for extending our dominion whenever and wherever such extension can peaceably and honorably, and with the approval and desire of all the parties concerned, be accomplished."[60]

Actually, Douglass's position on annexation reflected his adhesion to a certain idea of the United States as being "at the vanguard of modern development and civilization" and thus committed to expanding human rights—or at least abolitionist and egalitarian ideas—throughout the Americas and particularly the nonwhite nations of the Caribbean.[61]

Senator Charles Sumner was not the only one among Douglass's friends who opposed his new annexationist stance. William Lloyd Garrison and many Black activists disagreed with Douglass regarding the hypothetical blessings of the annexation of the Dominican Republic. On March 30, 1871, just a few days after the commission landed in Washington, a certain Reverend "Wyland Garnett" delivered a speech opposing the annexation of the Dominican Republic at the Cooper Institute in New York (better known as the Cooper Union for the Advancement of Science and Art) before a Black audience who had gathered to commemorate the ratification of the Fifteenth Amendment.[62] In this speech, he castigated the commission and especially Frederick Douglass, whom he accused of having taken part in the commission after having previously agreed to sign its report in favor of annexation. Not surprisingly, "an allusion to Senator Sumner as the man true of justice and equality was received with loud and continued cheering."[63] What was in fact particularly embarrassing for Frederick Douglass was that his name was then used by local and national newspapers to justify their support of the annexation of Santo Domingo and sometimes even to give credibility to their racist or prejudiced positions, which made it clear that the South was still highly prejudiced against Black people and was neither ready nor willing to enter an integrated postslavery society in which Black and white citizens would be equal. Drawing on statements supposedly made by the editor of the *Baltimore American*, who had been one of the journalists accompanying the commission, the *Richmond Whig* suggested in its April 7, 1871, issue that Santo Domingo be annexed and then colonized by American Black people and that Frederick Douglass be sent there as governor of this new state. The *Whig* considered Santo Domingo as "a place of refuge for the black population" of the United States. After all, according to *The Sun*, "the object of attaching [Douglass] to the expedition [was], on board, popularly supposed to be, to enable him, in case San Domingo is annexed, to describe in his beloved decasyllables the glories of the country to his sable [African American] friends in the Southern States, whom in consequence of their late symptoms of a Democratic tendency, it might be advisable to transplant." Annexation would open the way to the emigration of African Americans; the *Richmond Whig* stated that it "would furnish a good home for every freedman in the Southern States" and be "the only mode of restoring peace and order in the South." Newspapers also exploited the Douglass-Sumner controversy to justify their proannexation sentiment: Senator Charles Sumner "ought to see in the proposed annexation of Santo Domingo the surest and most practical mode of escape from Ku Klux outrages."[64]

Because Douglass had affixed his signature at the bottom of the commission's proannexation report, newspapers felt free to use his name not only to justify their proannexation opinions but also to give credit to their anti–Fifteenth Amendment propaganda. It must not be forgotten that the Fifteenth Amendment had been ratified a few months before the expedition to Santo Domingo and that the South was particularly reluctant to enforce it. Most southerners did not want to grant the right to vote to the Black population, whom they considered as inferior, uneducated, and unable to use the suffrage properly, especially since a large part of the white population of the former Confederate states was still deprived of this right. Therefore, southern newspapers such as the *Georgia Weekly Telegraph* gladly circulated "proof" of Black people's inferiority and took delight in quoting supposed statements by Frederick Douglass asserting Dominican and/or Haitian people's "barbarism": "Frederick Douglas [*sic*] returned ... with tears of sorrow in his eyes at the evidence of the backward progress of his race in civilization, if not their near return to barbarism." In an article entitled "Negro Barbarism and Suffrage," the *Georgia Weekly Telegraph* attributed to Douglass thoughts and sentiments he probably never had and used them to spread its racist propaganda, militating against equal rights and against the "vicious" Black suffrage: "What Douglass saw in Santo Domingo conforms to universal experience and observation over the whole earth, from the earliest historical records of the negro. Nowhere on the face of the earth has he made the slightest improvement, except under the tutillage [sic] and control of a superior race."[65]

The various attacks on Frederick Douglass made by some members of the Black community, on the one hand, and the hurtful use of his name by malicious white newspapers, on the other, forced Douglass to react. While regularly publishing articles in the *New National Era* in favor of the annexation of the Dominican Republic, Douglass was forced to justify himself and answer his opponents in the newspapers that incriminated him.[66]

Actually, all of Douglass's arguments in favor of annexation can be found in an undated speech entitled "Santo Domingo."[67] In this very long speech, which he undoubtedly delivered after the return of the commission, the Sage of Anacostia gave a very enthusiastic description of Santo Domingo and of its population (as well as that of Haiti) and was very optimistic about its annexation. He thus explained why he was in favor of the annexation of Santo Domingo to the United States. "First: Latin civilization ... is in Santo Domingo a wretched failure. It has, after more than three centuries, conducted one of the most beautiful and productive countries in the world to the very verge of barbarism." Second, Douglass assured his listeners that the climate of Santo Domingo was an ideal climate in which to "live, work and be happy." Moreover, he held that, according to Dominicans themselves, "there is no remedy for this state of things, except by the friendly intervention of some power outside of itself." Then, he also dismantled one by one all the arguments of his opponents and answered all their objections, including that made by Sumner that annexation "would put an end to a colored nationality ... and that the measure would be another humiliation of the colored race." He "den[ied] the alleged humiliation or degradation" and contended that "the trouble with Santo Domingo is that it is both too small and too weak to maintain a respectable national government." The people of Santo Domingo "want to join their country to the United States and become citizens of the United States" because "wherever that flag waves there is protection for every American citizen of whatever color." As he would write in his autobiography a decade later, Douglass did not deny that there was a time when he was opposed to the expansion of the United States. "That was the time when extension meant more slavery, more ignorance and barbarism," but he insisted that "that time is now gone by. Extension now means freedom, knowledge and progress," and he concluded that the United States was "the hope of freedom throughout the world." He was "one of those who gladly see its power and influence extended to all the adjacent islands and capes of this continent and throughout the world."[68]

Douglass was not writing or thinking as a Black man or an activist of the Black cause but rather as a good Republican, which did not stop him from talking about Santo Domingo's race issue. On the contrary, in his undated speech on Santo Domingo, Douglass tried to give a fair account of the racial composition of the country. Some of his ambiguous remarks concerning the people of color in Santo Domingo may partly explain why Henry Highland Garnet attributed to him the statement that "the people of Hayti are an inferior race to those of Santo Domingo."[69] Indeed, noting that there was "much superstition" on the island, Douglass asserted that "the colored people of this country are very religious, but they do not invent steam plows, electric telegraphs, sewing machines, and many other useful things in the way of human wellbeing"; he concluded that the Dominican civilization was a "feeble" civilization. Douglass also tried to explain the "spirit of caste," which governed race relations in Santo Domingo ("the mulattoes and Black people quarrel and fight among themselves"), and concluded that "the true cure for this spirit of caste, in our country and in Santo Domingo, has been found in the fifteenth amendment of the Constitution of the United States. The spirit of that amendment makes national sympathy possible to all colors and races of men."[70] Again, Frederick Douglass believed that annexing the small nation to the United States would solve all of Santo Domingo's problems, including the racial problem, and enable the Dominicans to progress.

In fact, in his lectures and articles highlighting the benefits of the annexation of Santo Domingo, Douglass mainly emphasized the economic aspect of this annexation (he praised the fabulous resources of the island, in both wood and fruit and in other commodities), but he also listed its strategic aspects—all benefits for the United States—which made him a good imperialist. Of course, he did not forget to praise its humanitarian or humanist advantages. Douglass was indeed convinced that by annexing Santo Domingo and thus having a physical and permanent presence in the Caribbean, the United States could and would effectively fight for the abolition of slavery in the Caribbean area, particularly in Cuba: "There is reason to believe that that measure would powerfully tend to the speedy abolition of slavery in Cuba and throughout the western world."[71] Although Douglass did not include Haiti or Cuba in his own annexationist scheme, he still hoped that the example set by a prosperous Santo Domingo would radiate so that "Cuba, Hayti, Puerto Rico and Jamaica shall someday seek shelter under our wing."[72]

Conclusion

Frederick Douglass, who did not hide his support for the Republican Party, certainly adhered to the imperialist ideology of his time. In the post-slavery era, the United States still claimed its intention to bring freedom to oppressed peoples and spread its (superior) civilization, as well as its democratic and republican ideals, throughout the world. Douglass was convinced that Santo Domingo should not be left by itself, because it was too weak to be able to resist any potential invasions or attacks from a European power such as France, Spain, or Great Britain. He thought that annexing the Dominican Republic and incorporating it into the Union would bring civil peace and progress to the island and its inhabitants, who he felt had been impoverished by years of slavery and then years of devastating civil wars. To Douglass, annexation "meant the alliance of a weak and defenseless people, having few or none of the attributes of a nation, torn and rent by internal feuds, unable to maintain order at home, or command respect abroad, to a government which would give it peace, stability, prosperity, and civilization" and would serve the interests of both countries.[73]

Thus, Douglass may have sincerely believed that the protection of the American government and access to American citizenship could bring stability and prosperity to this "weak and defenseless people," just as it had brought freedom and equal civil rights to Black Americans. Rejecting "the idea that annexation meant degradation to a colored nation," Douglass placed Santo Domingo at the same level as any other territories of the American continent whose incorporation into the Union advantageously lifted "what must be despised for its isolation into an organization and relationship which would compel consideration and respect." Simply (and cunningly) stated, he considered that "there was no more dishonor to Santo Domingo in making her a State of the American union, than in making Kansas, Nebraska, or any other territory such a State."[74]

His attitude toward the Dominican Republic and the Dominican people and his support for the Republican Party's expansionist and imperialist ideology show Douglass in a new light. The ex-abolitionist and champion of the Black cause had turned into a laid-back imperialist. Was he blinded by his desire to see the Republican Party continue to dominate the American political landscape? After all, the Republican Party had abolished slavery and granted equal civil rights and the right to vote to Black Americans, so Douglass had no reason to fear any malice from the Grant administration toward the black Caribbean people. Anyway, the Frederick Douglass of the early 1870s seemed to have relegated the struggle for the progress of the Black community to the background.

Douglass probably did not perceive at the time that the rights his community had recently acquired were still fragile and that they needed—more than ever—to be ardently defended. Perhaps he did not perceive that the Reconstruction era was coming to an end and that the Republican Party was gradually turning away from its commitment to the Black community, especially in the southern states, in order to strengthen the Union and focus on the concerns of the white majority of the population—for evident electoral reasons. Perhaps Douglass did not realize that at the international level, the Republicans were moving toward aggressive imperialism at the expense of the autonomy of the Caribbean peoples. It must be said that his appointment to the commission happened at a key moment in the history of Black Americans—a period when, free at last but not quite equal to their white counterparts, African Americans were trying to secure their rightful place within American society, accessing state, federal, or, to a lesser extent, international positions. But the illusion of the success of some Black people "hid the forest" of discrimination and segregation many others were enduring. If this mission to Santo Domingo obviously revealed the personal paradoxes of a man, Frederick Douglass, it also revealed a lot about the ambiguous behavior of the American government, which seems to have praised and wheedled some of the most influential African Americans—the Black elite—in order to secure the votes of Black people and, in the present case, to lure or cajole black Caribbean peoples while serving the imperialist cause and the interests of the Republican Party.

Alas, the situation of African Americans only deteriorated throughout the rest of the decade as racism, corruption, and political opportunism put an end to Reconstruction, "America's unfinished Revolution."[75] "By the law and the constitution, the negro is a man and a citizen, and has all the rights and liberties guaranteed to any other variety of the human family, residing in the United States," Douglass declared in his 1880 Elmira speech—a speech he made on the anniversary of the emancipation of Black people in the West Indies. "But to-day, in most of the Southern States, the fourteenth and fifteenth amendments are virtually nullified. The rights which they were intended to guarantee are denied and held in contempt. The citizenship granted in the fourteenth amendment is practically a mockery, and the right to vote, provided for in the fifteenth amendment, is literally stamped out in face of government." Yet Douglass was then still convinced that the Republican Party had not abandoned its commitment to the Black cause, and this speech was even the occasion for him to make up with Charles Sumner: "This was seen and felt by Thaddeus Stevens, Charles Sumner, and leading stalwart Republicans, and had their counsels prevailed, the terrible evils from which we now suffer would have been averted."[76]

It would take another longer stay in Haiti and a bitter experience as a diplomat on the Caribbean island of Hispaniola for Douglass to realize how deeply racial prejudice was rooted within the institutions of his nation and how wrong he was in thinking that Republicans were fully committed to the progress and independence of people of color at home and abroad.[77]

NOTES

1. Eric Foner, *The Tocsin of Freedom: The Black Leadership of Radical Reconstruction* (Gettysburg, Pa.: Gettysburg College, 1992).

2. John S. Durham, the last Black ambassador to Haiti in the nineteenth century, was recalled in November 1893. His successor was General Henry M. Smythe from Virginia.

3. On the African American migration movements to Haiti in the antebellum period, see Claire Bourhis-Mariotti, "African American Emigrationists and the Voluntary Emigration Movement to Haiti, 1804–1862," in *Undoing Slavery: American Abolitionism in Transnational Perspective (1776–1865)*, ed. Michaël Roy, Marie-Jeanne Rossignol, and Claire Parfait (Paris: Éditions Rue d'Ulm, 2018), 41–56; and Claire Bourhis-Mariotti, *L'union fait la force: Les Noirs américains et Haïti, 1804–1893* (Rennes: Presses Universitaires de Rennes, 2016).

4. Walter LaFeber, *The American Age: United States Foreign Policy at Home and Abroad since 1750* (New York: W. W. Norton, 1989), 157–61.

5. Ibid., 161.

6. See Rayford W. Logan, *The Diplomatic Relations of the United States with Haiti 1776–1891* (New York: Kraus Reprint Co., 1969), 315–33. On the various attempts by the United States to annex Santo Domingo, see also Charles C. Tansill, *The United States and Santo Domingo, 1798–1873* (Baltimore, Md.: Johns Hopkins Press, 1938).

7. See Laurent Dubois, *Haiti: The Aftershocks of History* (New York: Metropolitan Books, 2012), 139–42.

8. "The St. Domingo Question in Congress—a Decisive Victory for General Grant," *New York Herald*, January 11, 1871, 6.

9. Frederick Douglass, "The Haytian Emigration Movement," *Douglass' Monthly*, July 1861.

10. Frederick Douglass, "Hayti," *North Star*, April 21, 1848, 2.

11. Frederick Douglass, "A Trip to Hayti," *Douglass' Monthly*, May 1861.

12. For a history of the Dominican Republic, see Frank Moya Pons, *The Dominican Republic: A National History* (Princeton, N.J.: Markus Wiener Publishers, 1998).

13. American Council of Learned Societies, *Dictionary of American Biography* (New York: C. Scribner's Sons, 1943), 15:88.

14. Bruce W. Jentleson and Thomas G. Paterson, eds., *Encyclopedia of U.S. Foreign Relations* (New York: Oxford University Press, 1997), 2:28.

15. Logan, *The Diplomatic Relations*, 333.

16. Jean Price-Mars, *La République d'Haïti et la République dominicaine: Les aspects divers d'un problème d'histoire, de géographie et d'ethnologie* (Port-au-Prince: Collection du Tricinquantenaire de l'Indépendance d'Haïti, 1953), 2:294. Unless otherwise noted, all translations are the author's.

17. Ibid.

18. Ibid., 2:301.

19. Logan, *The Diplomatic Relations*, 335–37.

20. Jacques Nicolas Léger, *Haïti, son histoire et ses détracteurs* (New York: Neale Publishing Company, 1907), 216.

21. *Dominican Republic. Report of the Commission of Inquiry to Santo Domingo, with the Introductory Message of the President, Special Reports Made to the Commission, State Papers Furnished by the Dominican Government, and the Statements of Over Seventy Witnesses* (Washington, D.C.: Government Printing Office, 1871), 62, 61.

22. Daniel Brantley, "Black Diplomacy and Frederick Douglass' Caribbean Experiences, 1871 and 1889–1891: The Untold History," *Phylon* 45, no. 3 (1984): 197–209, 202.

23. Logan, *The Diplomatic Relations*, 345–46; Léger, *Haïti*, 219.

24. Senator Charles Sumner was a strong opponent to annexation, as he was convinced that the annexation of the Dominican Republic would inevitably lead to the fall of Haiti and its subsequent annexation. On Sumner's dispute with Grant and opposition to annexation, see Dennis Hidalgo, "Charles Sumner and the Annexation of the Dominican Republic," *Itinerario* 21, no. 2 (1997): 51–65.

25. See Nicholas Guyatt, "Race, Reconstruction, and the Santo Domingo Debate," *Journal of American History* 97, no. 4 (2011): 974–1000, 978.

26. Merline Pitre, "Frederick Douglass and the Annexation of Santo Domingo," *Journal of Negro History* 62, no. 4 (1977): 390–400, 391–92.

27. "The Good News from Santo Domingo," *New York Herald*, February 21, 1871, 6.

28. "The Island of San Domingo," *National Opinion*, February 10, 1871, 1.

29. "Manifest Destiny vs. Annexation of St. Domingo," *New York Herald*, January 5, 1871, 3.

30. "The St. Domingo Question," 6.

31. Pitre, "Frederick Douglass," 391; Frederick Douglass, *Life and Times of Frederick Douglass* (1881; repr., Radford: Wilder Publications, 2008), 238.

32. *Report of the Commission*, 36; "Santo Domingo," *New York Daily Tribune*, February 21, 1871, 1; "The Good News," 6. Frederick Douglass also appears in fifth position on the title page of the official report published by the commission as "F. Douglass, Assistant Secretary." The secretary attached to this commission was a white man, Allan A. Burton, a former U.S. envoy to Colombia. Anyway, it would have been impossible for Grant to appoint Douglass as a secretary. Indeed, the resolution passed by Congress stipulated that the secretary should "be versed in the

English and the Spanish languages," and Douglass did not speak Spanish. See *Report of the Commission*, 4.

33. "San Domingo," *Cincinnati Daily Gazette*, March 17, 1871, 1.

34. "Fred Douglass and the Santo Domingo Commission," *New York Tribune*, August 10, 1872, 1.

35. Douglass, *Life and Times*, 239, italics in the original.

36. Ibid., 240.

37. See William S. McFeely, *Frederick Douglass* (New York: Norton, 1995), 276–77. Sumner would later receive a gold medal from the Haitian authorities for his opposition to annexation. An avenue in Port-au-Prince even bears the name of the senator.

38. Douglass, *Life and Times*, 239.

39. *Report of the Commission*, 4–5.

40. "The St. Domingo Question," 6.

41. *Report of the Commission*, 4.

42. "Santo Domingo," 8.

43. "The Good News," 6.

44. "Santo Domingo," 8.

45. *Report of the Commission*, 11, 231, 232.

46. Ibid., 232.

47. Ibid., 13, 15, 220, 227. On the complexity of racial identity, racial thinking, and racism in the Dominican Republic, see Silvio Torres-Saillant, "The Tribulations of Blackness: Stages in Dominican Racial Identity," *Latin American Perspectives* 25, no. 3 (1998): 126–46.

48. "The Good News," 6.

49. Louis Joseph Janvier, *Les constitutions d'Haïti (1801–1885)* (Paris: C. Marpon et E. Flammarion, 1886), 301.

50. "Hayti," *New York Daily Tribune*, March 17, 1871, 2.

51. *Report of the Commission*, 71, 38, 231–32.

52. *Supplement to Frank Leslie's Illustrated Newspaper*, March 11, 1871. On the voluntary emigration movement of thousands of free Black people to Haiti in the 1820s, see Bourhis-Mariotti, *L'union fait la force*, 42–55.

53. *Frank Leslie's Illustrated Newspaper*, 1; "The Tennessee Safe," *The Sun*, February 21, 1871, 1.

54. "St. Domingo," *New York Herald*, February 21, 1871, 3.

55. "The Good News from St. Domingo—the Letters from Our Special Correspondents—a Very Interesting Budget," *New York Herald*, February 21, 1871, 6.

56. *Report of the Commission*, 56.

57. Henry Highland Garnet agreed with Sumner that the annexation of Santo Domingo would threaten Haitian sovereignty. Like Senator Sumner, Garnet reacted strongly to Douglass's support of an annexationist project that potentially threatened not only the independence of a Black population (the Dominicans) but also, through a domino effect, the independence of Toussaint Louverture's home-

land, a nation that he admired very much. In April 1871 Douglass answered Garnet's accusation in a letter that was published in the *New York Daily Tribune*: "If I am for annexing Santo Domingo, and am not for annexing Hayti, it is because the one is in favor of being annexed while the other is not" ("Frederick Douglass on the Haytiens," *New York Daily Tribune*, April 3, 1871, , 5).

58. "Fred. Douglass on Sumner," *New National Era*, March 30, 1871, 2. In another issue, the *New National Era* relates that during one of his lectures, Douglass "paid a glowing tribute to the character and services of Charles Sumner, but held that in his opposition to the annexation of San Domingo he was wrong—honest, but mistaken. He next noticed the heterogeneous character of the materials of which the opposition to San Domingo was made up. Upon this question Sumner, Schurz, Davis, Bayard, and Saulsbury come together, but only touch the Ku-Klux, and they fly apart like the fragments of an exploded shell" ("San Domingo," *New National Era*, May 25, 1871, 3).

59. Douglass had stood up for Haiti very early in his abolitionist career. On April 15, 1846, while he was in Glasgow, Scotland, Douglass wrote a letter to Horace Greeley in which he denounced the expansionist (and thus annexionist) designs of the American government toward Haiti. Douglass thought that the Polk government wanted to "exterminate" the Black republic to better preserve, expand, and perpetuate slavery. This letter was published in the *New York Tribune*, the organ of the Whig (and later Republican) Party, of which Greeley, a moderate antislavery activist, was the editor: "It seems, in the language of John Quincy Adams, that the preservation, propagation, and perpetuation of slavery is the vital and animating spirit of the American Government. Even Hayti, the black Republic, is not to be spared; the spirit of Freedom, which a sanguinary and ambitious despot could not crush or extinguish, is to be exterminated by the American Republic, because that spirit is dangerous to slavery" (Frederick Douglass to Horace Greeley, April 15, 1846, Series: General Correspondence, Frederick Douglass Papers, Library of Congress).

60. Douglass, *Life and Times*, 239.

61. See Millery Polyné, *From Douglass to Duvalier: U.S. African Americans, Haiti, and Pan Americanism, 1870–1964* (Gainesville: University Press of Florida, 2010), 25–43.

62. It is highly probable that this "Wyland Garnett" was no other than Henry Highland Garnet. The journalist of the *Richmond Whig*, reporting on this meeting, may simply have misspelled his name.

63. "Colored Sentiment against San Domingo Annexation," *Richmond Whig*, April 4, 1871, 4.

64. "The Tennessee Safe," *The Sun*, February 21, 1871, 1; "Coming to the Point," *Richmond Whig*, April 7, 1871, 4. This view of Santo Domingo as a potential refuge for terrorized southern Black people was shared by Grant and Howe (see Guyatt, "Race, Reconstruction").

65. "Negro Barbarism and Suffrage," *Georgia Weekly Telegraph*, April 11, 1871, 4.

66. Douglass was one of the financial partners of the *New Era*, which was founded at the beginning of 1870. In early September 1870 the newspaper took the name *New National Era*, and Douglass became its "Mr. Editor," that is, editor in chief. See McFeely, *Frederick Douglass*, 270–73. Historian Merline Pitre states that Douglass had become so "fully convinced that its people [the people of Santo Domingo] should be made American citizens" that he published six consecutive articles in favor of annexation in the *New National Era* in 1871. Some of these articles, published between March 30 and October 26, 1871, were republished in various local and national newspapers. See Pitre, "Frederick Douglass," 393. Actually, the *New National Era* published tens of articles about Santo Domingo in its 1871 issues. If all were not signed by Frederick Douglass himself, they did support annexation and endlessly repeated Douglass's arguments. These could be, for example, articles summarizing Douglass's lectures on the subject or transcriptions of other annexionists' speeches, letters to the editor, or correspondence with opponents.

67. Douglass probably gave this speech on several occasions in 1871. The *New National Era* summarizes a "lecture on San Domingo delivered in the Congregational Church by Hon. Fred. Douglas" in its May 25, 1871, issue. The summary includes all the arguments that can be found in this undated speech.

68. Douglass, *Life and Times*, 238–39; Frederick Douglass, "Santo Domingo," n.d., 30–37, folder 4 of 5, manuscript / mixed material, speech, article, and book file Douglass Papers.

69. "Frederick Douglass on the Haytiens," *New York Daily Tribune*, April 3, 1871, 5.

70. Douglass, "Santo Domingo," 15–17, 27–28.

71. *Weekly Louisianian*, May 28, 1871, 3.

72. Douglass, "Santo Domingo," 35.

73. Douglass, *Life and Times*, 239.

74. Ibid.

75. Eric Foner, *Reconstruction: America's Unfinished Revolution, 1863–1877* (New York: Harper Perennial Modern Classics, 2002).

76. Douglass, *Life and Times*, 295–96.

77. Frederick Douglass was appointed minister resident and consul general to Haiti by the administration of Republican president Benjamin Harrison in 1889. Douglass resigned two years later after he and Admiral Bancroft Gherardi failed to obtain the lease of the Môle-Saint-Nicolas and the U.S. government unfairly gave Douglass full responsibility for the failure of the negotiations. Douglass's bitter Haitian experience as a diplomat made him realize how fragile the situation of Black people truly was in the United States and abroad and aroused within him a renewed sense of militancy. On Douglass and the Môle-Saint-Nicolas affair, see Bourhis-Mariotti, *L'union fait la force*, 163–88.

PART 4

Europe

CHAPTER 10

African American Women in Europe

PIA WIEGMINK

In *African American Travel Narratives from Abroad: Mobility and Cultural Work in the Age of Jim Crow* (2015), Gary Totten examines processes of African American identity formation in the context of discourses of mobility in African American travel literature. He argues that "the cultural work that the genre undertakes in order to understand and represent African American mobility generates specific discursive spaces for the construction of identity." In his analyses of travel narratives by Zora Neale Hurston and Ida B. Wells, Totten puts special emphasis on the role of women authors in the genre of African American travel writing.[1] The itineraries and the printed narratives of Harriet Jacobs, Nancy Prince, and Eliza Potter, which I examine in this chapter, must be considered antebellum precursors to and possible role models for subsequent African American women's travel and travel writing of the Jim Crow era. The transatlantic travels of Jacobs, Prince, and Potter—like those of Hurston and Wells decades later—provided them with geographical, moral, intellectual, and literary grounds for exploring, redefining, and reinventing their identities.

In the slave narrative *Incidents in the Life of a Slave Girl* (1861), Harriet Jacobs's first visit to England comprises only one brief chapter of her narrative but addresses most major themes of the narrative.[2] Her experience abroad profoundly influenced her critique of American slavery and enabled her to claim a Black female subject position in transatlantic discourses on slavery. Nancy Prince's *A Narrative of the Life and Travels of Mrs. Nancy Prince*, self-published in three editions with minor changes in 1850, 1853, and 1856 to provide an income for the author, chronicles Prince's trip to Russia in 1824 with her husband; two journeys to Jamaica, which she conducted on her own; and her final, hazardous return to the United States. Eliza Potter's *A Hairdresser's Experience in High Life* (1859) is the autobiography of a Black hairdresser for Cincinnati's elite white women that reads like a travel narrative because it recounts Potter's extensive travels throughout the United States, Canada, France, and England. Like Harriet Jacobs's brief chapter on her trip to England, Prince's and Potter's narratives highlight a lack of prejudice abroad. All three book-length autobiographical works by African American women who traveled to England, France, Russia, Canada, Jamaica, and the American South prior to the Civil War chronicle Black mobility, reflect on notions of African American womanhood, and give evidence of (Black) antislavery sentiment.

Jacobs, Prince, and Potter wrote their accounts of travel during the time of Judge Roger B. Taney's infamous Supreme Court ruling in *Scott v. Sandford*, which denied citizenship to African Americans. As historian Elizabeth Stordeur Pryor explains, "Taney indicted black allegiance and freedom of mobility. Taney's argument employed frustrating circular logic. He asserted that people of color were not citizens of the United States because they had never been treated as citizens in the United States."[3] In other words, Taney argued that the enslavement of Black people in the United States and the long history of curtailing their free movement justify why African Americans should not be considered American citizens. Jacobs's, Prince's, and Potter's transatlantic travels must be read as refutations of enslaved African Americans' forced migration and immobility.[4] Taking into account that relatively few African Americans crossed the Atlantic, and considering that even fewer African American women undertook this voyage (let alone women traveling on their own), the accounts of the travels of Harriet Jacobs, Nancy Prince, and Eliza Potter bring to the fore a hitherto understudied genre of African American autobiography: antebellum African American women's travel writing.

In contrast to the forced migration of enslaved women, I examine women's deliberate, uncompelled journeys and how these journeys affected their sense of African American identity. The writings Jacobs, Prince, and Potter published about their travels represent declarations of independence; their travels provided them with an extranational frame of reference from which they were able to perceive slavery, their own social position as African American women, and their sense of (national) belonging with fresh pairs of eyes. Examining these three examples of early African American women's travel narratives as an ensemble not only brings to the fore continuities and common tropes but also draws attention to the multifariousness with which the women approach issues like slavery, national belonging, and Black womanhood.

Revisiting the Slave Narrative: Discourses of Travel in Harriet Jacobs's *Incidents*

From forced transportation across the Atlantic, further movement imposed by slaveholders, the restriction and denial of mobility by regulatory laws and practices, to the final travel toward freedom during the escape north, slave narratives contain various discourses of African American mobilities.[5] Accordingly, Virginia Whatley Smith observes, "The ship, which served as the prison for the Black body during the slave trade, assumes a different meaning in the emancipatory travel literature of escaped slaves and freedmen."[6] In his first autobiography, *Narrative of the Life of Frederick Douglass, an American Slave, Written by Himself* (1845), Douglass presents his view of the "beautiful vessels" he sees in the Chesapeake Bay as an epiphanous moment that channeled the yearning for freedom (to travel) the sight of the vessels aroused in him into the concrete decision to escape the condition of containment, that is, slavery.[7]

The same year Douglass wrote his narrative, Harriet Jacobs traveled to England for the first time.[8] Discourses of travel loom large in *Incidents*: Jacobs skillfully contrasts the restraint of her life as an enslaved woman with her mobility in the North, where she frequently moves between New York, Boston, and Rochester. During her seven-year, self-imposed incarceration at her "loop hole of retreat" at her grandmother's house, which is marked by extreme physical immobility, Jacobs created letters about her fictional free movement in Boston and New York in order to make her enslaver believe she had escaped to the North. Her subsequent escape from Edenton, North Carolina, to Philadelphia in 1842 is made in a small vessel on which Jacobs traveled most of the time concealed below deck because of her fear of being captured. In contrast, her trip across the Atlantic, which took roughly the same amount of time, is referred to as "a pleasant voyage."[9] Having escaped from slavery only three years earlier, Jacobs accompanied Nathanial Parker Willis to take care of his baby daughter, Imogen, on a ten-month trip to England in 1842. Jacobs's biographer Jean Fagan Yellin recounts that boarding the steamship *Britannic* changed Jacobs's life, as it "had little in common with the vessel in which Jacobs had escaped from Edenton.... Now she was traveling in style—albeit as a servant—as one of an international grouping of passengers that included the citizens of a dozen countries."[10] Jacobs recalls her first night in "a pleasant room" in a hotel in London as follows: "I felt as if a great millstone has been lifted from my breast.... I laid my head on my pillow, for the first time, with the delightful consciousness of pure, unadulterated freedom."[11] Although not yet legally free, Jacobs experiences in England her first genuine feeling of freedom.

In this brief chapter about her stay abroad, Jacobs employs characteristics of the genre of travel writing, namely, the outsider's perspective on a culture and society.[12] Her perspective on England is a decidedly comparative one: she contrasts the Edenton Episcopal Church services by slaveholding ministers, which she refers to as a "mockery and a sham," with the services provided by "a true disciple of Jesus" she witnessed in England; she compares the immobility and "stagnation of our Southern towns" to the vitality and dynamic life of London; and she compares the condition of "the poorest poor" in Europe to that of the enslaved in the United States. Jacobs uses her visit to Steventon in Oxfordshire to once more illustrate the horrors of slavery at home, coming to the conclusion that "the most ignorant and destitute of these peasants was a thousand fold better off than the most pampered slave at home." After this series of comparisons between the Old World and her home country, she concludes the chapter with an observation that is often found in African American travel accounts: "During all that time, I never saw the slightest symptom of prejudice against color. Indeed, I entirely forgot it, till the time came for us to return to America."[13] This observation not only condenses her previous comparisons between England and the United States but also evokes a stark contrast to her report of a previous voyage within the United States, which she writes about in a chapter closely preceding "A Visit to England." In this chapter, entitled "Prejudice against Color," Jacobs chronicles the racial discrimination she endures during a steamboat voyage to Albany with her former employer, Mrs. Willis.[14] Jacobs, Prince, and Potter, like so many African American travelers before and after them, emphasize the absence of "prejudice of color" abroad; it is only once they traveled outside the United States that they were able to experience freedom from discrimination.

With regard to nineteenth-century Anglo-American women's writing, Mary Suzanne Schriber remarks that "travel rewrote 'home' in new and more appealing terms."[15] Although going abroad may have been a daring move for American women in the nineteenth century, their ventures were often used to reaffirm the ideals of domestic tranquility of their home and home country. However, for African American women travelers, the notion of "home" is a profoundly troubled one. Jacobs clearly presents the foreign as much more appealing than home; her travel abroad even results in the observation that "it is a sad feeling to be afraid of one's native country."[16] Jacobs, as well as Prince and Potter, grappled with the notion of "home" in her account of traveling abroad.

In all three works discussed in this chapter, the journey across the Atlantic provided African American women with a geographical and psychological distance that allowed them to critically inquire what it meant to be African American in the United States; traveling abroad thus functioned as a form of self-scrutiny and an exploration of identity and belonging. In nineteenth-century African American travel writing, Europe was repeatedly stylized and romanticized as an alternative space marked by the absence of American racism and by a greater freedom of movement. Jacobs's account of her travel in England affirms the antislavery fashioning of Europe and Great Britain, respectively. In Jacobs's comparison of England and the United States, England always emerges as superior in regard to religion, lifestyle, and manners. Jacobs here performs what Elisa Tamarkin referred to as "Black anglophilia": "What the black cosmopolitan does in pursuing the 'cause'... is analogize antislavery to a world of high sociability and extreme politesse, which like antislavery itself, has little patience for narrow souls and the rudeness of local ways."[17] It is thus no coincidence that Jacobs compares vibrant London to the stagnant southern rural small town (and not to New Orleans or other urban southern hubs) because she intends to demonstrate, to adopt Tamarkin's observation from another context, how "abolitionism become[s] a *kind* of cosmopolitanism."[18]

While her stay abroad decidedly sharpened her critique of slavery because it provided her with a comparative frame of reference, Jacobs also used her account of her experience abroad to present herself as a participant in a transatlantic public debate. In her observations concerning the British working class, she explicitly responds to what British travelers reported about American slavery. More precisely, Jacobs refutes the observations the British traveler and maid of honor to Queen Victoria, Amelia M. Murray, made in her travel narrative, *Letters from the United States, Cuba, and Canada* (1856), an autobiographical account of Murray's fifteen-month transatlantic travels. In her travel narrative, Murray employs a common trope of antebellum proslavery arguments, namely, the comparison between England's and Ireland's working class and American bondspeople.[19] Murray downplays slavery as an institution fostering "civilization and Christianity" and producing bondspeople "who are orderly, quiet, contented, and industrious." Wage labor, according to Murray, is the greater evil, as the Englishman's "penalty for severing his bonds is *starvation*."[20] Jacobs, in turn, recounts her impression of her own travels and explicitly disagrees with Murray: "I do not deny that the poor are oppressed in Europe. I am not disposed to paint their condition so rose-colored as the Hon. Miss Murray paints the condition of the slaves in the United States. A small portion of *my* experience would enable her to read her own pages with anointed eyes."[21] Whereas, in the typical fashion of the travel report, Murray's account represents a supposedly "authoritative observation of the people and customs" of a foreign country, Jacobs's account is the more reliable voice, since she speaks both from personal experience (having experienced slavery firsthand) and as a traveler in a foreign country.[22] Inextricably connected to the recollection of her travel abroad, Jacobs presents herself as an informed participant in a transatlantic discourse on (anti)slavery: she presents herself as a formerly enslaved person turned Black traveler who saw the working poor in England and read Murray's travel account. It is due to her own experience and travel that Jacobs is able to counter Murray's authoritative voice.

Samantha M. Sommers observed in another approach to Jacobs's narrative that "under slavery she is a subject of print; in freedom she becomes an author and arranger working in the medium." According to Sommers, Jacobs participates in what she refers to as a "recirculation of print." Sommers analyzes several instances in which Jacobs makes use of the practice of "recirculation," that is, the deliberate reprinting of previous textual material, such as letters, advertisements, and her bill of sale. "When we ground our reading of *Incidents in the Life of a Slave Girl* in Jacobs's recirculation of print," Sommers argues, "we see her as a critic keenly attuned to her vexing position as subject, author, and arranger of printed matter."[23] Complementing Sommers's observation, I would argue that although Jacobs's referencing of Murray's travel narrative is not an explicit recirculation of her travel account, it is nonetheless an intertextual strategy with which Jacobs further models her autobiographical self from victim to author. By referencing and, more importantly, by countering Murray's travel narrative with her own experience in *Incidents*, Jacobs also claims Black female agency in a transnational political debate on slavery. As Angela Shaw-Thornburg observes with regard to the genre of the slave narrative, "The achievement of mobility in the text is the achievement of agency for the narrator."[24] In addition to the achieved mobility inherent in the move from enslavement to freedom and from object to author, Jacobs's physical travels abroad and her experiences in

England further refined this agency because they equipped her with a comparative perspective from which she was able to reflect on her political, cultural, and psychological position as an African American woman.

Traveling beyond the Slave Narrative: The Autobiographies of Nancy Prince and Eliza Potter

In contrast to slave narratives, which were usually published by antislavery societies, free Black women's autobiographical writings of the period such as *The Life and Religious Experience of Jarena Lee* (1836), *Productions of Mrs. Maria Stewart* (1935), Zilpha Elaw's *Memoirs* (1846), Prince's *Narrative* (1850), and Potter's *Hairdresser's Experience* (1859) were often self-published and receive less scholarly attention today than the popular genre of the slave narrative.[25] Attempting to revise the prevalent notion that the genre of the slave narrative is the most dominant and representative genre of nineteenth-century African American literature, scholars like Xiomara Santamarina, Frances Smith Foster, and Kimberly Blockett argue for the need to pay more attention to and, above all, disseminate knowledge about texts that do not primarily focus on African Americans as victims of slavery. Blockett, for example, contends that in African American literary history there is a "dearth of textual frameworks other than those of impoverished, undereducated, enslaved, and profoundly victimized Africans in America."[26] Blockett cautions us not to use the fact that the majority of works authored by African Americans in the antebellum period were first and foremost critiques of slavery as evidence for arguing that antebellum African American culture can be trimmed down to discourses of enslavement. Such an endeavor, Blockett argues, would "conflate geographic and class concerns and engender distorted readings and understandings of nineteenth-century American and Atlantic culture both then and now."[27] My following analysis both builds on and argues against Blockett's observation. It is certainly crucial to continue to promote and disseminate a more nuanced understanding of the heterogeneity of nineteenth-century African American (print) culture. It is for this reason that I examine the discourses of travel in the life writing of African Americans such as Nancy Prince and Eliza Potter. Nevertheless, the ways these two women narrate their travels in relation to their autobiographical selves force readers to consider race-based slavery as a major literary, social, and political discourse in antebellum African American literature and autobiography. Although Nancy Prince and Eliza Potter were freeborn women, they addressed the issue of slavery in multifaceted ways, and their critiques of slavery are inextricably connected to their transatlantic travels. The narrative, editorial, and argumentative choices made in both texts profoundly trouble common perceptions of Black mobility and womanhood, and they highlight the ways in which free Black women reflected upon and participated in the transatlantic political discourse of abolition.

A Black Woman's Odyssey through Russia and Jamaica

It is remarkable that Nancy Prince's *Narrative* was not only published but also republished in a revised second edition in 1853 and reprinted in a revised third edition in 1856.[28] As Frances Smith Foster and Larose Davis explain, autobiographical personal texts by African American women comprise a rare literary genre in the nineteenth century: "One reason that the personal narratives and private thoughts of African American women writers were rarely made public is because nineteenth-century gender conventions required modesty for respectability."[29] Accordingly, Prince declares in her preface, "My object is not a vain desire to appear before the public."[30] In particular at the beginning of her *Narrative*, despite several hardships, she presents herself as a modest, caring, and virtuous woman who tries to take care of her mentally unstable mother and several of her younger siblings until she decides "to do something for [her]self." She then recounts how she learned "a trade" and that a couple of years later she "made up [her] mind to leave [her] country." In addition to these two crucial personal decisions, which are mentioned in one breath, she then adds: "September 1st, 1823, Mr. Prince arrived from Russia. February 15th, 1824, we were married. April 15th, we embarked as passengers on board the ship Romulus, captain Epes Sergeant commander, for Russia; no woman but myself, in company with my husband, there was one man who stopped at Copenhagen."[31]

The chronology in which she presents these important events in her life is striking. She first articulates her decision to take more care of her personal well-being, which then results in her decision to leave the United States. It is only then that she informs her reader about her decision to marry Mr. Prince. Nancy Prince presents these three resolutions in three subsequent sentences in a matter-of-fact style that reads more like notes than prose. Mr. Prince is her future husband, but up to this point, he has not been mentioned in the narrative. Without further ado, Mr. Nero Prince is introduced first and foremost as a welcome rescue from the economic hardship and instability of Nancy's single life. She straightforwardly presents her marriage as the result of her wish to finally stop sacrificing herself—a wish, she also implies, that can only be fulfilled by leaving the United States.

In the three editions of her *Narrative*, Prince made two small but crucial changes in the excerpt quoted above. First, in her 1850 edition it reads, "I made up my mind to leave this country."[32] In the 1853 and 1856 editions, Prince changed the pronoun "this" to the personal pronoun "my" and thus obviously decided to add an emphasis on her affiliation to the United States as her home country. Sandra Gunning, who first observed this editorial change, points out that what seems to be a minimal alteration in the second edition of Prince's *Narrative* nonetheless "acknowledges an equivocal national identification but also some anxiety inherent in the decision to abandon [her] native place."[33] The second change Prince made in this passage occurred only in the 1856 edition of her *Narrative*. In the two previous editions, Prince did not include the observation that she had been the only woman on board the *Romulus*. It might have only been due to the stark increase of female passengers on steamships crossing the Atlantic in the 1850s that Prince suddenly considered this fact worth pointing out when she revised her *Narrative*.[34] Nevertheless, the inclusion of this detail signals how much Prince was aware of her extraordinary status as a woman, let alone a Black woman, traveling to Russia. Taken together, both these editorial changes emphasize the perspective of the woman traveler who, by traveling abroad, begins to reflect on her attitude toward her native country and who becomes aware of herself as a traveling female subject.

Why Russia? Despite the order in which Prince presents her decisions in her *Narrative*, Russia became the destination of her travel because she accompanied her husband, who "served ... one of the noble ladies of the [tsarist] Court" in Saint Petersburg.[35] Reminiscent of tourist guide books, her account of her nine-year stay (1824–33) in Russia begins with a chronological report of important public holidays, which is interspersed a few times with significant historical occurrences such as the Saint Petersburg Flood of 1824 and the Decembrist revolt in 1825. Given the fact that Prince presents herself as an ardent observer of postemancipation race relations in her account of her travels to Jamaica, it seems odd that there are only two remarks on the culture and customs in Russia that hint at her antislavery attitude and her African American identity. First, Prince recounts how Emperor Alexander I and Empress Elizabeth received her and gave her and her husband a valuable wedding present. It is in this context that she observes that in Russia "there was no prejudice against color, there were there all casts, and the people of all nations."³⁶ Despite its very different cultural context, this incident echoes Jacobs's writings about England in that both women use the exact same parameter, namely, "prejudice of color," to distinguish racial oppression at home from other forms of social oppression and inequality in Europe.³⁷

Tamarkin's observations concerning the ways in which Black abolitionists fashioned the absence of racial prejudice in British genteel culture as a natural component of "cultivated tastes" seem also a relevant argument to describe Prince's account of her interaction with Russian nobility. Tamarkin describes Black abolitionists' fashioning of British gentility as follows: "Prejudice or no prejudice, the British are too decorous to show prejudice, in an expedience that removes antislavery from the demands of principle or conscience and makes it the sure expression of cultivated tastes."³⁸ In a similar fashion, in Russia, Prince experienced not only the absence of prejudice but acceptance by Russian nobility, evident in her receiving gifts from Empress Elizabeth. Prince also presents herself as a respected member of Russian society, able to earn a decent living and to educate herself—in short, she describes a social upward mobility and respect that were denied to her at home.³⁹

Second, in a brief comparative passage about housing in Russia, she includes a comment on the indentured peasants of Russia. "This class of people till the land," Prince recounts, "most of them are slaves and are very degraded. The rich own the poor, but they are not suffered to separate families or sell them off the soil. All are subject to the Emperor, and no nobleman can leave without his permission."⁴⁰ Her use of negation must be read as a reference to her home country, where enslaved families were separated at the will of their slaveholders. However, whereas Harriet Jacobs uses her experience abroad to draw attention to the peculiar institution at home and to point out the cruelties of this institution, Prince only implicitly establishes a comparison between Russian serfdom and American slavery. This is even more astounding because this was a comparison that (like Jacobs's assessment of the British working poor in relation to American slavery) has often been made in American antislavery literature, a body of literature Prince was presumably very familiar with.

We know from the archives that after she had returned without her husband from Russia her writings appeared in the *National Anti-Slavery Standard* and in William Lloyd Garrison's *Liberator*. Prince was a member of the mixed-race Boston Female Anti-Slavery Society, and she was involved in preventing a fugitive man from being recaptured by his enslaver in Boston.⁴¹

Interestingly, the time period back home between her return from Russia in 1833 and her departure to Jamaica in 1840 is merely presented as a brief, intermediary phase between two foreign locations in which her abolitionist activities are only noted in passing: "There had been an Anti-Slavery Society established by W. L. Garrison, Knapp and other philanthropists of the day.... These meetings I attended with much pleasure until a contention broke out among themselves." The distance with which she narrates her involvement in abolitionist work is even more astounding because she signed a petition that contributed to this "contention," namely, a debate about the ways in which women should participate in abolitionist political work. This disappointment with the abolitionist movement in Boston and her experience of "the weight of prejudice [that] has again oppressed [her]" then triggers a reflection on her sense of belonging, which culminates in her decision to travel to Jamaica: "God has in all ages of the world punished every nation and people for their sins. The sins of my beloved country are not hid from his notice." As I have argued elsewhere, her musing about God's wrath again emphasizes her sense of displacement and alienation from her home country and constitutes a moment of both national and personal self-reflection. Immediately after this reflective insertion, she articulates her desire to go to Jamaica. She informs her readers, "My mind, after the emancipation in the West Indies, was bent upon going to Jamaica. A field of usefulness seemed spread out before me."[42] Prince's decision to work in Jamaica must thus be considered an important moment in her *Narrative* that expresses her dissatisfaction with her national affiliation to the United States.

Yet despite the feeling of alienation that characterizes her brief account of her nine-year interim in the United States, her stay in Jamaica did not seem to offer her the possibility to explore extranational forms of identification with, for example, the Black diaspora in the West Indies. Instead, it is Prince's outsider status and her Americanness that she explicitly emphasizes in her account of Jamaica. In the Jamaica section of her *Narrative*, the traveler's ethnographic perspective, that is, the perspective of an outsider observing a foreign society and culture, is maintained throughout the text. Rather than presenting herself as an active participant and supporter of local Black community life—after all, Prince wanted to build a "Free Labor School" for girls and orphans on the island—her observations of black Jamaicans are recounted with the narrative distance of a foreign visitor. Whereas almost all foreign missionaries are mentioned by name, local Black people are only referred to as, for example, "a respectable looking man" or "the poor colored people."[43] Accordingly, Prince does not present her idea as part of a collaborative or communal endeavor with local black Jamaicans but instead highlights her African American identity when she warmly refers to the immigrants on the island as "my colored friends from America."[44] As Gunning observes, "Although Prince shared a racial alliance with the ex-slaves, her Americanness made her equally an outsider to the black Jamaicans."[45] In her account, Prince's sense of alienation from the United States, which drove her to travel to Jamaica, reverses and transforms into a conscious endorsement of her African American identity. She does so, for example, by explicitly urging her African American readers not to emigrate to Jamaica and by appealing to their sense of national U.S. belonging: "I called on many Americans and found them poor and discontented,—rueing [sic] the day they left their country, where, notwithstanding many obstacles, their parents lived and died,—a country they helped to conquer with their toil and blood; now shall their children stray abroad and starve in foreign lands."[46] Disregarding any possibility of a Black diasporic identity, Prince states that African Americans belong to the United States and should not be lured to distant countries that have nothing to offer them.

With her remarks on tsarist Russian culture and postemancipation Jamaican society, Prince presents herself as an independent Black female traveler and social commentator. However, upon her return to the United States, this mobility was decisively curtailed. During her return trip to the United States after her second stay in Jamaica, Prince experienced how much she was subject to U.S. racial discrimination. During the unexpected stops in Key West and New Orleans, Prince repeatedly juxtaposes her own curtailed mobility with that of enslaved workers unloading the ships. At each stop, she refuses to leave the vessel out of fear of being put in custody and is intimidated by white southerners.[47] Whereas, as Carla Peterson observed so aptly, in Russia and Jamaica "Prince insists on positioning herself as the subject authorized to scrutinize the Other, refusing to be gazed at, or at least letting the reader see her being gazed at," on her return voyage to the United States Prince painstakingly acknowledges how she herself becomes a "spectacle for observation": white southerners, deeply disturbed by the sight of her, closely watched her every step because they feared that the free and single traveling Black woman might function as a negative role model to the enslaved workers at the docks.[48]

Her travels and her experiences in Jamaica, just like her time in Russia, altered Nancy Prince's perspective on her home country. Prince had previously positioned herself as an observer who compared Russian serfdom with U.S. chattel slavery, who assessed race relations in postemancipation

Jamaica, and who warned her fellow countrymen of the dangers of emigration. Rather than maintaining this agency once she returned to the United States, Prince experienced a series of disappointments after her return to Boston: the lack of support from supposed friends, economic hardships, and the decline of her health. At the end of her *Narrative*, Prince presents herself as a subject of racial oppression who experiences "disadvantages and stigma" and who is robbed, "embarrassed," and "obliged to move." Rather than maintaining the mobility of the cosmopolitan traveler that informed most of her narrative, Prince's only remaining refuge at the end of her narrative is her faith in God, whose promise she presents as "a sure retreat for the weary and way worn traveller." At the end of her narrative, Prince's physical travels are superseded by a spiritual journey.[49] As Kristin Fitzpatrick poignantly observes, "God, not America, is her refuge."[50] The narrative ends with a poem in which the lyrical I repeatedly praises the belief in God as a "hiding place." Faith becomes a safe space "amid this world's tumultuous noise."[51] In contrast to the self-assurance and sense of identity Prince gained from her physical and intellectual mobility, her faith in God might have been a spiritual shelter and sanctuary but ultimately did not provide her with a home space. At the end of Prince's *Narrative*, her objective is no longer to come to terms with her national identity as a Black woman in the United States but merely to "enter safe [her] hiding place."[52]

"A Desire to See the World": Eliza Potter's Travels

Like Prince's *Narrative*, Eliza Potter's *A Hairdresser's Experience in High Life* (1859) is a hybrid between autobiography and travel narrative. Eliza Potter was a free Black woman who had, by the time her autobiography was published in Cincinnati, worked for several years as a hairdresser in that city. In *A Hairdresser's Experience*, Potter writes about her experiences with upper-class women in Cincinnati, New York, Kentucky, New Orleans, and Saratoga. She chronicles many confidential conversations she witnessed or engaged in with her customers while she did their hair and styled them in the domestic sphere of their homes for balls and weddings. At the same time, and more importantly for this chapter, Potter's autobiography also reads like a travel narrative because it chronicles Potter's extensive travels throughout the southern United States and then in Canada and France and from France to Great Britain. Her text thus testifies to the exceptional mobility of a free Black woman in the antebellum United States.

While Jacobs and Prince begin their narratives by providing information about their family and racial background, and while Jacobs's slave narrative chronicles a journey from bondage to freedom, Potter already claims her "liberty" and independence in the second paragraph.[53] She writes: "Being at liberty to choose my own course, I determined to travel, and to gratify my long-cherished desire to see the world—and especially the *Western world*: so I started as soon as possible toward the setting sun."[54] Her deliberate and self-confident emphasis on traveling, specifically her desire to see the "*Western world*," mimics the rhetoric of Westward expansionism. As critics have pointed out, with this itinerary of her travels, Potter presents herself as an active participant in and economic profiter of the national endeavor of Manifest Destiny.[55] Potter's travels indeed take her first westward from New York but also north to Canada, south to New Orleans, and across the Atlantic to France and England. Yet, rather than populating the frontier, her destinations are industrial Cincinnati, Ohio, and the lucrative recreational resort at Drennon Springs, Kentucky. Furthermore, when read in the context of her subsequent comments on marriage and, in particular, when considering her use of italics in these comments, Potter's remark could also be interpreted as a playful mocking of the gendered parameters that tag the myth of westward expansion as a process of male technological progress and frontier life: "At Buffalo, however, my journey was suddenly arrested by a sort of ceremony called *matrimony*, which I entered into very naturally, and became quieted down under it for a length of time, *just as naturally*.... [A]fter a season of quiet, or unquiet, just as you please to call it, the desire for roving again took possession of me; and I determined to visit Canada."[56]

Maintaining the playful tone of her description of travel, Potter presents marriage as a woe that distracted her from her travels. Accordingly, there are only two more and very minor references to a husband in the entire autobiography.[57] Whereas Jacobs laments that she has not yet achieved the domestic ideal of "a hearthstone of my own," for Potter and Prince, domesticity was something both women wanted to escape.[58] For Nancy Prince, getting married represented a necessary step to be able to leave the United States. Potter refers to marriage as a kind of obstacle, a "weakness" that happened accidentally and that hindered her in her westward route. Potter's opening of her autobiography highlights unrestricted professional and spatial mobility and presents a narrator who seems to be freed from the constraints of race, class, and gender.

The reviewers of her autobiography clearly identified Potter as an African American woman.[59] Yet, compared to the opening chapters written by

Harriet Jacobs and Nancy Prince, Potter's first chapter does not explicitly state her African American identity but first presents her desire to travel. Harriet Jacobs, in typical fashion of the genre of the slave narrative, opens her autobiography with the identification of her social status, declaring, "I was born a slave," and describes the complexion of her parents and next of kin in great detail.[60] Nancy Prince begins her narrative by providing details about her parents. Sharon G. Dean comments on the peculiarity of Potter's narrative in comparison to other nineteenth-century African American female autobiographies: "The autobiography lacks an overt interest in defining a black self, or in struggling to appreciate that identity. Instead, Potter's story is an affirmation of her artistry and her success, not merely of her survival."[61] It could be easily argued that rather than presenting herself as a member and representative of an African American community, Potter's life writing instead focuses on the lives of the elite white women whom she works for and on whom she frequently comments. As a professional hairdresser, she positions herself as an expert on white womanhood, a process in which her own racial affiliation can easily be obfuscated. Rafia Zafar argues that Potter chose this "tactical anonymity" in order to divert attention away from herself and toward the women she writes about.[62]

When considered more closely, however, Eliza Potter does in fact repeatedly reflect upon her own at times precarious status as an African American woman, albeit in a much more subtle fashion than other African American (female) authors of that time. It is "on the steamer to Toronto," mentioned in her opening chapter, that Potter first comments on her racial identity as an African American woman and on the discrimination she is prone to experience. After her marriage in Buffalo, her longing to travel resurfaced, and Potter added a detour to Toronto on her westward journey to Ohio. On the boat, Potter is overcome with loneliness. She feels "self-exiled from home and friends" and "isolated." Yet this feeling soon dissolves when the governor general of Canada and his family, who happen to be on the boat, take care of her and help her overcome her anxiety: "I had never before been associated with those who considered themselves my superiors—*at table*; but upon this occasion, I was invited to sit and take my meal with those who, had they been educated in my own country, would have indignantly repudiated any such arrangement." Potter describes the process of becoming acquainted with a group of people she has formerly not been part of. While the other passengers on the boat are perceived by Potter as her "superiors," at the end of the trip they are referred to as "new-found friends." Her initial feeling of isolation yields to a sense of "fe[eling] perfectly at home." The reason for this transformation is generated by "the gentle treatment" Potter experiences by the Canadian passengers on board and the "gentle and pleasant" atmosphere. This experience of feeling at home among foreigners and her subsequent positive experiences in Toronto have Potter struggling with her American identity. However, in contrast to Jacobs and Prince, who straightforwardly address their African American identity and the lack of "prejudice of color" they experience outside the United States, Potter only vaguely hints at how these experiences relate to her racial identity. It is only thanks to Canadian good manners, which ignore "color or condition," that she finally feels at ease.[63] Her use of the term "condition" together with the reference to "color" must be read as an indicator of her racial identity. As Zafar points out, the term "previous condition" has often been used in nineteenth-century legal discourses as a "term for former enslavement."[64]

Comparable to how Nancy Prince reports about Jamaica, Potter also takes a clear stance against discrimination and slavery but repeatedly refuses to explicitly establish a connection between her own subject position and that of the enslaved. Early in her narrative, shortly after she reported on her voyage to Toronto, Potter recounts an incident that aptly illustrates this point. On her way down the Ohio River from Pittsburgh to Cincinnati, Potter remembers that a *"negro trader"* came on board. Potter observes how all the enslaved are shackled together and stay below deck; one beautiful enslaved woman, however, receives a cabin on deck. Potter refuses to sit with her at the same table and complains about the unequal treatment of the enslaved. She then explains, "Mr. W. [the trader] was highly indignant that *I* should have questioned his right to treat his *goods and chattels* as he pleased."[65] It is only by means of italicizing certain words—*"negro trader," "I,"* and *"goods and chattels"*—that Potter subtly establishes a relation between herself, the enslaved woman, and the trader. For the attentive reader, these incidents, presented in the opening chapter of Potter's narrative, hint at the vulnerability of Black traveling women in the United States and the volatile condition of their mobility.[66]

In her introduction to the annotated edition of Potter's narrative, Santamarina remarks that there exists different census information about Eliza Potter. Whereas one census lists her as a native of New York, the other indicates that she was born in Virginia. Considering the fact that Potter is traveling to visit relatives in Canada, her praise for Canadian good manners, which make her feel at ease, might even suggest the possibility that Potter could be the offspring of former bondspeople who emigrated to Canada to escape slavery.[67] However, in this episode, as in many others in the narrative,

Potter does not straightforwardly identify herself as African American, nor does she mention any reference to former enslavement.

Whereas Harriet Jacobs's fugitive journey has her first head to the North and then across the Atlantic, Potter's narrative reverses fugitive slave itineraries. The opening chapter begins with her travels to Canada and then France and England. Potter's life was decidedly influenced by her travel to France, even though her description of it constitutes only a relatively small part of her autobiography. She explicitly positions and reflects upon her experiences in France as transformative events. In France, Potter acquired the skill of hairdressing that would ignite her professional career as a hairdresser for America's white elite women. Her time in France would also provide her with the financial means and social recognition that would enable her intranational travels, in particular, those to Natchez and New Orleans. The acquisition of "the art of hairdressing," which she learned in France from one of "the best hair-dressers in Paris," thus provided her with economic independence, a crucial requisite for a person who describes herself as someone with "a rather vagabond disposition" and a "desire to see the world."[68] Her autobiography is not structured chronologically, but, as Hannah Spahn observes, Potter "emphasize[s] space over time, her meandering first-person narrative is mainly structured, like a travel narrative, by the places she decides to visit."[69] Potter mostly resists a chronological presentation of events and travels in her narrative. It is thus important that her trip to France is positioned in the first chapter of her autobiography and forms the basis of both her future career and her social commentary.

In her brief account of her time in Paris, Potter strategically positions herself as an expert in French fashion and ostentatious display. Like Harriet Jacobs, Potter originally arrived in Paris as a baby nurse. However, it is no coincidence that she explicitly mentions her walks along the Champs-Élysées, the exceptional beauty of Versailles, and witnessing the ultimate "scene of splendor": the baptism of the count of Paris. She emphasizes the "weeks of leisure," which gave her "the opportunity of enjoying many of the amusements of Paris—concerts, balls, hippodromes, theaters, operas, and *fêtes champêtre*, without number," that is, the kinds of social activities that would further confirm her expertise in European high manners, style, and fashion and that are essential for her career as a hairdresser. Curiously, despite the glamour of these sights, Potter also repeatedly chronicles her "long[ing] for home." Reminding her readers that she "had learned the art in Paris" in later chapters, she will repeatedly refer back to her experiences in France and England. In addition, her frequent use of French fashion terminology aims at further validating the unique competence with which she performs her profession.[70]

In her accounts of her stays in both France and England, Potter repeatedly emphasizes her interest in royal and genteel culture, which is similar to Prince's reports about the tsarist court. When she recounts her first arrival in England in chapter 2 of her narrative, the first thing she describes is her view of "grand doings," that is, "Prince Albert was to lay the cornerstone of the Royal Exchange." She then recounts how she got lost in the new city, and it was only due to the help of a gentleman that she was able to find her way back to her hotel. She comments on this as follows: "On thanking the gentleman for his kindness in bringing me home, I cried with a joy I never felt before, and wondered what rich or grand person in America would have done so charitable an act."[71] Here, Potter performs a form of "black anglophilia" as described by Tamarkin, in which "abolitionist sentiments . . . become the index to a larger system of class protocols, an attempt to consolidate a genteel consensus by equating the antislavery platform with a primer in British courtesies, hoping to produce, in broad effect, a kind of snobbery towards racism."[72] Although Potter—again—does not explicitly reference her racial identity in this passage, she strongly suggests that the kindness she experienced from the English gentleman would be denied to her in the United States. Martha Schoolman argues that "the story of the African American cosmopolitan may be said to reside in the discovery that the promise of equality laid out by the nation's founding documents has been realized, ironically, on European rather than American soil." Travel experiences to Europe thus often resulted in the "discover[y] that all people are *indeed* created equal," and upon their return home, travelers "claim[ed] those rights."[73]

Potter's account of her experiences in France and England affirms Schoolman's description of Black cosmopolitanism, because Potter's narrative deliberately emphasizes her interaction with genteel culture and the possibility to learn the art of French hairdressing. In Europe rather than in the United States, Jacobs's, Prince's, and Potter's narratives seem to suggest that Black women experienced kindness and respect from white (genteel) culture that were denied to them at home. Potter, it seems, deliberately positions her accounts of her stay in France, which provided her with the essential skill of French hairdressing, securing her economic independence, and her travels to England in the first two chapters of her narrative; they thus function as a foil for her experiences and travels within the United States. Positioned at the beginning of Potter's narrative but *after* she recounts her experiences on the steamer to Toronto and her encounter with the *"negro trader,"* they also function as empowering experiences that enable Potter to by and large circumvent restrictions on her freedom of movement in the United States: after her return to the United States, Potter became a well-respected and well-known hairdresser for the white elite, among whom she gained a certain popularity and status. She was able to extensively travel to and within the United States, including the American South.[74] While Prince's return voyage to the United States marks the beginning of continuous racial oppression, which results in the decline of her economic and physical well-being, Potter self-confidently epitomizes her travels within the United States and in particular to the South and thus celebrates her unrestrained freedom of movement.

Conclusion

My discussion of African American women's transatlantic travels examined the transnational dimension inherent in nineteenth-century Black women's life writing. Angela Shaw-Thornburg emphasizes that "African Americans have long thought of and written about themselves in transnational contexts, and ... there are significant continuities in the way that individual writers have addressed the issue of what it means to be an African American vis-à-vis non-American geographies."[75] Inquiring "what it means to be African American" via Jacobs's, Prince's, and Potter's travel writing highlights travel, mobility, and transnational encounters as key elements of African American self-fashioning. Although each autobiography is characterized by the individual and unique trajectory of each woman's life, a comparative analysis of the discourses of travel in the three autobiographies makes it possible to identify recurring themes and common tropes that unite Jacobs, Prince, and Potter as writers who were deeply engaged in questions concerning slavery, national belonging, and female identity. Their transatlantic travels allowed the authors to physically and mentally experience the absence of "prejudice" abroad. This, in turn, made them reflect on the modes and mindsets of racial discrimination and, related to that, the curtailing of mobility at home. Thus, it is no coincidence that by putting their travels center stage, antebellum life writing by both formerly enslaved and free African American women adhered to what Edlie L. Wong considers "the profoundly American understanding of personal liberty as freedom of movement."[76] It is not astounding that when freedom is equated with mobility, the deprivation of mobility—one significant aspect of enslavement—becomes a powerful literary, personal, and political trope that all three writers vehemently criticized. Their travels provided the women with a comparative frame of reference that empowered them to position themselves in transatlantic discourses of slavery, abolition, and emigration. Furthermore, their writings not only substantially participated in abolitionist discourses in the United States but also complicate nationalist interpretive frameworks of nineteenth-century notions of Black womanhood and female agency.

Despite these similarities, the specific ways in which these women developed their sense of national belonging, how they attacked slavery, and how they perceived themselves as African American women vary tremendously. Thus, when looked at as an *ensemble*, the discourses of slavery, gender, and national belonging emerge as common but multifaceted tropes in these texts. First, while all three women take an explicit stance against slavery, their subject positions—former bondswoman, missionary, entrepreneur—and their intended readership vary immensely. The writings of Jacobs, Prince, and Potter give us Black women's perspectives on slavery, but they also draw attention to the heterogeneity of the canon of American antislavery literature.

Second, all three writers reflected the protocols of women's respectability, but while Jacobs largely adhered to these protocols by emphasizing children and domesticity, Prince and Potter expanded and eventually broke away from these protocols. For Prince and Potter, marriage was either a means to an end or an obstacle to travel, and both women valued their mobility over a family life at home. Despite the racial discrimination all women faced, their autobiographies also testify to the agency of Black women and to the broad range of Black female experiences in the antebellum period.

Finally, although all three travelers chronicle the attempts to come to terms with what it means to be African American both at home in the United States and abroad, their sense of national belonging could not have been more varied. Both Jacobs's and Potter's travels abroad reaffirmed their firm sense of American identity. Yet while Jacobs's visit to England reinforced her feeling of dispossession and repression at home, in France and England, Potter chronicles numerous instances of homesickness.[77] In between these two positions, Prince's travels to Jamaica represent an unsuccessful search for alternative geographies of identification. Thus, in addition to highlighting transnational tropes inherent in antebellum African American life writing, this chapter also demonstrates why it is essential to look at Jacobs's, Prince's, and Potter's travel accounts not only individually but as a set of works that, taken together, shed light on the heterogeneity of African

American women's life writing and on the multifarious experience of Black women's travel in the antebellum United States and beyond.

NOTES

1. Gary Totten, *African American Travel Narratives from Abroad: Mobility and Cultural Work in the Age of Jim Crow* (Amherst: University of Massachusetts Press, 2015), 5, 3.
2. Harriet Jacobs, *Incidents in the Life of a Slave Girl, Written by Herself*, ed. Jean Fagan Yellin (Cambridge, Mass.: Harvard University Press, 2009), 234–37.
3. Elizabeth Stordeur Pryor, *Colored Travelers: Mobility and the Fight for Citizenship before the Civil War* (Chapel Hill: University of North Carolina Press, 2016), 123.
4. Without explicitly referring to Sarah Parker Remond, Pryor argues that "the symbolism of traveling on a ship as an unchained person of African descent in the opposite direction of the dreaded Middle Passage could not have been lost on radical black intellectuals, who were familiar with its infamous horrors" (ibid., 127).
5. Alasdair Pettinger, "'At Least One Negro Everywhere': African American Travel Writing," in *Beyond the Borders: American Literature and Post-colonial Theory*, ed. Deborah Madsen (London: Pluto Press, 2003), 80. See also Mary G. Mason, "Travel as Metaphor and Reality in Afro-American Women's Autobiography, 1850–1972," *Black American Literature Forum* 24, no. 2 (1990): 339.
6. Virginia Whatley Smith, "African American Travel," in *The Cambridge Companion to American Travel Writing*, ed. Alfred Bendixen and Judith Hamera (New York: Cambridge University Press, 2009), 199.
7. Frederick Douglass, *Narrative of the Life of Frederick Douglass, an American Slave, Written by Himself*, ed. Robert B. Stepto (Cambridge, Mass.: Harvard University Press, 2009), 71.
8. Jean Fagan Yellin, *Harriet Jacobs: A Life* (New York: Basic Civitas Books, 2004), 136–39, 211–17. Throughout her life, Jacobs would cross the Atlantic two more times. In 1858 she traveled as an abolitionist activist in search of a publisher for her narrative, and ten years later she traveled with her daughter to collect money for the Savannah freedmen.
9. Jacobs, *Incidents*, 163–65, 202, 234.
10. Yellin, *Harriet Jacobs*, 83–84.
11. Jacobs, *Incidents*, 234–35.
12. Alfred Bendixen and Judith Hamera, introduction to Bendixen and Hamera, *The Cambridge Companion*, 2–3.
13. Jacobs, *Incidents*, "mockery and sham" and "a true disciple of Jesus," 237; "stagnation of our Southern towns," 235; "the poorest poor," 235; "the most ignorant and destitute," 236.
14. Throughout her autobiography, Jacobs uses fictional names to conceal the identities of those she describes in her narrative. Mrs. Willis is referred to as Mrs. Bruce, Jacobs introduces herself as Linda Brent, and so on.

15. Mary Suzanne Schriber, *Writing Home: American Women Abroad, 1830–1920* (Charlottesville: University Press of Virginia, 1997), 40.

16. Jacobs, *Incidents*, 238.

17. Elisa Tamarkin, "Black Anglophilia; or, The Sociability of Antislavery," *American Literary History* 14, no. 3 (2002): 461–62.

18. Ibid., 262, emphasis in original.

19. In *Incidents* Jacobs defies this comparison twice. See ibid., 38, 235–36.

20. Amelia M. Murray, *Letters from the United States, Cuba and Canada* (New York: Putnam, 1856), 407, emphasis in original.

21. Jacobs, *Incidents*, 236, emphasis in original.

22. Pettinger, "'At Least One,'" 81.

23. Samantha M. Sommers, "Harriet Jacobs and the Recirculation of Print Culture," *MELUS* 40, no. 3 (2015): 137, 137–38.

24. Angela Shaw-Thornburg, "Problems of Genre and Genealogy in African-American Literature of Travel," *Journeys* 12, no. 1 (2011): 49.

25. As William Andrews notes, up until the 1980s, the slave narrative, edited by white abolitionists, was still considered "the dominant mode of antebellum black narrative" ("The Novelization of Voice in Early African American Narrative," *PMLA* 105, no. 1 [1990]: 23). Likewise, Roger Rosenblatt observed in 1980 that "except for slave narratives, we have very few works [of Black autobiography and fiction] that go back before 1890" ("Black Autobiography: Life as the Death Weapon," in *Autobiography: Essays Theoretical and Critical*, ed. James Olney [Princeton, N.J.: Princeton University Press, 1980], 171).

26. Kimberly Blockett, "Disrupting Print: Emigration, the Press, and Narrative Subjectivity in the British Preaching and Writing of Zilpha Elaw, 1840–1860s," *MELUS* 40, no. 3 (2015): 94. In a similar vein, Xiomara Santamarina explains, "Students of nineteenth-century American literature are often quite surprised to discover that free African-Americans, even some former slaves, did not see the abolition of slavery as the only topic worth writing and publishing about" ("Antebellum African-American Texts beyond Slavery and Race," in *Beyond Douglass: New Perspectives on Early American Literature*, ed. Michael Drexler and Ed White [Lewisburg, Pa.: Bucknell University Press, 2008], 141). Along the same line, in her compelling essay on the early African American press, Frances Smith Forster cautions us to "particularly now with other extant texts, greater access to data, and other relevant questions, we should consider complementary narratives that work against the oversimplification or conflation of the early African-American press with the abolitionist press" ("A Narrative of the Interesting Origins and [Somewhat] Surprising Developments of African-American Print Culture," *American Literary History* 17, no. 4 [2005]: 719).

27. Blockett, "Disrupting Print," 95.

28. I borrow for this section the title of Ronald G. Walter's annotated edition of Prince's 1850 narrative published in 1989. See Ronald G. Walter, *A Black Woman's Odyssey through Russia and Jamaica: The Narrative of Nancy Prince* (New York: Wiener Publishers, 1989).

29. Frances Smith Foster and Larose Davis, "Early African American Women's Literature," in *The Cambridge Companion to African American Women's Literature*, ed. Angelyn Mitchell and Danille K. Taylor (New York: Cambridge University Press, 2009), 24.

30. Nancy Prince, *Narrative of the Life and Travels of Mrs. Nancy Prince. Written by Herself*, 2nd ed. (Boston: Published by the author, 1853), 3.

31. Nancy Prince, *Narrative of the Life and Travels of Mrs. Nancy Prince. Written by Herself*, 3rd ed. (Boston: Published by the author, 1856), 21–22.

32. Nancy Prince, *Narrative of the Life and Travels of Mrs. Nancy Prince. Written by Herself* (Boston: Published by the author, 1850), 14.

33. Sandra Gunning, "Nancy Prince and the Politics of Mobility, Home and Diasporic (Mis)Identification," *American Quarterly* 53, no. 1 (2001): 41.

34. For a more precise examination of changing women's roles and women travelers in the nineteenth century, see Mary Suzanne Schriber, *Telling Travels: Selected Writings by Nineteenth-Century American Women Abroad* (DeKalb: Northern Illinois University Press, 1995), 12–45.

35. Prince, *Narrative* (1853), 22. Her husband was one of twenty "colored men" who served as guards in the tsarist court of Alexander I (ibid., 23). For more information on African American presence in tsarist Russia, see Allison Blakely, "The Negro in Imperial Russia: A Preliminary Sketch," *Journal of Negro History* 61, no. 4 (1976): 354–56; Mina Curtiss, "Some American Negroes in Russia in the Nineteenth Century," *Massachusetts Review* 9, no. 2 (1968): 268–96.

36. Prince, *Narrative* (1856), 23.

37. Interestingly, this passage was not part of the first edition of 1850 but was added in the 1853 version. Prince, *Narrative* (1850), 17; Prince, *Narrative* (1853), 23.

38. Tamarkin, "Black Anglophilia," 265.

39. Prince, *Narrative* (1853), 26, 38. Prince ran an institution for "children boarders," and she reports having learned several languages in six months.

40. Prince, *Narrative* (1856), 38.

41. "Narrative of Mrs. Prince," *Liberator* (Boston, Mass.), May 17, 1850; "Lecture by Mrs. Nancy Prince," *Liberator*, March 8, 1839; "Another Brutal Outrage," *Liberator*, September 17, 1841; "State of Things in Jamaica," *Liberator*, November 5, 1841, reprinted in the *National Anti-Slavery Standard* (New York), November 11, 1841; "To the Benevolent," *Liberator*, November 12, 1841; "Notice," *Liberator*, February 11, 1842; "To the Public," *National Anti-Slavery Standard*, May 25, 1843; "The Undersigned, 78 Members of the Boston Female Anti-Slavery Society (BFAAS), Make the Following Statement," *Liberator*, November 15, 1839; Thos. B. Hilton, "Reminiscences: Woodfork and Nancy Prince," *Woman's Era* 1, no. 5 (1894), Emory Women Writers Resource Project, Emory University.

42. Prince, *Narrative* (1853), 42, 43. See also Pia Wiegmink, "Race, Slavery, and Emigration in Early Black Women's Life Writing," in *African American Literature in Transition, Volume 3, 1830–1850*, ed. Benjamin Fagan (New York: Cambridge University Press, forthcoming).

43. Prince, *Narrative* (1853), 56, 53, 58. At this point, it is worth pointing out that

prior to her autobiography, Nancy Prince published a pamphlet. In it, the (white) missionaries are usually mentioned by name. We learn, for example, that Mr. Abbott was the minister who hired Prince in Kingston, "Mr. Venning, the teacher, kindly received [her]," and she accompanied a Rev. J. S. Beadslee to other parts of the country (*The West Indies: Being a Description of the Islands, Progress of Christianity, Education, and Liberty among the Colored Population Generally* [Boston: Dow & Jackson, 1841], 46, 48). For discussion of the ethnographic characteristics of Prince's pamphlet, see Carla L. Peterson, *Doers of the Word: African-American Women Speakers and Writers in the North (1830–1880)* (New York: Oxford University Press, 1995), 91. Prince reprinted the entire pamphlet in her *Narrative*, albeit in a different order.

44. Prince, *Narrative* (1853), 55.

45. Gunning, "Nancy Prince," 55.

46. Prince, *Narrative* (1853), 51.

47. Ibid., 74, 79. Prince here experienced firsthand the effects of the southern Negro Seamen Acts, which were passed in the 1820s to curtail the mobility of Black seamen in southern ports. For a detailed discussion on the Negro Seamen Acts, see Edlie L. Wong, *Neither Fugitive nor Free: Atlantic Slavery, Freedom Suits, and the Legal Culture of Travel* (New York: New York University Press, 2009), 183–238.

48. Peterson, *Doers*, 97; Prince, *Narrative* (1853), 79.

49. Prince, *Narrative* (1853), 84, 85, 86. See 82–88 for the description of Prince's spiritual journey. Although the second and third editions still culminate in spiritual reflections, these are most prominent in the first edition of her *Narrative*. The entire final part is entitled "Divine Contentment" and consists of a spiritual reflection on her belief in God.

50. Kristin Fitzpatrick, "American National Identity Abroad," in *Gender, Genre, & Identity in Women's Travel Writing*, ed. Kristi Siegel (New York: Peter Lang, 2004), 277.

51. Prince, *Narrative* (1853), 88. The poem "The Hiding Place" seems to be a copy of a poem by the same title published in London in the *Sunday School Teacher's Magazine and Journal of Education* in the October 1840 issue. The poem is part of a two-part memoir written by the British Baptist Joseph Belcher about a Sunday school teacher, Joseph E. S., who is also referred to as the author of the poem. It seems likely that Prince came across this journal addressed to Sabbath school-teachers during her stay in Jamaica. See Joseph Belcher, "The Sunday Scholar; A Memoir of Joseph E. S. Part II," *Sunday School Teacher's Magazine and Journal of Education* 11 (October 1840): 660, courtesy of the J. F. C. Harrison Collection of Nineteenth-Century British Social History, Brigham Young University, Salt Lake City, Utah.

52. Prince, *Narrative* (1853), 88.

53. Xiomara Santamarina, "Introduction: Eliza Potter, Black 'Working Woman,' Author, and Social Critic," in *A Hairdresser's Experience in High Life*, by Eliza Potter, ed. Xiomara Santamarina (Chapel Hill: University of North Carolina Press, 2009), xiv. This edition will be cited throughout the notes.

54. Potter, *Hairdresser's Experience*, 3, emphasis in the original.

55. Santamarina, introduction, xv. See also Hannah Spahn, "Eliza Potter's '*barberous* profession': Self, Race, and Nation in *A Hairdresser's Experience In High Life*," in *American Lives*, ed. Alfred Hornung (Heidelberg: Universitätsverlag Winter, 2013), 192.

56. Potter, *Hairdresser's Experience*, 3, emphasis in the original.

57. Xiomara Santamarina, "Appendix A: Biographical Information on Eliza Potter (1820?–1893)," in Potter, *Hairdresser's Experience*, 179–81. The little information that is available indicates that Potter must have been married at least twice. In view of the scarcity of information about Potter's life, we can only speculate about her motivations to exclude any personal reference from her life writing. Her decision to not present any details on her marriage, children, or parents turns her autobiography into a document that chronicles her professional rather than her private life.

58. Harriet Jacobs adheres to the protocols of female respectability when she reminds her reader in the penultimate paragraph of her autobiography, "Reader, my story ends with freedom; not in the usual way, with marriage." Jacobs connects her freedom to an ideal of domesticity: "The dream of my life is not yet realized. I do not sit with my children in a home of my own, I still long for a hearthstone of my own, however humble. I wish it for my children's sake far more than for my own" (*Incidents*, 259).

59. Sharon G. Dean, introduction to *A Hairdresser's Experience in High Life*, by Eliza Potter, ed. Henry Louis Gates Jr. (New York: Oxford University Press, 1991), xlv. It must be kept in mind that Eliza Potter's autobiography had been published in Cincinnati and was assumedly read primarily by local Cincinnatians. Most of the readers personally knew Eliza Potter. As mentioned before, she was "extensively known and patronized by the ladies of [Cincinnati]" (Xiomara Santamarina, "Appendix B: Newspaper Reports of *A Hairdresser's Experience in High Life*," in Potter, *Hairdresser's Experience*, 183). It can thus be assumed that for the local readers who were aware of Potter's complexion, the first chapter, "My Debut," might have read differently than for a reader who did not know the author's race. Potter is also listed in the census of 1860 as an African American woman who held a significant amount of property.

60. Jacobs, *Incidents*, 5.

61. Dean, introduction, lvii.

62. Rafia Zafar, *We Wear the Mask: African Americans Write American Literature, 1760–1870* (New York: Columbia University Press, 1997), 160.

63. Potter, *Hairdresser's Experience*, 3, 4, 5, emphasis in the original.

64. Zafar, *We Wear the Mask*, 160. At the end of *Incidents*, for example, the now freed Harriet Jacobs reflects upon "the vast improvement of [her] condition" (259).

65. Potter, *Hairdresser's Experience*, 6.

66. Lisa Ze Winters, "'More Desultory and Unconnected Than Any Other': Geography, Desire, and Freedom in Eliza Potter's *A Hairdresser's Experience in High Life*," *American Quarterly* 61, no. 3 (2009): 462.

67. Santamarina, "Appendix A," 180.
68. Potter, *Hairdresser's Experience*, 3, 8, 12.
69. Spahn, "Eliza Potter's '*barber*ous profession,'" 191.
70. Potter, *Hairdresser's Experience*, 9–12, 18, 22, 121–22, emphasis in the original. Potter's use of words such as "*ton*," "*jet-d'eaux*," "*a la Grecque*," "*faux pas*," and "*moire antique*," as well as her repeated use of the term "*parvenu* woman," demonstrates her strategic use of French. See, for example, 2, 10, 41, 51, 31, 15, 36.
71. Ibid., 13.
72. Tamarkin, "Black Anglophilia," 465.
73. Martha Schoolman, *Abolitionist Geographies* (Minneapolis: University of Minnesota Press, 2014), 101–2.
74. The importance of travel and mobility in Potter's narrative is already indicated in the chapter titles. Seven out of nine chapter titles consist of or feature place-names. Particularly noteworthy is chapter 8, "Natchez–New Orleans," which is the longest chapter and extensively chronicles Potter's travels to and throughout the American South. Potter, *Hairdresser's Experience*, 84–115.
75. Shaw-Thornburg, "Problems of Genre," 54.
76. Wong, *Neither Fugitive*, 240.
77. Potter, *Hairdresser's Experience*, 12, 19.

CHAPTER 11

Black Abolitionists in Ireland and the Challenge of Universal Reform

ANGELA F. MURPHY

In 2013 award-winning author Colum McCann published a novel called *Transatlantic*. In it, he included an imagining of Black abolitionist Frederick Douglass's 1845–46 tour of Ireland, which happened to coincide with the initial stages of the Great Famine. Based on Douglass's own accounts, McCann described the way in which Douglass was unnerved by the poverty he witnessed in Ireland. He had never seen such want, and yet, in McCann's words, Douglass "would take the poverty of a free man. No whips. No chains. No branding marks." Although Douglass's rhetoric supported the idea of universal liberty for all men, McCann acknowledged the extent to which the Black leader kept his focus on the cause of American bondspeople throughout his Irish tour. The author imagined what Douglass thought during one speech when members of the audience shouted: "What about England? Would he not denounce England? . . . Was there not an underground railroad that every Irishman would gladly board to get away from the tyranny of England?" McCann's Douglass remained silent for a moment and decided that although he believed "in Erin's cause," he had to be judicious in his response, for "there were newspaper reporters scribbling down every word. It would lead back to Britain and America." He skirted the question with the general proclamation that "the cause of humanity is one the world over." Later McCann imagined Douglass consulting with Richard Davis Webb, the Irish Quaker who was a leader of the Hibernian Anti-Slavery Society and who had made arrangements for much of Douglass's tour. When Douglass took note of the starvation he witnessed in Ireland, Webb told him, "There was only so much a man could achieve: they could not give health to the fields. Such a thing happened often in Ireland. It was a law of the land, unwritten, inevitable, awful." When Douglass asked questions about oppressive British policies in Ireland and about the cause of Irish nationalism, Webb responded, "You cannot bite the hand that feeds." British elites were important supporters of the abolitionist movement. It would not be politic to criticize their government's policies in Ireland. McCann's Douglass agreed: "There would always have to be an alignment. There were so many sides to every horizon. He could choose only one. No single mind could hold it all at once. Truth, justice, reality, contradiction. Misunderstandings could arise. He had one cause only. He must cleave to it."[1]

Douglass in Ireland

Although McCann's version is a simplification of the issues involved, Frederick Douglass was indeed presented with such a dilemma when he visited Ireland, and he did choose to avoid engagement with Irish problems during his tour. Douglass described the Irish poverty he witnessed in a letter to William Lloyd Garrison, but he did not publicly address the problem while he was in Ireland.[2] Also, while he praised Irish nationalist leader Daniel O'Connell as a man "who loved liberty and hated oppression the world over," and he appeared at a meeting of O'Connell's Loyal National Repeal Association, where he was introduced as the "black O'Connell," Douglass never explicitly endorsed O'Connell's movement to repeal the parliamentary union between Ireland and Great Britain and promote Irish legislative independence within the British Empire. Instead, he focused on antislavery and support for the general idea of universal human liberty.[3] Later in life, after the American Civil War and the end of chattel slavery in the United States, he would become more outspoken—more ready to support the cause of Irish Home Rule and more willing to draw parallels between the condition of African Americans and the Irish poor—but during his antebellum Irish tour he generally kept mum.[4] In his few antebellum discussions of Irish poverty, such as the letter to Garrison, Douglass attributed the Irish condition to their own shortcomings—problems with alcohol, the limitations of Catholicism, and an unwillingness to strive to better themselves. He gave no attention to British policies in Ireland that might contribute to such suffering.[5]

What is going on here? Twenty-first-century scholars are beginning to ask that question. The interesting juxtaposition of America's most famous

Black abolitionist promoting the antislavery cause in a famine-ridden Ireland has garnered some interest in recent years. Articles by Patricia Ferreira, Lee Jenkins, John F. Quinn, Adrian N. Mulligan, Richard Hardock, and Jeffrey R. Kerr-Ritchie have focused on Douglass's tour of the island. Some of these authors argue that the visit enlarged his reform interests by stimulating a desire to help other groups that suffered under oppressive circumstances, while others correctly notice the way in which Douglass sought to avoid entangling his antislavery efforts with Irish problems during the course of his tour.[6] Biographies of Douglass also give attention to his visit, highlighting his Irish experiences as important in his development as a spokesman for African Americans.[7] Authors of books on Irish nationalism, Anglo-American abolition, and the larger transatlantic reform community of the mid-nineteenth century have discussed Douglass's Irish tour as a way to highlight various aspects of the complicated network of reform that developed across the Atlantic at this time.[8]

In addition to these scholarly treatments, Douglass's connection to Ireland has been an object of interest outside academia. McCann's 2013 book is one example of this. President Barack Obama also noted the connection. During a trip to Dublin in 2011, he discussed links between the African American and Irish freedom struggles, and in one of his speeches Obama referenced Douglass's statement that his time in Ireland "defined him not as a color but as a man." His tie to the island, the president said, "strengthened the non-violent campaign he would return home to wage."[9]

And the interest in Douglass's time in Ireland shows little sign of abating. In 2014 two books dedicated wholly to Douglass's Irish experiences were published: Tom Chaffin's *Giant's Causeway: Frederick Douglas's Irish Odyssey and the Making of an American Visionary* and Laurence Fenton's *Frederick Douglass in Ireland: The "Black O'Connell."*[10] Both books are narrative histories that chronicle Douglass's time in Ireland and discuss his reflections on Ireland later in life. Like the scholars who went before them, both Chaffin and Fenton address Douglass's reticence about Irish problems during his initial tour. Chaffin attributes it to Douglass's reluctance to anger British abolitionists, while Fenton is more interested in showing how Douglass's time in Ireland helped to bring about his later commitment to a broader platform of reform. These two works thus mirror the dichotomy in how earlier scholars have reflected on the tour. All agree that Douglass publicly ignored Irish problems during the tour, but some are more interested in interrogating the reasons for this, while others wish to minimize this narrowness and argue that the tour contributed to the broadening of Douglass's interests in the years after American emancipation. A common denominator in most of the studies, however, is the idea that Douglass's experiences of Ireland and his later reflections on those experiences shed light on our understanding of his personal character.

The Black Visitor's Dilemma

Lacking in most of these treatments of Douglass's trip is acknowledgment that his visit to Ireland actually took place within the context of a larger tradition of Black antislavery efforts in Great Britain and Ireland and that his reluctance to address Irish problems while in Ireland was not unique. His reticence thus says less about Douglass as a man than it does about the situation in which he found himself.[11] With this in mind, this chapter has two goals: the first is to place Douglass's visit within this larger context, giving attention to the experiences of other Black abolitionists who visited Ireland, and the second is to explain the reasons these visitors—whose antislavery rhetoric encouraged the liberty-loving Irish to look beyond their own difficulties and engage with the cause of others who suffered under oppression—were unable to look beyond their own cause and deal in a meaningful way with the question of economic suffering and limitations on political liberty in Ireland during the 1840s and 1850s.

In the decades before the outbreak of the American Civil War, African American travelers from the United States visited Great Britain in significant numbers. Some were fugitives from American enslavement, others came to study at British schools, and several of them were abolitionists who wished to bring international pressure to bear against the American institution of slavery. Whatever their purpose, all of them drew attention to the problems of slavery and racial inequality in the United States. As Richard Blackett has stated in his groundbreaking study of these visits, *Building an Antislavery Wall: Black Americans in the Atlantic Abolitionist Movement, 1830–1860*, African American visitors to the British Isles served as "living refutations of America's boasted freedom."[12] Black visitors told stories of their own enslavement and their experiences with American racism, and they contrasted the warm reception they received in Great Britain to the racial intolerance they experienced in the United States. A common theme in their overseas speeches and letters home was the hypocrisy of the American republic. Americans professed to be citizens of the freest nation on earth, but they allowed millions to be enslaved. Several Black overseas visitors asserted in their speeches that because imperial Britain had emancipated bondspeople in the West Indies, it was, ironically, more dedicated to human freedom than the republican United States. Black abolitionists thus tapped into the "moral capital" of antislavery in Great Britain in order to conduct what Van Gosse has called an "exercise in table turning" in which the British are described as freedom lovers and Americans are described as enslavers in the Atlantic world.[13]

During their visits to the British Isles, some of the more prominent Black abolitionists spent time in Ireland, where they attempted to further their agenda of gathering transatlantic support for the antislavery movement. The situation in mid-nineteenth-century Ireland, however, presented a unique problem for the abolitionist visitors. If Black Americans embodied a refutation of American boasts of freedom, then the oppressed Catholic peasants, the circumscription of their political freedom, and the widespread economic hardship in Ireland served up a similar refutation to British boasts. Because part of the mentality of Black abolitionists was to elevate the cause of universal freedom, the situation in Ireland aroused their sympathy. On the other hand, the widespread suffering of the oppressed Irish posed a predicament for Black American activists. Because the Irish problems were an affront to the moral prestige of Great Britain, which African American reformers wished to employ in the promotion of their own cause, they faced the dilemma of how to meld their own interests with those of another oppressed group. Amplifying their difficulties in this regard was the tendency of both slavery apologists and reformers interested in Irish problems to draw false parallels between slavery and the poverty and political oppression present in Ireland. Ireland thus presented a challenge to the Black abolitionists' vision of universal reform.

Who were some of these other Black visitors? Five decades before Douglass's trip, Olaudah Equiano toured Ireland to promote, as Douglass did during his own tour, the published narrative of his life. And just a few years before Douglass's visit, Charles Lenox Remond toured the island after attending the 1840 World's Antislavery Convention in London, creating antislavery societies in his wake. Remond brought back to America an Irish Address from antislavery supporters in Ireland to Irish immigrants who had settled in the United States, calling on them to look beyond their own interest in Irish liberty from British rule and participate in the antislavery movement. Remond's sister, Sarah Parker Remond, also conducted a lecture tour of Ireland in the late 1850s. Other visitors to Ireland were fugitives from slavery who made transatlantic journeys to avoid being returned to bondage after the passage of the Fugitive Slave Law of 1850. They raised money to purchase their freedom and to aid other fugitives, encouraged Irish antislavery efforts, and agitated for Black rights. This group included men like William Wells Brown, Henry Highland Garnet, Samuel Ringgold Ward, and Edmund Kelly. Others, like William Howard Day, appeared at antislavery meetings to raise money for Black refugees in British Canada. Finally, William G. Allen, a free Black educator in the United States, became a transatlantic exile after he married a white woman. For several years in the late 1850s his family settled in Dublin, where he taught and lectured about American slavery.

One of the reasons for the focus on Douglass to the exclusion of these other visitors is that, due to his prominence, there are more documents available on Douglass that shed light on his experiences and his point of view. It is more difficult for historians to investigate these other visitors, as most of their talks, impressions, and experiences overseas went unrecorded or, when recorded, lack a significant amount of detail. Black, antislavery, and reform-oriented newspapers on both sides of the Atlantic, however, do shed light on the experiences of some of these other visitors. Most notably, in addition to those of Frederick Douglass, the impressions of and experiences in Ireland of William Wells Brown, Samuel Ringgold Ward, Henry Highland Garnet, and Charles Lenox Remond in part have been preserved through letters, speeches, and reports that appear in these resources. And there are indeed many commonalities that exist in the experiences and the rhetoric of each of these visitors.

The Moral Example of Great Britain

Both Remond and Douglass, for example, contrasted the discrimination they faced on their transport across the Atlantic—both were required to travel in steerage—with their experiences in Great Britain and Ireland, where they were welcomed into the homes of the highest echelons of society. When Remond returned from his transatlantic journey, he discussed this contrast when he addressed the Massachusetts House of Representatives regarding segregated transportation in his state. A few years later, abolitionist presses printed reports of Douglass's journey on the steamship *Cambria*: he was required to travel in steerage, and a riot nearly erupted when he was invited to give a talk on his experiences of enslavement.[14] In 1849 Douglass spoke on segregation in the United States and noted that he traveled through all the British Isles "for nearly a year" on "railways, stagecoaches, omnibuses, steam boats, and putting up at hotels," and during that time he never had one resident indicate "a dislike to me on account of my complexion." He surmised that "across the Atlantic, men and women were free from all this matter of prejudice in this country."[15]

In fact, Black abolitionists frequently commented on the general lack of prejudice they encountered across the Atlantic in comparison to the prejudice they found in the United States. When Remond presented the aforementioned Irish Address at a meeting in Boston's Faneuil Hall, he addressed the crowd with a speech contrasting the respect he received abroad with the lack of respect he encountered in the United States.[16] In 1845 Douglass described his reception at a temperance meeting in Ireland, noting that "no one seemed to be shocked or disturbed by my dark presence. No one seemed to feel himself contaminated with contact with me." This he juxtaposed with all areas of the United States, even liberal New England, where the national history of slavery had corrupted white views of African Americans as inferior.[17] William Wells Brown also differentiated between his treatment in Ireland and Great Britain and his experiences in the United States. On his visit to the British Isles, he said, he was judged on his moral worth and not his skin color.[18] At an antislavery meeting in Syracuse in October 1854 Brown proclaimed: "Get out from under the stars and stripes and prejudice against color is not known."[19]

It was not just the perceived lack of racism that made Britain a moral example to the United States. It was the nation's commitment to ending slavery that was most important to these Black visitors. They praised British West Indian emancipation and the nation's continued antislavery efforts in the Atlantic world, and they used contrasts between American and British policies on slavery to bring shame on the United States. Their desire to use Britain's moral prestige to further their cause often placed Black abolitionists in the position of praising imperial Great Britain as morally superior to the republican United States. Some even expressed an acceptance of the idea that because of its role in spreading antislavery sentiment, the British Empire should be praised as a civilizing force in the world.

Irish scholar Fionnghuala Sweeney discusses this tendency in her treatment of Frederick Douglass's Irish trip. She describes the way in which Douglass's visit played into a British need for "moral displacement"—a process in which British elites glossed over human, civil, and labor rights issues at home by focusing on American slavery, a problem safely removed to foreign shores. She notes that in his antislavery speeches, Douglass appealed to British nationalism and praised the civilizing influence of Great Britain in the world, and he recognized a link between abolitionism and

"British moral expansion."[20] Similarly, Jeffrey R. Kerr-Ritchie's article on Samuel Ringgold Ward's transatlantic experiences argues that those experiences helped to transform him into an "imperial subject" who saw the British Empire as a place within which he and other Black exiles from the United States could achieve "legal equality for all people regardless of racial origin."[21]

Charles Lenox Remond was not immune to this sentiment either. Ideas expressed in a speech before the Hibernian Anti-Slavery Society illustrate his point of view. After communicating his "pride and pleasure" to be standing before an Irish audience made up of those who had assumed the title of "philanthropists," he proclaimed that he would rather know men who adopted that label than those "having the name of republicans and democrats" but who still "nurture slavery" and "countenance oppression." Although these Irish abolitionists had been "conditioned" to undemocratic "political influences," Remond argued that their commitment to the antislavery cause elevated them. "Give me a monarch—give me an oligarchy—give me an autocracy—yea, or even give me a despotic and tyrannical government," he said, "if ... I see the living spirit of liberty glowing bright and imperishable in the people's breast." This he preferred to "a republicanism whose watchwords are 'Equality to all, and mastery to none,' but whose deeds belie their splendid promises, and whose actions are those of oppression and persecution."[22]

During his tour of Ireland, Remond also repeatedly suggested that the British should exploit the cotton-growing possibilities of British India as a way of weakening American slavery.[23] When he made these recommendations, Remond displayed little discomfort with the British imperial relationship with India. In addition, he promoted British investments in Indian cotton even while abolitionists in Great Britain were publicizing the continued existence of unfree labor in India under British rule. Remond, however, felt that expanding cotton cultivation in the region would serve the cause of freedom. In a letter to William Lloyd Garrison, he expressed confidence that "England can and will abolish East India slavery. England can and will abolish American slavery."[24] Remond thus saw British imperial power as a civilizing force that would, in the end, promote freedom. During these years before American emancipation, slavery was deemed the great evil by men like Remond, and it was only after they had addressed that wrong that like-minded Black abolitionists began to question the morality of European imperialism.[25]

This lack of attention given to British power over other nations extended to Ireland in the 1840s and 1850s. Irish leader Daniel O'Connell was no critic of British imperialism per se, but he did oppose British governance in Ireland, and this sparked his mass movement for the repeal of the parliamentary union between England and Ireland in the 1840s. Although Black abolitionists in Ireland expressed admiration for O'Connell, they avoided identifying themselves closely with the repeal movement. For example, in Irish speeches both Douglass and Remond praised O'Connell for his commitments to liberty without explicitly endorsing repeal. Remond lauded him as a "good and mighty man, who has put himself forth the undaunted and fearless champion of liberty and the rights of man in every clime the sun adorns."[26] Douglass praised him as a person "who loved liberty and hated oppression the world over."[27] During their time in Ireland both men's praise centered on O'Connell's general commitment to freedom and reputation as an antislavery activist rather than his efforts for Irish uplift.

Even so, both Remond and Douglass explicitly reached out to O'Connell's nationalist supporters, beseeching them to embrace the cause of antislavery as their leader had. They reminded Irish audiences of the special love of liberty among the Irish in their antislavery speeches. In 1841 Remond proclaimed he was there "to advocate a cause which, above all others, be, and ever has been, dear to the Irish heart—the cause of liberty."[28] In an 1845 speech in Dublin, Douglass referenced O'Connell's activism before he set out to "appeal to his audience as Irishmen, as patriots, and as true lovers of liberty" to join with the antislavery movement.[29] Later visitors used similar rhetoric. In his antislavery speeches before Irish audiences in 1851, Henry Highland Garnet said that his subject was that of "universal emancipation," a cause that should be popular among the Irish people, who had a special "attachment to the principles of liberty."[30] Black abolitionists thus were not shy about making appeals to the idea of "universal emancipation" as they enlisted support for the transatlantic antislavery movement in Great Britain. In doing so, however, they were beseeching Irish men and women to look beyond troubles at home and support the cause of antislavery; they were not attempting to look beyond their own cause to agitate for change in Ireland.

Transatlantic Reform in the United States

In the United States, abolitionists also appealed to the concept of universal reform as they addressed visitors from overseas who crossed the Atlantic to gather money and moral support for social and political causes in Ireland and elsewhere in Europe. Despite their own reticence on Irish rights when visiting Ireland, Black abolitionists censured those visitors who, to avoid alienating southerners and other Americans with antiabolitionist sensibilities, chose to withhold denunciations of chattel slavery while on their tours of the United States. They roundly criticized exiled Hungarian nationalist leader Louis Kossuth, for example, when he avoided addressing the slavery issue during his 1849–51 American tour to promote support for Hungarian independence. When he heard of Kossuth's choice to avoid comment on slavery so that he would not damage his own cause, Black educator William G. Allen said that the Hungarian leader had forfeited his claim to the title of "Apostle of Liberty." To identify as such, Allen said, one "must have a heart not circumscribed by national lines" and must instead have "sympathies which can grasp the entire human family."[31]

Irish Catholic temperance advocate Father Theobold Mathew also drew criticism when he visited the United States to encourage pledges of abstinence from alcohol in 1849 and 1850. As Kossuth had, Father Mathew refused to address the problem of slavery while in the United States out of fear of damaging his primary mission. Father Mathew's decision felt like a betrayal to Black abolitionists, for in Ireland he had been outspoken on their behalf. He had hosted Frederick Douglass at temperance meetings and in his own home, actions that Douglass and others referenced in their rhetoric to shame Americans for their own refusals of African American social equality.[32] In 1841 Father Mathew's name also had appeared prominently alongside Daniel O'Connell's at the head of approximately seventy thousand other Irish signatures in the *Address from the People of Ireland to Their Countrymen and Countrywomen in America*, which Charles Lenox Remond brought home with him after his Irish tour. This Irish Address, a strongly worded plea for Irish Americans to join with the abolitionists in protesting American slavery, had little success in coaxing antislavery sensibilities out of the general Irish American population; but it did provide a vehicle for American abolitionists, Black and white, to point out the disconnect between Irish American rhetoric about human rights in Ireland and their lack of attention to human rights violations in the United States.[33] Understanding the general Irish American position on slavery in the United States and concerned about promoting temperance in the American South, Father Mathew had chosen to remain silent on slavery when he visited the United States. He did not address the topic in speeches, and he declined invitations to antislavery meetings. Abolitionists in the United States took special offense at Father Mathew's withdrawal from their cause during his visit. Not only did they feel betrayed, but they recognized that his decision to tamp down his views on slavery during his American tour tainted the use of Father Mathew as a symbol of racial egalitarianism among the Irish, which they had in the past employed in their rhetoric as a contrast to the racial intolerance found in the United States.[34]

Abolitionists thus prominently criticized Father Mathew in American antislavery publications throughout the duration of his tour.[35] Among those journals that expressed disdain for his position was Frederick Douglass's *North Star*. In 1849 an editorial in the paper expressed disappointment that Father Mathew had fallen prey to the tendency to "change his morality by changing his locality" and forsaken his antislavery views once he was in the United States. It referenced his support of the Irish Address, which, it pointed out, had denounced slavery as "the most tremendous invasion of the natural, inalienable rights of man" and had called on Irish Americans to unite with the abolitionists. "Such was Father Mathew's advice to his countrymen in America, when he stood under the shadow of the British monarchy," it asserted, "but oh! How different, how changed is his tune, when he treads the soil of this Republic!"[36]

The contradiction of Black abolitionists levying criticism at reformers in the United States who were silent on slavery while at the same time exhibiting hesitance to address Irish issues while promoting antislavery in Ireland illustrates how "the politics of resistance" was intricately linked to "the politics of location."[37] The same forces that made it difficult for Black abolitionists to live up to their rhetoric of universal reform when confronted with Irish suffering encouraged European reformers to remain silent on slavery while visiting the United States. These challenges illustrate the way in which local politics could erode the ability of those who spoke of, and for the most part genuinely desired, expanding the liberty for all humankind to advocate for other groups without damaging their own cause. Although reformers involved in these reform efforts were sympathetic to other movements for social justice and employed the rhetoric of universal emancipation, pragmatic concerns made it difficult to always be vocal when it came to bolstering support for their primary cause.

In addition to pressure placed on foreign visitors to the United States, abolitionists also urged American citizens who supported other freedom movements to expand their efforts and embrace abolitionism. Remond's presentation of the Irish Address was one such example of this. Samuel Ringgold Ward also called on Americans to give equal attention to those enslaved at home as they gave to the politically oppressed elsewhere. He criticized American willingness to support freedom movements in Greece,

Hungary, Ireland, and Poland while giving no thought to oppression at home, and he particularly condemned those who sent relief to Ireland in support of repeal or to alleviate the suffering of those affected by famine while ignoring slavery in the United States. "The Irish desired to free themselves [and] ... abundant was the American disposition to intervene," he pointed out. "Meetings were held, money raised, speeches made, everything done. But not a single flash of light came to the American mind touching the oppressions of Americans. When Ireland famished for want of bread," he said, "Americans intervened against hunger, while they drove the slave to starvation and death."[38]

Meditations on "Caste" and Color

These calls for an expanded vision of reform in the United States were, as they had been in Ireland, more about drawing attention to the movement for African American freedom and equality than a true vision of universal reform. Black Americans, for good reason, were deeply ambivalent about tying their arguments about Black freedom and equality to arguments against other forms of prejudice. For example, at the 1854 Syracuse meeting where William Wells Brown spoke on the lack of racial prejudice he encountered overseas in Ireland and Great Britain, he sparked a debate when he elaborated that it was "prejudice against condition" that one found in the British Isles rather than "prejudice against color." Brown's statement led to a heated discussion about whether this so-called prejudice against condition, or "caste," as one speaker labeled it, was any better than racial prejudice. Charles Lenox Remond was one of the more active participants in this debate. When white educator and abolitionist Beriah Green proclaimed that "colorphobia is what in Europe is called caste," Remond questioned "if he meant to imply that the condition of the indigent white man of England and the colored man in America was similar." Remond acknowledged that he had witnessed class prejudice during his visit to the British Isles, but he asserted that "no people in any part of the world were victims so complicated and withering of indignities as the colored American," reminding his audience that "avenues for elevation" were open to victims of class prejudice, whereas they were not to Black Americans. Frederick Douglass also was present at this meeting, and he pointed out that color prejudice "seemed to get stronger as the people were lower in class, even to the Irish just come over." He remarked that he encountered no such prejudice among the poor in Ireland and speculated that poor Irish immigrants in the United States were eager "to find someone lower than themselves" and that American slavery and racial prejudice created this possibility for them.[39] As this exchange shows, Black abolitionists plainly viewed the antislavery movement as their most important commitment, and they were reluctant to allow others to draw parallels between economic inequality on both sides of the Atlantic with slavery and color prejudice in America.

The discussion in Syracuse was not the first time the subject had come up for these Black reformers. Remond had engaged in similar conversations about class and race during his 1841 tour of Ireland. In September 1841, during a speech before the Hibernian Anti-Slavery Society in Dublin, a voice from the audience asked Remond, "What will you do for the white slaves?" Remond responded that the man making such a remark "could understand little of the principles of freedom, when he for a moment compared the hardships of any people of this country to that of the slave."[40] He explained his position: "It is not because the slave is a poor man, nor an ignorant man, nor a lowly man, that I profess myself his friend, it is because he is a despised man, an outraged man, a trampled man, a brutified man ... [who is] herded with the things that crawl and the beasts that grovel."[41]

Douglass also consistently took issue with any attempt to equate Irish oppression and poverty with chattel slavery, although he did recognize similarities in the living conditions among enslaved Americans and the impoverished Irish. In private correspondence and in later recollections of his 1845 tour of Ireland, Douglass compared the destitution he saw in Ireland with Black living conditions in the southern United States. In an 1854 speech in which he remembered his tour, Douglass proclaimed of the needy Irish he encountered: "Never did human faces tell a sadder tale.... [T]hese people lacked only a black skin and wooly hair, to complete their likeness to the plantation negro."[42] While he was in Ireland, he made no public comment concerning the poverty he encountered there, but he did discuss the brotherhood he felt with the suffering Irish during his travels in private communications with William Lloyd Garrison. Douglass wrote to Garrison: "I see much here to remind me of my former condition, and I confess I should be ashamed to lift up my voice against American slavery, but that I know the cause of humanity is one the world over."[43]

Even as his sympathy was aroused, however, Douglass felt it necessary to refute attempts to address Irish poverty and oppression with language similar to that used to describe American slavery. "There is no analogy between the two cases," he said. "The Irishman may be poor, but he is not a slave. He may be in rags, but he is not a slave.... The Irishman has not only the liberty to emigrate from his country, but he has liberty at home. He can write, and speak, and cooperate for the attainment of his rights and the redress of his wrongs."[44] Furthermore, he asserted that Americans who drew parallels between the Irish condition and that of American bondspeople were "influenced by no higher motive than that of covering up our national sins."[45]

It was not just in the United States that Douglass felt the need to refute such comparisons. Some Irish newspapers also referred to the "white slaves of Ireland" as they discussed Frederick Douglass's tour of the island in 1845. Douglass responded that these papers did not "sufficiently distinguish between certain forms of oppression and slavery."[46] In Limerick Douglass elaborated on this thought as he responded to assertions that Irishmen should be more concerned with oppression at home than abroad in the United States. Douglass disagreed and sought to make clear the reason the emancipation of enslaved Americans should be a priority to humanitarians everywhere. He said to his audience that "there was nothing like American slavery on the soil on which he now stood." He continued: "Negro slavery consisted not in taking away any of the rights of man, but in annihilating them all—not in taking away a man's property, but in making property of him, and in destroying his identity." He asked the Irish audience, "Could the most inferior person in this country be so treated by the highest?"[47] In Cork he also made clear his position that Black bondage in the United States should not be conflated with the "slavery" of political or economic oppression. "I stand here before you ... a slave," he said and clarified that he was "a slave not in the ordinary sense of the term, but in its real and intrinsic meaning."[48]

In the 1850s William Wells Brown and Henry Highland Garnet both took similar positions. In the travel narrative in which he described his time overseas, Brown sympathized with Irish poverty and acknowledged class prejudice in Great Britain, but he refused to legitimize any comparison between slavery and the troubles he witnessed across the Atlantic. Although he noted that both Ireland and the American South had equally deplorable conditions, he pointed out that an enslaved person in the United States was denied freedom and ownership over his or her own body and labor, while the impoverished person in Ireland was not.[49] Similarly, in 1850 Garnet pointed out that "the poorman of Great Britain may be compelled to toil hard for a livelihood; but he toils for himself. He may not own an inch of soil; but he owns himself. He may dwell in a humble tenement; but it is his home—sweet home! And no tyrant dares to separate his family or to intrude upon his domestic rights."[50]

Black abolitionists were sincere in their general calls for liberty for all men, but as Mitch Kachun argues in an article on Black transatlantic activism, "they were also cognizant of the tactical advantages connected to those ideas." References to Daniel O'Connell and Irish freedom movements were, Kachun writes, "tools for soliciting support from international activist leaders and the masses involved in these other movements."[51] The universalist rhetoric these leaders employed as they addressed members of other reform movements was in service of the antislavery cause rather than a pledge of support for those movements themselves, for in the period before the Civil War, Black abolitionists were reluctant to support any cause that might damage their cause by alienating prominent antislavery supporters in Great Britain or by diluting the importance of their abolitionism with hints at false equivalencies between slavery and political or class-based inequalities.

The Challenge of Universal Reform

The seeming contradiction of the employment of universalist rhetoric to strengthen a singular cause does not mean that Black abolitionists did not believe in that rhetoric, but it is important to recognize that neither did they consider other causes to be equivalent to their own. As Richard Blackett explains in *Building an Antislavery Wall*, although Black abolitionists were supportive of the idea of universal freedom, they also knew that drawing too close a comparison between slavery and other forms of oppression "ignored the salient feature of American slavery, the 'chattel principle,' and in the minds of many blacks, broadening the notion of slavery only allowed the slaveholder to escape the full force of international revulsion."[52] Frederick Douglass understood this, and so did other Black abolitionists who traveled to Ireland and other nations.

Consideration of the rhetorical choices that Black abolitionists made while in Ireland thus sheds light not so much on the individual sensibilities of Douglass or of any of the other Black abolitionist visitors in Ireland as on the moral complexity of the nineteenth-century network of transatlantic reform. Black abolitionist visions of universal freedom were genuine, but both the "politics of location" and the understanding that chattel slavery was a particular form of evil that stood above other forms of oppression necessarily guided the activism of Black reformers in the years before emancipation.

NOTES

1. Colum McCann, *Transatlantic: A Novel* (New York: Random House, 2013), 55, 64–65, 70–71, 75.

2. Frederick Douglass to William Lloyd Garrison, January 1, 1846, in *Life and Writings of Frederick Douglass*, ed. Philip Foner (New York: International Publishers, 1950), 1:125.

3. *Liberator*, November 17, 1845. For more on the interactions between Garrisonian abolitionists and the members of the Irish repeal movement, see Angela F. Murphy, *American Slavery, Irish Freedom: Abolition, Immigrant Citizenship, and the Transatlantic Movement for Irish Repeal* (Baton Rouge: Louisiana State University Press, 2010); W. Caleb McDaniel, "Repealing Unions: American Abolitionists, Irish Repeal, and the Origins of Garrisonian Disunionism," *Journal of the Early Republic* 28, no. 2 (2008): 243–69.

4. See Frederick Douglass, "Thoughts and Recollections of a Tour in Ireland," Frederick Douglass Papers, Library of Congress, http://hdl.loc.gov/loc.mss/mfd .24015. See also the discussion in Douglas Riach, "Ireland and the Campaign against American Slavery, 1830–1860" (PhD diss., University of Edinburgh, 1975), 441.

5. Douglass to Garrison, January 1, 1846. See also discussion in Fionnghuala Sweeney, *Frederick Douglass and the Atlantic World* (Liverpool: Liverpool University Press, 2007), 75; Riach, "Ireland," 439; Richard Hardock, "The Slavery of Romanism: The Casting Out of the Irish in the Work of Frederick Douglass," in *Liberating Sojourn*, ed. Alan J. Rice and Martin Crawford (Athens: University of Georgia Press, 1999), 115–40.

6. Patricia Ferreira, "All but 'a Black Skin and Wooly Hair': Frederick Douglass's Witness of the Irish Famine," *American Studies International* 37, no. 2 (1999): 69–83; Lee Jenkins, "Beyond the Pale: Frederick Douglass in Cork," *Irish Review* 24 (Autumn 1999): 80–95; John F. Quinn, "'Safe in Old Ireland': Frederick Douglass's Tour, 1845–46," *Historian* 64, no. 3–4 (2002): 535–50; Jeffrey R. Kerr-Ritchie, "Black Abolitionists, Irish Supporters, and the Brotherhood of Man," *Slavery & Abolition* 37, no. 3 (2016): 599–621; Adrian M. Mulligan, "'As a Lever Gains Power by Its Distance from the Fulcrum': Tracing Frederick Douglass in the Irish Atlantic World," *Social and Cultural Geography* 18, no. 3 (2017): 395–414; Hardock, "The Slavery of Romanism."

7. For example, see William S. McFeely, *Frederick Douglass* (New York: Norton, 1991), 119–30; L. Diane Barnes, *Frederick Douglass: Reformer and Statesman* (New York: Routledge, 2013), 45–54. Fionnghuala Sweeney gives special attention to Douglass's time in Ireland in Sweeney, *Frederick Douglass*.

8. For example, see Bruce Nelson, *Irish Nationalists and the Making of the Irish Race* (Princeton, N.J.: Princeton University Press, 2012), 86–120; Nini Rodgers, *Ireland, Slavery and Anti-slavery, 1645–1865* (New York: Palgrave Macmillan, 2007), 278–89; Kerr-Ritchie, "Black Abolitionists."

9. Office of the Press Secretary, "Remarks by the President at Irish Celebration in Dublin, Ireland," May 23, 2011, White House, http://www.whitehouse.gov/the-press-office/2011/05/23/remarks-president-irish-celebration-dublin-ireland.

10. Tom Chaffin, *Giant's Causeway: Frederick Douglass's Irish Odyssey and the Making of an American Visionary* (Charlottesville: University of Virginia Press, 2014); Laurence Fenton, *Frederick Douglass in Ireland: The "Black O'Connell"* (Cork: Collins Press, 2014).

11. An exception to this is Kerr-Ritchie, "Black Abolitionists." While Kerr-Ritchie focuses largely on Douglass and his relationship with Daniel O'Connell in an effort to show both men's internationalist sensibilities, he does spend some time discussing other black abolitionists who traveled in Ireland during the mid-nineteenth century and giving evidence of the widespread support for their pleas for black freedom on the island.

12. R. J. M. Blackett, *Building an Antislavery Wall: Black Americans in the Atlantic Abolitionist Movement, 1830–1860* (Baton Rouge: Louisiana State University Press, 1983), 5. On black efforts to internationalize the slavery movement, see Manisha Sinha, *The Slave's Cause: A History of Abolition* (New Haven, Conn.: Yale University Press, 2016), 340–42.

13. See Christopher Leslie Brown, *Moral Capital: Foundations of British Abolitionism* (Chapel Hill: University of North Carolina Press, 2006); Van Gosse, "'As a Nation, the English Are Our Friends': The Emergence of African American Politics in the British Atlantic World, 1772–1861," *American Historical Review* 113, no. 4 (2008): 1005–6.

14. *Liberator*, February 25, 1842, September 26, November 17, 1845.

15. *National Anti-Slavery Standard*, May 3, 1849.

16. *Liberator*, January 28, 1842.

17. *Liberator*, November 28, 1845.

18. *Pennsylvania Freeman*, November 8, 1849.

19. *Liberator*, October 27, 1854.

20. Sweeney, *Frederick Douglass*, 28–30.

21. Jeffrey R. Kerr-Ritchie, "Samuel Ward and the Making of an Imperial Subject," *Slavery and Abolition* 33, no. 2 (2012): 205–19.

22. *Liberator*, November 19, 1841.

23. *Liberator*, September 25, 1840, October 8, November 19, 1841; *Dublin Morning Register*, August 27, 1841; *Dublin Freeman's Journal* June 27, 1840, August 5, 1841; *Belfast Newsletter*, October 29, 1841.

24. *Liberator*, September 25, 1840.

25. Some abolitionists were more outspoken against imperialism. See Sinha, *The Slave's Cause*, 371–80.

26. *Liberator*, September 10, 1841.

27. *Liberator*, November 17, 1845.

28. *Liberator*, November 19, 1841.

29. *Liberator*, November 17, 1845.

30. *Belfast Newsletter*, January 22, 1851.

31. Blackett, *Building an Antislavery Wall*, 10–12.

32. *Liberator*, November 28, 1845.

33. For more on the Irish Address, see Murphy, *American Slavery*, 73–100; Sinha, *The Slave's Cause*, 360–62.

34. For more on Father Mathew's tour, see John F. Quinn, "Father Mathew's American Tour, 1849–1851," *Eire-Ireland* 30, no. 1 (1995): 91–104.

35. One may find reprints of antislavery newspaper editorials on Father Mathew along with its own in *Liberator*, March 24, September 7, October 25, November 16, 1849, January 25, 1850.

36. Excerpt from the *North Star* in *Liberator*, March 24, 1849.

37. Sweeney, *Frederick Douglass*, 2.

38. *Frederick Douglass' Paper*, February 19, 1852.

39. *Liberator*, October 27, 1854.

40. *Liberator*, September 10, 1841.

41. *Liberator*, November 19, 1841.

42. John Blassingame et al., eds., *The Frederick Douglass Papers* (New Haven, Conn.: Yale University Press), 2:520–21.

43. Foner, *Life and Writings*, 1:141.

44. "The Nature of Slavery: Extract from a Lecture on Slavery, at Rochester, December 1, 1850," in *My Bondage and My Freedom*, by Frederick Douglass (New York: Dover Publications, 1969), 433.

45. Frederick Douglass to W. L. Garrison, February 26, 1846, in Foner, *Life and Writings*, 2:139.

46. *Banner of Ulster*, December 9, 1845; Jenkins, "Beyond the Pale," 83.

47. *Limerick Reporter*, November 11, 1845.

48. *Cork Examiner*, October 15, 1845; Jenkins, "Beyond the Pale," 83.

49. Christine Buzinde and Iyunolo Osage, "William Wells Brown: Fugitive Subjectivity, Travel Writing, and the Gaze," *Cultural Studies* 25, no. 3 (2011): 405–25; William Wells Brown, *The American Fugitive in Europe* (New York: Jewett, Proctor and Washington, 1855), 44, 103–4, 140–41.

50. Quoted in Blackett, *Building an Antislavery Wall*, 23.

51. Mitch Kachun, "'Our Platform Is as Broad as Humanity': Transatlantic Freedom Movements and the Idea of Progress in Nineteenth-Century African American Thought and Activism," *Slavery and Abolition* 24, no. 3 (2003): 4.

52. Blackett, *Building an Antislavery Wall*, 24.

EPILOGUE

GERALD HORNE

This valuable volume engages with the most protean aspect of African American studies today: how the global has shaped the domestic. In an era when the term "globalization" has become au courant, it is well to explore the antecedents of what is often thought to be a relatively new twist and turn in history. Understandably, these pages give pride of place in this regard to the Haitian Revolution, which ignited a general crisis of the entire slave system that could only be resolved with its collapse—not least in North America, as London was induced to move toward abolition in order to forestall losing all lives and investments, most notably in such sites as Jamaica and Barbados, and was pressuring Washington to act similarly.

Raising the question of Haiti leads us inexorably to what is today referred to as "Francophonie," that is, the territories once colonized by France, and that leads us north of the U.S. border to Québec. Although the riveting article by Paz and Whitfield does not concern this still mostly French-speaking province, inferentially it raises the matter of the historic tie between African Americans and Québécois—though, strikingly, the authors do point to "Mathieu da Costa, an early free Black man in colonial Canada, [who] was a member of Pierre Dugua's 1605 exploratory party. He likely worked as a translator between the French and Mi'kmaq." This in turn leads us to a pioneer of the Black press, John Russwurm, who spent some of his formative years there.[1] That is to say, like any good book, the one at hand inexorably leads us down fruitful byways, and here, the contributions of Russwurm have been so vast that it stands to reason that he is not alone. That in turn brings us to a wizard of the keyboard, Oscar Peterson, the master musician in the genre known as "jazz," who was born in Montreal in 1925.[2] A considerable study could be done on his collaborations with African American artists and how those collaborations took this important contribution to global and musical culture to an entirely new level.

We already know about the fruitful collaborations between and among Canadians and African Americans, which manifested most dramatically not only during the heyday of the Underground Railroad but also during the War of 1812, when the enslaved often collaborated with redcoats in league with Canadians.[3]

Brandon Byrd also shines the spotlight on Haiti and urges scholars to eschew "well-trod sources." Instead, they should seek out the country's "robust archive of Black internationalism, a body of sources that testify to the intellectual and affective experiences of Black collaboration across national boundaries," when considering the trailblazing events there. This is all too true, and I would add that already there has been exploration of the vast records in Haiti itself, not to mention Paris and London and Santo Domingo, in sketching events in Hispaniola as a whole.[4] Haiti has been an independent nation for two hundred years, so there are bound to be Haitian records scattered globally. I would add to this list Brussels, The Hague, Berlin, Brasilia, Rio de Janeiro, Caracas, Bogotá, and Buenos Aires to begin. Similarly, Claire Bourhis-Mariotti reminds us of the blunder of Frederick Douglass and the failed annexation of the Dominican Republic. Though the events it describes are painful to contemplate, this informative chapter should remind those who may have forgotten that the adoption of U.S. nationality has not been penalty free, as participation in wars in Korea, Vietnam, Iraq, Afghanistan, and Libya of late have tended to illustrate. Fortunately, Douglass's crusade failed, though the same cannot be said for companion efforts spearheaded by the buffalo soldiers to liquidate Indigenous polities in North America. Douglass, says the author, "certainly adhered to the imperialist ideology of his time." Douglass's oversight is even more pronounced in the light of Angela F. Murphy's informing chapter. She describes the abolitionist's frequent presence in Ireland, which should have underlined to him the inherent dangers of annexation and colonialism.

Raising the matter of Québec, Canada, and even Ireland then leads us to a matter that this worthwhile volume effortlessly confronts: comparative settler colonialism. Unfortunately, since the publication decades ago of the work of Frank Tannenbaum, this important field has not advanced considerably, especially insofar as it concerns the southern neighbor of the United States during the antebellum epoch.[5] Thomas Mareite's estimable contribution opens an important door in this regard. For example, Tannenbaum sought to distinguish enslavement in the Spanish Empire from its counterpart in the British Empire by pointing to alleged theological differences between Catholicism (Madrid) and Protestantism (London), but in retrospect it is possible to aver that Spain opened a passageway for England when it sought to impose a religious test on arriving settlers, which narrowed the base for colonialism and led inexorably to the rise of a substantial free Negro population.[6] London, in response, checkmated Madrid by welcoming those whom Spain had shunned—especially the Sephardim, expelled from Iberia in 1492. Instead of using "Pan-Protestantism" to confront "Pan-Catholicism," Britain moved toward "Pan-Europeanism" or "whiteness," which created a wider base of support for the settler project, useful in overwhelming often rebellious indigenes and rambunctious Africans, including a much smaller free Negro population.[7] Thus, Moses Austin was slated to deliver "three hundred Catholic families on the Brazos and Colorado Rivers," an overly narrow base from which to confront Comanches poised to deliver an unfriendly welcome to invaders. And a choking bone of contention between Austin and his comrades, on the one hand, and abolitionist Mexico, on the other, was the latter's "lack of legal and moral support for institutionalized slavery on its northeastern periphery ... a constant source of annoyance for slaveholders in Texas" and an unbridgeable chasm that led to secession in 1836—a presentiment of what rocked the United States in 1861. Of course, Mexico elected what has been described as a Black Indian president during this era of tumult, almost two centuries before the United States moved in a similar direction.[8] Of course, the ability of African Americans to leverage events south of the border to our benefit did not cease magically with the conclusion of the nineteenth century.[9]

Mekala Audain's insightful words add smartly to this rewarding portrait begun by Mareite: "The Louisiana Purchase ushered in political and diplomatic changes that allowed freedom seekers from Louisiana to consider the Spanish-speaking world as a haven." This insight helps us to understand not only why conflict erupted between the settlers recruited by Austin and Mexico City but also why Washington felt compelled to wage war in 1846 in order to curtail an escape route often utilized by what was deemed to be a valuable commodity.

Given the ferocity of enslavement in the vast region stretching eastward from Texas, it was comprehensible why those of African descent in the United States began to cast their eyes farther east, that is, back to Africa itself. Lawrence Aje focuses heavily on Liberia (with a look at Haiti and

Canada too) in this regard, and in a chapter dripping with nuggets of wisdom, almost offhandedly he writes, "The expansion of white male suffrage in South Carolina led to the formulation of political demands by the laboring class. White mechanics expressed open hostility against free colored and hired-out enslaved labor, which they perceived as unfair competition." Dexter Gabriel, quoting Christopher Phillips, subsequently informs us that in Maryland during this time, policymakers warned that free blacks were "'withdrawing a large portion of employment from the laboring class of the white population,'" a "matter ... of 'grave consideration.'" In other words, contrary to generations of historians, advance for one racialized segment of labor did not form a precedent necessarily or create a template for the advance of another; in fact, it had the opposite effect. This helps us to understand the persistence of Black nationalism and, as well, the obdurateness of white nationalism, which continues to bedevil our country.

As those who had been enslaved in the United States fled to British jurisdictions—especially Jamaica and Canada—they were simultaneously denuding the republic and adding to the sinew of its prime antagonist in London, thus jeopardizing national security, an inevitable by-product of state-sanctioned racism. As they did in Mexico, in Canada, Black people and those of European descent enjoyed similar civil rights, which—again—impelled migration and the African American desire to align with London against Washington.

Although Caree A. Banton also deals with Liberia, she too adds to the cavalcade of discernment by observing that "when Haiti gained independence, Jean-Jacques Dessalines declared it a nation of Black people," a capacious contrast when juxtaposed to the "white republic," which defined the emblem of nationality and citizenship in a much narrower manner.[10] The author paves the path for new departures in scholarship when she discusses the 1849 visit of Liberian leader Joseph Roberts to Brussels: a new diplomatic history of Liberia is long overdue.

Scholarship has benefited immeasurably from recent interventions on the Congo, and the same could be said for Marcus Bruce's perusal of George Henry Jackson, a revealing companion to John Hope Franklin's remarkable depiction of yet another African American who made it to the Congo during this era: George Washington Williams.[11] I was struck by the revelation that Jackson "spoke and read six languages—English, French, Spanish, Hebrew, Latin, and Arabic—[and then] began studying Kikongo and other indigenous languages." Again, in terms of future scholarship, I would like to know to what extent was it common for African Americans in the nineteenth century to study various languages—including those of Europe, the Americas, and Africa too? And that brings us to the wider question: What does that tell us about the worldview and the global engagement of African Americans?

These latter points are also raised—at least by way of inference—quite capably by Pia Wiegmink. In reading about these women and their peregrinations, especially to Russia, I immediately thought—once more—of comparative history, this time the comparison of serfdom and slavery.[12] And then I thought of the great Alexander Pushkin, a man of African descent and deemed widely to be a father of the modern Russian language whose heralding reminds us again of the fact that the atrocious maltreatment of peoples of African descent is not necessarily normative globally. Like many histories, this inspires us to strive toward a better future that we know is possible.[13]

In a similar vein, this enlightening book concerns predominantly the Atlantic world, which has been a worthy prism through which to examine the many ties that continue to exist between and among the Americas, Europe, and Africa. Still, of late, there has been taking place an examination in the other direction, that is, the Pacific world, which raises the similarly significant point of how African Americans in the nineteenth century engaged with the South Seas and, most notably, Japan. Indeed, when comprehending nineteenth-century events that transformed the African American experience, assuredly the United States prying open Japan in 1853, which in turn led to Tokyo's helping to instigate the underexamined concept of the "Asiatic Black man" in the twentieth century, which shaped and propelled the Nation of Islam, should receive serious contemplation.[14]

In short, these diverse scholars are blazing a trail for others to follow, and, as a result, we are in their debt.

NOTES

1. Winston James, *The Struggles of John Brown Russwurm: The Life and Writings of a Pan-Africanist Pioneer, 1799–1851* (New York: New York University Press, 2010).

2. Gene Lees, *Oscar Peterson: The Will to Swing* (Rocklin, Calif.: Prima, 1990). See also Gerald Horne, *Jazz and Justice: Racism and the Political Economy of the Music* (New York: Monthly Review Press, 2019).

3. Gerald Horne, *Negro Comrades of the Crown: African-Americans and the British Empire Fight the U.S. before Emancipation* (New York: New York University Press, 2013).

4. Gerald Horne, *Confronting Black Jacobins: The U.S., the Haitian Revolution, and the Origins of the Dominican Republic* (New York: Monthly Review Press, 2015).

5. Frank Tannenbaum, *Slave and Citizen: The Negro in Americas* (New York: Knopf, 1947).

6. Gerald Horne, *Race to Revolution: The U.S. and Cuba during Slavery and Jim Crow* (New York: Monthly Review Press, 2014).

7. Gerald Horne, *The Apocalypse of Settler Colonialism: The Roots of Slavery, White Supremacy and Capitalism in 17th Century North America and the Caribbean* (New York: Monthly Review Press, 2018).

8. Theodore Vincent, *The Legacy of Vicente Guerrero: Mexico's First Black Indian President* (Gainesville: University Press of Florida, 2001).

9. Gerald Horne, *Black and Brown: African Americans and the Mexican Revolution, 1910–1920* (New York: New York University Press, 2005).

10. Alexander Saxton, *The Rise and Fall of the White Republic: Class Politics and Mass Culture in Nineteenth Century America* (London: Verso, 1990); Alexander Saxton, *The Indispensable Enemy: Labor and the Chinese Movement in California* (Berkeley: University of California Press, 1995).

11. Ira Dworkin, *Congo Love Song: African American Culture and the Crisis of the Colonial State* (Chapel Hill: University of North Carolina Press, 2017); John Hope Franklin, *George Washington Williams: A Biography* (Chicago: University of Chicago Press, 1985).

12. Peter Kolchin, *Unfree Labor: American Slavery and Russian Serfdom* (Cambridge, Mass.: Harvard University Press, 1990).

13. John Fennell, ed., *Pushkin* (New York: Penguin, 1964); A. S. Pushkin, *Pushkin: A Collection of First Editions* (London: Quaritch, 2006).

14. See Gerald Horne, *Facing the Rising Sun: African Americans, Japan, and the Rise of Afro-Asian Solidarity* (New York: New York University Press, 2018); Horne, *Race War! White Supremacy and the Japanese Attack on the British Empire* (New York: New York University Press, 2003); Horne, *The White Pacific: U.S. Imperialism and Black Slavery in the South Seas after the Civil War* (Honolulu: University of Hawai'i Press, 2007).

CONTRIBUTORS

LAWRENCE AJE is an associate professor of U.S. history at Paul Valéry University, Montpellier, France. He is the coeditor of *The Many Faces of Slavery: New Perspectives of Slave Ownership and Experiences in America* (Bloomsbury, 2019) and of *Traces and Memories of Slavery in the Atlantic World* (Routledge, 2019).

MEKALA AUDAIN is an assistant professor in the Department of History at the College of New Jersey. Her chapter "'Design His Course to Mexico': The Fugitive Slave Experience in the Texas-Mexico Borderlands, 1850–1853" appears in *Fugitive Slaves and Spaces of Freedom in North America*, edited by Damian Alan Pargas (University Press of Florida, 2018). She is currently completing her first book manuscript, tentatively titled "A Mexican Promised Land: Fugitive Slave Escapes and Contested Territory in the U.S. Southwest Borderlands, 1804–1865."

CAREE A. BANTON is an associate professor of history in the J. William Fulbright College of Arts & Sciences at the University of Arkansas. She specializes in abolitionism, the postemancipation Caribbean, colonization in the nineteenth century, the African diaspora, and the Atlantic world. She has authored several journal articles, including "'Nationalism and Not Racialism': Liberia in the Making and Un-making of Garveyism," *76 King Street: Journal of Liberty Hall: The Legacy of Marcus Garvey* 3, no. 1 (July 2017) and "'Inherited Benevolence?': Gerard Ralston and the Trans-Atlantic Colonization Movement," *A.M.E. Church Review* 126, no. 417 (March 2010). Her book, *More Auspicious Shores: Barbadian Migration to Liberia, Blackness and the Making of an African Republic*, was published by Cambridge University Press in 2019.

CLAIRE BOURHIS-MARIOTTI is an associate professor of African American history and the codirector of the research unit TransCrit at the University of Paris 8–Paris Lumières in France. Her main research concentrates on nineteenth-century African American history, particularly the emigration and colonization movements, the emergence of Black nationalism, and Black internationalism. She published her first monograph, *L'union fait la force: Les noirs américains et Haïti, 1804–1893* with the Presses Universitaires de Rennes in 2016. With Hélène Le Dantec-Lowry and Claire Parfait she coedited *Writing History from the Margins: African Americans and the Quest for Freedom* (Routledge, 2017). She has contributed essays to *Traces and Memories of Slavery in the Atlantic World* (Routledge, 2019), *Undoing Slavery: American Abolitionism in Transnational Perspective (1776–1865)* (Éditions rue d'Ulm, 2018), the *Revue française d'études américaines*, and *IdeAs/Idées d'Amérique*. Her upcoming book, *Isaac Mason, une vie d'esclave* (Presses Universitaires de Rouen et du Havre, 2020), is the French translation and critical edition of a postbellum slave narrative entitled *Life of Isaac Mason as a Slave* (1893).

MARCUS BRUCE is a professor of religious studies at Bates College and the author of *Henry Ossawa Tanner: A Spiritual Biography* (2002). He is currently working on a book manuscript exploring the life and work of George Henry Jackson, who participated in a number of nineteenth-century discourses with international visions, such as missionary movements, Ethiopianism, the Student Volunteer Movement, and Black folks, churches, and colleges (Spelman and Shaw University in particular) looking to "regenerate" or save Africa.

BRANDON R. BYRD is an assistant professor of history at Vanderbilt University. His research focuses on nineteenth- and twentieth-century Black intellectual and social history, with a special interest in Black internationalism. He is the author of *The Black Republic: African Americans and the Fate of Haiti* (University of Pennsylvania Press, 2019).

DEXTER J. GABRIEL is an assistant professor in the Department of History and the Africana Studies Institute at the University of Connecticut, where he teaches courses in the Atlantic world, the African diaspora, and the history of abolitionism and emancipation.

GERALD HORNE holds the Moores Professorship of History and African American Studies at the University of Houston. He is the author of more than thirty books, including *The Counter-revolution of 1776: Slave Resistance and the Origins of the United States of America* (NYU Press, 2014) and *Confronting Black Jacobins: The U.S., the Haitian Revolution, and the Origins of the Dominican Republic* (Monthly Review Press, 2015), and one hundred scholarly articles and reviews.

RONALD ANGELO JOHNSON holds the Ralph and Bessie Mae Lynn Chair of History at Baylor University and is an associate professor of history at Texas State University. He is a historian of early U.S. diplomacy, race, and religion in the Atlantic world. He is the author of *Diplomacy in Black and White: John Ad-*

ams, Toussaint Louverture, and Their Atlantic World Alliance (University of Georgia Press, 2014).

THOMAS MAREITE is a historian of slavery and slave resistance in the United States and Latin America during the eighteenth and nineteenth centuries. He has published articles in *Slavery & Abolition* and the *Journal of Global Slavery*. His PhD dissertation, "Conditional Freedom: Free-Soil and Fugitive Slaves from the U.S. South in Mexico's Northeast, 1803–1861" (Leiden University, 2020), proposes a social and political history of the contests over free-soil and the self-emancipated slaves from the U.S. South who settled down in Mexico's northeastern borderlands. It explores the development of southern routes of escape from slavery in the U.S. South and the experiences of self-emancipated slaves in the U.S.-Mexico borderlands.

ANGELA F. MURPHY is a professor of history at Texas State University. She specializes in nineteenth-century social reform movements of the United States and the Atlantic world, with an emphasis on antislavery, Ireland, and U.S. sectional politics. She has published two books, *American Slavery, Irish Freedom: Abolition, Immigrant Citizenship, and the Transatlantic Movement for Irish Repeal* (LSU Press, 2010) and *The Jerry Rescue: The Fugitive Slave Law, Northern Rights, and the American Sectional Crisis* (Oxford University Press, 2016).

FRANCO PAZ is a PhD student in the History Department at Harvard University.

OUSMANE K. POWER-GREENE is an associate professor of history at Clark University. He specializes in African American history with a focus on Black internationalism and comparative social and political movements. He is the author of *Against Wind and Tide: The African American Struggle against the Colonization Movement* (New York University Press, 2014). He is currently working on projects that study Hubert Harrison and the New Negro movement, white northern colonizationists, and African American emigration movements across the nineteenth century.

JAMES SIDBURY is the Andrew W. Mellon Distinguished Professor of Humanities at Rice University. He is a historian of race and slavery in the English-speaking Atlantic world from the seventeenth to the nineteenth century with a special interest in the ways that nonelite peoples conceived of their histories and, through their histories, their collective identities. He is the author of *Becoming African in America: Race and Nation in the English Black Atlantic, 1760–1830* (Oxford University Press, 2007) and *Ploughshares into Swords:*

Race, Rebellion, and Identity in Gabriel's Virginia, 1730–1810 (Cambridge University Press, 1997). He is currently at work on a synthetic book analyzing the era of the American Revolution as an era of race formation.

HARVEY AMANI WHITFIELD is a professor of history at the University of Vermont. His books include *North to Bondage: Loyalist Slavery in the Maritimes* (University of British Columbia Press, 2016), *The Problem of Slavery in Early Vermont, 1777–1810* (Vermont Historical Society, 2014), and *Blacks on the Border: The Black Refugees in British North America, 1815–1860* (University of Vermont Press / University Press of New England, 2006).

PIA WIEGMINK is currently interim chair of American studies at Regensburg University, Germany. She has published on various topics related to American antislavery literature and coedited the special issue of the journal *Atlantic Studies* 14, no. 4, entitled "German Entanglements in Transatlantic Slavery" (2017). In addition, she is the author of two monographs, *Theatralität und öffentlicher Raum* (Tectum, 2005) and *Protest EnACTed* (Universitätsverlag Winter, 2011) and coeditor of the essay collection *Approaching Transnational America in Performance* (Lang, 2016).

Race in the Atlantic World, 1700–1900

The Hanging of Angélique: The Untold Story of Canadian Slavery and the Burning of Old Montréal
BY AFUA COOPER

Christian Ritual and the Creation of British Slave Societies, 1650–1780
BY NICHOLAS M. BEASLEY

African American Life in the Georgia Lowcountry: The Atlantic World and the Gullah Geechee
EDITED BY PHILIP MORGAN

The Horrible Gift of Freedom: Atlantic Slavery and the Representation of Emancipation
BY MARCUS WOOD

The Life and Letters of Philip Quaque, the First African Anglican Missionary
EDITED BY VINCENT CARRETTA AND TY M. REESE

In Search of Brightest Africa: Reimagining the Dark Continent in American Culture, 1884–1936
BY JEANNETTE EILEEN JONES

Contentious Liberties: American Abolitionists in Post-Emancipation Jamaica, 1834–1866
BY GALE L. KENNY

We Are the Revolutionists: German-Speaking Immigrants and American Abolitionists after 1848
BY MISCHA HONECK

The American Dreams of John B. Prentis, Slave Trader
BY KARI J. WINTER

Missing Links: The African and American Worlds of R. L. Garner, Primate Collector
BY JEREMY RICH

Almost Free: A Story about Family and Race in Antebellum Virginia
BY EVA SHEPPARD WOLF

To Live an Antislavery Life: Personal Politics and the Antebellum Black Middle Class
BY ERICA L. BALL

Flush Times and Fever Dreams: A Story of Capitalism and Slavery in the Age of Jackson
BY JOSHUA D. ROTHMAN

Diplomacy in Black and White: John Adams, Toussaint Louverture, and Their Atlantic World Alliance
 BY RONALD ANGELO JOHNSON

Enterprising Women: Gender, Race, and Power in the Revolutionary Atlantic
 BY KIT CANDLIN AND CASSANDRA PYBUS

Eighty-Eight Years: The Long Death of Slavery in the United States, 1777–1865
 BY PATRICK RAEL

Finding Charity's Folk: Enslaved and Free Black Women in Maryland
 BY JESSICA MILLWARD

The Mulatta Concubine: Terror, Intimacy, Freedom, and Desire in the Black Transatlantic
 BY LISA ZE WINTERS

The Politics of Black Citizenship: Free African Americans in the Mid-Atlantic Borderland, 1817–1863
 BY ANDREW K. DIEMER

Punishing the Black Body: Marking Social and Racial Structures in Barbados and Jamaica
 BY DAWN P. HARRIS

Race and Nation in the Age of Emancipations
 EDITED BY WHITNEY NELL STEWART
 AND JOHN GARRISON MARKS

Vénus Noire: Black Women and Colonial Fantasies in Nineteenth-Century France
 BY ROBIN MITCHELL

City of Refuge: Slavery and Petit Marronage in the Great Dismal Swamp, 1763–1856
 BY MARCUS P. NEVIUS

In Search of Liberty: African American Internationalism in the Nineteenth-Century Atlantic World
 EDITED BY RONALD ANGELO JOHNSON
 AND OUSMANE K. POWER-GREENE

www.ingramcontent.com/pod-product-compliance
Lightning Source LLC
Chambersburg PA
CBHW010719300426
44115CB00020B/2958